16-12
22-171
29-23
3>-30

Econometric
Studies
of
Macro
and
Monetary
Relations

Papers presented
at the second
Australasian
Conference
of Econometricians
held at
Monash University,
9 - 13 August 1971

Econometric Studies of Macro and Monetary Relations

edited by

ALAN A. POWELL
Professor of Econometrics
Monash University

and

ROSS A. WILLIAMS
Senior Lecturer in Economics
Monash University

1973

NORTH-HOLLAND PUBLISHING COMPANY
AMSTERDAM · LONDON
AMERICAN ELSEVIER PUBLISHING CO., INC.
NEW YORK

North-Holland ISBN: 0 7204 3068 2

PUBLISHERS:
NORTH-HOLLAND PUBLISHING COMPANY – AMSTERDAM
NORTH-HOLLAND PUBLISHING COMPANY LTD. – LONDON

Sole distributors for the U.S.A. and Canada:
AMERICAN ELSEVIER PUBLISHING COMPANY, INC.
52 VANDERBILT AVENUE, NEW YORK, N.Y. 10017

PRINTED IN THE NETHERLANDS

PREFACE

In consultation with the Econometric Society, the Department of Economics of Monash University organized the second Australasian Conference of Econometricians which was held at Monash University from 9th–13th August, 1971. Cosponsors of the attendance of distinguished overseas guests at the Conference were Monash University, the University of Sydney, and the Reserve Bank of Australia. The theme of the Conference was aggregative econometric models, with special emphasis on macroeconometrics and the monetary sector. A selection of the conference papers on the latter two topics are collected in this volume – a complete listing of the papers presented appears on page 349.

As is usual, a number of acknowledgements should be made: of the generous manner in which the University placed its facilities at the disposal of the Conference; of the comments of all who participated in the presentation and discussion of papers; of the assistance towards the publication of this volume given by the Publications Committee of Monash University. The work of the Conference Committee – A.D. Brownlie, S.P. Burley, E.J. Hannan, W.P. Hogan, and F.G. Jarrett – was indispensable for the success of the Conference. Finally, special mention must be made of Anita Heislers' devoted hard work during the organizing of the Conference and the preparation of the papers for publication.

Alan A. Powell
Ross A. Williams
Editors

v

CONTENTS

PART 2: MONETARY SECTOR MODELS

Contents

PART 1

MACROECONOMETRICS

THE TREATMENT OF UNDERSIZED SAMPLES IN ECONOMETRICS

L.R. KLEIN

University of Pennsylvania

1. The degrees of freedom problem

One straight line can be passed through two points; one three-dimensional plane through three points; and one n-dimensional hyperplane through n points. These simple geometric facts imply, in linear correlation theory, a perfect fit of an n-parameter relationship to n sample points. The statistical inference problem does not arise unless there are more data points than parameters to be estimated. *Degrees of freedom* must be available in order to give rise to an inference problem.

In single equation regression analysis, the degrees of freedom problem does not generally arise in acute form since we rarely deal with more than ten or so unknown coefficients in a single equation and usually have more than ten data points. In fitting high order polynomials, the nonlinear function being estimated really falls under the heading of linear regression analysis since transformations of variables re-cast the problem in linear form, as far as parameter estimation is concerned, and shortage of degrees of freedom restrains the statistician from forcing a close or perfect fit by inclusion of more and more powers of regressor variables. The same situation prevails for lag distributions; more and more lag terms with unknown coefficients can force the fit of the regression equation. The use of orthogonal polynomials and few-parameter lag distributions are ways of coping with the degrees of freedom problems while obtaining estimates of high order terms.

In the case of equation systems the degrees of freedom problem is more serioùs and more common. The number of parameters in the system is often actually as large as or greater than the number of data points. Although this is not the proper way of looking at the numbers situation for calculation of degrees of freedom, it does raise the possibility of trouble in the estimation process. I assert that appropriate estimates can usually be made, even though there are fewer data points than system parameters, yet the argument is lengthy and round about.

That the pure counting problem is different in single equation linear regressions and in complete systems can be indicated by a simple pair of examples.

(i) The single equation

$$y_t = \alpha_1 x_{1t} + \alpha_2 x_{2t} + \ldots + \alpha_m x_{mt} + e_t \qquad (t = 1, 2, \ldots, T) \qquad (1.1)$$

must be estimated from a sample (of size T) with more than m data points, i.e.,

$$T > m;$$

otherwise a perfect fit can be obtained.

Write eq. (1.1) for each data point

$$y_1 = \alpha_1 x_{11} + \alpha_2 x_{21} + \ldots + \alpha_m x_{m1} + e_1$$

$$y_2 = \alpha_1 x_{12} + \alpha_2 x_{22} + \ldots + \alpha_m x_{m2} + e_2 \qquad (1.2)$$

$$\vdots$$

$$y_T = \alpha_1 x_{1T} + \alpha_2 x_{2T} + \ldots + \alpha_m x_{mT} + e_T .$$

If $T = m$, there is a vector $a' = (a_1, a_2, \ldots, a_m)$ that estimates $\alpha' = (\alpha_1, \alpha_2, \ldots, \alpha_m)$ with zero residuals

$$y = Xa + 0; \quad X = (x_{ij}), \qquad (1.3)$$

provided det. $X \neq 0$.

If $T < m$, a perfect fit can be obtained in an infinite number of ways by assigning $(m-T)$ arbitrary values to elements of a and solving for the remaining T elements from

$$y_1 - a^0_{T+1} x_{T+1,1} - \ldots - a^0_m x_{m1} = a_1 x_{11} + a_2 x_{21} + \ldots + a_T x_{T1} + 0 ,$$

$$y_2 - a^0_{T+1} x_{T+1,2} - \ldots - a^0_m x_{m2} = a_1 x_{12} + a_2 x_{22} + \ldots + a_T x_{T2} + 0 ,$$

$$\vdots$$

$$y_T - a^0_{T+1} x_{T+1,T} - \ldots - a^0_m x_{mT} = a_1 x_{1T} + a_2 x_{2T} + \ldots + a_T x_{TT} + 0 .$$

$$(1.4)$$

If

$$\det . \begin{bmatrix} x_{11} & \cdots & x_{T1} \\ \vdots & & \vdots \\ x_{1T} & \cdots & x_{TT} \end{bmatrix} \neq 0 ,$$

there will exist a truncated estimate $(a_1, a_2, \ldots, a_T)$ giving zero residual variation for any choice $a_{T+1}, \ldots, a_m$. This holds for any ordering of the coefficients.

(ii) The equation system

$$A y_t + B x_t = e_t \qquad (1.5)$$

with typical equation

$$\sum_{j=1}^{n} \alpha_{ij} y_{jt} + \sum_{j=1}^{m} \beta_{ij} x_{jt} = e_{it} \qquad \begin{array}{l} (i = 1, 2, \ldots, n) \\ (t = 1, 2, \ldots, T) \end{array} \qquad (1.6)$$

can be estimated with coefficients (a_{ij}) and (b_{ij}) that produce zero residuals if nT does not exceed the number of unknown parameters, provided the determinant of the appropriate data matrix does not vanish.

There are two specific aspects of this proposition that should be stressed. In the first place, the number of data points is not simply T; it is nT. This is the number of stochastic elements in the joint probability distribution of the system. It combines both the number of equations and the number of points at which sample observations are taken. Secondly, the number of unknown parameters in the system is not given by the number of elements in (A, B). From these $(n^2 + nm)$ elements we must subtract n for the rule of units normalization, i.e. the choice of one element of y_t to have a unit coefficient in each equation. We must also subtract the number of identifying restrictions on the equations of the system. This issue does not arise in the single equation regression model. The implicit effect of the identifying restrictions is to impose *a priori* values on some of the system's coefficients. If we write out each equation for each sample point, we shall have the nT equations

$$\alpha_{11} y_{11} + \dots + \alpha_{1n} y_{n1} + \beta_{11} x_{11} + \dots + \beta_{1m} x_{m1} = e_{11} \; ;$$
$$\vdots \qquad \qquad \vdots \qquad \qquad \vdots \qquad \qquad \vdots \qquad \qquad \vdots$$
$$\alpha_{11} y_{1T} + \dots + \alpha_{1n} y_{nT} + \beta_{11} x_{1T} + \dots + \beta_{1m} x_{mT} = e_{1T} ;$$
$$\vdots \qquad \qquad \vdots \qquad \qquad \vdots \qquad \qquad \vdots \qquad \qquad \vdots \qquad (1.7)$$
$$\alpha_{n1} y_{11} + \dots + \alpha_{nn} y_{n1} + \beta_{n1} x_{11} + \dots + \beta_{nm} x_{m1} = e_{n1} \; ;$$
$$\vdots \qquad \qquad \vdots \qquad \qquad \vdots \qquad \qquad \vdots \qquad \qquad \vdots$$
$$\alpha_{n1} y_{1T} + \dots + \alpha_{nn} y_{nT} + \beta_{n1} x_{1T} + \dots + \beta_{nm} x_{mT} = e_{nT} .$$

If there are nT or more unknown coefficients (α_{ij}) and (β_{ij}), we shall be able to find a set of estimates (a_{ij}) and (b_{ij}) that produce a perfect fit. This is obviously a different criterion than applied in the case of the single equation, and it does not involve a simple comparison of T with n, m, or the number of unknown coefficients.

A point that is not usually appreciated is that the number of degrees of freedom should be considered in relation to the method of estimation used. Some methods are more economical than others in the use of degrees of freedom. Let us first take up single-equation methods of estimating equations in complete interdependent systems.

The first stage calculation for either limited information (maximum likelihood) single equation (LISE) estimates or two-stage-least-squares (TSLS) estimates is the regression of each dependent variable on all the independent variables of the system. From (1.5), we obtain

$$y_t = -A^{-1} B x_t + A^{-1} e_t \qquad (1.8)$$

which is written as

$$y_t = \Pi x_t + v_t. \tag{1.9}$$

The first-stage regression calculations ignore the identities

$$\Pi = -A^{-1}B, \tag{1.10}$$

$$v_t = A^{-1}e_t, \tag{1.11}$$

and simply estimate the unrestricted regressions

$$y_{it} = \pi_{i1}x_{1t} + \ldots + \pi_{im}x_{mt} + v_{it} \quad \begin{array}{l} (i = 1,2,\ldots,n) \\ (t = 1,2,\ldots,T). \end{array} \tag{1.12}$$

From preceding arguments, it is evident that we must have $T > m$. If this inequality does not hold, we can obtain a perfect fit for (1.9), in which case the second stage of TSLS or LISE will collapse into ordinary single equation regression by the method of least squares (OLS).

This is, by far, the most commonly encountered problem of shortage in degrees of freedom, since many econometric systems now have large values for m if all the lagged values of dependent variables are classified as *predetermined* variables and placed in the x-vector for this calculation. We frequently find that $m > T$, in practice.

Another way of looking at this problem is to observe that

$$\det. (X'X) = 0,$$

where $X'X$ is the moment matrix of predetermined variables. The regression estimate of π_i in (1.12) is given by

$$\text{est. } \pi_i = (X'X)^{-1} X' y_i \; ; \tag{1.13}$$

therefore it is essential that $X'X$ be nonsingular.

It is instructive to look at the degrees of freedom problem from this point of view, since multicollinearity among elements of x_t also causes $X'X$ to be singular or at least "ill-conditioned". [1] Methods that will be suggested in section 2 for coping with a shortage of degrees of freedom will also be used for coping with the problem of multicollinearity. Both problems are manifestations of basic singularities.

So far, we have shown that for OLS calculations, the degrees of freedom restriction is

$$T > m_i ,$$

where m_i is the number of regressors (unknown coefficients) in the ith single equation. For TSLS or LISE calculations we must have

$$T > m.$$

This is a much stronger condition since $m \geqslant m_i$. The number of predetermined variables in a complete system will almost always be greater than the number in a single equation. In today's systems, the discrepancy between m_i and m is large.

Other methods of estimation, particularly three-stage-least-squares (3SLS) and full-information-maximum-likelihood (FIML) impose even stronger degrees of freedom requirements on a system. These will be examined now.

An important matrix in the calculation of full information estimators (3SLS and FIML), and indeed a matrix that is important by itself for stochastic simulation, evaluation of forecast error and other uses, is the estimated variance/covariance matrix of structural disturbances,

$$\text{est. } \Sigma = \text{est. } (E(e_{it}e_{jt})) . \tag{1.14}$$

The covariances of sample residuals form the estimate of the Σ-matrix,

---

[1] See L.R. Klein and M. Nakamura [7].

$$\text{est. } \Sigma = \left[\frac{1}{T} \sum_{t=1}^{T} (\text{res.})_{it} \, (\text{res.})_{jt} \right] . \tag{1.15}$$

This matrix appears directly in the concentrated likelihood function

$$\log (\det. A) - \frac{1}{2} \log (\det. \Sigma)$$

that is maximized for FIML estimates. The "normal equations" of 3SLS estimation make use of the elements of est. Σ^{-1} as weighting factors. It is evident, therefore, that est. Σ must be nonsingular in order that the likelihood function be finite or that the inverse of est. Σ exist. A necessary condition for the nonsingularity of est. Σ is

$$T > n .$$

The restriction

$$T > m$$

is obviously necessary for 3SLS estimation as long as that method uses TSLS estimation for the calculation of est. Σ^{-1}. It can easily be shown that the same restriction holds for FIML estimation. We may write

$$\text{est. } \Sigma = \text{est. } \frac{1}{T} \sum_{t=1}^{T} (A y_t + B x_t) (A y_t + B x_t)' . \tag{1.16}$$

Define

$$W = (Y|X) = \begin{bmatrix} y_{11} \cdots y_{n1} & x_{11} \cdots x_{m1} \\ \vdots \quad \vdots & \vdots \quad \vdots \\ y_{1T} \cdots y_{nT} & x_{1T} \cdots x_{mT} \end{bmatrix} , \tag{1.17}$$

$$\Gamma = (A|B) = \begin{bmatrix} \alpha_{11} \cdots \alpha_{1n} & \beta_{11} \cdots \beta_{1m} \\ \vdots \quad\ \vdots & \vdots \quad\ \vdots \\ \alpha_{n1} \cdots \alpha_{nn} & \beta_{n1} \cdots \beta_{nm} \end{bmatrix}. \tag{1.18}$$

It follows that

$$\text{est. } \Sigma = \text{est. } \frac{1}{T}(\Gamma W'\ W\Gamma'). \tag{1.19}$$

The moment matrix $W'W$ must be positive definite in order for the matrix in (1.19) to be nonsingular. In order for $W'W$ to be positive definite, we must have

$T > m + n.$

Since $Y'Y$ and $X'X$ are both principal minors of $W'W$, they must be positive definite. This implies the inequality

$T > m,$

which is the same one that holds for LISE and TSLS.

All the methods of estimation considered except OLS require that the number of predetermined variables be fewer than the number of sample points. In addition, the full information methods require that the number of equations (endogenous variables) also be fewer than the number of sample points. These are highly restrictive conditions.

These are not purely formal conditions. In large macroeconometric systems it is likely that we shall find a shortage of degrees of freedom in the sense that

$n > T, \quad m > T.$

In systems with large numbers of observations, these restrictions may not be consequential, but there are many situations in which they are effectively having an influence on estimation procedures. In the estimation of the Brookings Model [3], we have a case where there are fewer than 100 time series observations (quarters since 1948) ($T < 100$) but more than 200 equations ($n > 200$). Counting lag variables, there are more than 200 predetermined variables ($m > 200$). In a situation like this, straightforward applications of FIML, 3SLS, TSLS, and LISE are all precluded. There is, however, nothing to prevent OLS estimation of each equation. The Wharton Model and several others with 50–100 simultaneous stochastic equations usually violate one of the two restrictions, or come close to it.

Econometricians are usually loath to use data from the period of the Korean War and post World War II reconstruction or reconversion; therefore most samples effectively begin after 1953, and (limiting ourselves to consideration of quarterly models) this cuts significantly into sample size. Data are available for models like the Klein-Goldberger Model for a longer time period, but these are necessarily annual models and consist of no more than 35–40 observations. [2] In microeconomic cross section samples there are thousands of degrees of freedom, but not enough information to estimate a complete system.

For the near term, econometricians must face the fact that there is a shortage of degrees of freedom. In the case of the developing countries where model building is rapidly gaining popularity for planning growth, the degrees of freedom are even scarcer because samples are rarely available before 1950 and are only annual. In these cases and in the cases of large models for the industrial economies, application of FIML or 3SLS methods seem to be out of the question unless the whole model is split into mutually orthogonal blocks. These methods can be applied within small blocks provided one is prepared to make the strong assumption of block diagonality in the covariance matrix of errors. It seems more plausible, however, to modify single equation methods such as LISE or TSLS for the usual type models. These are the procedures that we take up in the next section.

---

[2] See L.R. Klein [6].

2. *Ways of coping with undersized samples*

To many econometricians it seems strange to work hard at getting estimates by consistent and efficient methods when degrees of freedom are scarce, data are often of dubious quality, and differences in numerical magnitudes of individual coefficients are often small. Because there are such great needs for improvement, I contend that we should be on the lookout for even modest gains wherever possible; all avenues should be explored. It also appears that small differences in individual coefficients may become magnified into significant differences in complete system solutions. Also, small inconsistencies or biases in complete system solutions may build up over time in dynamic simulations. This point is especially significant in striving for consistent estimation for models of the developing countries. The main issue is to make long run analyses, and in decade-length simulations there is much chance for error build-up to occur. There will always be build-up of *random* errors; it is avoidance of *bias* error build-up that is being pursued in the construction of consistent estimates for developing country models.

2.1. *Deletion of variables*

The simplest method of obtaining consistent estimates of the TSLS or LISE types for systems that have too few degrees of freedom in that

$$T < m$$

is to select subsets of predetermined variables to be used as regressors in the first-stage calculations.
From

$$\{x_{1t}, x_{2t}, ..., x_{m_1 t}, x_{m_1+1,t}, ..., x_{mt}\}$$

a subset

$$\{x_{1t}, x_{2t}, ..., x_{m_1 t}\}$$

is selected for which

$$m_1 < T.$$

Included in the selected subset are the predetermined variables that explicitly appear in the single equation to be estimated. This means that the first-stage regressions cannot be done once and for all for the whole system; they must be tailored to the estimation of specific structural equations.

This is an old procedure and was always in the "oral tradition" discussions at the Cowles Commission in the early days of development of simultaneous equation methods. It was then used for LISE calculations of the first postwar U.S. model and received formal justification (consistency) in the basic paper on LISE by Anderson and Rubin [1]. [3]

The drawback to this method is its arbitrariness and lack of uniqueness; there are many ways in which subsets of predetermined variables, sufficient for the estimation of any single equation, can be selected, and there is no simple criterion to indicate where to stop in this solution process. If it were feasible to search over all possible subsets for each equation, we could choose that combination of equation estimates that provided best system simulation performance, measured by some summary statistic, but this does not seem to be a practical suggestion for large systems.

Where collinear variables alone are omitted; i.e. where the omitted variables are highly correlated with retained variables, there should be little effect on the estimated residual variances and covariances in the reduced form. The two systems

$$y_{it} = \sum_{j=1}^{m} p_{ij} x_{jt} + (\text{res.})_{it} , \tag{1.20}$$

and

$$y_{it} = \sum_{j=1}^{m_1} p'_{ij} x_{jt} + (\text{res.})'_{it} , \tag{1.21}$$

[3] For an application see L.R. Klein [5].

will give rise to approximately the same covariance matrix

$$\text{est. } \Sigma_v = \left[\frac{1}{T} \sum_{t=1}^{T} (\text{res.})_{it} \, (\text{res.})_{jt} \right],$$ (1.22)

using either (1.20) or (1.21) as the estimates of the reduced forms in (1.12), if the omitted variables $x_{m_1+1,t}$, ..., x_{mt} are highly correlated with x_{1t}, ..., $x_{m_1,t}$. If the collinearity is strong enough and if the omitted set is large enough, both the problems of collinearity and shortage of degrees of freedom could be handled jointly by the appropriate deletion of first stage regressors. This is only a special case and is not typical, however.

2.2. Principal components

If instead of regressing on all the predetermined variables independently we were to carry out the first stage regressions on restricted combinations of predetermined variables we may be able to get round the degrees of freedom problems and the collinearity problem in a systematic way that is not open to personal choice or arbitrariness. Kloek and Mennes [8] proposed the use of principal components of predetermined variables as a procedure for dealing with a shortage of degrees of freedom. They suggested alternative ways of doing this, either by forming principal components of variables excluded from a given equation, principal components of certain residuals, or principal components of all the predetermined variables in the system. The last way has the advantage that the components need to be evaluated only once for an entire system.

Principal components of x_{1t},...,x_{mt} expressed as linear combination of the x's

$$(PC)_{it} = \sum_{j=1}^{m} q_{ij} x_{jt} \qquad (i = 1,2,...,m),$$ (1.23)

are mutually orthogonal and have the same generalized variance (in total) as that of the original set of variables. That is to say, the components each contribute to an "explanation" of the generalized variance of the x's. If we order them by percentage of variance accounted for individually, we may be able to find a small number of principal components that account for a large portion of the generalized variance of the predetermined variables. Principal component analysis may be regarded as a *data reduction* technique, by enabling us to replace a large number of predetermined variables by a small number of linear functions of these variables. The replacement set preserves, to a large extent, the generalized variance of the original set, and if the number of elements in the replacement set is small, as usually happens, we are likely to find that they do not exhaust the available degrees of freedom in the system when used as first stage regressors. They have the additional advantage of being orthogonal; therefore they are not collinear regressors.

Principal components have the disadvantage of not being invariant under a change in units of measurement of the original predetermined variables. If, however, we adopt a convention that they shall be evaluated as characteristic vectors of a correlation matrix

$$\left[\frac{\sum\limits_{t=1}^{T} (x_{it} - \bar{x}_i)(x_{jt} - \bar{x}_j)}{\sqrt{\sum\limits_{t=1}^{T} (x_{it} - \bar{x}_i)^2 (x_{jt} - \bar{x}_j)^2}} \right] = R, \tag{1.24}$$

$$|R - \lambda I| = 0, \tag{1.25}$$

we have a definite rule to follow that is independent of the units of measurement of the individual x_{it}.

Principal components, being linear functions of the original x_{it}, as in (1.23), can often be associated with particular types of movements in the variables that are responsible for movement of the economy. One component may give big weight, through large values of q-coefficients, to trend variables in $x_{1t}, ..., x_{mt}$; another to short-cycle variables; and still others to long-cycle variables; etc. In short, the data reduction methods of principal components analysis enable us to pick out leading groupings within $x_{1t}, ..., x_{mt}$. The fact that several variables among the predetermined set account for each of the dominant aspects of economic movement means that data reduction through principal component analysis enables us to pick out a small number of leading characteristics associated with a few principal components. This is the reason why collinearity is avoided at the same time that degrees of freedom are conserved.

2.3. Restricted reduced forms

The identifying restrictions on a system leave many "holes" or restrictions on elements in A and B, the matrices of the economy's structure. When the reduced form is derived as in (1.8)

$$y_t = -A^{-1}Bx_t + v_t \ ,$$

there will be corresponding restrictions on $-A^{-1}B$. These are ignored in the first stage regressions for TSLS or LISE estimators, and that is a basic reason why degrees of freedom considerations look so large, as do the multicollinearity problems as well. If we had some preliminary estimates of A and B, say $\hat{A}$ and $\hat{B}$, the estimated restricted reduced forms [4]

$$\hat{\hat{y}}_t = -\hat{A}^{-1}\hat{B}x_t \tag{1.26}$$

would provide values of y_t that could be used as regressors or instruments in the subsequent stages of TSLS or LISE estimation calculations.

If few degrees of freedom are used up in estimating each row of $(A|B)$, and (1.26) is derived from the row by estimates of the

---

[4] In (1.26), we denote computed values as $\hat{\hat{y}}_t$ instead of $\bar{\hat{y}}_t$, since the latter are customarily the values obtained from unrestricted reduced form regressions $\hat{y}_t = \hat{\Pi}x_t$.

whole system, then the values of $\hat{y}_t$ can be used at a final stage for the estimation of each single equation without using many degrees of freedom. All the economic information on coefficient structure is used in this approach. In that sense it is a full-information procedure, but covariance information on the structure of the random errors is not used; therefore this method is not as efficient as FIML or 3SLS, yet it makes few demands on degrees of freedom and in that sense has much to recommend it as a kind of full information method.

There are many ways of getting preliminary estimates $\hat{A}$, $\hat{B}$ for the calculation of instruments or regressors from (1.26). Three possible methods are [5]

(i) instrumental variables;

(ii) TSLS (or LISE) with arbitrarily selected subsets of predetermined variables;

(iii) TSLS (or LISE) with principal components of predetermined variables.

The method of instrumental variables is taken here to mean the arbitrary selection of n_{i-1} instruments for the formation of the "normal equations"

$$\sum_{t=1}^{T} y_{1t} z_{kt} = - \sum_{j=2}^{n_i} \alpha_{ij} \sum_{t=1}^{T} y_{jt} z_{kt} - \sum_{j=1}^{m_i} \beta_{ij} \sum_{t=1}^{T} x_{jt} z_{kt} \quad (k=2,3,...,n_i),$$

$$\sum_{t=1}^{T} y_{1t} x_{\varrho t} = - \sum_{j=2}^{n_i} \alpha_{ij} \sum_{t=1}^{T} y_{jt} x_{\varrho t} - \sum_{j=1}^{m_i} \beta_{ij} \sum_{t=1}^{T} x_{jt} x_{\varrho t} \quad \begin{array}{l} (\varrho=1,2,...,m_i); \\ (m_i \leqslant m; n_i \leqslant n). \end{array}$$

$$(1.27)$$

The outside instruments are $z_{2t}, ..., z_{n_i t}$; while the inside instruments are $x_{1t}, ..., x_{m_i t}$. The first dependent variable is assumed to have a normalized unit coefficient ($\alpha_{i1} = 1$), and the identifying restrictions are implied by the fact that n_i and m_i do not cover all dependent and independent variables of the system.

---

[5] OLS estimates of structural equations, though inconsistent, would also be suitable initial estimates and need not lead to inconsistency of the final estimates.

Since the selection of z_{kt} is arbitrary except for the fact that these variables must qualify as being proper instrumental variables, the preliminary estimates of A, B are inefficient. The procedure using the restricted reduced forms may be iterated, however, and this should lessen dependence on the starting estimates. Nevertheless, it is important to have good starting estimates that are economically plausible.

The method of instrumental variables applied as in (i) to single equations, one at a time, is simple, straightforward and no more demanding on degrees of freedom than is OLS, but it gives a *consistent* starting estimate. It is only slightly more laborious to use method (ii) in place of (i) for a starting estimate. Since TSLS (or LISE) can be given instrumental variable interpretations, (i) is a special case of (ii). Estimates based on starting values provided by (ii) should be more efficient than those based on (i) and somewhat less arbitrary because there are fewer ways in which subgroups of instruments appropriate to (ii) can be chosen than there are ways in which separate instruments for eq. (1.27) can be chosen.

A preferred way of obtaining preliminary estimates for the computation of values from restricted reduced forms is by estimating the entire system by TSLS (or LISE) using principal components of predetermined variables. The arbitrariness of selection of the components can be reduced by fixing a required percentage of total variance to be accounted for by the principal components or a minimal number of degrees of freedom to be preserved for the estimation of unrestricted reduced forms. [6]

The estimates of A and B obtained by (iii) are useful in themselves as estimates of the entire system, but there is some evidence that they can be improved upon through the use of restricted reduced forms. Asymptotically, we shall not be able to improve upon TSLS efficiency through iterative use of the restricted reduced forms, but there is some evidence that sample simulation

---

[6] When principal components are used as first stage regressors, in place of predetermined variables, there are, in fact, some restrictions placed on the reduced forms, but these are not economic theoretic restrictions.

performance of complete systems is improved in terms of mean square error if the ordinary estimates are iterated once. There is some evidence as well that post sample extrapolative performance is also improved, but that evidence is less impressive. [7]

2.4. Causal ordering

Soon after the introduction of the simultaneous equations approach to inference in econometric systems by the Cowles Commission, Bentzel and Wold [2] pointed out the enormous simplification in the whole procedure in the case where the model has the structure of the cobweb theory. For example, the system

$$q_t = \beta_0 + \beta_1 p_{t-1} + e_t$$
$$(1.28)$$
$$p_t = \alpha_0 + \alpha_1 q_t + u_t$$

can be efficiently estimated by regressing (OLS) q_t on p_{t-1} and p_t on q_t, separately, provided e_t and u_t are independent. The main feature of this system is that it is fully recursive, namely, the matrix of coefficients of dependent variables is triangular

$$A = \begin{bmatrix} 1 & 0 \\ -\alpha_1 & 1 \end{bmatrix},$$

and the covariance matrix of disturbances is diagonal

$$\Sigma = \begin{bmatrix} \sigma_e^2 & 0 \\ 0 & \sigma_u^2 \end{bmatrix}.$$

In this kind of system, through a proper recursive ordering of equations we can always form a set of efficient OLS estimates. These use no more degrees of freedom per equation than the number of unknown coefficients in each individual equation.

[7] See H.N. Johnston et al. [9].

There is, generally speaking, no degrees of freedom problem in estimating this system. Even if Σ is not diagonal, a variation on TSLS and OLS can be devised which is highly economical in the use of degrees of freedom. In this case, the first equation to be estimated by OLS is the one that has only one unlagged dependent variable and one or more predetermined variables. This would be the first equation in (1.28). In the second equation p_t should be regressed on the values of q_t computed from the first equation rather than observed q_t values. This, in fact, uses a restricted reduced form. Even if there were other predetermined variables in the second equation, these would not be used in the computation of q_t values for OLS purposes in the second; this is the sense in which a restricted reduced form is being used. Fisher [4] generalized the concept of a recursive system into one in which

A is block triangular;
Σ is block diagonal.

Within blocks the usual methods (OLS, TSLS, LISE, FIML, 3SLS) are to be used, but blocks may be small enough so that degrees of freedom problems are not serious. The predetermined variables of a block are those that appear explicitly in equations of the block and dependent variables that come from prior blocks in the recursive ordering. If the Σ matrix is block diagonal, actual values of dependent variables may be taken from prior blocks, but if Σ is not block diagonal, computed values of dependent variables may be taken from prior blocks. The dependent variables taken from prior blocks are added to the list of predetermined variables within a block.

If the Brookings Model or the Wharton Model is to be estimated by FIML or 3SLS techniques, some block decomposition must be introduced in order to satisfy the degrees of freedom restrictions. The same considerations hold for ordinary TSLS or LISE methods. Fisher's method, called Structurally Ordered Instrumental Variables (SOIV) takes account of the causal structure both from the point of view of economic lines of relationship and dynamics. Implicitly, however, this is done automatically when restricted reduced forms are used in the iteration of TSLS or LISE methods. The advantage of the latter methods based on the restricted reduced forms is that they do not require extensive prior searching for the recursive ordering into an optimal block structure lay out. Something like the SOIV method will be necessary for the application of FIML methods to large systems, but single-equation methods are probably better handled by the use of principal components and restricted reduced forms.

3. Some practical problems

One of the most important aspects of contemporary model building has been the extensive and intensive use of lag distributions to capture the economic dynamics of the system. It is no longer satisfactory to introduce simple delays of one or two periods for some leading variables. Similarly, we can do better than make simplifying transformations, as in the well-known Koyck case, by casting the specification into a linear problem with short lags. The issue has been to estimate lengthy complicated lag distributions on several variables simultaneously, and this has greatly improved the explanatory power of single equations. The preferred procedure has been to specify an equation such as an investment function

$$I_t = \sum_{i=0}^{s} w_i \left[\frac{P}{C}\right]_{t-i} + \sum_{i=0}^{u} q_i x_{t-i} + \sum_{i=0}^{v} r_i K_{t-i} + e_t \qquad (1.29)$$

and find distributed lag weights w_i, q_i, r_i together with length of lag s, u, v that minimize

$$\sum_{t=1}^{T} \hat{e}_t^2.$$

It has been a significant advance to be able to do this by search or iteration methods, and the results appear to be gratifying. Methods have not been extended yet to simultaneous equation systems, but even on a single equation OLS basis, much research was required in order to devise workable procedures for simultaneous estimation of several lag distributions within one equation. Simple Koyck transformations are not capable of putting this case into linear form. Working directly with the untransformed specification, we have not complicated the structure of the error term.

As a practical matter the estimation of equations like (1.29) and indeed all the preliminary specifications of a complete model have been explored by OLS methods. The usual procedure is to estimate by consistent methods after the preliminary specification by OLS methods. This is less than satisfactory, but it is the way models of any complexity are, in fact, constructed.

Two lag distributions that are capable of showing the types of dynamic reactions that we hypothesize for economic behavior are the rational polynomial and the (Almon) finite polynomial. The latter will form the basis of the present discussion. It will be assumed that w_i, q_i and r_i lie along polynomials

$$w_i = \alpha_0 + \alpha_1 i + \alpha_2 i^2 + \alpha_3 i^3 + ...;$$

$$q_i = \beta_0 + \beta_1 i + \beta_2 i^2 + \beta_3 i^3 + ...; \qquad (1.30)$$

$$r_i = \gamma_0 + \gamma_1 i + \gamma_2 i^2 + \gamma_3 i^3 + ...$$

The OLS estimates are obtained by searching the parameter space for values of s, u, v, α_j, β_j, γ_j, and the degrees of the polynomials. There are customarily some end point restrictions on w_i, q_i, and r_i.

What has all this to do with the problem of undersized samples? It is simply that when we come to the stage of developing TSLS or other consistent estimates for a large model with comparatively few sample points, we are going to be starting from a specification that is based on long lag distributions, for which we have OLS estimates. It is not practical to consider each lag variable

$$(P/C)_{t-1}, (P/C)_{t-2},...; \quad x_{t-1}, x_{t-2},...; \quad K_{t-1}, K_{t-2},...; \text{etc.}$$

as separate predetermined variables and search again for optimal parameter values in the context of consistent estimation methods. There are likely to be several long lags, and this will enormously extend the list of predetermined variables. There are two alternative simplifications that serve to reduce the computing burden associated with lag distributions in the context of consistent estimation. The composite variable

$$\sum_{i=0}^{u} q_i x_{t-i}$$

can be written as

$$q_0 \sum_{i=0}^{u} \frac{q_i}{q_0} x_{t-i} = q_0 x_t + q_0 \sum_{i=1}^{u} \frac{q_i}{q_0} x_{t-i},$$

$$= q_0 x_t + q_0 z_t. \tag{1.31}$$

The variable z_t will be constructed from lag values of x_t with coefficients (q_i/q_0) estimated from the OLS values and will appear as one single predetermined variable of the system. The scale parameter q_0 will be re-estimated by consistent methods, taking account of the fact that x_t and z_t are constrained to have identical coefficients.

The alternative procedure is to rewrite the equation being estimated as [8]

$$I_t = \alpha_0 \sum_{i=0}^{s} \left[\frac{P}{C}\right]_{t-i} + \alpha_1 \sum_{i=0}^{s} i \left[\frac{P}{C}\right]_{t-i} + \alpha_2 \sum_{i=0}^{s} i^2 \left[\frac{P}{C}\right]_{t-i} + \ldots$$

$$+ \beta_0 \sum_{i=0}^{u} x_{t-i} + \beta_1 \sum_{i=0}^{u} i x_{t-i} + \beta_2 \sum_{i=0}^{u} i^2 x_{t-i} + \ldots$$

$$+ \gamma_0 \sum_{i=0}^{v} K_{t-i} + \gamma_1 \sum_{i=0}^{v} i K_{t-i} + \gamma_2 \sum_{i=0}^{v} i^2 K_{t-i} + \ldots$$

$$+ e_t. \tag{1.32}$$

[8] This suggestion was made by Robert Rasche.

The predetermined variables are:

$$\sum_{i=1}^{s} i \left[\frac{P}{C}\right]_{t-i} , \; \sum_{i=1}^{s} i^2 \left[\frac{P}{C}\right]_{t-i} ,...;$$

$$\sum_{i=1}^{u} i x_{t-i} , \; \sum_{i=1}^{u} i^2 x_{t-i} ,...;$$

$$\sum_{i=1}^{v} i K_{t-i} , \; \sum_{i=1}^{v} i^2 K_{t-i} ,... .$$

These are more numerous than in the previous case. Also, the estimation of α_j, β_j, γ_j by consistent methods will re-introduce some searching again. To keep the number of predetermined variables from growing unusually large and to limit the amount of computation, the first alternative should be chosen. The method of principal components and restricted TSLS estimation applied to this kind of model is feasible.

An earlier version of the Wharton family of models was estimated by constructing 12 principal components of predetermined variables, regressing dependent variables on these principal components, and using the computed regressands as regressors in the second stage regressions of each structural equation. These estimates have also been iterated once by computing a new set of values from restricted reduced forms and using them as regressors in structural equations again. These are all feasible calculations in a system with 50 structural equations and 68 quarterly observations. The newer version of this model will have many more lags, a few more equations, and a few more variables. The methods of restricting the lag distributions by ratios of OLS estimates will be used. This method has been applied to the Wharton Annual and Industry Model, which has 150 structural equations and only 18 annual observations. Seven principal components were found to account for more than 75% of the variance of predetermined variables. Dependent variables were regressed on these, together with included predetermined variables from each equation. The computed regressands were then used as second stage regressors.

If the dependent variables of a system are regressed on a fixed set of principal components for an entire system, and on no other variables, in the first stage, the computed regressands should be used as instrumental variables in the second stage; otherwise consistency will not be obtained. If, however, the first stage regressions contain the included predetermined variables, the computed regressands may be used as either regressors or instruments in the second stage.

This issue arises in another way for LISE estimates. In that method, a difference between two covariance matrices is used

$$B = (Y'X)(X'X)^{-1}(X'Y) - (Y'X_i)(X_i'X_i)^{-1}(X_i'Y). \tag{1.33}$$

The matrix B is the difference between the covariance matrix of unrestricted reduced form residuals using only the components of x_t appearing explicitly in the ith equation and the same covariance matrix using all the components of x_t. Of course the first set of residuals dominate the second in the sense that B is positive semi-definite. If we replace the whole set of x_t by principal components, denoted as a data matrix P, we cannot be sure that

$$(Y'P)(P'P)^{-1}(P'Y) - (Y'X_i)(X_i'X_i)^{-1}(X_i'Y)$$

will be positive semi-definite. This problem can be avoided if P is augmented by x_i, i.e. if the first stage regressions contain the included predetermined variables for each structural equation, as well as the principal components.

Even though $X'X$ is singular or ill-conditioned, either through a shortage of degrees of freedom or collinearity, both of which are likely to occur in large dynamic systems, we can still extract principal components. Care must be taken to use much computational accuracy and to watch for multiple or close characteristic roots. Since it is not known in an absolute sense just how many roots to extract, we should experiment to the extent allowable by computing facilities to see which set of principal components gives the best system estimate, based on some overall statistic of simulation performance. Average (RMSE/mean) would seem to be a good indicator of performance. It has been found that a modest number of principal components seems to produce TSLS estimates that simulate best.

References

[1] T.W. Anderson Jr. and H. Rubin, "The asymptotic properties of estimates of the parameters of a single equation in a complete system of stochastic equations", *Annals of Mathematical Statistics* 21 (December 1950) 570–82.

[2] R. Bentzel and H. Wold, "On statistical demand analysis from the viewpoint of simultaneous equations", *Skandinavisk Aktuarictidskrift* (1946) 95–114.

[3] J. Duesenberry, et al., *The Brookings quarterly econometric model of the United States* (Chicago, Rand McNally, 1965).

[4] F.M. Fisher, "Dynamic structure and estimation in economy-wide econometric models", in: *The Brookings quarterly econometric model of the United States*, edited by J. Duesenberry et al. (Chicago, Rand McNally, 1965).

[5] L.R. Klein, *Economic fluctuations in the United States, 1921–1941* (New York, John Wiley and Sons, 1950).

[6] L.R. Klein, "Estimation of interdependent systems in macroeconometrics", *Econometrica* 37 (April 1969) 171–92.

[7] L.R. Klein and M. Nakamura, "Singularity in the equation systems of econometrics: some aspects of the problem of multicollinearity", *International Economic Review* 3 (September 1962) 274–99.

[8] T. Kloek and L.B.M. Mennes, "Simultaneous equations estimation based on principal components of predetermined variables", *Econometrica* 28 (January 1960) 45–61.

[9] H.N. Johnston, L.R. Klein and K. Shinjo, "Estimation and prediction in dynamic economic models", 1971, to be published.

SOME FEATURES AND USES OF THE
CANADIAN QUARTERLY MODEL RDX2

John HELLIWELL,
University of British Columbia

Fred GORBET, Ian STEWART and Don STEPHENSON
Bank of Canada

1. Introduction

In this paper we describe some of the main features and uses of RDX2, a quarterly model of the Canadian economy.

RDX2 has 142 behavioural and 116 technical relationships, divided into twenty-one sectors that can be grouped into five main categories. Table 1, showing the number of stochastic equations and technical relationships in each of the twenty-one sectors of RDX2, provides a convenient statement of the degree of disaggregation used in the various sectors. Because a full explanation of the structure may be found elsewhere [8], here we merely touch on a few of the more interesting mechanisms built into RDX2 (in sections 2—5), in order to set the stage for a discussion (in sections 6—8) of some of the simulation possibilities open to users of a model with a great deal of structural detail.

The aspects of RDX2 we stress in sections 2—5 are those that represent innovations designed to increase its ability to perform an expanded set of realistic policy simulations. For example, considerable care has been lavished on making aggregate supply depend in appropriate ways on the available factor supplies, and on using relationships between aggregate supply and demand to influence changes in prices, wages, trade flows, inventory stocks, and

J. Helliwell et al.

Table 1
RDX2 equations by sector

Sector	Number of equations		
	Behav.	Tech.	Total
1. Consumer expenditure	4	3	7
2. Residential construction	5		5
3. Business investment and output	3	13	16
4. Foreign trade	22	9	31
5. Business employment, hours, labour force, and population	7	6	13
6. Private sector wages	2	1	3
7. Prices	20	3	23
8. Income components	3	9	12
9. Direct taxes and other current transfers from persons			
Personal income tax	3	26	29
Transfers from persons to provincial-municipal governments	2	1	3
Corporation income tax	3	1	4
10. Indirect taxes and other government revenue	7	1	8
11. Transfers to persons	5	1	6
12. Federal current and capital expenditure on goods and services	4	1	5
13. Provincial-municipal current and capital expenditure on goods and services	6	2	8
14. Government asset and liability changes	5	8	13
15. Demand for liquid assets by nonfinancial sector	8	3	11
16. Chartered bank assets	6	5	11
17. Interest rates and mortgage approvals	10	1	11
18. The market value of real capital, wealth, the supply price of capital and the expected rate of inflation	1	6	7
19. Long-term capital flows	13		13
20. International portfolio positions		10	10
21. The foreign exchange market and short-term capital flows	3	6	9
Total number of equations	142	116	258

other mechanisms brought into play in disequilibrium situations. These developments are the subject of section 2.

The behaviour of governments (federal and provincial-municipal) is explained in some detail, so as to include a wider variety of policy instruments and to improve the realism of the model's dynamic structure. Some of the more novel features of these equations are mentioned in section 3.

In section 4 we describe the attempts that have been made to explain the flows of goods, services, people and capital between Canada and other countries, and in section 5 we explain some of the links between financial markets and goods markets within Canada.

The simulation contexts in which RDX2 is employed, the types of problem analysed, and some features of the simulations linking RDX2 with a model of the U.S. economy are dealt with in sections 6–8.

2. Aggregate supply and demand, derived factor demands, and some adjustment mechanisms

2.1. Supply and demand

The main aggregate supply and demand measures in RDX2 are based on the concept of gross private business output, defined as non-agricultural GNP less value added by governments and non-commercial institutions. Actual private non-agricultural business output is called UGPP. The aggregate demand measure is called UGPPA, and is equal to UGPP less unintended inventory accumulation. The two main aggregate supply measures are both based on an explicit production function and different definitions of factor supply. The current supply variable (UGPPS) represents the quantity of output that would be forthcoming if the capital stocks (of non-residential construction and of equipment treated separately), actual business employment, and current average weekly hours per man are all used at their average productivity levels, given the current state of Harrod-neutral technical progress. That is, UGPPS is what would be produced if the assumed production function held exactly, based on current input levels. The longer-term or "desired" level of output (UGPPD) is what would be produced if the production function held exactly using actual capital, "normal" employment, and "normal" average weekly hours. "Normal" employment is what business employment would be if the unemployment rate were at its average value, and "normal" hours follows a declining trend.

There are two further supply measures based on UGPP and employed in the factor-demand equations described in section 2.2.

UGPPANP is the level of output that would be forthcoming if the remaining portion of each vintage of construction-type capital were employed at the capital/output ratio that minimized expected costs at the time the original investment decision was taken. UGPPAMP is a parallel measure of preferred output in which each vintage of equipment works with its desired capital/-output ratio.

We now consider the ways in which the above measures of supply and demand are explained and used within the aggregate model.

2.2. Derived factor demands

The demands for construction, equipment, business employment and average weekly hours are jointly derived assuming minimization of expected costs and a three-factor (construction, equipment and man-hours) Cobb-Douglas production function with constant returns to scale and Harrod-neutral technical progress. We chose the production function exponents from a grid of alternatives, basing our choice on the relative success of the derived factor-demand equations. Data treated as given to the factor-demand decisions are expected output, and the expected prices of the services of construction capital, of equipment capital, and of man-hours. The expectations processes used have explicit time horizons, so that it is possible to model the incentive to substitute capital for labour that may result when there are increases in the expected rates of growth of both prices and wages.

Although the target inputs for all factors are consistently derived from a cost minimization process, the adjustment paths embody a hierarchy of dependence, with capital adjusting first, then employment, and finally hours worked.

The demand for each type of capital good depends on the gap between expected output and preferred output for that type of capital. This gap is then multiplied by the cost-minimizing value of the relevant capital/output ratio. The investment equations are fitted net of assumed replacement investment, and the time paths of adjustment from the actual to desired levels of capital stock depend on internally generated cash flow, interest rates, the availability of bank advances, and direct investment inflows. These latter variables are all represented as ratios to moving averages, so that they affect only the dynamics of investment response.

The business employment equation is at the next level in the hierarchy. The "desired" level of employment is the level of employment that would be required to produce UGPPA, given the stocks of available capital and normal average weekly hours. Straightforward inversion of the production function, with an adjustment for the trend in average weekly hours, gives a labour requirement in terms of men of unchanged efficiency. The difference between the trend of this series and the trend of actual business employment defines the labour efficiency factor (ELEFF). Dividing the labour requirement expressed in efficiency units by ELEFF gives an employment target, and the change in the level of employment is determined by the gap between the current employment target and the level of employment in the preceding quarter. This gap is referred to by us as the "short gap" to distinguish our concept of the desired level of employment from some alternative definitions. (See [8], pp. 97–98.)

Because only partial adjustment to the current employment gap takes place, there is room for a third level in the hierarchy of factor demands. The difference between actual average weekly hours and "normal" hours, measured as a ratio to "normal" hours, depends on the difference between the current employment target and the current actual level of employment, measured as a ratio to the target level. A coefficient of 1.0 on this variable would indicate that marginal factor adjustments were rapid enough to permit output, at normal levels of short-term productivity, to alter sufficiently to match demand. But the estimated coefficient is about 0.13, leaving a remaining gap (either positive or negative) between UGPPA and UGPPS.

The actual level of output (UGPP) falls part way between aggregate demand and the supply variable (UGPPS). UGPP differs from UGPPS to the extent that employed factors work at other-than-average productivity levels, and from UGPPA to the extent that inventories play a buffer-stock role in permitting final demand and output to differ.

The buffer-stock role of inventories is quantified by including the difference between UGPPS and non-inventory final demand (UGPP-IIB) as an independent variable in the equation for the change in non-farm business inventories. The coefficient on this variable (0.46) indicates a substantial buffer-stock role, and the coefficient times the variable defines the difference between UGPP and aggregate demand (UGPPA). We determine the intended portion of inventory accumulation by a flexible accelerator mechanism with different marginal stock/sales ratios for each of three main categories of final sales. So far we have not attempted to tie the desired level of inventories or of other elements of working capital into the network of factor-demand equations derived from the assumed production function.

2.3. Equilibrating devices

In this section we describe some of the mechanisms brought into play when there is an imbalance between aggregate supply and demand.

The basic measure of demand/supply imbalance is the ratio UGPPA/UGPPD. It enters directly in several price and trade equations. If prices are to play any role in restoring balance between demand and supply, then changes in the price level should depend upon the relationship between supply and demand at existing prices. The ratio UGPPA/UGPPD enters equations for both imports and exports; its largest impact is on the propensity to import goods from the United States. This non-linear safety-valve role for imports is a large part of the reason why real expenditure multipliers in the Canadian model are much higher at low levels of capacity utilization.

To the extent that any demand/supply imbalance is concentrated in the labour market, induced changes take place in wage rates and in labour supply. The principal business wage rate equation shows that the equilibrium real wage is determined chiefly by the labour efficiency factor, with price expectations and the square of the inverse of the unemployment rate exerting a modest influence. The main effect of differences between aggregate supply and demand on the supply of labour lies not in the domestic labour force participation rate equation but in the migration equations. Both immigration and emigration depend on the unemployment rate, while immigration also depends on the real wage differential between Canada and those countries that are the prime sources of migrants. In fact, the current specification of the immigration equation is so strongly dependent on the unemployment rate that when the model is simulated under expansionary shock there is very little net reduction in the unemployment rate. Part of the reason for this result may lie in the difficulty of disentangling the effect of labour market tightness from that of cyclical variations in government efforts to attract migrants.

If pressures in the labour market lead to higher wages, the cost-minimizing choice of factor proportions will lead to substitution of capital for labour. This substitution will be muted somewhat by the strong effect of unit labour costs on prices of capital goods.

As noted above, prices move fairly slowly to equilibrate supply and demand when there is imbalance at the existing prices. The factor-demand network provides handy measures of normal unit labour costs and normal unit capital costs. The former is the ratio of total private labour costs to UGPPS, whereas the latter is a marginal concept based on the replacement value of the capital stocks times their imputed rental prices, again divided by UGPPS. Any increase in wages, capital goods prices, or interest rates leads to higher prices through these unit factor cost variables. Higher domestic prices affect some categories of expenditure and lead to some financial constraints, but the main equilibrating effect of these higher prices operates through the balance of trade.

The various equilibrating mechanisms in the goods market and the labour market are supplemented by similar mechanisms in the financial sector, including endogenous monetary policy responses. The private financial sector is described in section 5. The endogenous monetary and fiscal policy responses are taken up in the following section concerned with the government sector of the model.

3. Government sector behaviour

3.1. Types of disaggregation

RDX2 separates federal government activities from those of the
provinces and municipalities. This split permits detailed asset and
liability accounting at the federal level and allows us to distinguish
the different constraints and policy motivations at the two levels
of government. For each level of government, there are equations
covering taxes, transfers, employment, wage rates, nonwage current expenditure, and capital expenditure. Some of the tax and
transfer models were used in RDX1 [6] and most of the rest have
been described elsewhere [3], so we shall restrict comment here to
monetary policy, employment and wages, other current expenditure, and capital expenditure. In the light of our concern in this
paper with the unusual features of RDX2, we shall emphasize the
ways in which demand and relative prices are combined with explicit policy variables in the explanation of government sector
behaviour.

3.2. Monetary policy

There are two main endogenous features of monetary policy. First
the interest rate on short-term government securities (1–3 year
bonds) is determined chiefly by recent rates of inflation, recent
rates of change in bank lending, a U.S. short-term interest rate,
and the rate of change in the outstanding stock of Government of
Canada direct market securities held by the general public. Second
the official demand equation for foreign exchange, which applies
to the fixed exchange rate period only, depicts the rules of the
Bretton Woods game along with other factors reflecting the wil-
lingness of the foreign exchange authorities to buy or sell foreign
exchange. Aside from these policy reactions, there are a number of
exogenous features of monetary and foreign exchange policy (e.g.
official forward exchange purchases, required secondary reserve
ratios for banks, direct lending in the mortgage market, and official long-term borrowing abroad), as well as many endogenous

implications of the chosen policies. For example, the asset and liability accounting of the federal government sector is made explicit, so that the choice of a particular interest rate, along with the chosen taxation and expenditure policies, serves to determine the size of the government debt and, less directly, the size of the banking system.

3.3. Government current expenditure

For both levels of government there is a split between current wage and nonwage expenditure, with the former derived as the product of calculated values for employment and wage rates. Employment in public administration at both levels of government depends on distributed lags on real personal income and relative costs. The relative cost variable is defined as the wage rate of each government divided by the price of government current nonwage expenditure and is used to model the substitution of 'in house' work for purchased goods and services in the face of changing relative costs. The other variables in the two employment equations illustrate the differences between the two levels of government. Provincial-municipal employment is affected by the ratio of national accounts revenues (including transfers from the federal government) to total uses of funds, a bank liquidity variable, and the long-term rate of interest. Federal employment, on the other hand, depends positively on a distributed lag of the unemployment rate, reflecting policy considerations rather than budget and borrowing constraints.

The equation for municipal employment in schools is estimated as a teacher/pupil ratio, with the main independent variables being current transfers per student from provinces to municipalities, lag distributions on real per capita personal income, the long-term interest rate, and the size and growth of the school population.

Wage rates at both levels of government are lagged functions of private and other government wage rates, with the response to these wage rates varying according to conditions in the labour market.

Current nōnwage expenditure at both levels of government reflects the mirror image of the substitution effects (determined by the wage rate for direct employment relative to the price of other purchased goods and services) appearing in the government employment equations. Government nonwage expenditures are positively influenced by distributed lags on aggregate real personal income. At the provincial-municipal level this effect is proportionate to the ratio of provincial-municipal national accounts income (including federal transfers) to total uses of funds, less the average value of the ratio over the estimation period. The federal equation also embodies strong effects from two variables reflecting recent values of two target variables — positive effects from the unemployment rate and negative effects from the expected rate of increase in consumer prices.

3.4. Government capital expenditure

There are three equations for government expenditure on non-residential construction — schools, other provincial-municipal construction, and federal construction. Equipment expenditure is left exogenous, because the expenditure is small and the preferred equations have scores of parameters. The construction equations all involve accelerator influences and reflect again the differences in behaviour at the two levels of government: the schools equation depends on transfers from provinces, the other provincial-municipal construction equation is influenced by real interest rates, while federal expenditure depends positively on current unemployment rates relative to their three-year moving average.

Taking the government equations as a group, it is clear that they contribute importantly to the dynamic behaviour of RDX2. The various income and accelerator influences tend to amplify, with sometimes lengthy lags, increases in real aggregate demand generated elsewhere. The revenue and relative price effects at the provincial-municipal level provide only moderate capacity constraints, whereas the important influence of unemployment rates and price expectations at the federal level illustrates how induced changes in government expenditure may help to equilibrate supply and demand. Only detailed dynamic simulations can show whether the modelled aspects of government expenditure act to increase or decrease the stability of the economy in response to various shocks. Given the large size of government expenditures, and their heavy dependence on other endogenous variables, it is clear from the outset that the behaviour of the model as a whole will depend on whether or not the government expenditure equations are used in particular simulations.

4. International linkages

From the outset, RDX2 was designed with a view to joint simulations with a model of the U.S. economy. Thus there is much breadth and detail in the ties between the separate national markets for goods, capital, and labour. In a progress report [7] on the bilateral linkage project the various mechanisms are described in some detail, as is the case in chapters 4, 10 and 11 of [8]. Here these mechanisms will only be briefly mentioned.

4.1. Trade flows.

There are 13 estimated equations for imports of goods and services and 9 for exports. More than half are for trade flows between Canada and the U.S.A. In these cases we are obviously aware that one country's imports are the exports of the other; thus our specifications take a more balanced account of conditions in both countries than is usual. We have explained with special care the interest and dividend flows, so as to model reasonably well the current account consequences of capital movements.

4.2. Capital markets

The links here are several. Capital flows of various sorts – new issues of provincial-municipal bonds, new issues of corporate bonds, trade in outstanding bonds, direct investment, trade in outstanding shares – are modelled for long-term flows between

Canada and the U.S.A. There is less detail in the explanation of long-term capital flows between Canada and other countries, primarily because it is not possible to make use of as much explanatory detail about the heterogeneous "other countries" category.

Short-term capital flows are explained as a by-product of a sub-model of the foreign exchange market. Separate equations for private and official excess demand for foreign exchange interact to determine (under the "fixed" exchange rate regime) the exchange rate and the change in foreign exchange reserves. Given the balance on trade and long-term capital accounts, explanation of the change in foreign exchange reserves leaves short-term capital flows to be determined, as they are in some part measured, as a residual in the balance of payments identity.

Long- and short-term interest rates and the supply price of capital influence capital flows; the capital flows themselves do little to eradicate the rate-of-return differentials unless the induced changes in foreign exchange rates and foreign exchange reserves lead to changes in domestic expenditure or money supply. For simulation purposes, it will be interesting to see what happens if the rules of the gold standard are substituted for the short-term interest rate equation.

4.3. Labour markets

Equations in the trade sector explain freight, shipping, tourism, and similar international purchases of services, but the key linkage between labour markets in Canada and elsewhere lies in the migration equations already described briefly in section 2.3.

5. The financial sector

This sector contains several interesting features, such as the constrained joint estimation of the lagged changes in the nonfinancial sector's holdings of nine liquid assets. A complete description of the financial sector may be found in chapter 9 of [8]. Here we describe only two features that are of key importance in linking the financial and real sides of the economy.

5.1. The role of bank assets and liabilities

One of the trickiest problems in financial model-building is how to develop measures of the extent to which prevailing interest rates are not a sufficient measure of the availability and cost of finance. In RDX2, the primary purpose of the equations for bank assets and liabilities (given the policy-determined rate of interest on short-term Government of Canada securities) is to determine the ratio of earning liquid assets to total bank assets. The difference between this ratio and its desired value, measured as a fraction of the actual value, plays a direct part in explaining new bond issues abroad, bank advances, housing investment, and employment by provincial and municipal governments. At times when the bank liquid asset ratio has reached abnormally low levels, there have apparently been quantitative restrictions on lending, and "drying up" of bond markets. These effects have transcended movements in our recorded series for interest rates and the supply price of capital.

5.2. The supply price of capital and price expectations

In another paper in this volume [9] an explanation is given of the model from which measures are derived of the supply price of capital and the expected rate of change in consumer prices. That paper also contains a description of how the supply price of capital is used in the explanation of investment and consumption expenditure, price formation, and capital flows. The equation used to define the supply price of capital is solved within the model to determine the market value of business fixed assets and inventories, an important component of the series for private sector wealth.

6. Simulation contexts for RDX2

In this section and in sections 7 and 8 we consider some of the uses to which RDX2 is to be put. RDX2 embodies scores of policy instruments, included either as exogenous variables or as parameters in behaviour equations. The primary purpose of the model is to use simulation techniques to consider the macroeconomic effects of policy changes, with international repercussions getting the attention they merit in an open economy. In the present section, the stage is set by a listing of the principal contexts in which simulations have been or will be run. We then list in section 7 some of the policy issues to be assessed using RDX2. We conclude in section 8 with a discussion of simulations involving the simultaneous solution of RDX2 and the MPS model (formerly known as the Federal Reserve-MIT-Penn model) of the U.S.A.

6.1. Historical context

The first experiments run with a model are usually "control" solutions to see how well the system "tracks" the historical course of the economy within and beyond the sample period. With RDX2 these simulations have been run for individual sectors, groups of sectors, and the whole model, so that the causes of puzzling behaviour can be fairly easily pinpointed. Our whole-model control solutions for RDX2, as reported in table 12.1 of [8], show the model to keep on track quite well within and beyond the estimation period. The within-sample simulations were run over the 21 quarters 4Q63–4Q68, and show the various aggregate demand and supply measures to have root mean square errors ranging between 0.54% for UGPPD and 1.32% for UGPPA. The root mean square error for actual output (UGPP) is 1.17% and that for aggregate current-dollar GNE is 1.01%. Outside the sample period, the errors generally increase. An eight-quarter simulation 1Q69–4Q70 produces errors of 1.37% and 1.06% for UGPP and current-dollar GNE, respectively. Among the components of GNE, the investment equations perform well in both simulations, and do even better outside than inside the sample period. This pattern is reversed for the consumption sector which does rather poorly in 1969 and 1970, with a root mean square error of 2.4% for total consumption. Throughout the rest of the model, simulation performance is good enough to suggest that we have avoided or removed any large and glaring errors in model structure.

At this stage, there are two further goals for simulations in the historical context. The model builder is always torn between using the period of history as a mould that the model must be shaped to fit and starting from the other side. To start from the other side is to assume that the model depicts the structure of the economy and to apply experimental techniques in order to understand better the workings of the model and of the economy. To some extent the two goals are compatible, as the experiments designed to show the properties of the model sometimes reveal features so incompatible with the actual structure of the economy that rebuilding is necessary. Beyond such rebuilding required by evidence of implausible dynamic properties, we are not inclined to rework RDX2 to capture all the events in the sample period, because exaggerated attempts to explain a particular sequence of events may lead to an overly specialized model of limited use for conditional or ex ante simulations.

If the model structure is treated as given, the model can be used to unravel history, recreating economic episodes by some rearranging of the exogenous impulses.

6.2. Ex ante context

The distinction between ex ante and historical simulations is that ex ante simulations require the use of forecasts rather than reported values for the exogenous variables. Given the frequency and magnitude of revisions in reported statistics, however, the boundary line between the two types is not always clear.

We plan to use RDX2 for the purpose of regular forecast simulations four to eight quarters ahead using detailed estimates of the values of exogenous variables. For longer-term simulations in a growth context, the values of exogenous variables forecast several years into the future will have mainly trend and seasonal variance. The sheer housekeeping effort in providing updated forecasts of the 321 exogenous variables in RDX2 will be very great, but one of the advantages of the structural detail in RDX2 is that most of the exogenous variables relate to policy variables and to slow-moving demographic and institutional characteristics. For long-term forecasts, of course, there will arise some real puzzles in finding a plausible set of internally consistent guesses about trends in the exogenous features of demography, technology and preferences.

6.3. Stationary context

It is in this context that we plan to undertake the main analysis of dynamic response patterns. In their paper in this volume, Zellner and Peck [11] suggest that tests for nonlinearity and asymmetry should be part of a model-builder's basic assessment of his model. We agree in principle, but do not think that such tests should be performed in the historical context. If a model is highly non-linear with numerous supply constraints coming into play at different levels of capacity utilization, the lagged effects of policy changes cannot be accurately traced within an historical period where the control solution exhibits different degrees of capacity utilization. Experiments for asymmetry of response in RDX1 revealed [6], predictably enough, that the degree of asymmetry, and of non-linearity, increases with the rate of capacity utilization. Thus it is important that the level of capacity utilization be held constant during the simulation run used to gather evidence for a test of asymmetry or nonlinearity. This requirement is even more important in the case of experiments assessing the dynamic response of the model to cyclical shocks, because the simulations must run for many periods. The experiments using RDX1 to test the efficiency of automatic stabilizers [4] were bedevilled by changes in the underlying economic situation during the simulation period.

For RDX2 we propose to get around this problem by developing sets of stationary data in which time stands still and the exogenous variables have all variance removed. Simulating the model with one of these data sets should lead to a steady-state control solution on which a battery of tests can be employed. Suitable steady-state solutions might not exist for a model with certain non-homogeneities. We hope that the emphasis on both stock and flow disequilibrium adjustment mechanisms in the equations of

RDX2 will make the model suitable for use in steady-state simulations.

In both the *ex ante* and stationary contexts, we plan to undertake stochastic simulations, hopefully encompassing the variances of important exogenous variables as well as of equation residuals. The stationary context has been employed by Vince FitzGerald in his stochastic simulations of the Australian NIF model, as reported in this volume [2].

7. Example issues for simulation studies

7.1. Multi-dimensional policy menus

Given assumptions about the most important targets and certain boundary conditions on instrument values, the model can be used to depict, for any set of initial conditions and time horizon, the alternative outcomes available measured in as many dimensions as desired. In some experiments with RDX1 a modest start was made in this direction, using pairs of values of a monetary and a fiscal policy instrument to trace out the sets of target outcomes (rates of unemployment and of price increase) consistent with the maintenance of a constant level of foreign exchange reserves [5]. As the number of instruments used and the number of targets considered increase, the problems of assessing and presenting the results grow rapidly. It is not enough just to map the results in terms of the target variables, because policy-makers are not indifferent as to which policy instruments have been changed and by how much.

The simulations described above ought to be conducted in both *ex ante* and stationary contexts. The *ex ante* results are more useful for analysis of current policy options, whereas the results in the stationary context illustrate the pure dynamics of the consequences. Our initial policy simulations of RDX2 were in the historical context, and are reported in [8]. They show that real expenditure multipliers are higher than those in RDX1. We also find that the size of the fiscal policy multipliers depends very much on the method of financing employed.

7.2. *The dynamic consequences of government sector behaviour*

Discussion of the stabilizing or destabilizing role of the spending behaviour of provincial-municipal governments has already been the subject of some study in Canada (see, e.g., [10]). The simulation of RDX2 in the stationary context will allow much more precise analysis than has been possible previously. Under any assumed set of exogenous impulses, the dynamic behaviour of RDX2 can be assessed with the various provincial-municipal equations either included or declared exogenous. Thus it will be possible not only to make overall assessments, but to trace the sources of any net effects.

Some similar experiments were carried out [4] for the combined tax and transfer network of RDX1. With RDX2 it is possible to consider the expenditure equations as well, and to make the important split between the two main levels of government. The great number and variety of government sector equations increases the variety of alternative behaviour rules to be assessed. Using policy instruments at the federal level, Fred Gorbet is engaged in a study of the dynamic efficiency of various rules for aggregate stabilization policy.

7.3. *Single-model simulations of international policies*

The detailed treatment of trade and capital flows, international indebtedness, and other links between Canada and other countries permits simulation treatment of a number of vexing issues.

What have been the effects of U.S. balance of payments guidelines on capital flows into and out of Canada? What would be the effects on trade and capital flows of alternative exchange rates linking Canada with other countries? What has been the relative importance of internal and external causes of price and wage movements in Canada? What would be the domestic economic effects of a change in migration policy? Some of these questions require a number of rather hair-raising assumptions to be made before the necessary simulations can be run, but in all cases the results from RDX2 promise to be considerably more detailed and plausible than those available from other national models.

Several of the questions listed above can be best treated by the linked simulation technique described in the next section, but the results from RDX2 simulated on its own provide at least a useful reference point.

8. Linked simulations

RDX2 has been designed for linkage with a recent version [1] of the MPS model of the U.S.A. When the two models are run as one, they provide a model of the North-American economy with four separate government sectors: the Canadian federal government, the U.S. federal government, the Canadian provincial-municipal governments, and the U.S. state and local governments. In the various simulations, the two federal governments are treated as policy-makers, and the other governments are represented by their usual expenditure and revenue equations.

Viewed as a model of the North-American economy, the RDX2-MPS linked system provides geographic disaggregation of a type not possible within national models. A range of preliminary simulations is underway to expose the "inter-regional" dynamics of changes originating on either side of the border. For these experiments, the U.S. government is assumed to "benignly neglect" its balance of payments, and the Canadian government buys or sells foreign currency at the rate indicated by the relevant equations. Various "regional" multipliers can be calculated showing the effects of each country's policies at home and in the other country. At present third countries are treated inadequately in the linked system. There are equations for most trade and capital flows between Canada and the "other countries" category, but only an aggregate U.S. import equation for flows between the U.S.A. and countries other than Canada. This means that the balance of payments consequences of the simulations are likely to be depicted more accurately for Canada than for the U.S.A.

The second phase of linked simulations involves constructing U.S. policy reaction functions taking some account of balance of payments considerations. These reaction functions might then trigger changes in monetary or fiscal policy, or changes in the regulations governing trade and capital flows. More sophisticated reaction functions could be designed for each country, in which the policies chosen depend not only on the balance of payments (and other targets) viewed by themselves but also on whether the other country has recently taken specific action directed at the balance of payments.

If satisfactory stationary state and extended *ex ante* solutions can be developed for the MPS model, the simulations of alternative balance of payments strategies could best be carried out in one or the other of these contexts. The more interesting features of the experiments involving interacting choices of balance of payments policies are the dynamic patterns of the results, and these can best be assessed in the stationary context or in extended *ex ante* simulations.

The interaction between policy decisions in the two countries may depend on issues beyond the immediate balance of payments: the presence of "imported inflation", "imported unemployment", or the scale of induced migration might also trigger policy responses. On the basis of crude assumptions about what constitutes "good" and "bad" economic outcomes, we could assess the size and distribution of any gains thought possible from the choice of co-operative rather than competitive policy reactions.

Most of the politically important international issues have too many facets to be adequately represented by joint simulations of even the most comprehensive econometric models. Nevertheless, we think that the sort of simulations possible with the linked RDX2-MPS system might capture enough of the substance of some genuinely open economic issues to give our games some possible utility to supplement the fun.

References

[1] A. Ando and R. Rasche, "Equations in the MIT-PENN-SSRC econometric model of the United States". Mimeographed manuscript, October 1971.

[2] V.W. FitzGerald, "Dynamic properties of a non-linear econometric model", in: this volume, p. 169.

[3] John F. Helliwell, R.G. Evans, F.W. Gorbet, Robert F.S. Jarrett and D.R. Stephenson, *Government sector equations for macroeconomic models*. Bank of Canada Staff Research Studies, No. 4 (Ottawa, Bank of Canada, 1969). 173 pp.

[4] John Helliwell and Fred Gorbet, "Assessing the dynamic efficiency of automatic stabilizers", *Journal of Political Economy* 79 (July/August 1971) 826–845.

[5] John F. Helliwell, Lawrence H. Officer, Harold T. Shapiro and Ian A. Stewart, "Econometric analysis of policy choices for an open economy", *The Review of Economics and Statistics* 51 (November 1969) 383–398.

[6] John F. Helliwell, Lawrence H. Officer, Harold T. Shapiro and Ian A. Stewart, *The structure of the RDX1; The dynamics of RDX1*. Bank of Canada Staff Research Studies, Nos. 3 and 5 (Ottawa, Bank of Canada, 1969).

[7] John F. Helliwell, Harold T. Shapiro, Gordon R. Sparks, Ian A. Stewart and Frederick W. Gorbet, "Comprehensive linkage of large models: Canada and the United States", in: *International linkage of national economic models,* edited by R.J. Ball (Amsterdam, North-Holland, forthcoming).

[8] John F. Helliwell, Harold T. Shapiro, Gordon R. Sparks, Ian A. Stewart, Frederick W. Gorbet and Donald R. Stephenson, *The structure of RDX2*. Bank of Canada Staff Research Studies, No.7 (Ottawa, Bank of Canada, 1971).

[9] John Helliwell, Gordon Sparks and Jack Frisch, "The supply price of capital in macroeconomic models", in: this volume, p. 261.

[10] T.R. Robinson and T.J. Courchene, "Fiscal federalism and economic stability: an examination of multi-level public finances in Canada, 1952–1965", *The Canadian Journal of Economics* 2 (May 1969) 165–189.

[11] Arnold Zellner and Stephen C. Peck, "Simulation experiments with a quarterly macroeconometric model of the U.S. economy", in: this volume, p. 149.

THE STRUCTURE OF A MODEL OF
THE AUSTRALIAN ECONOMY *

W.E. NORTON and J.F. HENDERSON

Reserve Bank of Australia

1. Introduction

A project to construct quarterly models of the Australian econo-my has been in progress for about three and a half years. In the first three years our attention was concentrated on building the model now referred to as RBA1. Over recent months RBA1 has been revised almost daily in response to two factors: the results of using various versions of RBA1 for both short-term forecasting and hypothetical policy exercises; and the findings of our recent research work. Currently, our efforts are shared between the test-ing and revising of RBA1 and the building of a new model, RBA2. Our present intention is that RBA2 will differ from RBA1 by making use of additional consistency constraints suggested by eco-nomic theory.[1] In 1972, we plan to complete RBA2 and to begin testing the two models together.

This paper discusses the structure of RBA1.[2] In section 2, the features of the model are outlined. In section 3, the structural equations are discussed. In section 4, some limitations of the pres-ent version of RBA1 are noted.

* This paper is the result of the efforts of a group in the Research Department of the Reserve Bank of Australia. But the opinions expressed by the authors are not necessarily those of the other members of the group or of the Reserve Bank of Australia.

[1] For a discussion of RBA2, see Helliwell and Norton [10].

[2] The sections on the dynamics of the model have been deleted because of a lack of space. For a discussion of the dynamics of RBA1, see Norton and Henderson [26]. The results of stochastic simulations with an earlier version of RBA1 are reported by Sowey [30].

2. Features of RBA1

The broad structure of RBA1 is depicted by figure 1. The model is basically neo-Keynesian. Thus, for instance, gross national product is essentially demand determined and interest rates have an important role in the demand equations for financial assets. But there are some neo-classical features too; for example, the presence of wealth and relative prices in the equations for personal consumption expenditure.

A variation of the stock adjustment model provides the theoretical basis for most of the behavioural relationships in RBA1. For instance, the equations for spending on consumer durables are based on a stock adjustment model modified to allow for a wealth constraint on consumer behaviour. The investment and employment equations and the demand equations for financial assets are based on other variations of the stock adjustment model. A price adjustment model is used for the equations for prices and average weekly earnings.

The main links between the financial and expenditure sectors of RBA1 are based on some theoretical work by Tobin [32] and the empirical example of the RDX2 model of the Canadian economy [12]. Two key variables are used to forge the links: private sector wealth; and the supply price of capital. Private sector wealth is defined as the sum of the market values of the business capital stock and government debt held by residents and the replacement values of consumer durables and dwellings. This variable has an important role in the equations for personal consumption expenditure and investment in dwellings. The supply price of capital, which is defined in nominal terms as the sum of the expected change in the consumer price index and the ratio of earnings to the business capital stock, is used as a measure of the cost of funds in the equations for capital inflow and business fixed investment.

Several policy instruments appear in RBA1. These include fiscal instruments, such as government expenditure and several tax rates; and monetary instruments, such as quantitative requests about advances and the interest rates on bank deposits, advances and government securities. Equations representing the behaviour of the

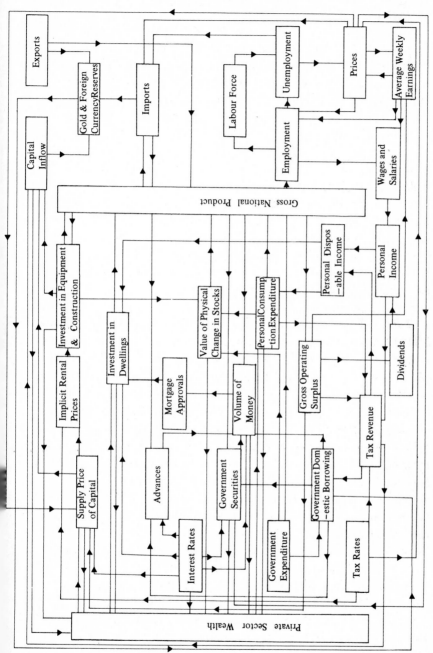

Fig.1. The structure of the model.

fiscal, monetary and wage-fixing authorities are not part of the model but some experiments are being made with such relationships. The use of several interest rates as policy instruments in RBA1 is worth further comment. In Australia, the authorities have generally preferred to set the interest rates, rather than the quantities, of government debt. Similarly, the maximum interest rates on bank deposits and advances are set by the authorities. Hence these interest rates are exogenous policy variables in the model and there are no explicit supply equations for cash, government securities, deposits or advances. But, as noted above, the supply price of capital is endogenous in the model.

The importance of explaining the financing of government spending within a macroeconomic model has been stressed by Christ [3]. In RBA1, there is a government budget identity to express the condition that (net) government expenditure must be financed by either taxation or borrowing. This constraint limits the independence of fiscal and monetary policies. Apart from the government budget identity, the equations in RBA1 to explain the financing of government spending include identities for government domestic borrowing and statutory reserve deposits and behavioural relationships for tax payments and for bank and non-bank holdings of government debt. The banks' stock of government securities is assumed to be the residual item in government financing and so, in a simple sense, is determined by the identity for government domestic borrowing rather than by a behavioural relationship. Similarly, in a formal sense, the level of deposits is determined by the banks' balance sheet identity.[3]

Lags receive a good deal of attention in RBA1. In particular, the length and shape of the lagged responses of investment, employment and imports to changes in output and relative prices have been measured by two methods: the Almon variable technique [1]; and the rational distributed lag function approach as general-

---

[3] This last assumption does not preclude the inclusion in RBA1 of behavioural relationships for current, fixed and savings deposits so long as these relationships are estimated subject to the condition that the sum of the three types of deposits (and any exogenous deposits) is equal to total deposits.

ized by Jorgenson [14]. One of the important conclusions of our work on RBA1 is that there are long lags in the response of some important macroeconomic variables to changes in their determinants and that the shape of these lag distributions is often not the commonly assumed geometric one.

3. The structural equations

RBA1 contains 79 equations of which 41 are behavioural relationships and 38 are identities. The equations are given in Appendix 1 below. The preferred equation for each behavioural relationship has been chosen from many estimates. Several criteria were used to choose the preferred equations: the sign and significance of the coefficients of the explanatory variables suggested by economic theory; where relevant, the shape and mean of the lag distribution on the explanatory variables; the results of *ex post* forecasts; and the values of the coefficient of determination (R^2), the standard error of estimate (*Se*), and the Durbin-Watson (*DW*) and Durbin statistics. The statistical tests afforded by these criteria are not strictly suited to choosing between many estimates of a single behavioural relationship, but are used due to the lack of suitable alternative criteria.

Quarterly seasonally unadjusted data are used. The maximum sample period is 1958(3) to 1969(4). This choice of data is discussed by Norton and Broadbent ([24], pp.6–7). The preferred behavioural relationships have been estimated by ordinary least-squares. Currently, these relationships are being estimated by two-stage least-squares using principal components of the predetermined variables.

To simplify the following discussion, the equations in the model are arranged into six groups: expenditure equations; labour and price equations; income equations; government financing equations; wealth equations; and other financial equations. Of course, the six groups are closely interrelated.

3.1. Expenditure equations

Expenditure identities for gross national product (eqs. 1–2)
The familiar identity for gross national product at current prices expresses this variable as equal to the sum of expenditures at current prices less imports at current prices. Similarly, gross national product at constant prices is set equal to the sum of expenditures at constant prices less imports at constant prices. In both identities, the main exogenous items are exports and (real) government expenditure. Government spending is assumed to be a policy variable but, as noted earlier, this does not preclude it from being endogenous. In later versions of RBA1, part of government spending is likely to be made endogenous. The volume and price of farm and mineral exports seem to be essentially independent of short-term movements in the non-farm sector of the ·Australian economy. But manufactured exports appear to be influenced by, among other things, the pressure of demand on capacity in Australia and the prices of these goods relative to their foreign-produced substitutes. These results, which are reported by Macfarlane [19], suggest that manufactured exports should be made endogenous in later versions of the model.

Personal consumption expenditure (eqs. 3–5)
Personal consumption expenditure is disaggregated into three categories: purchases of motor vehicles; household durables (that is, electrical goods and other household durables); and non-durables, an aggregate of the other ten categories of personal consumption expenditure in table 8 of the *Quarterly Estimates of National Income and Expenditure* [6]. As noted earlier, the behavioural relationships for spending on purchases of motor vehicles and household durables are based on a modified stock adjustment model. As shown by Norton and Broadbent [24], this model yields relationships of the form

$$C = a + bY - cX + eW - gK_{-1} \tag{3.1}$$

where C = consumption spending, Y = personal disposable income,

X = relative prices, W = private sector wealth, K = stock of consumption goods, and a, b, c, e and g are estimated coefficients.

For non-durables, the relationship is based on a flow adjustment model of the form

$$C = a + bY - cX + eC_{-1} \qquad (3.2)$$

with the notation being the same as for eq. (3.1).

According to these equations, rates of return have little direct effect on consumer spending. However, as shown below, rates of return have a substantial indirect effect on personal consumption expenditure due to, among other things, the effects of rates of return on the market value of private sector wealth.

Further work on the consumption equations is underway. This work, which is based on the approach used by RDX2 [12], has several interesting features: the disaggregation of personal disposable income into wage and non-wage components where one definition of the latter variable before tax is the product of private sector wealth and the relevant rates of return; the introduction of a measure of capital gains, defined as the sum of changes in the market values of the stocks of capital and government securities less the sum of the face value of physical changes in capital and the face value of changes in holdings of government securities; and the use of the supply price of capital to reflect the relative attractiveness to persons of spending and saving.

Gross private fixed capital expenditure (eqs. 6–8)

Gross private fixed capital expenditure is disaggregated into the three categories in table 4 of the *Quarterly Estimates of National Income and Expenditure* [6]: dwellings; "other new building and construction", which it is convenient to refer to as construction investment; and "all other", which is referred to as equipment investment.

Construction investment and equipment investment are explained by relationships derived from the neo-classical theory used by Jorgenson [15]. This theory yields investment equations of the form

$$I = dK_{-1} + \sum w_i \Delta \left[\left(\frac{PY}{PRK} \right)^{\lambda} Y \right]_{-i} , \tag{3.3}$$

where I = gross investment, K = stock of capital, PY = price of output, Y = output, PRK = implicit rental price of capital services, λ = elasticity of desired capital stock with respect to relative prices, and the w_i and d are estimated coefficients.

The variable PRK is defined as

$$PRK = [d(1 - a.RCS - c.RIA.RCS)$$

$$+ 0.0025\, RHO(1 - e.RCS)(1 - c.RIA.RCS)]\, \frac{PI}{1 - RCS} ,$$

where d = rate of depreciation of capital stock, RHO = supply price of capital, PI = price of investment goods, RCS = company tax rate, RIA = investment allowance, and a, c and e are the proportions allowable for tax purposes of depreciation, new investment and the total cost of capital respectively.

For both construction and equipment, the lags between investment and its determinants are long. The relationship for construction investment has a maximum lag of 18 quarters. The implied average lag in the response of construction investment to changes in output and relative prices is about 9 quarters. For equipment investment the maximum lag is 17 quarters and the average lag is 10 quarters. Moreover, the shapes of the lag distribution are very different from the geometric lag distribution assumed in many investment equations. The values for the λ_i, the elasticities of the desired stocks of construction capital and equipment capital with respect to relative prices, are found by a search procedure. Experiments with these equations are discussed by Mackrell et al. [22] and McLaren [23].

Private investment in dwellings is explained by a relationship based on a model formally similar to that used by Jorgenson [15] for business investment. This model, which is explained by Kelly and Norton [16], produces an equation in which the explanatory variables are personal disposable income, relative prices, mortgage approvals, interest rates, wealth and the lagged stock of dwellings. There are lag distributions on the first four of these variables: for instance, for mortgage approvals, the distribution has a maximum lag of 5 quarters and a mean lag of 2 quarters. Note that the effects on investment in dwellings of wealth, mortgage approvals and interest rates provide further important links between the financial and expenditure sectors.

Value of the physical change in non-farm stocks (eq. 9)

This equation is based on an extension of the stock adjustment model used by Lovell [18]. In this model, investment in stocks is assumed to be a fraction of the difference between the desired and actual levels of stocks less a fraction of the difference between actual and expected sales. Desired stocks are assumed to depend on, among other things, expected sales. Following Duesenberry et al. [8], this model is extended by adding the lagged dependent variable to the set of explanatory variables so as to allow for the effects of aggregating investment in stocks over several levels of manufacturing and distribution. Finally, as suggested by Lovell [18], expected sales are approximated by a weighted average of current and lagged sales, with sales defined as non-farm gross national product plus imports less investment in non-farm stocks.

The coefficient of the lagged level of non-farm stocks indicates that there is a moderately rapid adjustment of the actual level of stocks towards the desired level. If one assumes that expected sales are equally dependent on current and lagged sales, then the estimated coefficients in this equation imply a quarterly ratio of non-farm stocks to sales of about 0.85 and a moderately rapid response of output to unexpected changes in sales. Further details of experiments with this equation are given by Lightfoot [17].

Imports (eq. 10)

Total imports have moved erratically in recent years due to the influence of imports of defence equipment and civil aircraft. The size and timing of these imports is not likely to be explained by reference to the determinants of other imports. Moreover, oil imports have been subject to unusual movements in recent years due to the government's policy of encouraging the use of locally-produced oil instead of imported oil. Hence the dependent variable in this equation is total imports net of government imports and imports of civil aircraft and oil.

The theory underlying this relationship is outlined by Norton et al. [27]. The equation implies that the level of imports at any time is the result of, among other things, successive lagged values of gross national product, that is

$$M = w_1\, GNP_{-1} + w_2\, GNP_{-2} + w_3\, GNP_{-3} + \dots . \qquad (3.4)$$

The average lag is approximately 2 quarters.

Two other implications of this equation may be of some interest. The significant negative coefficient on unemployment suggests that imports increase particularly rapidly when there is a high pressure of demand on capacity. Secondly, the dock strike in the United Kingdom in 1967 seems to have caused a shift of imports of about $75 million from the last quarter of 1967 into the first quarter of 1968. Similarly, the U.S. dock strike in November 1968 to March 1969 appears to have shifted about $33 million of imports from the first quarter of 1969 to the second and third quarters of that year.

3.2. Labour and price equations

Labour force, employment and unemployment (eqs. 11–13)

Civilian employment is explained by a behavioural relationship based on Jorgenson's neo-classical theory of factor demands [15]. This theory yields an equation of the form

$$NE = \sum w_i \left[\left(\frac{PY}{PL}\right)^{\beta} Y\right]_{-i}, \qquad (3.5)$$

where NE = employment, PY = price of output, PL = price of labour, Y = output, β = elasticity of desired employment with respect to relative prices, and the w_i are estimated coefficients.

A dummy variable is added to this equation to allow for the

break in the employment series in 1966. The value for β is found by a search procedure. Some results of other experiments with this equation are discussed by Norton and Sweeny [29].

The labour force is defined in RBA1 as the sum of employment and unemployment. This identity serves as the equation for unemployment in the model. In the same simple sense, the labour force is determined by an equation in which the main explanatory variables are employment, time and the lagged value for the labour force. These variables are intended to reflect the effects of both cyclical and secular influences on the labour force, including the short and long term effects of changes in participation rates.

Average weekly earnings (eq. 14)

Average weekly earnings are explained by prices, unemployment and profits. There is a lag distribution on each of these variables; for instance, profits has a maximum lag of 10 quarters and a mean lag of 4 quarters. Thus there are substantial differences between the direct short term (one quarter) and long term effects on average weekly earnings of a change in one of its immediate determinants; for example, an increase of $100 million in company profits is expected to cause short term and long term increases in earnings of 2 and 8 index points respectively.

Implicit deflators for expenditures (eqs. 15–22)

These price equations contain variables representing both cost and demand influences. Average weekly earnings, unemployment, price expectations and the lagged dependent variable are the main explanatory variables in most equations. Appropriate indirect tax rates are added to the relationships for the prices of motor vehicles and other durables.

The high positive coefficient on the lagged dependent variable in most of these relationships suggests that there are long lags in the response of prices to changes in their determinants. However, these lags are consistent with the findings of similar studies for other countries. Further comments on these relationships are made by Norton et al. [28].

Identities for prices (eqs. 23–29)

There are six price identities. The implicit deflator for gross national product is defined as the ratio of gross national product at current prices to gross national product at constant prices. Similarly the implicit deflator for the business capital stock is equal to the ratio of that stock at current prices to its value at constant prices. The consumer price index is set equal to a weighted average of the implicit deflators for spending on motor vehicles, other durables, non-durables and dwellings. The expected change in prices is defined as a weighted average of current and lagged changes in the consumer price index. Finally there are definitions of the implicit rental prices for the services of construction capital and equipment capital and for the supply price of capital.

3.3. Income equations

Wages, salaries and supplements (eq. 30)

Conceptually, total wages should be equal to the product of employment and earnings per man. But, empirically, wages, salaries and supplements are not equal to the product of civilian employment and average weekly earnings due to the use of different bases of measurement. Average weekly earnings, for instance, is defined in terms of male units and the series for civilian employment excludes employees in domestic service, rural industries and the armed forces. Thus, wages, salaries and supplements is explained by an estimated relationship in which the main explanatory variable is the product of employment and average weekly earnings.

Dividends (eq. 31)

The equation for dividend payments is based on the Lintner model discussed by Mackrell and Broadbent [21]. This partial adjustment model reflects the underlying assumption that habit persistence and institutional constraints prevail in company dividend policy. The desired level of final dividends is assumed to be based on company profits for the past financial year, whereas the desired level of interim dividends depends on company profits for the first three quarters of the current financial year. For about 80% of companies, the financial year ends at 30th June. Seasonal dummy variables are used to capture other effects of the timing of dividend payments after declaration and differences in timing between companies, including the effects of budget constraints.

Income of other unincorporated enterprises *(eq. 32)*

Incomes of unincorporated enterprises are disaggregated into two components in table 32 of the *Australian National Accounts* [4]: income of farm unincorporated enterprises; and income of other unincorporated enterprises. The former component is exogenous in RBA1 but the latter is explained by an estimated relationship in which the explanatory variables are wages, salaries and supplements and the gross operating surplus of companies.

Income identities *(eqs. 33–36)*

There are four identities in the income sector. The most important is the national income identity which defines gross national product as the sum of wages, salaries and supplements, gross operating surplus of companies, the other components of the gross operating surplus of trading enterprises and indirect taxes less subsidies. Within RBA1, this identity serves to determine the gross operating surplus of companies. The other three identities define personal income, personal disposable income and the personal income of non-PAYE (pay-as-you-earn) taxpayers.

3.4. Government financing equations

Taxation *(eqs. 37–45)*

The equations for tax payments and tax liabilities are essentially empirical relationships. As expected, the appropriate tax base, statutory tax rate and administrative arrangements explain most movements in tax payments and liabilities. The tax payments equations are discussed by Mackrell [20].

Government securities *(eqs. 46–47)*

Government securities are disaggregated by holder into bank

and non-bank private sector holdings. As noted on page 52, the banks' stock of government securities is the residual item in government financing and, in a simple sense, is determined by the identity for government domestic borrowing. Following Deane [7], non-bank private sector holdings of government securities are explained by a behavioural relationship based on a modified stock adjustment model. This model yields an equation of the form

$$\Delta G = a + bW + c(RG - RC) - ePCE + gGDB - hG_{-1} ,\qquad (3.6)$$

where G = holdings of government securities, W = wealth or permanent income, RG = interest rates on government securities, RC = interest rates on competing assets, PCE = expected change in prices, and GDB = government domestic borrowing.

A dummy variable is added to this equation to allow for strong expectations of a rise in interest rates in 1969.

Notes, coin and cash balances (eqs. 48–49)

Holdings of cash are explained by two behavioural relationships: one for the trading banks' holdings of notes, coin and cash balances; and the other for the non-bank private sector's holdings of notes and coin. As shown by Norton et al. [25], both relationships are based on a modified stock adjustment model similar to eq. (3.6) above. The trading banks' holdings of cash depend on deposits, changes in (adjusted) statutory reserve deposits and lagged holdings of cash. Non-bank holdings of cash are explained by gross national product, domestic official borrowing, the interest rate on fixed deposits, a pre-decimal currency dummy variable and lagged holdings of cash. The savings banks' holdings of cash are exogenous in the present version of RBA1.

Identities for government financing (eqs. 50–52)

Apart from the government domestic borrowing identity (eq..48), there are three other identities relating to government financing: the government budget identity; and two identities concerning statutory reserve deposits. Of these identities, the most important is the government budget identity which expresses the condition that (net) government expenditure must be financed by either taxation or borrowing. In RBA1, this identity serves to determine government domestic borrowing which then, with other variables, feeds into eq. 48 to determine the banks' holdings of government securities.

3.5. Wealth equations (eqs. 53–69)

With one exception, these equations are a set of identities to define private sector wealth and its components. The exception is a behavioural relationship that serves to determine the market value of the business capital stock and the series used for the supply price of capital and the expected change of consumer prices. In this relationship, the difference between the interest rate on government securities and the supply price of capital is explained by current and past changes in consumer prices and an average of foreign supply prices of capital. Experiments with this equation are reported by Helliwell et al. [13] and, in more detail, by Boxall and Helliwell [2].

Private sector wealth is presently defined as an unweighted sum of its components. But, as suggested by Helliwell et al. [9], alternative definitions are to be tried in which wealth will be a weighted sum of its components.

Depreciated stocks of motor vehicles, household durables, dwellings, construction capital, equipment capital and non-farm inventories are generated by identities of the form

$$K = (1-d)K_{-1} + (1-q)I , \qquad 0 \leqslant q < d < 1 , \qquad (3.7)$$

where K = depreciated stock at end of period t, I = expenditure in period t, and d = depreciation rate.

For motor vehicles and household durables, the value for q is derived from the value of d by the formula used by Stone and Rowe ([31], p.430). For the other stocks, the value of q is assumed to be zero. Several values for d have been tried for each category except inventories for which d is assumed to be zero. The choice of the preferred values for d and the calculation of the base period stocks are discussed by Helliwell et al. [9].

Finally, permanent gross national product is defined as a weighted average of current and past values of gross national product in current dollars. Following Norton et al. [25] and Deane [7], permanent gross national product is used as a proxy for wealth in the non-bank private sector's demand equations for advances and government securities respectively. But experiments are planned in which permanent gross national product is replaced by some weighted average of the components of private sector wealth.

3.6. Other financial equations

Mortgage approvals (eqs. 70–72)

Mortgages for spending on dwellings are mainly issued by four types of financial institutions: trading banks; savings banks; building societies; and life insurance offices. In RBA1, private investment in dwellings depends on, among other things, total mortgage approvals but, so far, only mortgage approvals by trading banks and savings banks are endogenously determined. Further work is proceeding in this area.

Deposits (eqs. 73–75)

As explained on page 52, total deposits are determined by the banks' balance sheet identity. The division of total deposits between savings banks deposits and trading bank deposits is determined by two other equations: a behavioural relationship for savings bank deposits; and an identity which defines trading bank deposits as the difference between total deposits and savings bank deposits. The explanatory variables in the behavioural relationship for savings bank deposits include gross national product, the interest rates on savings bank deposits and government securities, and lagged savings bank deposits.

Advances (eq. 76)

Advances by the trading banks are essentially demand determined. However, the non-bank private sector's demand for advances is assumed to be modified by official requests to the banks about the level of advances outstanding or the rate of new lending. Thus, dummy variables for these requests are used in addition to other variables, such as permanent gross national product and the interest rates on advances and government securities, to explain movements in advances. This relationship is discussed in more detail by Norton et al. [25]. Advances by the savings banks are exogenous in the present model.

Foreign reserves and private capital inflow (eqs. 77–78)

Private capital inflow is split into three components in the *Balance of Payments* [5]: undistributed income; other direct investment; and portfolio investment and institutional loans. Undistributed income is exogenous in RBA1. This may not be an important omission as changes in this variable have no direct effect on the level of gold and foreign currency reserves because undistributed income appears in the balance of payments as both a current account outflow and a private capital inflow. Following Helliwell and Schott [11], other direct investment is explained by a behavioural relationship based on a modified stock adjustment model. This model yields an equation of the form

$$\frac{FIOD}{K} = a + b\,\frac{TYC}{K} + c\,\frac{BFR}{K} - e\left(\frac{LDI}{K}\right)_{-1} + \sum w_i(RHO - RHOF)_{-i},$$

(3.8)

where $FIOD$ = other direct investment, K = capital stock, TYC = company tax payments, BFR = business financing requirements, LDI = liability on direct investment account, RHO = supply price of capital, $RHOF$ = supply prices of capital in foreign countries, and a, b, c, e and the w_i are estimated coefficients.

By contrast, portfolio investment and institutional loans is exogenous in the present version of RBA1. No satisfactory behavioural relationship has been found for this component of private capital inflow, perhaps because of the sharp variations in the respective proportions of the two parts of this series. But sufficient quarterly data on these two parts will be available soon so further work is planned.

Holdings of gold and foreign currency reserves are explained, in a simple sense, by an identity. This identity expresses the condition that the change in foreign reserves must equal the sum of exports, private capital inflow and other net capital inflows minus imports.

4. Some limitations

There seem to be two main limitations to the present version of RBA1: some important sectors are missing or seriously incomplete; and some variables may be poorly defined.

The missing or incomplete sectors include the farm sector, the government sector and the capital account of the balance of payments. Work is underway in each of these areas: on the farm sector by a group at Macquarie University; and on the government sector and the capital account of the balance of payments by our group at the Bank.

Some variables in RBA1 may be poorly defined. For instance, some components of private sector wealth may be subject to large errors. These components may include the market value of the capital stock for which the valuation ratio is based on only a relatively small sample of firms. Similarly, the stocks of dwellings, household durables and motor vehicles are entered at their replacement values rather than market values due to a lack of sufficient information about the market valuations of these assets. A further problem with the wealth variable is that it currently excludes some conceptually important components such as land. Formally similar reservations should be expressed about several other variables such as, for instance, our measure of the supply price of capital.

Another possible limitation of RBA1 is that it makes relatively slight use of consistency constraints suggested by economic theory. As noted earlier, RBA2 will make fuller use of such constraints. Since evidence on their empirical value is sparse, comparisons between the results generated by RBA1 and RBA2 should be particularly interesting.

Appendix 1: The equations of RBA 1 [4]

A. Expenditure equations

Expenditure identities for gross national product:

1. $GNP\$ = CND.PCND + CHD.PCHD + CMV.PCMV + ID.PID + IC.PIC + IE.PIE$
   $+ IINF\$ + GEC.PGEC + GEK.PGEK - M.PM - ME + X\$ + ZA\$.$

2. $GNP = CND + CHD + CMV + ID + ID + IE + IINF + GEC + GEK - M$
   $- ME/PM + X + ZA.$

Personal consumption expenditure:

3. $CND = 1281 - 0.1050\ S1.CND_{-1} - 0.0490\ S3.CND_{-1} + 0.8695\ CND_{-1}$
   $\qquad\qquad (23.32) \qquad\qquad (14.91) \qquad\qquad (26.91)$

   $+ 0.1799\ (YPD/PCPI) - 1433\ (PCND/PCPI).$
   $\quad (12.30) \qquad\qquad\quad (2.66)$

   $Se = 19.42, R^2 = 0.997, DW = 2.14, CV = 0.007; 1958(4) - 69(4)$

4. $CHD = 74 - 0.0045\ S1.KHD_{-1} - 0.0032\ S2.KHD_{-1} - 0.0327\ KHD_{-1}$
   $\qquad\qquad (2.76) \qquad\qquad (2.05) \qquad\qquad (1.21)$

   $+ 0.0720\ (YPD/PCPI) + 0.00252\ J2A(WP/PCPI) - 102\ (PCHD/PCPI).$
   $\quad (9.58) \qquad\qquad\quad (2.60) \qquad\qquad\qquad (0.79)$

   $Se = 11.08, R^2 = 0.953, DW = 1.17, CV = 0.048; 1958(4) - 69(4)$

5. $CMV = 220 + 0.0168\ S1.KMV_{-1} + 0.0208\ S2.KMV_{-1} + 0.0209\ S3.KMV_{-1}$
   $\qquad\qquad (1.96) \qquad\qquad (2.50) \qquad\qquad (2.75)$

   $- 0.0984\ KMV_{-1} + 0.0774\ (YPD/PCPI) + 0.002015\ J2A(WP/PCPI)_{-1}$
   $\quad (2.73) \qquad\qquad (3.42) \qquad\qquad\qquad (1.74)$

   $- 257(PCMV/PCPI).$
   $\quad (2.63)$

   $Se = 13.77, R^2 = 0.890, DW = 0.82, CV = 0.088; 1958(4) - 69(4)$

---

[4] The notation used in the equations is listed in alphabetical order in Appendix 2. The constants in eqs. 24 and 25 are defined in the text. The sample period utilized is indicated as the final item in the reporting of each fitted equation. – The absolute values of Student's t statistics are given in parentheses beneath the coefficients and adjacent to the distributed lag weights. CV refers to the coefficient of variation, i.e. the standard error of estimate (Se) divided by the mean of the dependent variable.

Gross private fixed capital expenditure:

6. $ID = 79 + 0.0005\ S3.KD_{-1} + 0.0101\ KD_{-1} + 0.0021\ (WP/PCPI)_{-1}$
       (2.91) (3.66) (3.73)

       $+ JW[\Delta(YPD/PID)] + JW(RMOR) + JW(MA/PCPI).$

JW weights on

$\Delta(YPD/PID)$		$RMOR$		$(MA/PCPI)$	
w_0	0.01041(1.66)	w_3	−2.245(0.72)	w_0	0.19221(2.65)
w_1	0.01950(2.16)	w_4	−5.504(1.80)	w_1	0.28777(3.69)
w_2	0.02514(2.67)	w_5	−8.343(4.70)	w_2	0.30623(5.95)
w_3	0.02530(3.11)	w_6	−9.328(4.47)	w_3	0.26714(5.11)
w_4	0.01753(3.37)	w_7	−7.025(2.91)	w_4	0.19004(2.40)
				w_5	0.09448(1.29)

$Se = 6.24, R^2 = 0.988, DW = 1.44, CV = 0.027;\ 1960(2)\text{-}69(4)$

7. $IC = -19 - 0.0059\ S1.KC_{-1} + 0.0241\ KC_{-1} + JW(\Delta\left[(\frac{PGNP}{PRKC})^{\lambda}GNP\right])$
            (5.97) (9.92)

JW weights on $(\Delta\left[(\frac{PGNP}{PRKC})^{\lambda}GNP\right])$

w_0	0.01054(3.31)	w_7	0.04607(4.20)	w_{14}	0.03037(2.84)
w_1	0.01959(3.47)	w_8	0.04645(4.16)	w_{15}	0.02532(2.59)
w_2	0.02721(3.64)	w_9	0.04585(4.04)	w_{16}	0.01956(2.35)
w_3	0.03345(3.80)	w_{10}	0.04433(3.86)	w_{17}	0.01342(2.14)
w_4	0.03840(3.95)	w_{11}	0.04196(3.63)	w_{18}	0.00688(1.95)
w_5	0.04211(4.08)	w_{12}	0.03880(3.37)		
w_6	0.04465(4.17)	w_{13}	0.03492(3.10)		

$\lambda = 0.12$
$Se = 11.46, R^2 = 0.919, DW = 1.71, CV = 0.046;\ 1963(2) - 69(4)$

8. $IE = 146 - 0.0077\ S1.KE_{-1} - 0.0055\ S3.KE_{-1} + 0.0312\ KE_{-1}$
            (7.33) (4.99) (9.27)

       $+ JW(\Delta\left[(\frac{PGNP}{PRKE})^{\lambda}GNP\right]).$

JW weights on $(\Delta\left[(\frac{PGNP}{PRKE})^{\lambda}GNP\right])$

w_0	0.00190(0.66)	w_6	0.02172(2.12)	w_{12}	0.03210(2.90)
w_1	0.00446(0.86)	w_7	0.02500(2.35)	w_{13}	0.03059(2.90)
w_2	0.00752(1.10)	w_8	0.02786(2.55)	w_{14}	0.02775(2.89)
w_3	0.01093(1.34)	w_9	0.03016(2.70)	w_{15}	0.02343(2.86)
w_4	0.01453(1.61)	w_{10}	0.03173(2.80)	w_{16}	0.01746(2.83)
w_5	0.01818(1.87)	w_{11}	0.03243(2.87)	w_{17}	0.00970(2.79)

$\lambda = 0.32$
$Se = 22.90, R^2 = 0.914, DW = 1.41, CV = 0.058;\ 1963(1) - 69(4)$

Value of physical changes in non-farm stocks:

9. $IINF = 100 - 0.0129\ S1.KINF_{-1} + 0.0170\ S2.KINF_{-1} + 0.0215\ S3.KINF_{-1}$
    $\qquad\qquad\quad (0.84)\qquad\qquad\quad (3.60)\qquad\qquad\qquad (2.83)$

$\qquad - 0.2455\ KINF_{-1} + 118\ QINF + 0.2089\ SALNF - 0.2999\ \Delta SALNF$
$\qquad\quad\ (4.85)\qquad\qquad (3.30)\qquad\quad (4.94)\qquad\qquad (3.24)$

$\qquad + 0.4633\ IINF_{-1}.$
$\qquad\quad (4.35)$

$Se = 46.19, R^2 = 0.682, DW = 2.15, CV = 0.762;\ 1958(4) - 69(4)$

Imports:

10. $M = 385 + 0.0783\ S2.M_{-1} + 0.0998\ S3.M_{-1} + 0.3817\ M_{-1} + 0.0776\ GNP_{-1}$
    $\qquad\qquad (4.46)\qquad\qquad (5.50)\qquad\qquad (3.14)\qquad\qquad (4.31)$

$\qquad + 75\ QSUK + 11\ QSUS - 1.045\ NU_{-1} - 275\ (PM/PGNP_{-1}).$
$\qquad\quad (4.07)\qquad (1.51)\qquad\quad (2.59)\qquad\quad (1.09)$

$Se = 23.68, R^2 = 0.975, DW = 1.34, CV = 0.029;\ 1961(4) - 69(4)$

B. Labour and price equations

Labour force, employment and unemployment:

11. $NE = 1062 + 40\ S1\ + 22\ S2\ + 8\ S3\ + 132\ QNE + JW\left[(\dfrac{PGNPNF}{WE})^{\beta}GNPNF\right].$
    $\qquad\qquad (19.15)\quad (10.59)\quad (4.49)\quad (34.85)$

$JW\ weights\ on\ \left[(\dfrac{PGNPNF}{WE})^{\beta}GNPNF\right]$

w_0	0.139065(25.59)	w_6	0.032965(15.76)	w_{11}	$-0.015610(\ 9.34)$
w_1	0.119501(37.39)	w_7	0.019373(9.20)	w_{12}	$-0.018462(11.42)$
w_2	0.100420(59.92)	w_8	0.007511(3.74)	w_{13}	$-0.018536(12.28)$
w_3	0.082012(69.09)	w_9	$-0.002414(1.29)$	w_{14}	$-0.015624(12.39)$
w_4	0.064494(42.04)	w_{10}	$-0.010191(5.84)$	w_{15}	$-0.009515(12.12)$
w_5	0.048075(25.24)				

$\beta = 0.47$
$Se = 7.45, R^2 = 0.999, DW = 2.11, CV = 0.0008;\ 1962(2) - 69(4)$

12. $NL = 1343 - 9\ S1\ - 21\ S2 - 36\ S3 + 53\ QNE + 7.32\ (TIME)$
    $\qquad\qquad\quad (1.53)\quad (3.50)\quad (6.39)\quad (4.24)\qquad (4.45)$

$\qquad + 0.0793\ (TIME)^2 + 0.4137\ NE + 0.1561\ NL_{-1}$
$\qquad\quad (2.72)\qquad\qquad\ (6.31)\qquad\quad (1.57)$

$Se = 11.94, R^2 = 0.999, DW = 1.26, CV = 0.003;\ 1958(4) - 69(4)$

13. $NU = NL - NE.$

Average weekly earnings:

14. $WE = 0.407 - 0.063\,S1 - 0.017\,S2 - 0.023\,S3 + JW(PCPICE) + JW(YGOSC)$
          (9.00)   (2.60)   (3.95)

         $+ JW(NU)$.

JW weights on

PCPICE		YGOSC		NU	
w_0	0.0012(2.80)	w_0	0.000182(4.36)	w_3	−0.00004(1.22)
w_1	0.0021(2.80)	w_1	0.000125(6.04)	w_4	−0.00006(1.23)
w_2	0.0026(2.80)	w_2	0.000087(6.34)	w_5	−0.00006(1.23)
w_3	0.0028(2.79)	w_3	0.000065(4.18)	w_6	−0.00004(1.22)
w_4	0.0026(2.80)	w_4	0.000055(3.20)		
w_5	0.0021(2.80)	w_5	0.000053(3.04)		
w_6	0.0012(2.80)	w_6	0.000055(3.14)		
		w_7	0.000057(3.14)		
		w_8	0.000057(3.00)		
		w_9	0.000049(2.83)		
		w_{10}	0.000032(2.69)		

$Se = 0.0088,\, CV = 0.0095,\, R^2 = 0.997,\, DW = 2.00;\, 1961(1) - 69(4)$

Implicit deflators for expenditures:

15. $PCND = 0.0776 + 0.0024\,S2.PCND_{-1} + 0.0043\,S3.PCND_{-1} + 0.8329\,PCND_{-1}$
              (1.28)   (2.14)   (22.89)

         $+ 0.0974\,WE - 0.000098\,NU + 0.0022\,PCPICE$.
          (4.99)   (2.45)   (1.17)

      $Se = 0.0047,\, R^2 = 0.997,\, DW = 2.36,\, CV = 0.005;\, 1958(4) - 69(4)$

16. $PCHD = 0.1053 - 0.0035\,S3.PCHD_{-1} + 0.8704\,PCHD_{-1} + 0.0110\,WE$
              (1.84)   (14.17)   (1.43)

         $+ 0.1437\,RHD + 0.0034\,PCPICE$.
         (2.92)   (1.62)

      $Se = 0.0055,\, R^2 = 0.861,\, DW = 2.62,\, CV = 0.006;\, 1958(4) - 69(4)$

17. $PCMV = 0.1310 - 0.0115\,S1.PCMV_{-1} + 0.8305\,PCMV_{-1} + 0.0098\,WE$
              (2.75)   (10.37)   (0.68)

          $+ 0.1434\,RMV$.
           (1.62)

      $Se = 0.0121,\, R^2 = 0.894,\, DW = 2.28,\, CV = 0.012;\, 1958(4) - 69(4)$

18.　$PID = 0.1287 + 0.0099\ S1.PID_{-1} + 0.0048\ S2.PID_{-1} + 0.0025\ S3.PID_{-1}$
　　　　　　　　　(3.18)　　　　　　　　(2.55)　　　　　　　(1.18)

　　　$+ 0.7658\ PID_{-1} + 0.1096\ WE - 0.00011\ NU + 0.0034\ PCPICE.$
　　　　(10.27)　　　　　(3.49)　　　　　(4.01)　　　　　(2.30)

　　　$Se = 0.0030,\ R^2 = 0.998,\ DW = 2.52,\ CV = 0.003;\ 1958(4) - 69(4)$

19.　$PIC = 0.2684 + 0.0317\ S1.PIC_{-1} + 0.0123\ S2.PIC_{-1} + 0.0144\ S3.PIC_{-1}$
　　　　　　　　　(5.01)　　　　　　　　(3.07)　　　　　　　(3.49)

　　　$+ 0.3819\ PIC_{-1} + 0.3352\ WE - 0.00006\ NU + 0.0056\ PCPICE.$
　　　　(3.20)　　　　　(5.37)　　　　　(1.10)　　　　　(2.07)

　　　$Se = 0.0061,\ R^2 = 0.995,\ DW = 1.67,\ CV = 0.007;\ 1958(4) - 69(4)$

20.　$PIE = 0.0525 + 0.0044\ S3.PIE_{-1} + 0.9111\ PIE_{-1} + 0.0404\ WE$
　　　　　　　　　(3.29)　　　　　　　　(21.09)　　　　　(3.06)

　　　$- 0.00002\ NU + 0.0012\ PCPICE.$
　　　　(0.67)　　　　　(0.90)

　　　$Se = 0.0034,\ R^2 = 0.996,\ DW = 2.36,\ CV = 0.004;\ 1958(4) - 69(4)$

21.　$PGEC = -0.4501 + 1.4537\ PGNP.$
　　　　　　　　　　　　　(67.88)

　　　$Se = 0.0123,\ R^2 = 0.990,\ DW = 1.93,\ CV = 0.014;\ 1958(3) - 69(4)$

22.　$PGEK = -0.1124 + 0.0071\ S1 + 0.0079\ S2 + 1.1083\ PGNP.$
　　　　　　　　　　　(2.46)　　　　(2.74)　　　　(80.23)

　　　$Se = 0.0079,\ R^2 = 0.993,\ DW = 1.05,\ CV = 0.009;\ 1958(3) - 69(4)$

Identities for prices:

23.　$PGNP = GNP\$/GNP.$

24.　$PRKC = [0.010 + 0.0025\ RHO\ (1 - e.RCS)]\ PIC/(1 - RCS).$

25.　$PRKE = [0.030(1 - a.RCS - c.RIA.RCS) + 0.0025\ RHO\ (1 - e.RCS)$
　　　$(1 - c.RIA.RCS)]\ PIE/(1 - RCS).$

26.　$PCPI = 0.008 + 0.991\ PCPI_{-1} \sum_{j=1}^{4}\left[\sum_{i=1}^{4} w_{ji}p_i \middle/ \sum_{i=1}^{4} w_{ji}p_{i,-1}\right],$
　　　　　　　　　(77.37)

　　　where $p_1 = PCMV,\ p_2 = PCHD,\ p_3 = PCND,\ p_4 = PID,$ and w_{ji} = exogenous weights.
　　　$Se = 0.0039,\ R^2 = 0.996,\ DW = 2.11,\ CV = 0.004;\ 1963(1) - 69(4)$

27.　$PCPICE = JW.J4P(PCPI),$ where the JW weights on $J4P(PCPI)$ are obtained from
　　　the estimated eq. 54.

28. $PKCEI = (KC\$ + KE\$ + KINF\$ + KIF\$)/(KC + KE + KINF + KIF)$.

29. $RHO = 100 \left[\dfrac{J4S(YGOSC - YDEPC - TYCL)}{VKCEI} \right] + PCPICE$.

C. Income equations

Wages, salaries and supplements:

30. $YWSS = 178 - 36\ S1 - 34\ S2 - 17\ S3 - 62\ QNE + 2.82\ (TIME)$
             (8.26)   (8.70)   (4.44)   (10.61)   (6.39)

          $+ 0.703667\ NE.WE.$
           (93.92)

       $Sc = 8.66,\ R^2 = 0.999,\ DW = 1.97,\ CV = 0.004;\ 1958(3) - 69(4)$

Dividends:

31. $YDIV = 42 - 32\ S1 - 37\ S2 - 43\ S3 + 0.0291\ S2.J3S.(YGOSC - YDEPC - TYCL)$
             (1.41)   (1.69)   (1.71)   (1.57)

          $+ 0.0720\ S2.J3S(YGOSC - YDEPC - TYCL)_{-1}$
          (1.57)

          $+ 0.0313\ S3.J4S(YGOSC - YDEPC - TYCL)_{-1}$
          (3.15)

          $+ 0.0454\ S4.J4S(YGOSC - YDEPC - TYCL)_{-2} + 0.4039\ YDIV_{-4}.$
          (1.99)   (1.89)

       $Se = 9.63,\ R^2 = 0.952,\ DW = 1.23,\ CV = 0.098;\ 1959(4) - 69(4)$

Income of other unincorporated enterprises:

32. $YUO = 106 - 14\ S1 - 11\ S2 - 8\ S3 \ \ + 0.0831\ YWSS + 0.0662\ YGOSC$
            (6.03)   (5.60)   (4.52)   (14.48)   (3.69)

       $Sc = 4.06,\ R^2 = 0.997,\ DW = 1.09,\ CV = 0.012;\ 1958(3) - 69(4)$

Income identities:

33. $YP = YWSS + YDIV + YUO + YCB + YPO$.

34. $YPNP = YDIV + YU\dot{O} + YPO$.

35. $YPD = YP - TYPLP - TYPLNP - TPO$.

36. $YGOSC = GNP\$ - YWSS - TXC - TXP - TXS - YUO - ZD$.

D. Government financing equations

Taxation:

37. $TYPLP = -127 - 0.0114 \, S1.YWSS - 0.0187 \, S2.YWSS - 0.0126 \, S3.YWSS$
     $\qquad\quad$ (4.75) $\qquad\qquad$ (8.34) $\qquad\qquad$ (5.74)

     $\qquad + 0.1652 \, RPS.YWSS.$
     $\qquad\quad$ (42.28)

     $Se = 12.29, R^2 = 0.986, DW = 1.28, CV = 0.040; 1963(1) - 69(4)$

38. $TYPLNP = 13 + 0.0156 \, S1.YPNP + 0.0301 \, S2.YPNP + 0.0258 \, S3.YPNP$
     $\qquad\qquad$ (2.51) $\qquad\qquad$ (4.13) $\qquad\qquad$ (3.97)

     $\qquad + 0.1057 \, RPS.YPNP.$
     $\qquad\quad$ (11.97)

     $Se = 8.82, R^2 = 0.881, DW = 0.93, CV = 0.062; 1963(1) - 69(4)$

39. $TYCL = 16 + 0.8344 \, RCS.(YGOSC - YDEPC).$
     $\qquad\qquad$ (48.51)

     $Se = 7.42, R^2 = 0.982, DW = 1.40, CV = 0.040; 1958(3) - 69(2)$

40. $TYPPP = -147 + 0.0360 \, S1.YWSS + 0.0361 \, S2.YWSS - 0.0361 \, S3.YWSS$
     $\qquad\qquad$ (17.63) $\qquad\qquad$ (18.92) $\qquad\qquad$ (19.37)

     $\qquad + 0.1557 \, RPS.YWSS.$
     $\qquad\quad$ (46.75)

     $Se = 10.47, R^2 = 0.993, DW = 2.35, CV = 0.034; 1963(1) - 69(4)$

41. $TYPPNP = 13 + 0.0180 \, S1.RPS.J4S(YPNP_{-3}) + 0.1020 \, S2.RPS.J4S(YPNP_{-4})$
     $\qquad\qquad$ (12.91) $\qquad\qquad\qquad$ (73.21)

     $\qquad + 0.0107 \, S3.RPS_{-1}J4S(YPNP_{-5}).$
     $\qquad\quad$ (7.71)

     $Se = 11.61, R^2 = 0.994, DW = 1.50, CV = 0.091; 1960(2) - 69(4)$

42. $TYCP = 28 + 0.1810 \, S1.RCS.J4S(YGOSC_{-3}) + 0.3899 \, S2.RCS.J4S(YGOSC_{-4})$
     $\qquad\qquad$ (29.21) $\qquad\qquad\qquad$ (63.90)

     $\qquad + 4QTC1 + 23QTC2$
     $\qquad\quad$ (0.91) $\quad$ (5.20)

     $Se = 17.27, R^2 = 0.991, DW = 2.39, CV = 0.096; 1960(2) - 69(4)$

43. $TXC = -12 - 0.0076 \, S1.MG - 0.0096 \, S2.MG + 0.1352 \, MG.$
     $\qquad\qquad$ (2.87) $\qquad\quad$ (3.76) $\qquad\qquad$ (24.32)

     $Se = 3.77, R^2 = 0.947, DW = 0.69, CV = 0.056; 1961(3) - 69(4)$

44. $TXS = -1 + 12\,S1 + 4\,S2 \; +0.0951\,RND.CND.PCND$
             (7.42) (2.58) (6.72)

         $+ 0.9885\,RHD.CHD.PCHD + 0.8021\,RMV.CMV.PCMV.$
         (5.65)   (4.64)

     $Se = 4.25, R^2 = 0.947, DW = 1.97, CV = 0.047;\ 1958(3) - 69(4)$

45. $TXP = 4 + 0.0018\,S1.YWSS + 0.0012\,S2.YWSS + 0.0016\,S3.YWSS$
            (10.97)   (7.89)   (10.41)

         $+ 0.0123\,YWSS.$
         (54.76)

     $Se = 0.98, R^2 = 0.988, DW = 1.77, CV = 0.027;\ 1958(3) - 69(4)$

Government securities:

46. $\Delta GSP = 124 - 0.0108\,S1.GSP_{-1} + 0.0423\,S2.GSP_{-1} + 0.0090\,S3.GSP_{-1}$
              (1.67)   (2.80)   (1.46)

         $- 0.3357\,GSP_{-1} + 0.1868\,GNPP + 0.3542\,GDB$
         (3.64)   (3.80)   (5.18)

         $+ 99.49\,(RGM - RFD2) - 10.28\,PCPICE - 97\,QG.$
         (2.34)   (0.61)   (3.90)

     $Se = 42.18, R^2 = 0.733, DW = 2.18, CV = 0.013;\ 1959(1) - 69(4)$

47. $\Delta GSB = GDB - \Delta NCCP - \Delta NCCT - \Delta SRD - \Delta GSP - ZB.$

Notes, coin and cash balances:

48. $\Delta NCCP = 39 - 0.0751\,S1.NCCP_{-1} - 0.0118\,S2.NCCP_{-1} - 0.0232\,S3.NCCP_{-1}$
              (14.32)   (1.24)   (5.45)

         $- 0.0458\,NCCP_{-1} + 0.0136\,GNP\$ + 0.0354\,GDB - 7.49\,RFD1$
         (1.34)   (5.39)   (3.02)   (2.79)

         $- 19\,QDC.$
         (7.67)

     $Se = 8.16, R^2 = 0.945, DW = 2.27, CV = 0.009;\ 1959(1) - 69(4)$

49. $\Delta NCCT = 84 - 0.1957\,S1.NCCT_{-1} - 0.1505\,S2.NCCT_{-1} - 0.1871\,S3.NCCT_{-1}$
             (7.58)   (7.94)   (10.23)

         $- 0.5503\,NCCT_{-1} + 0.0049\,DEPT - 0.0464\,\Delta SRDA.$
         (3.80)   (4.13)   (2.37)

     $Se = 5.79, R^2 = 0.905, DW = 2.04, CV = 0.037;\ 1959(1) - 69(4)$

Identities for government financing:

50. $GDB = GEC.PGEC + GEK.PGEK - TYPPP - TYPPNP - TYCP - TXC - TXP$
$- TXS + \Delta FR - ZC.$

51. $SRD = U.DEPT.$

52. $\Delta SRDA = \Delta SRD - \Delta SRDTF.$

E. Wealth equations

53. $WP = VKCEI + VGS + NCCP + NCCS + NCCT + SRD + TFDLF$
$+ KMV.PCMV + KHD.PCHD + KD.PID - \left(\dfrac{LDI + LPI}{KCEIR}\right).VKCEI$

54. $RGM - 100\left[\dfrac{J4S(YGOSC - YDEPC - TYCL)}{VKCEI}\right] = -1.2416 - 0.5042\,RHOUKUS$
$+ JW.J4P(PCPI).$ (8.90)

JW weights on J4P(PCPI)

w_0	0.00190(0.06)	w_4	0.07096(6.15)	w_8	0.01380(1.56)
w_1	0.03798(2.38)	w_5	0.06208(5.86)	w_9	−0.00049(0.05)
w_2	0.06162(6.65)	w_6	0.04779(5.51)	w_{10}	−0.00936(0.89)
w_3	0.07170(6.83)	w_7	0.03079(4.00)	w_{11}	−0.01010(1.36)

$Se = 0.4177, R^2 = 0.738, DW = 0.71; 1958(3) - 69(4)$
R^2 for $VKCEI = 0.956, DW = 1.11.$

55. $VGS = RVG.(GSP + GSB).$

56. $KHD = 0.9425\,KHD_{-1} + 0.9713\,CHD.$

57. $KMV = 0.9350\,KMV_{-1} + 0.9675\,CMV.$

58. $KD = 0.9956\,KD_{-1} + ID.$

59. $KC = 0.9900\,KC_{-1} + IC.$

60. $KE = 0.9700\,KE_{-1} + IE.$

61. $KINF = KINF_{-1} + IINF.$

62. $KC\$ = KC\$_{-1} + IC\$ - 0.010\,KC_{-1}\,PIC.$

63. $KE\$ = KE\$_{-1} + IE\$ - 0.030\,KE_{-1}\,PIE.$

64. $KINF\$ = KINF.PKINF.$

65. $YDEPC = H.(0.010\ KC_{-1}\ PIC + 0.030\ KC_{-1}\ PIE).$

66. $KCEIR = KC.PIC + KE.PIE + KINF\$ + KIF\$.$

67. $LDI = LDI_{-1}\ \dfrac{PKCEI}{PKCEI_{-1}} + FIOD + FIUY.$

68. $LPI = LPI_{-1}\ \dfrac{PKCEI}{PKCEI_{-1}} + FIPL.$

69. $GNPP = J12W(GNP\$)$, where $w_i = 0.1394(0.9)^i$.

F. Other financial equations

Mortgage approvals:

70. $MA = MAS + MAT + MABL.$

71. $MAT = 1.2 + 0.0002\ S2.DEPT + 0.0005\ S3.DEPT + 0.0030\ DEPT.$
               (1.11) (2.95) (9.50)

     $Se = 2.31, R^2 = 0.706, DW = 0.50, CV = 0.143; 1958(4) - 69(4)$

72. $MAS = -6.7 - 0.0005\ \ S2.DEPS + 0.0090\ DEPS.$
                (1.14) (14.71)

     $Se = 5.44, R^2 = 0.830, DW = 0.61, CV = 0.162; 1958(4) - 69(4)$

Deposits:

73. $DEPB = NCCS + NCCT + GSB + ADVO + TFDLF + SRD + ONAB.$

74. $\Delta DEPS = 138 + 0.0085\ S2.DEPS_{-1} + 0.0244\ S3.DEPS_{-1} - 0.0331\ DEPS_{-1}$
              (4.38) (14.42) (3.28)

         $+ 0.0384\ GNP\$ + 77\ (RSD - RGM) + 16\ QDC + 16\ QDS.$
           (3.91) (6.25) (2.76) (1.54)

     $Se = 20.68, R^2 = 0.873, DW = 1.15, CV = 0.004; 1959(1) - 69(4)$

75. $DEPT = DEPB - DEPS.$

Advances:

76. $\Delta ADVO = 290 - 0.0184\ S1.ADVO_{-1} + 0.0211\ S2.ADVO_{-1}$
 (3.54) $\phantom{S1.ADVO_{-1} + }$ (1.47)

$+ 0.0237\ S3.ADVO_{-1} - 0.3261\ ADVO_{-1} + 0.2101\ GNPP$
 (4.91) $\phantom{S3.ADVO_{-1} - }$ (4.74) $\phantom{ADVO_{-1} + }$ (5.40)

$- 0.1596\ GDB - 80\ RADV + 51\ RGS - 34\ QA - 59\ QNL.$
 (2.92) (3.51) (2.62) (1.09) (4.16)

$Se = 28.17, R^2 = 0.915, DW = 2.07, CV = 0.011; 1959(1) - 69(4)$

Foreign reserves and private capital inflow:

77. $\Delta FR = X\$ - M.PM - ME + FIUY + FIOD + FIPL + ZE.$

78. $FIOD/KCEIR = 0.02411 - 0.00155\ S1 + 0.20837\ (TYCP/KCEIR)$
 (1.63) (2.84) (5.02)

$- 0.08891\ (LDI/KCEIR)_{-1} + 0.09620\ (BFR/KCEIR)$
 (1.65) $\phantom{(LDI/KCEIR)_{-1} + }$ (2.76)

$+ JW(RHO - RHOUKUS).$

JW weights on $(RHO - RHOUKUS)$

w_0	0.000089(0.27)	w_3	0.000022(0.27)
w_1	0.000062(0.27)	w_4	0.000010(0.27)
w_2	0.000040(0.27)	w_5	0.000003(0.27)

$Se = 0.122, R^2 = 0.651, DW = 2.08, CV = 0.36; 1962(4) - 69(4)$

Identity for business financing requirement:

79. $BFR = IC\$ + IE\$ + IINF\$ + IIF\$ - 0.030\ KE_{-1}.PIE - 0.010\ KC_{-1}.PIC.$

Appendix 2: Notation

The notation used in the equations of RBA1 is listed below in alphabetical order. Each endogenous variable is indicated by an asterisk. All indexes are based on 1966–67 = 1.00.

ADVO * other advances; loans, advances and bills discounted by All Trading Banks less term loans, farm development loans and temporary advances to wool-buyers, current $m.

BFR * business financing requirement, current $m.

CHD * personal consumption expenditure on household durables, $m at 1966–67 prices.

CMV *   personal consumption expenditure on purchases of motor vehicles, $m at 1966−67 prices.
CND *   personal consumption expenditure on non-durables, $m at 1966−67 prices.
DEPB *   total deposits, the sum of DEPS and DEPT, current $m.
DEPS *   deposits of the public with All Savings Banks, current $m.
DEPT *   deposits of the public and government and interbank deposits with All Trading Banks, current $m.
FIOD *   other direct investment, a component of private capital inflow, current $m.
FIPL   portfolio investment and institutional loans, a component of private capital inflow, current $m.
FIUY   undistributed income, a component of private capital inflow, current $m;
FR *   foreign reserves; holdings of gold and foreign currency reserves, current $m.
GDB *   domestic borrowing by the Commonwealth Government, current $m.
GEC   government current expenditure, $m at 1966−67 prices.
GEK   government capital expenditure; the sum of gross fixed capital expenditure by public enterprises and public authorities, $m at 1966−67 prices.
GNP *   gross national product at market prices, $m at 1966−67 prices.
GNP$ *   gross national product at market prices, current $m.
GNPF   farm gross national product at market prices, $m at 1966−67 prices.
GNPF$ *   farm gross national product at market prices, current $m.
GNPNF *   non-farm gross national product at market prices, defined as GNP − GNPF, $m at 1966−67 prices.
GNPP *   permanent gross national product, current $m.
GSB *   face value of the holdings of Commonwealth government securities by All Trading Banks and All Savings Banks, current $m.
GSP *   face value of the public's holdings of Commonwealth government securities, current $m.
H   ratio of company depreciation to total depreciation.
IC *   construction investment; gross private fixed capital expenditure on other new buildings and construction, $m at 1966−67 prices.
IC$ *   construction investment, defined as IC.PIC, current $m.
ID *   dwellings investment; gross private fixed capital expenditure on dwellings, $m at 1966−67 prices.
IE *   equipment investment, the "all other" component of gross private fixed capital expenditure, $m at 1966−67 prices.
IE$ *   equipment investment, defined as IE.PIE, current $m.
IIF$ value of the physical increase in farm stocks, current $m.
IINF *   value of the physical increase in non-farm stocks, $m at 1966−67 prices.
IINF$ *   value of the physical increase in non-farm stocks, defined as IINF.PKINF + $KINF_{-1}\Delta PKINF - ISVANF$, current $m.
ISVANF   valuation adjustment for non-farm stocks, current $m.
J   is an operator. The J is always followed by a numeral or by W. The numeral refers to the number of quarters, including the current quarter, involved in the operation. The following operations are defined in the case where J is followed by some numeral:

	J2A is a two-quarter unweighted moving average starting in the current quarter.
	J4P is a four-quarter percentage change.
	J3S is a three-quarter moving sum.
	J4S is a four-quarter moving sum.
	The *JW* operator is a weighted moving average. The weights are listed under the equation in which the operator is used.
KC *	depreciated constant-dollar stock of construction capital, $m at 1966−67 prices.
KC$ *	depreciated current-dollar stock of construction capital, current $m.
KCEIR *	replacement value of stocks of capital and inventories, current $m.
KD *	depreciated constant-dollar stock of dwellings, $m at 1966−67 prices.
KE *	depreciated constant-dollar stock of equipment capital, $m at 1966−67 prices.
KE$ *	depreciated current-dollar stock of equipment capital, current $m.
KHD *	depreciated constant-dollar stock of household durables, $m at 1966−67 prices.
KIF	constant-dollar value of farm stocks, $m at 1966−67 prices.
KIF$	book value of farm stocks, current $m.
KINF *	constant-dollar value of non-farm stocks, $m at 1966−67 prices.
KINF$ *	book value of non-farm stocks, current $m.
KMV *	depreciated constant-dollar stock of motor vehicles, $m at 1966−67 prices.
LDI *	liability to overseas residents on direct investment account.
LPI *	liability to overseas residents on portfolio investment and institutional loans account.
MA *	mortgage approvals of All Trading Banks, All Savings Banks, Building Societies and Life Offices, current $m.
MABL	mortgage approvals of Building Societies and Life Offices, current $m.
MAS *	mortgage approvals of All Savings Banks, current $m.
MAT *	mortgage approvals of All Trading Banks, current $m.
M *	imports of goods and services excluding exogenous imports, $m at 1966−67 prices.
ME	exogenous imports; that is, the sum of government imports and imports of civil aircraft and oil, current $m.
MG *	imports of goods, defined as *M.PM − MO*, current $m.
MO	imports of services less oil imports, current $m.
NCCP *	notes and coin in the hands of the public, current $m.
NCCS	notes, coin and deposits with the Reserve Bank of All Savings Banks, current $m.
NCCT *	notes, coin and cash balances with the Reserve Bank of All Trading Banks; current $m.
NE *	employment; non-farm civilian employees, thousands.
NL *	labour force; non-farm civilian labour force, thousands.
NU *	unemployment; persons registered for employment with Commonwealth Employment Service, thousands.
ONAB	other net assets of All Trading Banks and All Savings Banks; holdings of other assets net of other liabilities, current $m.

PCHD *   implicit deflator for personal consumption expenditure on household dura-
              bles.
PCMV *   implicit deflator for personal consumption expenditure on purchases of
              motor vehicles.
PCND *   implicit deflator for personal consumption expenditure on non-durables.
PCPI *   consumer price index.
PCPICE *   expected change in consumer price index.
PGEC *   implicit deflator for government current expenditure.
PGEK *   implicit deflator for government capital expenditure.
PGNP *   implicit deflator for gross national product at market prices.
PGNPNF *   implicit deflator for non-farm gross national product at market prices,
              defined as $[(GNP\$ - GNPF\$)/(GNP - GNPF)]$.
PIC *   implicit deflator for gross private fixed capital expenditure on construc-
              tion.
PID *   implicit deflator for gross private fixed capital expenditure on dwellings.
PIE *   implicit deflator for gross private fixed capital expenditure on equipment.
PKINF   implicit deflator for the level of non-farm stocks.
PM   implicit deflator for imports of goods and services.
PRKC *   implicit rental price of the services of construction capital.
PRKE *   implicit rental price of the services of equipment capital.
QA   dummy variable for requests by the Reserve Bank to All Trading Banks
              about advances outstanding.
QDC   dummy variable for the changeover to decimal currency.
QDS   dummy variable for the increase in the maximum limit on holdings of
              interest-bearing deposits at All Savings Bank.
QG   dummy variable for expectations about a rise in interest rates.
QINF   dummy variable for suspected error in the series for *IINF*.
QNE   dummy variable for a change in the measurement of the series for *NE*.
QNL   dummy variable for requests by the Reserve Bank to All Trading Banks
              about new lending commitments.
QSUK   dummy variable for the dock strike in the United Kingdom in September—
              October 1967.
QSUS   dummy variable for the dock strike in the U.S.A. in November 1968 to
              March 1969.
QTCi   dummy variables for changes in the seasonal pattern of company tax pay-
              ments.
RADV   maximum interest rate on advances by All Trading Banks, percentage.
RCS   statutory tax rate on taxable company profits, percentage.
*RFD*1   interest rate on fixed deposits with twelve months term, percentage.
*RFD*2   interest rate on fixed deposits with two year term, percentage.
RGM   theoretical yield on Commonwealth government securities with ten years
              to maturity, percentage.
RGS   theoretical yield on Commonwealth government securities with two years
              to maturity, percentage.
RHD   rate of sales tax on household durables, percentage.
RHO *   supply price of capital in nominal terms, percentage.
RHOUKUS   average supply price of capital for United Kingdom and U.S.A., percentage.
RIA   rate of the investment allowance, percentage.

RMOR	interest rate on private first mortgages registered in New South Wales, percentage.
RMV	rate of sales tax on purchases of motor vehicles, percentage.
RND	rate of sales tax on non-durables, percentage.
RPS	statutory tax rate on taxable personal income, index.
RSD	interest rate on deposits with All Savings Banks, percentage.
RVG	valuation ratio for government securities, as estimated by Helliwell et al. [9], p.45.
SALNF *	non-farm sales, defined as $GNPNF + M + (ME/PM) - IINF$, \$m at 1966–67 prices.
Si	seasonal dummy variables: = 1 in calendar quarter i; = 0 otherwise.
SRD *	statutory reserve deposits of All Trading Banks with the Reserve Bank, current \$m.
$\Delta SRDA$ *	change in statutory reserve deposits excluding changes due to transfers to the Term Loan Fund and Farm Development Loan Fund Accounts, current \$m.
$\Delta SRDTF$	change in statutory reserve deposits due to transfers to the Term Loan Fund and Farm Development Loan Fund Accounts, current \$m.
TIME	time trend: = 1 in 1958(3) ..... 46 in 1969(4).
TFDLF	term and farm development loan funds of All Trading Banks, current \$m.
TXC *	payments of indirect taxes: customs duties, current \$m.
TXP *	payments of indirect taxes: payroll tax (net), current \$m.
TXS *	payments of indirect taxes: sales tax, current \$m.
TYCL *	company income tax liabilities, current \$m.
TYCP *	company income tax payments, current \$m.
TYPLP *	personal income tax liabilities of PAYE taxpayers, current \$m.
TYPLNP *	personal income tax liabilities of other taxpayers, current \$m.
TYPPP *	personal income tax payments by PAYE taxpayers, current \$m.
TYPPNP *	personal income tax payments by other taxpayers, current \$m.
TPO	miscellaneous personal tax payments (other direct taxes, fees, fines, etc.), current \$m.
U	statutory reserve deposit ratio.
VGS *	market value of non-official holdings of Commonwealth government securities, current \$m.
VKCEI *	market value of the stocks of construction capital, equipment capital and inventories, current \$m.
WE *	average weekly earnings per employed male unit, index.
WP *	private sector wealth, current \$m.
X	exports of goods and services, \$m at 1966–67 prices.
X\$	exports of goods and services, current \$m.
YCB	cash benefits to persons from public authorities, current \$m.
YDIV *	dividends by persons, current \$m.
YDEPC *	depreciation allowance of companies, current \$m.
YGOSC *	gross operating surplus of companies, current \$m.
YP *	personal income, current \$m.
YPD *	personal disposable income, current \$m.
YPNP *	personal income of non-PAYE taxpayers, current \$m.

YPO	other personal income; includes rent, interest received, personal remittances from overseas and income of farm unincorporated enterprises, current $m.
YUO *	income of other unincorporated enterprises, current $m.
YWSS *	wages, salaries and supplements, current $m.
ZA	other exogenous expenditures: the sum of the value of the physical increase in farm stocks, expenditure by financial enterprises and the statistical discrepancy, $m at 1966–67 prices.
ZA$	other exogenous expenditures, current $m.
ZB	other net borrowing by the Commonwealth government, current $m.
ZC	other net revenue of the Commonwealth government, current $m.
ZD	other components of the National Income identity; that is, the gross operating surplus of trading enterprises less the sum of the gross operating surplus of companies, the income of unincorporated enterprises and subsidies, current $m.
ZE	other net capital movements, current $m.

References

[1] Shirley Almon, "The distributed lag between capital appropriations and expenditures", *Econometrica* (January 1965).

[2] P.J. Boxall and J.F. Helliwell, *The share market value of business assets, the supply price of capital and price expectations.* Reserve Bank of Australia, Research Discussion Paper No.23, December 1971.

[3] C.F. Christ, "A simple macroeconomic model with a government budget restraint", *Journal of Political Economy* (January–February 1968).

[4] Commonwealth of Australia, Commonwealth Statistician, *Australian national accounts.* Canberra, Commonwealth Bureau of Census and Statistics, annually.

[5] Commonwealth of Australia, Commonwealth Statistician, *Balance of payments.* Canberra, Commonwealth Bureau of Census and Statistics, quarterly.

[6] Commonwealth of Australia, Commonwealth Statistician, *Quarterly estimates of national income and expenditure.* Canberra, Commonwealth Bureau of Census and Statistics, quarterly.

[7] R.S. Deane, *A model of the market for Australian government securities.* Reserve Bank of Australia, Research Discussion Paper No.14, August 1970.

[8] J.S. Duesenberry, O. Eckstein and G. Fromm, "A simulation of the United States in recession", *Econometrica* (October 1960).

[9] J.F. Helliwell et al., *Quarterly estimates of private sector wealth.* Reserve Bank of Australia, Research Discussion Paper No.18, August 1971.

[10] J.F. Helliwell and W.E. Norton, *Prospectus for RBA2.* Reserve Bank of Australia, Research Discussion Paper No.19, August 1971.

[11] J.F. Helliwell and Kerry E. Schott, *Some causes and consequences of direct investment inflows to Australia.* Reserve Bank of Australia, Research Discussion Paper No.20, August 1971.

[12] J.F. Helliwell, H.T. Shapiro, G.R. Sparks, I.A. Stewart, F.W. Gorbet and D.R. Stephenson, *The structure of RDX2*. Ottawa, Bank of Canada Staff Research Studies No.7, 1971.

[13] John Helliwell, Gordon Sparks and Jack Frisch, "The supply price of capital in macroeconomic models", in: this volume, p. 261.

[14] D.W. Jorgenson, "Rational distributed lag functions", *Econometrica* (January 1966).

[15] D.W. Jorgenson, "Anticipations and investment behaviour", in: *The Brookings quarterly econometric model of the United States*, edited by J.S. Duesenberry et al. (Chicago, Rand-McNally, 1965).

[16] G.P. Kelly and W.E. Norton, "Investment in dwellings: An econometric analysis", in: *Three studies of private fixed investment*, edited by W.E. Norton. Reserve Bank of Australia, Occasional Paper No.3E, June 1971.

[17] R.E. Lightfoot, *Stocks, expected sales and production flexibility*. Reserve Bank of Australia, Research Discussion Paper No.21, September 1971.

[18] M.C. Lovell, "Manufacturers' inventories, sales expectations and the acceleration principle", *Econometrica* (July 1961).

[19] I.J. Macfarlane, *Equations for exports of goods*. Reserve Bank of Australia, Research Discussion Paper No.17, March 1971.

[20] N.C. Mackrell, *Equations for tax payments*. Reserve Bank of Australia, Occasional Paper No.3C, April 1970.

[21] N.C. Mackrell and Jillian R. Broadbent, *Equations for factor shares*. Reserve Bank of Australia, mimeo., February 1970.

[22] N.C. Mackrell, J. Frisch and P. Roope, "Equations for business fixed investment", in: *Three studies of private fixed investment*, edited by W.E. Norton. Reserve Bank of Australia, Occasional Paper No.3E, June 1971.

[23] K.R. McLaren, "Equipment investment: an alternative approach", in: *Three studies of private fixed investment*, edited by W.E. Norton. Reserve Bank of Australia, Occasional Paper No. 3E, June 1971.

[24] W.E. Norton and Jillian R. Broadbent, *Equations for personal consumption expenditure*. Reserve Bank of Australia, Occasional Paper No.3B, March 1970.

[25] W.E. Norton, A.M. Cohen and K.M. Sweeny, *A model of the monetary sector*. Reserve Bank of Australia, Occasional Paper No.3D, July 1970.

[26] W.E. Norton and J.F. Henderson, *The structure and dynamics of RBA1*. Reserve Bank of Australia, Occasional Paper, forthcoming.

[27] W.E. Norton, G.H. Jackson and K.M. Sweeny, "A demand equation for imports", *Economic Record* (December 1969).

[28] W.E. Norton, Kerry E. Schott and K.M. Sweeny, "Price equations", in: *Employment and prices*, edited by W.E. Norton, K.E. Schott and K.M. Sweeny. Reserve Bank of Australia, Occasional Paper No.3F, July 1971.

[29] W.E. Norton and K.M. Sweeny, "A short term employment function", in: *Employment and prices*, edited by W.E. Norton, K.E. Schott and K.M. Sweeny. Reserve Bank of Australia, Occasional Paper No.3F, July 1971.

[30] Eric R. Sowey, "Stochastic simulation of macroeconometric models: methodology and interpretation", in: this volume, p. 195.

[31] J.R.N. Stone and D.A. Rowe, "The market demand for durable goods", *Econometrica* (July 1957).

[32] J. Tobin, "A general equilibrium approach to monetary theory", *Journal of Money, Credit and Banking* (February 1969).

MACROECONOMETRIC RELATIONSHIPS WITHIN NEW ZEALAND: A PRELIMINARY EXAMINATION *

R.S. DEANE
Reserve Bank of New Zealand

1. Introduction

This paper describes some initial results of an optimistic attempt to examine macroeconometric relationships in the New Zealand economy within the framework of a quarterly model. In its present preliminary form the model contains 63 equations including 44 behavioural and empirical relationships and 19 identities. The structure of the model and the formulation of the individual equations reflect the difficulties involved in constructing a model in the face of some unusual problems.

First, a model of the New Zealand economy must not only incorporate the traditional policy variables — tax rates, bank reserve ratios, government expenditure, and so on — but also take account of a multitude of direct controls, many of which are exceedingly difficult to quantify in an objective statistical manner. These include quantitative import restrictions, ceilings on bank credit, hire-purchase regulations, variable government security ratios for non-banks, building industry "programming" restrictions, officially controlled interest rates and, more recently, wage

*The model described in this paper is being constructed by the Research Section of the Economic Department of the Reserve Bank of New Zealand. Other members of the Research Section who have assisted with the work are M.A. Lumsden, D.E.A. Giles, D. Grindell and R.C. Jackson. Little progress could have been made without the help of A.B. Sturm, who constructed the Bank's Database and associated computer programs. However, the views expressed in this paper are the author's own; in particular, they do not purport to represent those of the Bank. A more extensive description of the model is contained in Deane [1].

and price "guidelines". Accordingly, rather more policy dummy variables appear in the model than would normally be expected. The background to these direct controls should perhaps be borne in mind. They are the product of a special mix of social, political and economic factors. More specifically, they are in part the product of a desire for a securely protected, fully employed, egalitarian society. But they also reflect rather unorthodox (economic) ideas about how an economy can and should be managed.

The second major problem, and one which is particularly relevant to the monetary sector, is the extent of institutional change which occurred during the model's estimation period. These changes were associated with the desire of the authorities to maintain an adequate flow of cheap funds to the government sector by creating a series of new financial assets and institutions, and extending the net of official controls to non-bank intermediaries.

Thirdly, New Zealand suffers from a disconcertingly large number of data deficiencies. For instance, official quarterly published statistics in the following areas are either completely non-existent or of only partial coverage: national accounts, including all non-salary and wage incomes and constant price expenditures, balance of payments, central and local government accounts, labour force, wage rates, wealth and stock series other than trade inventories and liquid financial assets, and aggregate production. On the other hand, there is a reasonable number of proxy variables available covering current expenditures in partial fashion, such as retail trade turnover and building permit issues; overseas exchange transactions, covering all foreign receipts and payments on a cash basis; surveyed employment (70% of the labour force); and so on. Beyond this, investigation of unpublished information has resulted in the availability of data covering salary and wage income (the model's private income proxy), the government accounts, including suitably disaggregated tax series, and additional financial statistics.

Within the limitations imposed by difficulties such as those mentioned, the model is orthodox in most respects. A specially constructed aggregate expenditure series, Y, fulfils the role normally adopted by gross national product. The model is essentially demand orientated being concerned primarily with explaining the components of Y: disaggregated consumption, investment and imports. At this stage, government expenditure and exports are treated as entirely exogenous. In addition, there are equations for salary and wage income, prices, employment, taxation receipts of government and a range of financial assets and liabilities. It is hoped that once sufficient developmental work has been undertaken, the model will be used to study the behaviour of the New Zealand economy, to generate short-term estimates and forecasts of magnitudes which the policymakers regard as important, and perhaps to assist them in examining hypothetical alternative courses of policy action.

2. Empirical considerations

Inevitably, the model makes extensive use of proxy variables. This leads to many complications and some rather heroic assumptions, most of which are spelt out in a series of Research Papers[1] which describe the model in more detail. But there is perhaps one compensation which accrues through using proxy data instead of a full set of national accounts. In terms of the quality of the basic statistics, the proxies may be individually superior to their corresponding national aggregates. Moreover, the quality of the data becomes a better known factor, a point which has some not inconsiderable advantages when a model is to be used in an essentially applied manner.

In order to provide the model with a meaningful framework an aggregate expenditure series was prepared based on existing and newly extracted proxy data.[2] While this does not purport to represent gross national expenditure, it nevertheless provides an identity to serve a role not dissimilar to that of the GNP identity in an orthodox economy-wide model. This series, Y, is the sum of ex-

---

[1] Published by the Reserve Bank of New Zealand, Wellington, New Zealand.
[2] Full descriptive details of this series and other data constructed specially for use in the model are contained in Deane et al. [2].

penditures in the following sectors: consumption (retail turnover and wholesale automotive sales), building and construction (private sector work put in place), plant and equipment (imports), government (aggregate expenditure adjusted for transfers except those to local authorities), changes in trade (non-farm) stocks, exports and other current overseas exchange receipts less imports and other current foreign payments. A comparable constant price series, YR, was prepared by the simple procedure of summing the various components after deflation of the latter by the price indexes which seemed most suitable. Full details are given in the relevant identities (eqs. 60–62).

Wherever possible the ordinary single stage least squares equations in this paper are based on quarterly seasonally unadjusted data for the period 1960(2)–1970(1), a total of 40 observations. The commencement date of the estimation period was determined solely by data availability while the closing date was chosen to enable *ex post* forecast tests to be carried out. Where the time period varies from the standard, it is expressly noted beneath the relevant equation. In the selection of equations the standard statistical tests were applied by considering, among other things, the coefficient of determination (R^2), the standard error of the estimate (SEE) and its relationship to the mean of the dependent variable (% SEE), the Durbin-Watson statistic (DW) and Durbin's unbiased statistic to detect autocorrelation (D), the t-values of the individual regression coefficients (shown in brackets beneath the equations) and the pattern of the residuals over the estimation period.

The theoretical underpinnings of the individual equations and other structural considerations are discussed briefly in the next section on an equation-by-equation basis. It will be seen that the partial adjustment model, assuming either a flow or stock adjustment process modified at times by short-term constraint variables, is used in many cases. Most of the major behavioural functions suggest the importance of lags in the economic process although often the specification of these lags rests on a common but possibly oversimplified geometric distribution. Future work will include a more sophisticated approach to the study of lags.

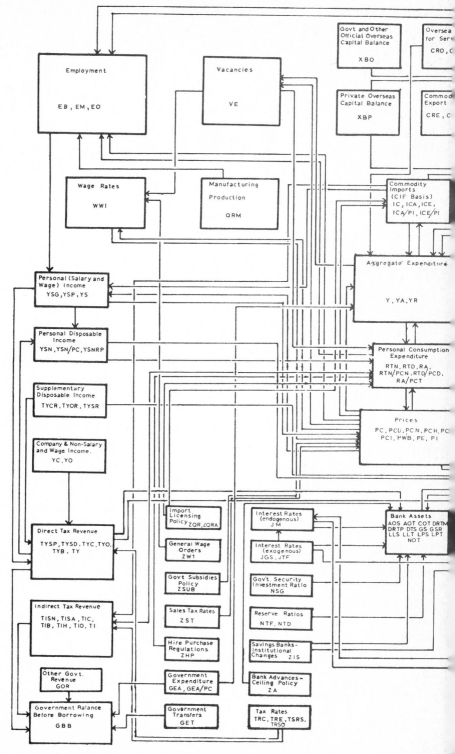

Fig. 4.1. Flow diagram for reserve bank

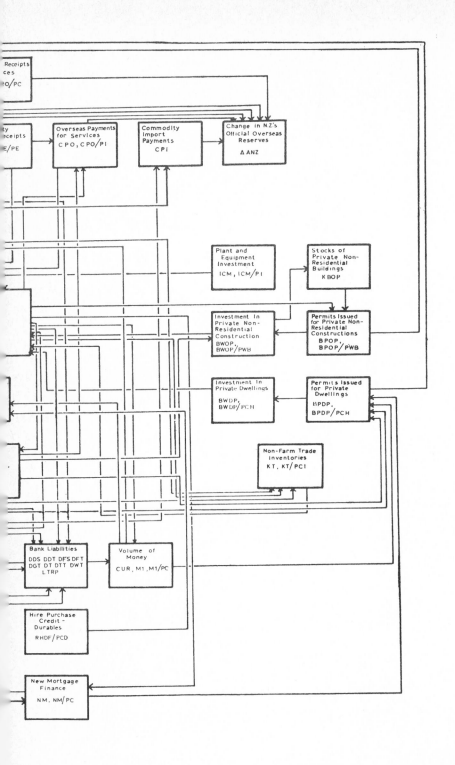

reliminary model of the N.Z. economy.

The equations are set out in Appendix 1 and the notation is listed in Appendix 2, where endogenous variables are denoted by an asterisk.

3. Equation specification

3.1. Private demand

The durable and non-durable consumption equations, which use appropriately price deflated data, assume that these expenditures are determined primarily by permanent disposable income (an eight quarter weighted moving average of net salary and wage income serving as the proxy variable), relative prices and other variables peculiar to each category. To increase the sensitivity of the non-durables equation to significant changes in current income, a transitory income concept is introduced (this being the difference between current and permanent income). A cyclical variable, notified vacancies, is also added to help overcome deficiencies in the rather narrowly defined income series. Over the estimation decade vacancies have tended to move in sympathy with non salary and wage income, suggesting a positive coefficient on vacancies in this role. The demand for durable goods, on the other hand, is expected to be influenced by the availability of funds to finance the expenditure − the volume of money and the flow of hire-purchase credit are both considered relevant − and the terms on which such credit is granted. As minimum deposits and maximum repayment periods are regulated by the monetary authorities, a specially constructed dummy variable is used to represent the impact of these factors. The peculiar nature of the traditionally undersupplied New Zealand car market necessitates a slightly different approach in the determination of automotive sales, where three explanatory variables are considered important: the national income proxy, YR (chosen to provide a broader income definition to account for corporate and commercial vehicle sales as well as those to private individuals), the previous level of automotive sales, to represent the stability of consumption behaviour as a result of accumulated habits, and a policy constraint variable to account for government's import licensing policy. The latter variable is based on annual licence allocations with quarterly interpolations. The unimportance of other factors, such as relative prices and liquid wealth, is probably attributable to the combination of persistent excess demand and official price control. Thus, according to the model, government policy can potentially influence consumption expenditure in three major ways: first, through changes in personal tax rates; secondly, via variations in monetary policy; and thirdly, by way of direct controls.

Turning to the investment sector, it can be noted that the residential construction sub-model at present includes four equations. These explain new issues of building permits for private dwellings, link permits to actual investment, and establish the demand for and the supply of new mortgage finance. Throughout most of the estimation period there appeared to be an excess demand for new housing, with the major constraint being the availability of finance. Hence it is not surprising to find that the major factors explaining building permits issued for private sector dwellings are private disposable income, new mortgage registrations and a liquid wealth proxy, the volume of money. A derived series for the stock of dwellings proved to be statistically insignificant. The demand for new mortgages is assumed to depend on aggregate expenditures (the national income proxy), adjusted to exclude changes in stocks and the balance of payments items, and the average mortgage interest rate. A broadly defined income proxy seemed necessary in view of the fact that the demand for mortgages is spread across a wide spectrum of economic units. The interest rate on mortgages is linked to the volume of new registrations and the short-term yield on government securities, with due allowance for lags. The inclusion of the official short-term bond rate is designed to help establish the link between exogenous and endogenous rates, and to reflect the influence of government policy and attitudes on the institutions which help determine the mortgage rate. The direct impact of interest rates on dwelling investment comes through the following chain: mortgage registrations, dwelling permits and work put in place.

Private sector "other" building permits depend on the lagged stock of these buildings and a distributed lag of changes in the national income proxy, Y, to give an accelerator type approach to the determination of net investment. Pending further development work, current price data unfortunately must be used. The second stage in explaining other construction investment is to link building work put in place to permits issued, incorporating a price variable to allow for escalation clauses. In each case, the Almon distributed lag procedure is employed, assuming the lag weights to lie on a polynomial curve. It is planned to use this technique much more extensively in future versions of the model.

Subject to modification in the light of further tests which are currently under way, changes in trade stocks are explained by the level of aggregate sales, the availability of imports (a constraint variable to account for the effect of licensing) and the lagged stock of inventories.[3] The coefficient on the lagged stock variable implies a fairly slow adjustment of actual to desired inventories; a finding similar to that of others.

Although imports of plant and machinery at present serve as the proxy for investment in this area, a new series is being constructed and this will be explained endogenously once the data become available. In the meantime this category of investment is treated as exogenous.

The final category of spending is imports, which are explained by a two stage procedure whereby, first, physical imports are related to aggregate expenditure, the price of imports relative to domestic prices, lagged holdings of liquid wealth (to account for monetary policy influences) and, to account for lags, the level of imports in the previous quarter. Dummy variables account for the impact of quantitative import restrictions, the 1966–67 United Kingdom dock strike and a statistical classification change. The second step in the importing chain involves the determination of current payments for imports as a function of the value of c.i.f.

---

[3] Two further variables seem to be required: a stock valuation adjustment factor and a buffer stock concept. As for the latter, the change in sales was not significant as an additional variable in the present equation.

imports in the current and immediately preceding quarters, with allowance being made for bank credit constraints and the effect of the dock strike. Current payments other than for imports depend on both external and domestic trade influences and the explanatory variables are chosen accordingly. The import equations illustrate again the way in which the model attempts to capture the impact of economic policy on expenditures. There is, for example, the potential effect of a change in government expenditure through YR, the influence of monetary policy, and the impact of direct controls.

3.2. Employment, income and prices

The shortage of satisfactory quarterly data in the fields of output, employment, wages and incomes generally necessitates a somewhat unorthodox treatment of this sector. Private sector employment (disaggregated into building and construction, manufacturing and all other) and notified job vacancies are assumed to be determined basically by a series of corresponding output indicators, with time trends added where necessary to overcome data (and hence specification) inadequacies and, in the case of vacancies, to account for employers' efforts to overcome a perpetual shortage of labour. Although a manufacturing production function is still under development, the other output proxies are endogenous to the model. Two of these equations assume a geometric lag distribution while the other two employ a probability distribution method. Given the usually exceedingly low levels of unemployment prevailing in New Zealand, it has not proved possible to develop a realistic explanation for unemployment within the model.

Because the product of employment and nominal award wage rates (the only quarterly wage series available) yields quite unacceptable estimates of private sector salary and wage income (YSP) a rather unusual three stage procedure is adopted to determine YSP. First, nominal wages are expressed as a function of prices, the excess demand for labour and an index of Arbitration Court general wage orders. Secondly, in the absence of ruling wage rate statistics, nominal wages are used to help explain prices changes. Finally, *YSP* becomes directly dependent in a linear relationship on employment and prices with allowance for lags and an indicator of pressures on domestic resources (imports). Later, it is hoped to introduce *YSP* divided by employment as the wage variable.

Pending the development of better data[4], prices in turn are driven mainly by unit labour costs (the ratio of salary and wage income to aggregate real expenditures, the output proxy) and award wages (the latter variable being required to help overcome statistical and definitional problems in respect of unit labour costs). This also means that the equations reflect at least indirectly the pressure of demand on supply, via the inclusion of vacancies in the wage equation. Other variables are incorporated as necessary in the various price relationships. These include indirect tax rates and import prices. The inclusion of an all-groups consumer price index equation implies that estimation errors in the component series are forced into the relatively unimportant residual categories, although this treatment is likely to be altered in the future.

3.3. Monetary sector

The structure of the monetary sector equations and their justification is described in detail elsewhere [3]. In summary, the monetary relationships of the model concentrate on the demand for a number of financial assets and liabilities in a series of markets: cash (including both currency and cash balances), demand deposits, term deposits, bank advances and mortgages, and central and local government securities. In a normal market situation it would also be necessary to develop supply functions. However, in New Zealand, many interest rates are subject to official regulation. Accordingly, supply equations are dropped from the model and interest rates are assumed to be exogenously determined by government. The implication of this assumption is, of course, that banks will accept any volume of deposits at the going rate; a position which is in fact very close to reality.

[4] Especially with respect to "normal" output and capacity utilisation.

A modified stock adjustment theory of portfolio behaviour is used as the basis for most of the behavioural equations in this section. Under this approach, the quarterly change in a sector's holdings of a financial asset is assumed to depend on the wealth of that sector, rates of return on the asset itself and on other competing assets, the level of holdings of the asset at the end of the previous period, and any relevant short-term constraints on the adjustment process. For banks, total deposits are treated as representing wealth, whereas for the non-bank private sector the national income proxy, Y, is used in this role, given the absence of any wealth estimates. An important short-term constraint for the private sector in New Zealand seems to be the highly seasonal flow of taxation payments to government.

Several special features which are incorporated in the monetary sector should be noted although their underlying rationale cannot be elaborated here. For the trading banks, New Zealand's peculiar institutional arrangements justify the treatment of the sum of net free cash and government security holdings as the balance sheet residual. On the other hand, private sector lending is the savings banks' residual, mainly as a result of the special captive market arrangements which demand that these intermediaries hold substantial minimum amounts of relatively low yielding official securities. Direct controls over trading bank advances (credit ceilings, etc.) are represented by a dummy variable, with a substantial implied lag in the operational effectiveness of this policy. The omission of lagged stock variables in the savings banks' deposit equations is on the grounds of lack of statistical significance. This is presumably a reflection of the passiveness in holdings of small savings. Quarterly flows represent, in effect, the "tip of an iceberg". Finally, it can be seen from the equations that both reserve cash ratios and government security investment ratios are built in as policy variables.

A more adequate linkage between the monetary and government sectors in the model (particularly with respect to the former's holdings of securities) is dependent on the availability of data currently being extracted to explain fully the financing of the Government's deficit before borrowing. Although the major linkage between these two sectors at present comes from the inclusion of the aggregate expenditure series (of which government spending is an important component) and the tax flow variables in the private non-bank sector's monetary equations, it is planned to amend this approach at a later stage by substituting a domestic official borrowing requirement variable for the tax series. In other words, the latter currently serve as a proxy for a more broadly defined governmental constraint variable. In addition, the monetary sector's holdings of securities will directly influence the government sector on the financing side when the government's borrowing and investment transactions are fully integrated in the model.

3.4. Government sector

The tax equations are relatively straight forward, covering disaggregated income tax as well as indirect and other tax flows. On the income side, taxation payments are expressed in each case as the product of a specially constructed tax rate variable and the corresponding income base.[5] The statutory tax rate indexes incorporate both the schedule of tax rates and the percentage distribution of income. The specifications reflect also the institutional arrangements existing in New Zealand. The other tax equations – sales tax, customs duties, highways tax, and so on – employ tax bases which seem appropriate to the individual categories and which are endogenous to the model as a whole. The absence of tax rate variables in these relationships is explained simply by the fact either that the tax base itself effectively incorporates any change in rates or that no significant alteration in rates occurred during the period under discussion. Thus, in contrast perhaps to the income tax equations, the indirect tax estimates may be of rather limited applicability in assessing the potential impact of changes in

---

[5] Company and non salary and wage incomes are at present exogenous to the model, being available only on an annual basis. It is planned to incorporate quarterly interpolated income variables for these categories as endogenous at a later stage. Hopefully, this will allow for a broader definition of private income in the relevant expenditure equations.

Table 1. Dynamic sim

Variable name [a]	Variable symbol	Units
Overseas reserves	ANZ	$m
Building permits, dwellings, real	$BPDP/PCH$	$m
Building permits, other	$BPOP$	$m
Building work, dwellings	$BWDP$	$m
Building work, other	$BWOP$	$m
Current payments, imports	CPI	$m
Current payments, other	CPO	$m
Currency	CUR	$m
Savings banks' demand deposits	DDS	$m
Trading banks' demand deposits	DDT	$m
Savings banks' fixed deposits	DFS	$m
Trading banks' fixed deposits	DFT	$m
Trading banks' minimum balances	$DRTM$	$m
Trading banks' total deposits	DT	$m
Savings banks' cash	DTS	$m
Employment in building	EB	000 pe
Employment in manufacturing	EM	000 pe
Employment in other industries	EO	000 pe
Government's balance before borrowing	GBB	$m
Trading banks' cash and securities	$GDRTN$	$m
Savings banks' government securities	GS	$m
Savings banks' required securities	GSR	$m
Imports, c.i.f., adjusted, real	ICA/PI	$m
Imports, c.i.f., current total	IC	$m
Mortgage interest rate	JM	%
Stocks of other buildings	$KBOP$	$m
Non-farm trade stocks, real	KT/PCI	$m
Savings banks' local body securities	LLS	$m
Savings banks' private lending	LPS	$m
Trading banks' advances, etc.	LPT	$m
Money supply	MI	$m
New mortgage registrations	NM	$m

[a] Variable names are abbreviated for convenience; full definitions are given in the list of nota
Appendix 2.

equation model

			Final quarter of estimation period 1970(1) Base remains 1965(3)		
uarter 1965(3)					
	Solution	Residual	Actual	Solution	Residual
300	210.537	− 1.737	332.700	350.040	−17.340
179	48.581	1.598	37.052	38.449	− 1.397
940	36.925	0.015	41.965	47.602	− 5.637
768	49.547	3.221	46.743	49.275	− 2.532
798	36.245	1.553	36.326	39.805	− 3.479
040	184.293	6.747	212.232	216.311	− 4.079
414	59.424	− 5.010	82.540	83.380	− 0.840
800	140.612	1.188	168.700	161.043	7.657
000	985.818	− 3.818	1125.100	1131.132	− 6.032
600	592.991	−22.391	608.300	611.644	− 3.344
400	263.847	5.553	555.900	554.121	1.779
700	101.024	12.676	230.800	239.334	− 8.534
070	71.637	− 1.567	21.070	17.269	3.801
900	711.615	− 9.715	881.400	893.278	−11.878
200	25.302	− 1.102	48.400	48.703	− 0.303
240	63.083	0.157	61.430	62.521	− 1.091
820	216.730	0.090	234.720	236.290	− 1.570
630	409.572	0.058	467.910	468.846	− 0.936
500	− 57.231	− 7.269	214.300	214.296	0.004
336	39.611	− 6.275	41.201	77.046	−35.845
300	1128.367	4.933	1458.100	1463.069	− 4.969
600	1117.200	1.400	1475.100	1479.651	− 4.551
627	206.289	7.338	173.475	182.619	− 9.144
300	207.967	7.333	223.500	235.082	−11.582
960	5.954	0.006	6.810	6.970	− 0.160
230	428.215	0.016	1073.180	1096.844	−23.664
344	806.687	2.657	933.499	943.784	−10.285
700	30.318	0.382	45.500	45.004	0.496
200	83.678	− 2.478	155.200	154.676	0.524
400	491.370	0.030	685.800	661.408	24.392
400	733.604	−21.204	777.000	772.687	4.313
598	136.189	8.409	125.162	126.212	− 1.050

Variable name	Variable symbol	Units
Trading banks' note holdings	*NOT*	Sm
Consumers' price index, all groups	*PC*	1965 =
Consumers' price index, durables	*PCD*	1965 =
Retail trade implicit price deflator	*PCI*	1965 =
Consumers' price index, non-durables	*PCN*	1965 =
Consumers' price index, transport	*PCT*	1965 =
Wholesale price index, building	*PWB*	1965 =
Wholesale automotive turnover, real	*RA/PCT*	$m
Retail trade turnover, durables, real	*RTD/PCD*	$m
Retail trade turnover, non-durables, real	*RTN/PCN*	$m
Retail trade turnover, total	*RT*	$m
Total indirect taxation	*TI*	$m
Indirect tax, beer duty	*TIB*	$m
Indirect tax, customs duty	*TIC*	$m
Indirect tax, estate duty	*TIE*	$m
Indirect tax, highways tax	*TIH*	$m
Indirect tax, automotive sales tax	*TISA*	$m
Indirect tax, non-automotive sales tax	*TISN*	$m
Total direct income tax	*TY*	$m
Company income tax	*TYCG*	$m
Other persons' income tax	*TYOG*	$m
Salary and wage earners tax deductions	*TYSD*	$m
Salary and wage tax payments to Government	*TYSP*	$m
Notified vacancies	*VE*	000 per
Nominal weekly wage rate index [b]	*WWI*	1965 =
Aggregate expenditure	*Y*	$m
Aggregate expenditure, adjusted	*YA*	$m
Real aggregate expenditure	*YR*	$m
Net salary and wage income	*YSN*	$m
Private gross salaries and wages	*YSP*	$m
Permanent salary and wage income, real	*YSNRP*	$m

[b] *WWI* was treated as exogenous in this simulation for reasons explained in the text.

inued)

	quarter 1965(3)		Final quarter of estimation period 1970(1) Base remains 1965(3)		
ıl	Solution	Residual	Actual	Solution	Residual
196	34.056	− 1.860	29.296	33.587	− 4.291
005	1.003	0.002	1.232	1.229	0.003
003	1.004	− 0.001	1.140	1.141	− 0.001
006	1.004	0.002	1.209	1.204	0.005
006	1.004	0.002	1.216	1.210	0.006
997	1.009	− 0.012	1.278	1.289	− 0.011
006	1.000	0.006	1.221	1.218	0.003
043	57.042	0.001	54.836	57.205	− 2.369
663	35.838	− 0.175	32.886	33.218	− 0.332
712	331.631	− 1.919	353.734	363.174	− 9.440
460	368.876	− 1.416	467.630	477.382	− 9.752
300	81.187	− 1.887	110.100	111.357	− 1.257
200	7.365	− 0.165	10.000	10.301	− 0.301
300	23.691	− 2.391	28.300	28.222	0.078
900	5.389	− 0.489	7.200	6.506	0.694
400	18.998	1.402	23.200	24.180	− 0.980
308	10.230	0.078	12.139	12.860	− 0.721
189	9.514	− 0.325	17.784	17.788	− 0.004
539	116.682	− 5.143	451.778	449.639	2.139
250	9.164	− 0.914	213.547	215.000	− 1.453
280	55.333	− 3.053	130.482	127.914	2.568
108	62.173	− 0.065	98.614	97.181	1.433
790	61.966	− 1.176	105.996	104.972	1.024
718	7.817	− 0.099	4.988	5.622	− 0.634
997	0.997	0.000	1.241	1.241	0.000
800	727.875	4.925	976.400	972.314	4.086
500	753.727	2.773	911.000	930.435	−19.435
300	716.880	2.420	826.200	830.881	− 4.681
965	403.366	− 5.401	533.115	543.928	−10.813
694	402.160	− 5.466	553.155	562.533	− 9.378
920	390.001	− 1.081	436.530	436.871	− 0.341

policy as conveyed through tax rate variations. However, they are still likely to be useful for forecasting purposes.

4. Simulation[6]

As a first step towards assessing the likely structural stability and forecasting ability of the present model, and with a view to examining ways of improving some of the more difficult areas, a series of dynamic simulation experiments have been carried out. These tests covered the period 1965(3)–1970(1) with *ex post* forecasts being generated for three further quarters to 1970(4). All endogenous values beyond the initial lags supplied for 1965(3) were generated within the model[7] and carried forward where necessary. Generally speaking, the preliminary simulation results were quite pleasing in the sense that most of the variables recorded solution values which moved closely in line with their actual historical values. Where divergencies occurred, they tended usually to be self-correcting rather than self-perpetuating. Accordingly, by the end of the estimation period, 1970(1), and in most cases even at the end of the forecast period, 1970(4), the differences between solution and actual values were quite small. This is illustrated in table 1. Several areas suggested the need for further work including, for example, wages and inventories. The proposed introduction of supply constraints, such as potential employment series and a capacity utilisation variable, may assist in picking up domestic inflationary movements rather better than at present.[8]

---

[6] For fuller details, see Deane [1].

[7] The only exception was *WWI* which was treated as exogenous as a result of the substantial institutional-type change which occurred in 1969–70 when many wage awards were altered in such a way as to bring award rates (i.e. *WWI*) up to parity with ruling rates.

[8] Some of these improvements, as well as others not mentioned here but on which work is proceeding, were suggested by J.F. Helliwell.

5. Conclusion

It will be clearly apparent that this paper is very much in the nature of a report on work in progress. Many of the equations are at an early stage of development; much of the detailed work has yet to be carried out. Improvements should include more satisfactory specifications of the equations, particularly with respect to lag distributions, the incorporation of new data in many areas (substantial amounts of new data are still being extracted), the adoption of more consistent estimation techniques, the inclusion of additional endogenous variables, further examination of deflation procedures, closer study of the linkages between various sectors of the model, and more extensive tests with model and sector simulations.

Nevertheless, some of the potentially more interesting features of the model are evident in the present version. First, the work represents an attempt to put together a macroeconometric model on the basis of, at least in some respects, exceedingly slender data resources. This gives rise to some rather heroic assumptions and the problems inevitably associated with them. But whether these assumptions are sustainable or not will be decided more on practical than theoretical grounds. In other words, the relevant question seems to be this: is such a model, despite imperfections, likely to be a useful additional tool for the forecaster and policymaker? It is hoped to set about finding an answer to this question in the reasonably near future.

Secondly, the model contains a wide range of policy variables not only of the orthodox type but also in the form of a series of policy dummy variables to account for direct controls. Simulation work should help throw some light on the meaningfulness of the way in which such policy considerations are handled in the model. Hopefully, some reverse causation may also be present, in which case the model may lead to improved understanding of the way in which policy measures influence economic activity. It is of interest to observe that, despite extensive use by government of non-market policy instruments over the past decade, relatively orthodox specification of the behavioural equations still gives reasonable statistical results.

Thirdly, the linkages between the monetary and real sectors undoubtedly warrant further study. On the face of it, monetary variables play significant roles in determining a range of expenditures including consumption of durables, spending on dwellings, imports of goods and payments for these imports. Interest rates, through their impact on the financial aggregates, also indirectly influence spending decisions.

The role of interest rates in the monetary sector of the model is particularly notable in view of widely-held beliefs in New Zealand about the unimportance of these rates in determining asset-holders' behaviour. The equations suggest that the potential role of interest rates in a policy sense has been underestimated by government. But, given orthodox economic theory, the significance of interest rates should not be too surprising. The popular assumption of a lack of responsiveness on the part of New Zealanders to changes in relative prices, including interest rates, seems to be based more on political than economic grounds. At least relative prices can be claimed to be important in an econometric model of the New Zealand economy, despite politicians' feelings about the true state of affairs.

Appendix 1: Equations and identities [9]

A. Private demand

Consumption:

1. $\dfrac{RTN}{PCN} = 0.5438\ YSNRP + 0.1409 \left(\dfrac{YSN}{PC} - YSNRP \right)$
    (10.38)   (1.53)

$\qquad - 1253.3080\ \dfrac{PCN}{PC} + 4.2553\ VE - 43.4435\ S_1$
$\qquad\quad (6.91) \qquad\qquad (5.98) \qquad\quad (12.76)$

$\qquad - 32.3480\ S_2 - 39.3346\ S_3 + 1378.1779$
$\qquad\quad (10.03) \qquad (11.79)$

$R^2 = 0.980,\ SEE = 5.57,\ \%SEE = 1.67,\ DW = 1.62$ (period 1961(I)–1970(I); 37 observations).

[9] Unless otherwise stated, the estimation period is 1960(2)–1970(1); a total of 40 observations. Numbers in parentheses are absolute values of Student's t ratio.

2. $\dfrac{RTD}{PCD} = \underset{(2.12)}{0.05031}\ YSNRP - \underset{(3.95)}{81.1282}\ \dfrac{PCD}{PC} + \underset{(8.42)}{0.05736}\ \dfrac{M1_{-1}}{PC_{-1}}$

$\quad + \underset{(4.91)}{1.5977}\ \dfrac{RHDF}{PCD} + \underset{(1.53)}{0.7586}\ ZHP - \underset{(8.75)}{7.9631}\ S_1 - \underset{(6.29)}{4.0150}\ S_2$

$\quad - \underset{(6.54)}{4.6648}\ S_3 + 46.6749.$

$R^2 = 0.942, SEE = 1.07, \%SEE = 3.15, DW = 1.95$ (period 1962(2)–1970(1); 32 observations).

3. $\dfrac{RA}{PCT} = \underset{(4.26)}{0.03832}\ YR + \underset{(5.28)}{0.4981}\ \dfrac{RA_{-1}}{PCT_{-1}} + \underset{(3.75)}{3.0156}\ ZQRA$

$\quad - \underset{(4.59)}{5.6407}\ S_1 + \underset{(1.93)}{2.3510}\ S_3 - 3.1199.$

$R^2 = 0.869, SEE = 3.06, \%SEE = 6.55, DW = 2.29, D = -1.16.$

Investment:

4. $\dfrac{BPDP}{PCH} = \underset{(2.36)}{0.03410}\ \dfrac{YSN}{PC} + \underset{(6.14)}{0.1388}\ \dfrac{NM}{PC} + \underset{(6.17)}{0.04648}\ \dfrac{M1_{-1}}{PC_{-1}} - \underset{(1.88)}{1.8754}\ S_1 - 20.1024.$

$R^2 = 0.860, SEE = 1.63, \%SEE = 3.97, DW = 1.57$ (period 1962(2)–1970(3); 34 observations).

5. $BWDP = \underset{(9.45)}{0.4442}\ (BPDP + BPDP_{-1}) - \underset{(3.86)}{3.7598}\ S_1 + 6.6340.$

$R^2 = 0.877, SEE = 1.85, \%SEE = 3.83, DW = 2.29$ (period 1965(3)–1970(3); 21 observations).

6. $NM = \underset{(7.75)}{0.3993}\ YA - \underset{(4.44)}{0.02518}\ (JM * YA) + \underset{(5.01)}{12.8554}\ S_2 + \underset{(11.81)}{30.2372}\ S_3 - 82.0102.$

$R^2 = 0.945, SEE = 6.56, \%SEE = 6.22, DW = 2.22.$

7. $JM = \underset{(2.63)}{0.00410}\ NM + \underset{(1.82)}{0.1195}\ JGS_{-1} + \underset{(13.77)}{0.8265}\ JM_{-1} + \underset{(3.29)}{0.1777}\ S_1 - \underset{(1.53)}{0.07674}\ S_3$

$\quad + 0.05858.$

$R^2 = 0.973, SEE = 0.11, \%SEE = 1.82, DW = 2.48, D = -1.64.$

8. $BPOP = \displaystyle\sum_{i=0}^{11} W_i\ \Delta Y_{t-i} + \underset{(2.53)}{0.00974}\ KBOP_{-1} - \underset{(2.97)}{6.3090}\ S_2 + 18.0213.$

$R^2 = 0.740, SEE = 4.74, DW = 1.92$ (period 1964(1)–1970(3); 27 observations). Almon variables *t*-values: $A1, 4.58; A2, 4.02; A3, 2.40.$

W_0	0.0539	W_4	0.1256	W_8	0.0850
W_1	0.0902	W_5	0.1215	W_9	0.0677
W_2	0.1123	W_6	0.1125	W_{10}	0.0482
W_3	0.1233	W_7	0.1001	W_{11}	0.0259

9. $$BWOP = \sum_{i=0}^{6} W_i \, BPOP_{t-i} + \underset{(2.85)}{18.2426} \, PWB - \underset{(4.04)}{4.8100} \, S_1 + \underset{(1.75)}{1.8521} \, S_3 - 12.1776.$$

$R^2 = 0.903, SEE = 2.06, DW = 2.75$ (period 1965(2)–1970(3); 22 observations).
Almon variables t-values: $A1$, 3.71; $A2$, 2.80; $A3$, 1.64.

W_0	0.0984	W_3	0.1606	W_5	0.0675
W_1	0.1567	W_4	0.1201	W_6	0.0203
W_2	0.1759				

10. $KBOP = BWOP + KBOP_{-1}$.

11. $$\Delta\left(\frac{KT}{PCI}\right) = \underset{(5.75)}{0.1966} \, YR + \underset{(3.69)}{0.2123} \frac{ICA}{PI} - \underset{(6.98)}{0.1662} \frac{KT_{-1}}{PCI_{-1}} + \underset{(12.25)}{36.5348} \, S_1 + \underset{(5.29)}{16.8679} \, S_2$$
$$+ \underset{(13.96)}{42.4771} \, S_3 - 63.9656.$$

$R^2 = 0.928, SEE = 6.19, DW = 1.99$ (period 1960(4)–1969(4); 37 observations) .

Imports:

12. $$\frac{ICA}{PI} = \underset{(2.28)}{0.08916} \, YR - \underset{(2.93)}{113.7220} \frac{PI}{PC} + \underset{(2.19)}{0.09379} \frac{M1_{-1}}{PC_{-1}} + \underset{(4.55)}{11.7947} \, ZQR$$
$$- \underset{(2.80)}{21.5364} \, ZDS + \underset{(3.10)}{22.2002} \, ZIC + \underset{(3.91)}{0.3746} \frac{ICA_{-1}}{PI_{-1}} + \underset{(4.73)}{18.9475} \, S_3$$
$$- \underset{(1.59)}{6.9612} \, S_1 + 87.0679.$$

$R^2 = 0.868, SEE = 9.42, \%SEE = 5.67, DW = 1.79, D = 0.84.$

13. $$CPI = \underset{(20.32)}{0.8638} \, (0.75 \, ICA + 0.25 \, ICA_{-1}) + \underset{(2.13)}{0.0578} \, \Delta LPT_{-1} + \underset{(2.31)}{12.2911} \, ZDS + 15.4995.$$

$R^2 = 0.923, SEE = 7.44, \%SEE = 4.46, DW = 1.69$ (period 1960(3)–1970(1);
39 observations) .

14. $$CPO = \underset{(14.54)}{0.0796} \, YA + \underset{(8.67)}{0.1913} \frac{CRE}{PE} + \underset{(3.25)}{9.8668} \, ZCP - \underset{(4.37)}{6.9473} \, S_1 - \underset{(2.92)}{5.0133} \, S_2 - 34.7371.$$

$R^2 = 0.976, SEE = 2.75, \%SEE = 4.70, DW = 2.16.$

15. $\Delta ANZ = CRE + CRO - CPI - CPO + XBP + XBO.$

B. Employment, income and prices

Employment:

16. $EB = 0.07081 \left(\dfrac{BPDP}{PCH} + \dfrac{BPOP}{PWB} \right) + 0.8197 \, EB_{-1} + 0.6391 \, S_1 - 0.5280 \, S_3 + 5.8258.$
    (5.53)   (21.08)   (2.64)   (2.06)

    $R^2 = 0.966, SEE = 0.58, \%SEE = 0.97, DW = 2.01, D = -0.04$ (period 1962(1)–1970(3); 35 observations).

17. $EM = 0.1081 \, QRM + 0.1284 \, ZT + 1.5065 \, EM_{-1} - 0.6985 \, EM_{-2} + 1.4407 \, S_2$
          (2.64)   (2.61)   (11.00)   (5.63)   (2.76)

    $+ 24.9205.$

    $R^2 = 0.989, SEE = 1.12, \%SEE = 0.51, DW = 1.78$ (period 1964(1)–1970(2); 26 observations).

18. $EO = 0.09161 \left(\dfrac{RTN}{PCN} + \dfrac{RTD}{PCD} \right) + 0.5131 \, ZT + 0.7222 \, EO_{-1} - 9.0881 \, S_1$
         (4.92)   (2.94)   (10.30)   (4.55)

    $- 17.4944 \, S_2 - 14.9083 \, S_3 + 82.9545.$
       (10.36)   (11.41)

    $R^2 = 0.999, SEE = 1.17, \%SEE = 0.28, DW = 2.20, D = -0.70.$

19. $VE = 0.01508 \, YR + 1.1604 \, VE_{-1} - 0.4117 \, VE_{-2} - 0.1251 \, ZT - 2.0671 \, S_1$
         (4.74)   (9.71)   (3.81)   (5.21)   (7.85)

    $- 2.0111 \, S_2 - 0.5792 \, S_3 - 5.4640.$
       (7.67)   (2.35)

    $R^2 = 0.956, SEE = 0.51, \%SEE = 8.36, DW = 2.34.$

Wage income:

20. $YSP = 0.2476 \, (EB + EM + EO) + 265.0249 \, PC + 0.2217 \, ICA + 0.5599 \, YSP_{-1}$
         (2.29)   (3.16)   (2.32)   (4.35)

    $- 0.1227 \, (S_1 * YSP_{-1}) - 0.0732 \, (S_2 * YSP_{-1}) - 0.1068 \, (S_3 * YSP_{-1})$
       (7.62)   (5.53)   (7.33)

    $- 263.8242.$

    $R^2 = 0.988, SEE = 10.67, \%SEE = 2.65, DW = 2.07.$

21. $YSN = YSP + YSG - TYSD.$

22. $YSNRP = 0.176 \sum\limits_{i=0}^{7} 0.9^i \left(\dfrac{YSN}{PC} \right)_{t-i}.$

23. $WWI = 0.8856\, PC + 0.0466\, ZW1 + 0.00322\, VE + 0.00610\, S_3 - 0.4228.$
    $\quad\;\;(12.97)\qquad(3.90)\qquad\quad(3.18)\qquad\quad(1.72)$

    $R^2 = 0.994, SEE = 0.010, \%SEE = 0.97, DW = 1.62.$

Prices:

24. $PCN = 0.1091\, \dfrac{YSP + YSG}{YR} + 0.1978\, WWI + 0.07038\, PI + 0.02112\, ZSUB$
    $\qquad\;\;(3.12)\qquad\qquad\qquad(3.26)\qquad\quad(3.09)\qquad\quad(2.88)$

    $\qquad + 0.6418\, PCN_{-1} + 0.00470\, S_1 + 0.00452\, S_2 + 0.00633\, S_3 + 0.02311.$
    $\qquad\quad(7.85)\qquad\qquad(1.46)\qquad\quad(1.18)\qquad\quad(2.11)$

    $R^2 = 0.997, SEE = 0.006, \%SEE = 0.60, DW = 1.99, D = 0.05.$

25. $PCD = 0.07434\, WWI + 0.06683\, PI + 0.8013\, PCD_{-1} - 0.00259\, S_1 + 0.06052.$
    $\qquad\;\;(2.78)\qquad\qquad(3.82)\qquad\;\;(11.36)\qquad\quad(1.53)$

    $R^2 = 0.994, SEE = 0.005, \%SEE = 0.46, DW = 1.87, D = 0.45.$

26. $PCT = 0.3798\, WWI + 0.00841\, ZST + 0.6296\, PCT_{-1} + 0.0057\, S_1 + 0.0108\, S_2$
    $\qquad\;\;(3.32)\qquad\qquad(1.99)\qquad\quad(4.89)\qquad\quad(1.51)\qquad\;(2.82)$

    $\qquad - 0.0841.$

    $R^2 = 0.995, SEE = 0.010, \%SEE = 0.95, DW = 1.63, D = 2.00.$

27. $PC = 0.07189\, \dfrac{YSP + YSG}{YR} + 0.1134\, WWI + 0.02924\, PI_{-1} + 0.8387\, PC_{-1}$
    $\qquad\;\;(2.71)\qquad\qquad\qquad(2.02)\qquad\quad(1.89)\qquad\quad(13.70)$

    $\qquad + 0.01497\, ZSUB + 0.00491\, S_1 + 0.00414\, S_2 + 0.00413\, S_3 - 0.02220.$
    $\qquad\quad(2.72)\qquad\qquad(2.02)\qquad\quad(1.44)\qquad\quad(1.81)$

    $R^2 = 0.999, SEE = 0.005, \%SEE = 0.46, DW = 1.92, D = 0.29.$

28. $PCI = \dfrac{RTN + RTD}{RTN/PCN + RTD/PCD}$

29. $PWB = 0.2823\, WWI + 0.1763\, PI + 0.4862\, PWB_{-1} + 0.00283\, S_1 + 0.05956.$
    $\qquad\;\;(6.11)\qquad\qquad(6.85)\qquad\;\;(5.83)\qquad\qquad(1.43)$

    $R^2 = 0.997, SEE = 0.005, \%SEE = 0.53, DW = 1.64, D = 1.33.$

C. Monetary sector:

30. $\Delta CUR = 0.00756\, Y - 0.2466\, CUR_{-1} - 11.2533\, ZDC1 + 14.1484\, ZE$
    $\qquad\quad(1.92)\qquad\;\;(2.21)\qquad\qquad(3.15)\qquad\qquad(6.06)$

    $\qquad - 35.7818\, S_1 - 22.0304\, S_2 - 19.1265\, S_3 + 49.6643.$
    $\qquad\quad(13.02)\qquad\quad(14.16)\qquad\;\;(12.64)$

    $R^2 = 0.954, SEE = 3.35, DW = 2.24.$

Trading banks:

31. $\Delta DDT = 0.0686\ Y - 0.1650\ (TYCG + TYOG) - 0.3231\ DDT_{-1} - 23.7593\ JGS$
        (3.56)   (6.79)   (2.99)   (3.50)

        $+ 1.6620\ XBP - 37.8764\ S_3 + 22.5365\ S_4 + 265.7405.$
         (2.86)   (8.37)   (4.52)

    $R^2 = 0.935, SEE = 10.38, DW = 2.13.$

32. $\Delta DFT = 0.1524\ Y + 0.05610\ (JTF * Y) - 0.02560\ (JGS * Y) - 0.8152\ DFT_{-1}$
        (1.55)   (2.95)   (2.42)   (4.78)

        $- 15.6645\ S_1 - 20.1572\ S_2 - 7.5999\ S_3 - 73.8983.$
         (2.33)   (3.30)   (1.45)

    $R^2 = 0.876, SEE = 8.45, DW = 2.64$ (period 1965(3)–1970(3); 21 observations).

33. $DT = DDT + DFT + DGT + DTT + DWT.$

34. $\Delta LPT = 0.1505\ Y + 0.3474\ (TYCG + TYOG) - 0.3590\ LPT_{-1} - 7.3014\ ZA_{-2}$
        (2.96)   (12.79)   (3.53)   (1.90)

        $+ 50.3217.$

    $R^2 = 0.902, SEE = 15.69, DW = 1.86.$

35. $\Delta NOT = 0.0502\ (DDT + DFT + DGT) - 0.0498\ LPT - 0.8712\ NOT_{-1}$
        (3.84)   (1.98)   (6.08)

        $- 0.0121\ (ZE * (DDT + DFT + DGT)) + 4.9386\ ZDC3 - 12.4258\ S_1$
         (3.87)   (3.28)   (3.13)

        $- 17.7017\ S_2 - 16.1849\ S_3 + 10.0973.$
         (11.20)   (9.74)

    $R^2 = 0.965, SEE = 3.11, DW = 2.24.$

36. $DRTM = ((DDT + DGT) * NTD) + (DFT + NTF) - NOT.$

37. $LTRP = DRTP.$

38. $GDRTN = DT + LTRP - (NOT + COT + LPT + LLT + DRTM + DRTP + AOT).$

39. $M1 = CUR + DDT.$

Savings banks:

40. $\Delta DDS = 0.03200\ Y - 0.2215\ TYOG - 0.00831\ (Y * JGS) + 10.8945\ ZIS2$
        (2.20)   (3.33)   (2.89)   (4.72)

        $+ 25.6538\ S_1 - 7.2539\ S_2 + 8.6001\ S_3 + 17.7412.$
         (4.00)   (4.30)   (2.29)

    $R^2 = 0.822, SEE = 3.68, DW = 2.23.$

41. $\Delta DFS = 0.03412\ Y - 0.1797\ TYOG + 0.8986\ (TYOR + TYSR) + 0.01382\ (Y * ZJSI)$
          (3.13)   (2.45)   (2.93)   (3.39)

$$- 4.2107\ JTF - 12.7218\ ZIS1 + 18.8590\ S_1 + 4.9529\ S_2 + 11.6903\ S_3$$
          (2.80)   (5.37)   (2.76)   (2.75)   (2.95)

$$- 4.3064$$

$R^2 = 0.870, SEE = 3.73, DW = 2.36.$

42. $\Delta DTS = 0.04266\ (DDS + DFS) - 0.9231\ DTS_{-1} - 12.3557\ ZIS3 - 11.9087\ S_1$
          (6.48)   (6.77)   (3.91)   (5.58)
$$- 8.5829\ S_2 - 13.7761\ S_3 - 16.0756.$$
          (6.07)   (8.97)

$R^2 = 0.919, SEE = 2.95, DW = 1.55.$

43. $GSR = (DDS + DFS) * NSG.$

44. $(GS - GSR) = 4.0914\ (JGS - JM) - 1288.20\ \dfrac{\Delta NSG}{NSG_{-1}} + 0.3544\ (GS_{-1} - GSR_{-1})$
              (2.65)   (2.97)   (3.13)

$$- 9.6829\ S_1 + 5.1284\ S_3 + 6.1618.$$
          (4.27)   (2.31)

$R^2 = 0.664, SEE = 5.74, DW = 2.37.$

45. $LLS = 0.0061\ (DDS + DFS) - 0.9438\ JM + 0.8828\ LLS_{-1} - 0.4897\ S_1 + 2.4489.$
              (2.54)   (2.03)   (12.66)   (3.59)

$R^2 = 0.998, SEE = 0.365, DW = 1.62.$

46. $LPS = DDS + DFS - (DTS + GS + LLS + AOS).$

D. Government sector

Direct taxation [10]

47. $TYCG = 0.02289\ (TRC * YC_{-1A}) + 0.8778\ (S_1 * TRC * YC_{-1A})$
              (2.73)   (192.41)
$$+ 0.00820\ (S_2 * TRC * YC_{-1A}) + 0.02120\ (S_3 * TRC * YC_{-1A}) + 0.05978.$$
          (1.80)   (4.65)

$R^2 = 0.999, SEE = 1.95, \%SEE = 4.17, DW = 2.53.$

[10] The sub-script $-1A$ in the company and other persons tax equations implies that the income variable relates to the immediately preceding annual March year aggregate.

48. $TYOG = 0.0586 \ (TSRO * YO_{-1A}) + 0.3536 \ (S_1 * TSRO * YO_{-1A})$
    (1.21)   (53.62)

    $+ 0.0158 \ (S_2 * TSRO * YO_{-1A}) + 0.1774 \ (S_3 * TSRO * YO_{-1A})$
    (3.27)   (36.69)

    $+ 3.9724 \ ZTT - 10.8079.$
    (7.74)

$R^2 = 0.998, SEE = 2.13, \%SEE = 4.34, DW = 2.01$ (period 1965(1)–1970(1); 21 observations).

49. $TYSD = 0.4825 \ (TSRS * YS) + 0.0035 \ (S_1 * YS) - 0.0023 \ (S_2 * YS) - 7.4684.$
    (84.18)   (3.22)   (3.22)

$R^2 = 0.995, SEE = 1.32, \%SEE = 2.15, DW = 2.09.$

50. $TYSP = 0.9176 \ TYSD + 0.1610 \ (S_1 * TYSD) + 0.0557 \ (S_2 * TYSD)$
    (69.27)   (17.02)   (5.49)

    $+ 0.0766 \ (S_3 * TYSD) + 0.1529.$
    (7.77)

$R^2 = 0.995, SEE = 1.42, \%SEE = 2.32, DW = 2.96.$

51. $TY = TYCG + TYOG + TYSP - TYCR - TYOR - TYSR + TYB.$

Indirect taxation:

52. $TISN = 0.0239 \ (RTN + RTD) + 0.0119 \ (S_1 * (RTN + RTD))$
    (7.63)   (8.73)

    $- 0.0141 \ (S_2 * (RTN + RTD)) + 0.6980.$
    (11.30)

$R^2 = 0.927, SEE = 1.17, \%SEE = 11.46, DW = 2.49$ (period 1963(2)–1970(4); 31 observations).

53. $TISA = 0.1735 \ RA + 0.1803 \ TISA_{-1} - 1.5677 \ S_1 - 0.4353 \ S_3 - 1.0630.$
    (9.35)   (2.36)   (4.21)   (1.50)

$R^2 = 0.943, SEE = 0.634, \%SEE = 6.29, DW = 1.79, D = 0.62$
(period 1963(2)–1970(3); 30 observations).

54. $TIC = 0.06237 \ IC - 0.02494 \ (S_1 * IC) - 0.02879 \ (S_2 * IC) - 0.01340 \ (S_3 * IC)$
    (4.82)   (5.01)   (6.77)   (2.69)

    $+ 0.5199 \ TIC_{-1} + 2.9011.$
    (3.91)

$R^2 = 0.824, SEE = 1.75, \%SEE = 7.67, DW = 2.38, D = -2.29$
(period 1960(2)–1970(2); 41 observations).

55. $TIB = 0.01015\ (RTN + RTD) + 0.2278\ S_1 - 1.7104\ S_2 - 1.6071\ S_3 + 5.2281.$
       (11.81)   (1.31)   (10.06)   (9.06)

$R^2 = 0.920, SEE = 0.38, \%SEE = 4.63, DW = 1.45$ (period 1960(1)–1970(2);
42 observations).

56. $TIE = 0.0036\ Y + 39.5035\ TRE - 1.1960\ S_2 - 1.4978.$
       (4.82)   (5.23)   (6.60)

$R^2 = 0.684, SEE = 0.469, \%SEE = 8.79, DW = 2.17$ (period 1961(2)–1970(1);
36 observations).

57. $TIH = 0.2358\ RA + 4.5631\ S_1 - 2.3878\ S_2 + 3.1294\ S_3 + 2.2352.$
      (15.50)   (8.99)   (4.72)   (6.22)

$R^2 = 0.932, SEE = 1.12, \%SEE = 7.48, DW = 2.04.$

58. $TI = TISN + TISA + TIC + TIB + TIE + TIH + TIO.$

59. $GBB = TY + TI + GOR - GEA - GET.$

E. Aggregate expenditure identities

60. $Y = RTN + RTD + RA + BWDP + BWOP + ICM + \Delta KT + GEA + CRE + CRO$
      $- ICA - ICE - CPO.$

61. $YR = \dfrac{RTN}{PCN} + \dfrac{RTD}{PCD} + \dfrac{RA}{PCT} + \dfrac{BWDP}{PCH} + \dfrac{BWOP}{PWB} + \dfrac{ICM}{PI} + \dfrac{KT}{PCI} - \dfrac{KT_{-1}}{PCI_{-1}} + \dfrac{GEA}{PC} + \dfrac{CRE}{PE}$

      $+ \dfrac{CRO}{PC} - \dfrac{ICA}{PI} - \dfrac{ICE}{PI} - \dfrac{CPO}{PI}.$

62. $YA = Y - \Delta KT - (CRE + CRO - ICA - ICE - CPO).$

63. $IC = ICA + ICE.$

Appendix 2: Notation [11]

ANZ *	New Zealand's official overseas reserves, $m.
AOS	Savings banks, net other assets, $M.
AOT	Trading banks, net other assets, $m.

[11] Endogenous variables are denoted by an asterisk.

BPDP *	Building permits issued, private dwellings, $m.
BPOP *	Building permits issued, private other buildings, $m.
BWDP *	Building work put in place, private dwellings, $m.
BWOP *	Building work put in place, private other buildings, $m.
COT	Trading banks' holdings of coin, $m.
CPI *	Current payments, imports, *OET*, $m.
CPO *	Current payments, other than imports, *OET*, $m.
CRE	Current receipts, exports, *OET*, $m.
CRO	Current receipts other than exports, *OET*, $m.
CUR *	Currency; notes and coin held by the public, $m.
DDS *	Savings banks' demand deposits, $m.
DDT *	Trading banks' demand deposits, excluding government, $m.
DFS *	Savings banks' fixed deposits, $m.
DFT *	Trading banks' fixed deposits, $m.
DGT	Trading banks' government deposits, $m.
DRTM *	Trading banks' statutory minimum balance at Reserve Bank, $m.
DRTP	Trading banks' deposits at Reserve Bank to meet penal requirements, $m.
DT *	Trading banks' total deposits, $m.
DTS *	Savings banks' cash plus savings banks' deposits at trading banks, $m.
DTT	Trading banks' Treasury deposits, $m.
DWT	Trading banks' wool retention accounts fixed deposits, $m.
EB *	Total employment in private sector building and construction, as at end of quarter, 000 persons.
EM *	Total employment in private sector manufacturing excluding seasonal manufacturing, as at end of quarter, 000 persons.
EO *	Total all other employment, including seasonal manufacturing employment, in private sector, as at end of quarter, 000 persons. (Seasonal manufacturing includes meat processing, fruit and vegetable preserving and dairy factories.)
GBB *	Government's balance before borrowing and investment transactions, $m.
GDRTN *	Trading banks' net free cash plus holdings of government securities, $m.
GEA	Government expenditure, adjusted to exclude transfers (except those to local authorities), $m.
GET	Government expenditure on transfers other than transfers to local authorities, $m.
GOR	Government all other current revenue, i.e. all current revenue other than direct income tax and indirect tax, $m.
GS *	Savings banks' holdings of government securities, $m.
GSR *	Savings banks' required minimum holdings of government securities, $m.
ICA *	Total c.i.f. imports, excluding ships, air, rail (i.e. excluding *ICE*), $m.
ICE	c.i.f. imports, exogenous component (ships, air, rail), $m.
IC *	Total c.i.f. imports (*ICA* + *ICE*), $m.
ICM	c.i.f. imports, plant and machinery, $m.
JGS	Yield on government securities, short-term, %.
JM *	Average rate of interest on new mortgages, %.
JTF	Non-carded short-term interest rate, trading banks' fixed deposits, %.
KBOP *	Stock of private non-residential buildings, $m.

KT *	Total non-farm trade stocks, $m.
LLS *	Savings banks' holdings of local authority securities, $m.
LLT	Trading banks' holdings of local authority securities, $m.
LPS *	Savings banks' lending to private sector (excluding holdings of local authority securities), $m.
LPT *	Trading banks' lending to private sector including advances, term loans, discounts, etc. but excluding holdings of local authority securities, $m.
LTRP *	Trading banks' penal borrowing from Reserve Bank, $m.
M1 *	Volume of money, defined as the sum of currency plus trading banks' demand deposits (excluding government deposits), $m.
NM *	Total value of new mortgage registrations, $m.
NOT *	Trading banks' holdings of notes, $m.
NSG	Savings banks' weighted average government securities ratio, %.
NTD	Trading banks' reserve ratio on demand deposits, %.
NTF	Trading banks' reserve ratio on fixed deposits, %.
OET	Overseas exchange transactions basis.
PC *	Consumers' price index, all groups, base 1965 = 1.000.
PCD *	Consumers' price index, all durables except automobiles, base 1965 = 1.000.
PCH	Consumers' price index, home ownership, base 1965 = 1.000.
PCI *	Implicit total retail trade turnover price deflator, base 1965 = 1.000.
PCN *	Consumers' price index, non-durables, base 1965 = 1.000.
PCT *	Consumers' price index, private transport, base 1965 = 1.000.
PE	Export price index, base 1965 = 1.000.
PI	Import price index, base 1965 = 1.000.
PWB *	Wholesale price index, building and construction, base 1965 = 1.000.
QRM	Reserve Bank quarterly manufacturing production index (unpublished).
RA *	Wholesale sales, motor vehicles, parts and accessories, $m.
RHDF	Value of durable goods (excluding motor vehicles and plant and machinery) financed under hire-purchase agreements, $m.
RTD *	Retail trade turnover, durables, $m.
RTN *	Retail trade turnover, non-durables, $m.
S_i	Seasonal dummy; = 1 calendar quarter i, = 0 elsewhere.
TI *	Total indirect taxation, $m.
TIB *	Indirect tax, beer duty, $m.
TIC *	Indirect tax, customs duty, $m.
TIE *	Indirect tax, estate duty, $m.
TIH *	Indirect tax, highways taxation, $m.
TIO	All other indirect tax, $m.
TISA *	Indirect tax, automotive sales tax, $m.
TISN *	Indirect tax, sales tax other than for the automotive group, $m.
TRC	Effective annual tax rate on company income, $ %.
TRE	Effective tax rate, estate duty, $ %.
TSRO	Statutory tax rate, other persons' income, $ %.
TSRS	Statutory tax rate, salary and wage earners, $ %.
TY *	Total direct income tax, $m.
TYB	Balancing residual, all other net direct income tax, $m.
TYCG *	Gross direct income tax, companies, $m.

TYCR	Refunds of income tax to companies, $m.
TYOG *	Gross direct income tax, other persons, $m.
TYOR	Refunds of income tax to other persons, $m.
TYSD *	Gross PAYE income tax (deductions from pay), salary and wage earners, $m.
TYSP *	Gross PAYE income tax (payments into the Public Account), salary and wage earners, $m.
TYSR	Refunds of income tax to salary and wage earners, $m.
VE *	Notified vacancies, as at end of quarter, 000 persons.
WWI *	Nominal weekly wage rate index (total, all jurisdictions), base 1965 = 1.000.
XBO	Capital balance, other than private, *OET*, $m.
XBP	Capital balance, private, *OET*, $m.
Y *	Aggregate expenditure (current prices), $m.
YA *	Aggregate expenditure, adjusted to exclude changes in trade stocks and balance of payments items, $m.
YC	Company annual income, national account basis, $m.
YO	Other persons' annual income, national account basis, $m.
YR *	Aggregate real expenditure (constant 1965 prices), $m.
YS	Total gross salary and wage income, $m.
YSG	Government sector gross salaries and wages, $m.
YSN *	Total net salary and wage income, $m.
YSP *	Private sector gross salaries and wages, $m.
YSNRP *	Permanent real net salary and wage income, $m (see eq. 22).
ZA	Dummy variable to represent official monetary policy in respect of trading bank advances. Assumes the following values: 0 = policy, passive or permissive; 1 = policy, caution; 2 = policy, firm restraint; and 3 = policy, severe restraint.
ZCP	Dummy, adjustment for wool price fall in 1966–67; takes the value 1 in 1967(1).
ZDC1	Dummy variable to account for dishoarding of currency during the decimal currency changeover period. Takes the value 1 in 1967(2).
ZDC3	As for *ZDC1*, except takes the value 1 from 1967(3) to 1969(1).
ZDS	Dummy variable to account for United Kingdom dock strike; takes the value 1 in 1967(4), −1 in (1968(1).
ZE	Dummy variable representing balance date adjustment to account for Easter falling at the end of March; takes the value 1 in the March quarters of 1961, 1964 and 1970.
ZHP	Dummy policy variable to account for changes in hire-purchase regulations; takes the value +1 when policy is one of ease, 0 when policy is moderate, −1 when policy is tight.
ZIC	Dummy, accounting break in c.i.f. imports data; takes the value +1 in 1962(2), −1 in 1962(3).
ZIS1	Dummy variable to account for period prior to introduction of private savings banks; takes the value 1 up to and including 1964(3).
ZIS2	Dummy variable to account for the influence of the opening of the private savings banks; takes the values 1, 1, 1, 0.7, 0.3 in successive quarters, commencing in 1964(4).
ZIS3	Dummy variable to account for a statistical discrepancy in the data for savings banks' cash; takes the value 1 in 1962(4).

ZJSI   Dummy variable to account for the immediate impact of a change in the savings banks' investment account interest rate; takes the value 1 in 1962(4) and 1966(3).

ZQR   Dummy variable to account for quantitative import restrictions; takes the value +1 for relaxed control, 0 for moderate control and −1 for tight control.

ZQRA   Dummy variable to account for quantitative import restrictions in respect of the automotive group; values assigned on same basis as for *ZQR*.

ZST   Dummy variable to account for changes in motor vehicle sales tax, expressed as an index on base 1965 = 10.000.

ZSUB   Dummy variable to account for the partial removal of government food subsidies; takes the value 1 in 1967(2).

ZT   Dummy, linear time trend on successive quarters; starts as 1 in 1960(2).

ZTT   Dummy, linear time trend on successive March quarters; starts as 0 in 1965(1).

ZW1   Dummy variable to account for general wage orders; index base 1960(1) = 10.000. Percentage wage orders are added cumulatively to this base throughout the estimation period.

Note: The sub-script −1 on a variable implies a lag of one quarter; −2, a lag of two quarters. The sub-script −1*A* in the company and other persons tax equations implies that the income variable relates to the immediately preceding annual March year aggregate. Apart from *YC* and *YO*, all data in the model are quarterly.

References

[1] R.S. Deane, *Towards a model of the New Zealand economy.* Research Paper No.1, Reserve Bank of New Zealand (Wellington, September 1971).

[2] R.S. Deane, D. Grindell and M.A. Lumsden, *New data for economic research.* Research Paper No.3, Reserve Bank of New Zealand (Wellington, February 1972).

[3] R.S. Deane and M.A. Lumsden, *A model of the New Zealand monetary sector.* Research Paper No.2, Reserve Bank of New Zealand (Wellington, December 1971).

A WAGE-PRICE SECTOR FOR A QUARTERLY AUSTRALIAN MODEL *

C.I. HIGGINS

Commonwealth Treasury, Canberra

1. Scope of the study

Under conditions of maintained full employment the determinants of the rate of change of prices are of considerable importance in the study of short-term changes in aggregate economic activity. Thus the wage and price relationships to be incorporated into a quarterly econometric model deserve considerable attention; this is all the more so because of the generally disappointing results obtained in this sector of macro-models (e.g. [4], pp. 11–12; [5], pp.495–500; [6], pp.14–31).

Because of the interrelationships between wage payments, incomes, excess demand and prices, any ultimate assessment of alternative sets of wage-price relationships must utilize a complete model. For exploratory work this is not practicable and most of the results herein assume that the explanatory variables are exogenous. This single equation approach produces results which can be compared with other Australian work in the field [7, 11, 12,

* This paper reports on some of the research being done in a model building project in the Australian Commonwealth Treasury and in the Bureau of Census and Statistics. C.I. Higgins and V.W. FitzGerald are the respective principal investigators. The analysis herein is that of the author and does not necessarily reflect the opinion of the employing organisation. Kathryn Moore assisted with data preparation and background research and provided valuable comments on an earlier draft of the wages parts of this paper. The author was visiting the Reserve Bank of Australia when part of this research was undertaken and is grateful to the Bank for the provision of facilities, and to staff members and Professor J. Helliwell for helpful discussion.

13, 14]. After detailed exploratory work, the wage-price sector is embedded in a quarterly econometric model of the Australian economy in order to analyse the short-run dynamics of wage-price adjustment. The conclusions reached are preliminary in that a wage-price sector has been added to a model theoretically not well suited to the purpose.

1.1. General features of the model

Underlying the model as a whole is a standard Keynesian framework as applied in quantitative models by Klein, and to a greater or lesser extent by the subsequent mainstream of model builders. Income is determined by expenditure flows (effective demand) with endogenous expenditure functions being driven chiefly by incomes. This general view of direction of causal influence is supplemented by detailed specification of the time lags involved in the causal mechanism.

In models of this type expenditure decisions are usually framed in real terms. Prices are determined, chiefly, by a relatively fixed mark-up on unit labour costs – money wages adjusted for (actual or normal) average product per worker. This is one of the features which leads to the characterization of the present analysis as short-run: although periods in excess of two or three years will be examined, the mark-up factor will not be subject to variation as a result of altered competitiveness due to changes in protection, restrictive trade practices, etc.

Because of historical reasons, not least the previous lack of official constant price quarterly national accounts, the particular model into which the wage-price sector has been incorporated has expenditure flows determined at current prices. Under simulations of the type envisaged, in which changes in wages and prices occur, endogenous expenditure components can adjust to appropriately altered money income flows. Some of the exogenous components, e.g. exports and farm production, can be properly regarded as fixed in money terms since their prices are exogenous. For others, chiefly government spending, prices should be allowed to adjust and the pre-existing model has been so extended.

Money wages are the key determinant of prices; but what determines money wages? Most macro-models are closed with respect to wages by relating them to pressure of demand in the labour market, productivity, prices and, more recently, price expectations. Some models determine the *real* wage by the non-price factors in a neo-classical formulation. The position taken here is to interpret the wage equation as modelling the factors in the bargaining process which sets the *money* wage.

In the institutional framework of Australian wage determination it seems permissible, at least for some purposes, to regard a significant proportion of money award wages — those covered by major Arbitration Commission decisions — as exogenous. Under this assumption the model is relatively open with respect to wages compared with models of other market economies. There is, of course, considerable evidence that the decisions of the tribunals are not independent of short-term economic conditions, particularly price changes and "capacity to pay". Consequently, for some conditional historical simulations it might be desirable to close the system with respect to major awards. Such relationships, i.e. completely endogenous awards dependent on labour market conditions, productivity and prices, have been developed[1] but are not used in the present study. This paper is primarily concerned to trace the process of adjustment to money wage changes and therefore assumes that major award decisions are exogenous.

2. Award wages and earnings

2.1. Structure of the wage sector

Quarterly series can be obtained for the following variables: average weekly earnings per employed male unit (E) and weighted average minimum (determined by awards) weekly rates of wage

---

[1] These results are contained in [9] and [10] (available from the author on request) which contain a more detailed report on award wages and earnings than can be given here.

(adult males) (W). The former series, in contrast to the weekly wage rate series, is inclusive of overtime, over-award and piece rate payments, bonus allowances and salary incomes. In addition, the average earnings series reflects structural and compositional changes in the work force. All of these sources of changes in earnings, over and above the changes in awards, comprise the widely analysed phenomenon of earnings drift. Given the three measures: rate of change of earnings $(\dot{E})$, rate of change of wages $(\dot{W})^2$ and the drift between them (D), what is the appropriate structure for the wage rate equations?

There is the possibility that changes in awards may be partly absorbed in drift, which gives rise to the need to consider explicitly

(1) the flow-on *from* awards to earnings; the pattern over time of changes in $\dot{E}$ consequent upon changes in $\dot{W}$ and whether or not these changes are fully reflected in $\dot{E}$.

There is also the possibility of

(2) flow-on *within* the award structure itself. Changes in award rates are the result of a myriad of individual arbitration decisions and other agreements. It is generally thought, nonetheless, that changes in awards are largely the result of several major decisions. Prior to 1967 the key wage cases were (1) Federal Basic Wage judgments and (2) Metal Trades margins cases. The latter tended to set the pace for margins increases throughout industry in general. In 1967, with the adoption of a "total wage" concept (total wage = basic wage + margins), the above system was replaced by National Wage Cases, where total wages are adjusted. It is of interest to represent the pattern and extent of flow-on from these major decisions within the award structure.

The wage sector therefore consists of two equations: one for award wage changes $(\dot{W})$ and one for earnings $(\dot{E})$.

---

² The choice of rate of change specifications for dependent variables is discussed below.

2.2. Specification of the wage equations

1. Basic (national) wage cases

An annual percentage change specification for award wages was chosen on *a priori* grounds as the specification most nearly reflecting the characteristics of the major award wage decision. Federal basic (now national) wage judgments have tended to be annual since the abandonment of automatic quarterly adjustments. Since minor awards are continuously changing however, quarterly observations rather than annual ones have been used for the award wage equation. Some form of change specification (as opposed to levels) seems more appropriate for representing the way in which economic factors are perceived by the Court in making the basic wage decision and, of course, national wage decisions are themselves handed down only as increases. The percentage change form seems most natural from this decision modelling point of view. It also enables consistent scaling to be easily applied under the basic and national wage systems so that the coefficients on decision variables have the same meaning over time.

The basic wage decision magnitude is defined as the percentage increase in average awards which would result if the basic wage increase applied to all awards (see table 1 for values). Since the variable to be explained is the percentage increase in award wages over the same quarter a year earlier, the decision variable is included in the equation for four *whole* quarters. If the award does not occur at the beginning of a quarter, the decision magnitude is given a weight of less than one in the quarter of the decision and one minus that weight in the corresponding quarter a year later. Although not all awards are covered by the national wage case there is generally flow-on to the bulk of awards. This flow-on is fairly rapid but preferred forms incorporate short distributed lags on the decision variable.

2. Metal trades awards

The initial impact of a metal trades margins decision is confined to those trades. Typically, however, including the 1967 work value

Table 1
Percentage increase in major awards

Basic or national wage case (date of effect)	Percentage increase in average awards (six capitals) [a]	Metal trades margins or work value (date of effect)	Percentage increase in metal trades award (fitter) [b]
June 1959	4.6	December 1959	6.0
April 1960	–		
July 1961	3.4	April 1963	2.6
February 1962	–		
February 1963	–	July 1965	1.5
June 1964	5.3		
June 1965	–	January 1967	2.5
July 1966	4.9		
July 1967	2.3		
October 1968	2.9	January 1968 } [c]	4.8 } 6.0
December 1969	3.0	August 1968 }	1.2 }

[a] Absolute increases in the basic or national wage have been expressed as percentages of *average award* wages in the month prior to the decision.

[b] Metal trades decisions refer to margins for a number of specific trades. Data pertaining to fitters and several other trades can be obtained. Except for the 1967 work value increases the percentage increase in total awards as a result of the margins decisions has not been greatly different for the trades considered. For all margins cases prior to and including 1966 the percentage increase in the total fitter's award has been taken as the metal trades decision magnitude. As a result of the 1967 work value case the fitter improved his relative position. For this decision an increase slightly less than that of the second class machinist was assumed to be representative.

[c] Part (30%) of any increase in excess of $1.60 p.w. awarded in January was deferred until late August; 20% effective average deferment has been assumed.

case[3], which was not intended to initiate a round of other award increases, there has been flow-on to other awards. Thus some form of lag response to the metal trades decision must be included in the relationships.

In any full quarter subsequent to the decision, the effect on $\dot{W}$ is assumed to be a constant function of the time elapsed since the decision, i.e., the time profile of adjustment (a_i, $i = 0,1, ..., q$) is the average pattern estimated from

$$\dot{W}_t = \sum_{i=0}^{q} a_i \, MI_{d,t-i} + Z \,,$$

[3] The decision in this case became operative during 1968.

where Z represents other variables and $MI_{d,t-i}$ is the value at time $t-i$ of decision magnitudes operative at that time. (As for the basic wage magnitude, the metal trades magnitude appears in the equation for four quarters.) Since decisions are infrequent the correlation between successive lagged values of $MI_{d,t-i}$, $i=0, 1, ..., q$ is quite high. To alleviate this problem the number of lag weights to be estimated $(q+1)$ is reduced by assuming that they lie on second degree polynomials with $a_{q+1} = 0$. The full sequence of $\{a_i\}$ is related to the two estimated parameters by Lagrangean interpolation (the method of S. Almon [1]). This form of lag specification is also used for the basic wage variable.

3. Pressure of demand and prices

The ratio of job vacancies to registered unemployment (VAC/U) has been used as an indicator of pressure of demand in the labour market. This variable is non-linear in unemployment, and when vacancies approach zero, unemployment can continue to rise. Conversely, as unemployment reaches its frictional floor vacancies can continue to rise. The rate of change of VAC/U has also been employed. These are the only demand pressure variables incorporated; others suggested — utilization, hours worked and strike activity etc. — have been excluded for reasons of data availability. (As noted below, part of the pressure of demand effect on *total* awards may operate via *major* awards.)

As shown in [9] and [10], basic wage decisions bear some relationship to the size of price increases between those decisions. There is a similar, though much less marked, influence of prices on metal trades awards. There are, in addition, price effects via other miscellaneous awards and hence a general price change variable, with at least a one quarter lag, is introduced uniformly in all quarters.

2.3. Awards with major awards known

Eq. 5.1 in table 2 is the preferred equation for $\dot{W}$ with major awards known. The variables used are as follows:

$\dot{W}$　　$= 100(W - W_{-4})/W_{-4}$ = rate of change of award rates; quarterly figures are weighted averages of four end-month figures to quarter-end with weights 1/6, 1/3, 1/3, 1/6.

VAC　= job vacancies registered with the Commonwealth Employment Service (CES) (average of end-month seasonally adjusted figures).

Table 2
Rate of change of awards and earnings

Eq. 5.1		Eq. 5.2	
Explanatory variable	Dependent variable $\dot{W}$ (4.099)	Explanatory variable	Dependent variable $\dot{W}H$ (5.492)
VAC/U	0.8050	VAC/U	1.6222
(0.636)	(1.225)	(0.650)	(3.627)
$P\dot{C}L$	0.0790	$VA\dot{C}/U$	0.007854
(2.741)	(1.552)	(19.311)	(4.898)
BD　−0	0.5833	$P\dot{C}L$	0.1574
(2.204) −1	0.2917	(2.698)	(1.943)
Sum	0.8751		
$MTDC$　−0	0.4074	$W\dot{W}H$　−0	0.5775
(1.583) −1	0.2232	(3.400) −1	0.2951
−2	0.0939	−2	0.1026
−3	0.0195	Sum	0.9753
Sum	0.7440	Constant	0.5388
Constant	0.3032		(1.839)
	(0.596)		
$\hat{u}_{-1}$	0.647		
$\bar{R}^2$	0.903	$\bar{R}^2$	0.895
SEE	0.64	SEE	0.72
D	2.09	D	1.78

Note: $\bar{R}^2$ = multiple correlation coefficient adjusted for degrees of freedom. *SEE* = standard error of estimate. D = Durbin-Watson d-statistic.

Figures in parentheses under coefficients are Student's *t*-ratios; under variables they are sample period means.

Eq. 5.1 is estimated with sample period December 1958 to June 1970 (plus lags) and incorporates correction for first order serial correlation in the residuals.

Eq. 5.2 is estimated with sample period June 1959 to June 1970 (plus lags).

U = number registered for employment with the CES (average of end-month seasonally adjusted figures).

$$VA\dot{C}/U = 400\,\frac{VAC/U - (VAC/U)_{-1}}{(VAC/U)_{-1}}.$$

$P\dot{C}L$ = $400\,\dfrac{PC_{-1} - PC_{-2}}{PC_{-2}}$; PC = implicit deflator for seasonally adjusted personal consumption expenditure, 1966–67 = 1.0.

BD = the sum of basic wage decision magnitudes operative in a given quarter.

$MTDC$ = the sum of metal trades decision magnitudes operative in a given quarter.

Eq. 5.1 indicates that 88% of basic wage changes are reflected in movements in average awards and 74% of metal trades changes are reflected. (On a comparable basis the 74 would be lower as metal trades changes have not been expressed as percentages of average awards.) If VAC/U and $P\dot{C}L$ are excluded, so that $\dot{W}$ depends only on major award decisions, then these estimates of reflection (flow-on within awards) are increased. Since some variation in $\dot{W}$ has to be attributed to VAC/U and $P\dot{C}L$, independent of their influence via major awards, eq. 5.1 is preferred but, because of collinearity, the coefficients of the award variables may underestimate the extent to which award changes reflect basic wage and metal trades decisions.

2.4. Earnings with awards known

Initial investigation of relationships for earnings employed the Commonwealth Statistician's series of average weekly earnings per employed male unit (E). Because of the requirement to link the wage-price sector with the overall model based on the national accounts, earnings were redefined as [4]

---

[4] Lack of suitable data precludes the use of an *hourly* earnings type variable.

$$WH = \frac{\text{Non-farm wages, salaries and supplements (seasonally adjusted)}}{\text{Non-farm wage and salary earners (seasonally adjusted)}}.$$

$$\dot{W}H = 100\,\frac{WH - WH_{-4}}{WH_{-4}};\ \text{defined to conform with } \dot{W} \text{ to best reflect decision timing effects.}$$

Eq. 5.2 is the selected equation for $\dot{W}H$.

Investigation indicated that it is preferable to relate $\dot{W}H$ to a short distributed lag on $\dot{W}$ rather than to current $\dot{W}$ alone. Because of earlier evidence of absorption of award increase in drift, the sum of weights on $\dot{W}$ in an equation for $\dot{W}H$ was expected to be less than unity, and such a result did ensue. In [9] an estimate of about 20% absorption was obtained. Hancock [7] obtained a figure of 11% using annual data for the period 1948–49 to 1964–65.

Because of a tendency for award increases to be reflected as absolute ($ value), rather than percentage, increases in earnings, part or all of this absorption is an arithmetic phenomenon (since both $\dot{W}H$ and $\dot{W}$ are expressed as percentage changes).[5] To ascertain the importance of this effect $\dot{W}$ was redefined as

$$W\dot{W}H = 100\left(\frac{W - W_{-4}}{WH_{-4}}\right),$$

i.e. the percentage change in earnings was related to the absolute change in awards expressed as a percentage of earnings.

Eq. 5.2 indicates that absolute increases are approximately fully reflected. It can be concluded that any absorption indicated by the usual functional form, which relates the rate of change of earnings to $\dot{W}$, may be predominately an arithmetic phenomenon due to a tendency for award increases to pass-on to earnings as absolute ($ value) amounts.

---

[5] Hancock [7] is well aware of this possibility but does not quantify it. I am indebted to Ted Sieper, Australian National University, for indicating the method of assessment referred to here.

Earnings equations contain fairly large constant terms indicating the presence of earnings drift of ½–1% per annum, which is unrelated to the pressure of demand as here defined. The inclusion of this pressure of demand variable and/or price variables considerably reduces the constant term in earnings equations; the fit is also improved. The introduction of a short distributed lag on $\dot{W}$ lowers the constant term and improves the fit still further. These changes in specification reduce the estimate of residual drift by at least 50%. When discussing estimates of residual drift, attention must therefore be given to the particular specification of variables and functional forms.

2.5. Summary single equation findings[6]

(1) Even given the magnitudes of major award decisions (basic wage and metal trades), variables representing pressure of demand in the labour market and price changes significantly influence the rate of change of awards ($\dot{W}$). $\dot{W}$ equations show some evidence of structural change and the above effects in equations for longer periods are largely a result of the experience of the late 1950's and early 1960's.

(2) There are significant non-zero order lags in the flow-on within the award structure of changes in major awards. The flow-on from the basic (national) wage case is represented as occupying 2 quarters, while that from metal trades decisions occupies 4 quarters.

(3) When major award decision magnitudes are unknown their representation in terms of productivity and/or price movement variables provides some explanation of annual percentage changes in award wages; the standard error is about 1.0 percentage point. When major awards are assumed known the standard error is 0.64 percentage points.

(4) When pressure of demand and price change variables are included, a 1% change in the national wage gives rise to a 0.88%

---

[6] This summary includes some results obtained in [9] and [10], but not included in detail herein.

increase in average awards and a 1% increase in the metal trades award leads to a 0.74% increase in average awards.

(5) It seems preferable to relate the rate of change of earnings ($\dot{W}H$) to (a function of) the rate of change of awards. The chief reason for this is to give prominence to the fact that the total of pressure of demand and price effects on $\dot{W}H$ consists of two parts: the effects on $\dot{W}$, transmitted to WH via $\dot{W}$, and the separate effects on drift ($\dot{W}H-\dot{W}$).

(6) There are significant non-zero order lags in the flow-on from award changes to earnings changes.

(7) After these lagged adjustments are complete, percentage increases in awards are less than fully reflected in earnings but absolute increases in awards are approximately fully reflected.

(8) Earnings equations are more stable than those for $\dot{W}$. Comparison of individual coefficients indicates, as for $\dot{W}$ equations though not as markedly, that the rate of change of earnings has become less sensitive to pressure of demand variables in recent years.

(9) In tests of the hypothesis that, for given conditions in the labour market, higher award increases are more fully absorbed than lower ones, the opposite finding was obtained.

3. Prices

3.1. Structure of the price sector

Attention has been focussed on a central, or key, price variable. The series chosen is the implicit deflator (PHG) for home produced gross national expenditure ($HGNE$), where

$HGNE = GNE$ – Statistical discrepancy – Change in farm
stocks – Imports of goods and services.

PHG is the deflator of broadest scope which reflects domestic influences on domestic prices. Other aggregate deflators can be obtained from PHG using the constant and current price flows, valued at exogenous prices, of other components of the aggregate in question. For example[7] ,

$$PGNE = \frac{PHG.HGNE + PFS.FS + PIM.IM}{HGNE + FS + IM} .$$

The aggregate consumption deflator (*PC*) is the price variable used in the award wages and earnings relationships described above. Consequently a relationship is also provided for that price variable. Preferred forms arising from the investigation of *PHG* are used to estimate equations for *PC*.

Before the empirical results are presented, the following section discusses the variables to be included and some aspects of their detailed specification.

3.2. Specification of the price equations

1. Treatment of import prices

An alternative treatment of the effect of foreign prices on domestic prices to that adopted here is to include import prices among the explanatory variables in, say, the (*GNE–DIS–FS*) deflator equation. Such an approach implies that a change in import prices will have a constant effect on the aggregate expenditure deflator regardless of changes in the import content of that aggregate. Whereas this restriction seems reasonable for narrow expenditure categories, it cannot be sustained for a broad aggregate such as *GNE*, where shifting import content is of considerable importance. (Only the most highly aggregated models would embody a fixed import/*GNE* ratio.)

On the other hand the form including import prices would capture, at least to some extent, the direct effect on prices of competition between domestic and imported goods. Some domestically produced goods may be priced to compete at the world price and, conversely, domestic mark-ups on imported goods may

---

[7] Where *FS* represents changes in farm stocks and *IM* imports, both measured at constant prices, and *PFS* and *PIM* are their respective deflators.

be adjustable in response to domestic price movements. If an
import price index is included in the price equation, then its coefficient will reflect these competitive effects in the sample period
along with the average direct content effect. It is assumed that
allowing for flexibility in content effect is more important than
reflecting the direct competitive effect on price determination. (Of
course, in the method adopted, changing relative domestic/import
prices could conceptually affect the GNE price via their effects on
relative domestic/import expenditure flows.)

2. Cost influences

Unit labour cost has played the dominant cost factor role in
models of price determination. In recent applied work use has
been made of wider, more appropriate, measures of total factor
cost, either by including unit capital cast as a separate variable, as
in [14], or jointly with labour cost to yield total factor cost as
given by a production function, as in [8].

At the present stage of development of the model, of which the
present equations form part, a production function—factor demand sector is not fully specified. For the time being then, attention is focussed on labour among the variable costs. (For data
reasons it is also impossible to consider materials costs.)

In competitive models price responds to variations in current
labour cost. In target return and mark-up theories prices do not
adjust in direct response to changes in current labour cost but to
"normal" or "standard" unit labour cost. This model of macro-
pricing has considerable support in single equation and interview
studies of pricing behaviour. It has also been noted [8] that, since
employment is generally slower to adjust than output, short-term
demand changes are partly reflected in productivity movements.
Hence current unit labour costs may fall when output increases,
leading to the result that prices may initially fall in response to an
increase in demand. The use of normal unit labour cost, which
abstracts from short-term productivity movements, generally
provides a more accurate simulation result.

A method of defining short-run productivity changes and consequently normal unit labour cost, which is theoretically satisfy-

ing, by virtue of being adequately integrated into a complete model, is that of the RDX2 model of the Canadian economy [8]. Normal factor cost is there defined as the ratio of total factor cost to the quantity of output which would be produced if the capital stock, employment and hours were combined according to the aggregate production function.

For reasons already stated this approach cannot yet be fully implemented in the present study. However, the same methodology can be applied to a production-input system with only labour input.

Assume the production function is a relationship which holds between output and the labour input normally required to produce it given a trend rate of technical change. Thus

$$Q = A e \rho^t N_N^\gamma . \tag{5.3}$$

Assume that actual (observed) labour input responds to changes in normally required labour according to the simple partial adjustment scheme

$$\frac{N}{N_{-1}} = \left(\frac{N_N}{N_{-1}} \right)^\lambda , \tag{5.4}$$

where Q = output, N = actual labour input, ρ = rate of technical change, λ = rate of adjustment of labour input, N_N = normal labour input, A = scale factor, and γ = elasticity of output with respect to normal labour input. (Lack of suitable data precludes the inclusion of average hours of work in the formulation.)

Substituting for N_N from (5.4) in (5.3) yields an estimating equation. Using seasonally adjusted quarterly data for the period September 1958 to June 1970, this estimating equation has been fitted for

Q = non-farm product at factor cost at constant 1966—67 prices, $m.
N = employed non-farm wage and salary earners, millions.
t = 100, 101, 102, ... (100 in September 1958).

With a first order serial correlation the following result was obtained:

$$\ln Q = \begin{array}{cccc} 6.3540 + & 0.0047t + & 2.7188 \ln(N/N_{-1}) \\ (78.231) & (2.571) & (6.077) \end{array}$$

$$+ \; 1.0520 \ln(N_{-1}) + 0.628\hat{u}_{-1} \; ; \qquad\qquad (5.5)$$
$$(4.544)$$

$$\bar{R}^2 = 0.9997, SEE = 0.008, D = 1.93.$$

This yields

$$\hat{\rho} = 0.0047; \quad \hat{\gamma} = 1.0520; \quad \hat{\lambda} = 0.3869.$$

Normal unit labor cost ($ULCN$) is then defined as

$$ULCN = WH\frac{N_N}{Q} , \qquad\qquad (5.6)$$

where WH = compensation per employee per quarter, as defined above, and N_N is obtained from (5.3) given $\hat{\rho}$ and $\hat{\gamma}$. (Current, as distinct from normal, unit labour cost would be $ULC = WH$ (N/Q).)

Thus $ULCN$ is affected only by changes in compensation per employee, economies of scale and the trend rate of technical change.

Even though there is averaging involved in the definition of $ULCN$ most studies have found significant lags between $ULCN$ and prices. Thus rather than the model

$$P = (1 + k) ULCN$$

they obtain

$$P = W(L) ULCN ,$$

where $W(L)$ is a lag generating function.

To allow for the possibility of a mixed system of pricing (with both competitive and mark-up elements), Eckstein and Fromm [2] suggest using (*ULC–ULCN*) as a separate additional variable.

3. Incidence of indirect taxes

Two alternative specifications of the influence of the rate of indirect taxation (*ITR*) were employed. In the first, ITR is included as a separate variable on the right, thus

$$P = W_1(L) ULCN + W_2(L) ITR . \tag{5.7}$$

The alternative (see [8]) is

$$\frac{P}{1 + ITR} = W_1(L) ULCN + W_2(L) ITR . \tag{5.8}$$

In this formulation any change in *ITR* will immediately be fully reflected in *P*. If there is absorption in subsequent periods the sum of coefficients in W_2 will lie between 0 and -1. A similar dynamic pattern – initial passing on greater than final passing on – can be obtained with form (5.7) as well.

Elsewhere in the model tax yield functions are defined as

$$IT = e(ITI)(BASE) , \tag{5.9}$$

where *ITI* is a quasi-statutory rate index (see [10]), and *BASE* is some set of current price expenditure flows distinguished within the model. $e(ITI)$ is then an estimate of the relevant scaled quasi-statutory tax rate.

The following definition of *ITR* has been used:

ITR = scaled quasi-statutory rate of sales, excise and payroll taxes and customs duties
 = $0.0708(ITI)$ on *HGNE*; $0.1122(ITI)$ on *C*.

ITI includes the rates of customs duty on excisable products; the bulk of customs duties are, however, included in the *e* coefficients as average effective rates. This is because the information to construct a statutory rate index is not conveniently available.

4. Pressure of demand

If prices play any role in clearing the aggregate goods market then a measure of demand-supply imbalance in that market is required. In most macro-models some measure of utilization, either of the capital stock or of potential output, is used for this purpose. A theoretically satisfying treatment of unintended inventory accumulation has recently been empirically implemented [8] to improve the definition of the aggregate demand variable. Unfortunately, not even the less sophisticated method is available in the present application and use is made of labour market proxies.

Australian wage rate functions, obtained above, have included the ratio of job vacancies to registered unemployment (VAC/U) as a pressure of demand indicator. This variable has also been used in the price equations. The rate of change of VAC/U was employed in exploratory estimation but has not been retained in any of the equations reported herein.

3.3. Empirical results

Additional variables introduced into the constant mark-up specification – indirect taxes and pressure of demand – can be regarded as linear approximations to a form in which the mark-up is functionally dependent on such variables. Some experimentation was conducted with the mark-up itself as the dependent variable, i.e.

$$\frac{P}{ULCN} = W_2(L)ITR + W_3(L) VAC/U + a VA\dot{C}/U$$

$$+ b \frac{ULC - ULCN}{ULCN} + c, \tag{5.10}$$

or in the more general form with $P/[W_1(L) ULCN]$ as dependent variable (where W_1 was obtained from estimates of the form of

(5.7). These results were generally inferior to the simple linear form (5.7) and no equations of form (5.10) are presented. The estimation forms presented in table 3 are thus

$$y = W_1(L) \, ULCN + W_2(L) \, ITR + W_3(L) \, VAC/U$$
$$+ aVA\dot{C}/U + b(ULC - ULCN) + c \,, \qquad (5.11)$$

in which y is either P or $P/(1 + ITR)$.

3.4. Summary single equation findings

(1) Aggregate price levels are better represented as a mark-up on normal unit labour cost than on current unit labour cost. Similar relationships to those of table 3 were estimated with ULC replacing $ULCN$ and with $(ULC-ULCN)$ as an additional variable; on all counts these were inferior. Even when the normal concept is used, prices adjust slowly to changes in wage costs. The preferred equations show an adjustment process occupying eight quarters with an average lag of about eight months.

(2) Estimates of mark-up on normal unit labour cost can be obtained from the fitted equations. Subsuming the constant terms into the mark-up factor, the estimates are about 62% for PHG and 57% for PC.

(3) The properties of the residuals in ordinary least squares equations led to adjustment for first order serial correlation. Since the correction factors are high, the adjusted equations are quasi-first difference forms.

(4) A labour market proxy was used to represent the effect on prices of demand-supply imbalance. In most equations this variable was insignificant and showed a very weak effect on prices. (When the price equations are combined with the wage equations, there will be significant price adjustment in response to pressure of demand since wage rates are sensitive to VAC/U.) Direct goods market measures of imbalance might well indicate significant market clearing price adjustment for given wages. The inclusion of VAC/U generally provided a superior specification for the effect

Table 3
Equations for prices of home produced GNE (PHG) and consumption (PC)

Explanatory variable	Lag in quarters	Dependent variable			
		PHG (0.9627)	$\dfrac{PHG}{(1+0.0708ITI)}$ (0.9022)	PC (0.9658)	$\dfrac{PC}{(1+0.1122ITI)}$ (0.8737)
Eq. no.		5.12	5.13	5.14	5.15
VAC/U (0.6603)		0.009029 (1.147)	0.007382 (1.080)	−0.00003831 (0.006)	0.0004908 (0.086)
ULCN (0.5842)	0	0.3043	0.2988	0.2705	0.2280
	1	0.2985	0.2867	0.2475	0.2117
	2	0.2835	0.2674	0.2214	0.1919
	3	0.2592	0.2409	0.1922	0.1687
	4	0.2258	0.2071	0.1599	0.1419
	5	0.1831	0.1662	0.1245	0.1117
	6	0.1313	0.1180	0.0861	0.0779
	7	0.0702	0.0626	0.0446	0.0407
Sum		1.7559	1.6476	1.3467	1.1724
0.0708ITI (0.0665) (PHG)	0	0.0917	−0.2084	0.7955	0.0251
	1	0.0780	−0.1595	0.2969	0.0192
	2	0.0650	−0.1172	−0.0113	0.0141
	3	0.0526	−0.0814	−0.1671	0.0098
	4	0.0408	−0.0521	−0.2089	0.0063
0.1122ITI (0.1054) (PC)	5	0.0296	−0.0293	−0.1749	0.0035
	6	0.0191	−0.1030	−0.1032	0.0016
	7	0.0092	−0.0033	−0.0322	0.0004
Sum		0.3859	−0.6642	0.3948	0.0800
Constant		−0.09189 (1.175)	−0.1869 (0.309)	0.1364 (1.748)	0.1783 (2.541)
$\hat{u}_{-1}$		0.785	0.775	0.920	0.949
$\bar{R}^2$		0.995	0.995	0.994	0.991
SEE		0.0039	0.0037	0.0033	0.0030
D		2.10	2.06	1.81	1.78

Note: Sample period is September 1960 to June 1970 (plus lags).
$\bar{R}^2$ = multiple correlation coefficient adjusted for degrees of freedom. SEE = standard error of estimate. D = Durbin-Watson d-statistic.

Figures in parentheses under coefficients are Student's t-ratios; under variables they are sample period means.

of indirect taxes and it has been retained in preferred equations.

(5) Considerable experimentation was undertaken with indirect tax rate variables and their dynamic specification. There is little sample period variation in tax rates and the results are sensitive to alternative specifications. Although some of the preferred equations seem reasonable, no emphasis is placed on the implied estimates of the extent to which indirect tax rate changes are reflected in prices.

4. Simulations of the wage-price sector in the macro-economy

4.1. The macro-model and adjustments to incorporate a wage-price sector

The wage-price sector developed above has been incorporated into an operational version of the quarterly National Income Forecasting (*NIF*) model which is being constructed at the Commonwealth Treasury and Bureau of Census and Statistics. A complete listing of this model is contained in the Appendix to this paper. As outlined in the introductory section, a number of extensions were made to the pre-existing NIF model to simulate price disturbances more adequately. These extensions are a stop-gap measure pending reformulation of the whole model at constant prices using the newly available official quarterly estimates.

The price sector above provides relationships for the prices of home produced GNE and personal consumption. Using these two deflators and the associated money flows, an implicit deflator for the difference between the two has been derived; it is called *PBAL*. Actual values of *PBAL* are used to deflate historical values of government capital (*PCAP*) and current (*PCUR*) spending, net current expenditure by financial enterprises (*FE*) and public building (*PCAB*) (which is a subtraction from the expenditure variable influencing imports). *PC* is used to deflate cash benefits (*CB*). These constant price values become the exogenous variables and replace their former current price values. In simulation the current price counterparts are obtained by applying solution values for *PBAL* and *PC* as appropriate.

Because of the incompleteness of the government sector in the pre-existing model there was no budget identity and a variable reflecting the budget outcome (*PLIQ*, change in primary liquidity of private sector) was exogenous. (It was adjusted in an ad hoc manner for simulation, and so in fact was partly endogenous.) This treatment has been changed by deriving from relevant government revenues and outlays included in the model, an endogenous component of *PLIQ*, called *PLEN*. The remainder of *PLIQ* is still regarded as exogenous.

Eqs. 5.1, 5.2, 5.12 and 5.14, from above, form the wage-price sector. Only a small number of simulations of the complete model have so far been undertaken; these and other subsequent results are being used to establish the characteristics of the model, which may be unsatisfactory.[8] The actual numerical results of the disturbed simulations presented below must be interpreted in this light.

4.2. Simulations with actual exogenous data

Mean errors (actual values minus simulated values) and mean absolute errors, as percentages of mean actual values of the endogenous variables, from simulations over the period March 1962 to June 1970 are shown in table 4.

In dynamic simulation the model displays a tendency for early overestimation to be replaced by underestimation later in the sample period but there is no tendency for errors to grow proportionately over time. By usual standards, the dynamic simulation performance of the wage-price sector in the macro-model is satisfactory.

Ex-post forecasts for three quarters beyond the sample period, i.e. to March 1971, display a continued tendency to underestimation.

---

[8] Some simulations of the wage-price sector with no feedback to the macro-economy are contained in [10]. Simulation properties of a version of the complete model are contained in V.W. FitzGerald's contribution to this volume [3].

Table 4
Percentage errors in simulation

Endogenous variable	One period		Dynamic	
	Mean error	Mean absolute error	Mean error	Mean absolute error
W	0.04	0.46	−1.00	1.26
WH	−0.20	0.73	−1.20	1.53
PHG	−0.03	0.37	−1.20	1.20
PC	0.03	0.23	−0.36	0.57

4.3. Simulations with altered historical data

Experiment 1: The effects of an additional 1% in a basic (national) wage decision in an initially
  (a) relatively tight labour market,
  (b) relatively slack labour market
were explored.

The basic wage decisions operative in (a) September quarter 1964 and (b) September quarter 1967 were assumed to be 1% above their actual historical values. Percentage effects are shown in table 5.

Table 5
Percentage effects of an additional 1% basic wage

Quarter after disturbance	W		WH		PHG		PC	
	(a)	(b)	(a)	(b)	(a)	(b)	(a)	(b)
0	0.55	0.55	0.25	0.24	0.00	0.00	0.00	0.00
3	0.85	0.85	0.71	0.70	0.41	0.38	0.31	0.29
7	0.88	0.87	0.80	0.77	0.81	0.74	0.61	0.55
11	0.90	0.88	0.86	0.79	0.88	0.80	0.69	0.62

The changes in earnings and prices in tight and slack labour markets differ by the order of 0.07 (about 10%) eleven quarters after the 1.0 change in the basic wage.

It is of interest to compare such results with those obtained by Pitchford [12] using a reduced form relationship for the quarterly rate of a change of consumer prices for the period 1947–68. His preferred equation (11) was

$$Y_t = 0.44 + 0.33\,X_{4(t-2)} + 0.16\,X_{1(t-3)} + 0.033\,X_{2(t-3)}$$
$$\quad\;(3.66)\quad(5.76)\qquad\quad(2.66)\qquad\qquad(2.82)$$

$$\quad + 0.15\,X_{32(t-1)} + 0.12\,X_{32(t-2)}$$
$$\qquad(3.66)\qquad\qquad(3.08)$$

$$R^2 = 0.77,\, D = 1.82$$

where Y_t = rate of change of consumer price index, X_{4t} = registered vacancies–unemployment, as a percentage of employment plus unemployment, X_{1t} = rate of change of import price index, X_{2t} = rate of change of export price index, and X_{32t} = rate of change of minimum hourly wage rates adjusted for changes in the terms of trade.

The coefficients on X_{32} indicate that a 1% increase in the rate of change of minimum (award) wages leads to a 0.15% increase in the rate of change of the consumer price index in the following period and a 0.27% increase after two periods, the adjustment being then complete.

The present analysis agrees fairly closely with these initial effects, obtaining a 0.2% and 0.3% increase in the rate of change of the consumption deflator after two and three quarters, but indicates a continuing process of adjustment leading to an effect in excess of 0.7% after 11 quarters.[9]

Experiment 2: In the second experiment the effects of basic wage decisions being determined by the trend rate of growth of average product per wage earner were investigated.

Basic (and national) wage decisions over the complete simulation period have been assumed to occur at their actual historical dates but to have been at a constant magnitude per annum, on average. In addition, no metal trades decisions were assumed to have occur-

---

[9] These estimates are obtained by pro-rating table 5 figures to correspond to a 1% increase in the rate of change of average awards.

Table 6
Effects of simple productivity rules (annual percentage changes)

Solution	W	WH	PHG	PC
Control	4.8	6.8	4.0	3.0
Rule 1: 1.9%	3.1	5.6	2.8	2.1
Rule 2: 2.5%	3.8	5.9	3.3	2.5

red. Thus, rather than their historical average of about 3.6% per annum, major award decisions have been assumed to be either 1.9% or 2.5% per annum. The 1.9% per annum corresponds to the trend rate of growth in product in the fitted production function (5.5), above. In that function labour input displayed increasing returns to scale and so a trend line fitted to average product per worker would grow somewhat more rapidly, i.e. at about 2.5% per annum.

Table 6 sets out, for the control and disturbed solutions, annual (arithmetic) percentage increases for the period 1961 to 1969–70.

Under the 1.9% rule the annual rate of average earnings increase would have been reduced by about 1.2% and that of consumer prices by 0.9%. Under the 2.5% rule the reductions would have been 0.9% in earnings and 0.5% in consumer prices.

The share of non-farm wages etc. in non-farm product at factor cost under the experimental regimes is as shown in table 7.

Insufficient experiments have been conducted with the model to indicate the complete set of reasons for these results. It may in large part be due to the relative importance of transitional effects in periods as short as the one considered. Prices take much longer to adjust to changes in the basic wage than do earnings and,

Table 7
Percentage share of non-farm wages in non-farm product

Solution	1961	1969–70
Control	63.9	61.6
Rule 1: 1.9%	63.9	60.7
Rule 2: 2.5%	63.9	61.1

in consequence, over any period which includes the initial adjustments, prices will change proportionately less than earnings. This effect is more or less symmetric so that if experiment 2 had assumed an increase greater than the actual historical average, the wage share would have increased.

Appendix: National income forecasting model with wage-price sector incorporated, July 1971

Behavioural equations (exogenous variables are overlined)

1. $CMV = 0.0923\ Y + 0.0754\ M_{-1} - 0.2033\ KMVD_{-1} - 15.7888\ \overline{RMFD}$
    $(2.088)\quad\ (3.282)\qquad (4.014)\qquad\qquad (1.591)$

    $- 43.1723\ \overline{STMV} - 100.1889 + 0.934\ \hat{u}_{-1}\ .$
    $\ \ (0.456)\qquad\qquad (1.193)$

    $\bar{R}^2 = 0.955,\ SEE = \$8.83\text{m},\ D = 2.41.$

2. $COD = 0.0447\ Y + 0.0395\ M_{-1} - 0.0773\ KODD_{-1} - 12.2456\ \overline{RMFD}$
    $(2.903)\quad\ (5.377)\qquad (4.760)\qquad\qquad (3.439)$

    $- 23.9254\ \overline{STOD} + 128.9906 + 0.831\ \hat{u}_{-1}\ .$
    $\ \ (0.379)\qquad\qquad (6.528)$

    $\bar{R}^2 = 0.995,\ SEE = \$3.09\text{m},\ D = 1.60.$

3. $\dfrac{CND}{Y} = -0.5364\ \dfrac{Y}{YPP} + 0.9560\ \left(\dfrac{CND}{Y}\right)_{-1} + 0.5769.$
    $\phantom{\dfrac{CND}{Y} =}\ \ (8.460)\qquad\ \ (43.146)\qquad\qquad\quad\ (8.338)$

    $c\bar{R}^2 = 0.979,\ c\ SEE = \$11.28\text{m},\ c\ D = 2.28.$

4. $ID = 0.1030\ Y + 0.0189\ M_{-1} + 0.7787\ \left(\dfrac{\overline{CPIR}}{\overline{RGS}}\right)_{-1} - 0.3910\ VAC_{-1}$
    $(3.536)\quad\ (3.904)\qquad (1.854)\qquad\qquad\quad (3.934)$

    $- 0.0541\ KIDD_{-1} + 0.8100\ ID_{-1} + 158.9394.$
    $\ \ (5.163)\qquad\quad (8.588)\qquad\ \ (4.775)$

    $\bar{R}^2 = 0.996,\ SEE = \$4.54\text{m},\ D = 2.12.$

5. $IOB = -1.2339\ VAC + 0.008821\ KIOB_{-1} + 57.3275 + W(L)\ (GPNF - GPNF_{-1}).$
    $(2.558)\qquad\ \ (0.816)\qquad\quad (1.044)$

    $\bar{R}^2 = 0.971,\ SEE = \$8.41\text{m},\ D = 1.92.$

    $W(L)$ Sum = 1.3337; Ave. = 5.678

W_0 0.0000	W_5 0.1659 (3.614)	W_{10} 0.0686 (2.132)
W_1 0.0727 (3.315)	W_6 0.1563 (3.424)	W_{11} 0.0454 (1.653)
W_2 0.1222 (3.531)	W_7 0.1393 (3.169)	W_{12} 0.0253 (1.142)
W_3 0.1519 (3.673)	W_8 0.1175 (2.872)	W_{13} 0.0098 (0.688)
W_4 0.1655 (3.704)	W_9 0.0933 (2.534)	W_{14} 0.0000

6. $IOPE = 0.0232\ KIOP_{-1} + 156.7759 + W(L)\ (GPNF - GPNF_{-1}).$
        (3.763)   (5.261)

   $\bar{R}^2 = 0.960,\ SEE = \$17.29\text{m},\ D = 2.02.$

   $W(L)$ Sum = 1.4488; Ave. = 7.322

W_0 0.0000	W_5 0.1480 (4.079)	W_{10} 0.1415 (3.839)
W_1 0.0136 (0.470)	W_6 0.1711 (4.653)	W_{11} 0.1072 (2.901)
W_2 0.0427 (1.064)	W_7 0.1827 (4.821)	W_{12} 0.0683 (1.961)
W_3 0.0791 (1.931)	W_8 0.1813 (4.768)	W_{13} 0.0303 (1.215)
W_4 0.1159 (3.045)	W_9 0.1671 (4.482)	W_{14} 0.0000

7. $(IMN - \overline{DSSK}) = 0.1117\ (GNEA + NFS) + 3.1517\ VWFB$
                (7.034)   (4.869)

   $$+ 0.3045\ (IMN - \overline{DSSK})_{-1} + 5.6021.$$
          (3.070)   (0.399)

   $\bar{R}^2 = 0.989,\ SEE = \$17.67\text{m},\ D = 1.76.$

8. $\dfrac{YPNW}{GPFC} = \underset{(752.162)}{0.9957}\ \left(\dfrac{YPNW}{GPFC}\right)_{-1} - 0.392\ \hat{u}_{-1}\ .$

   $c\bar{R}^2 = 0.946,\ c\ SEE = \$9.96\text{m},\ c\ D = 2.14.$

9. $\dfrac{TPL}{\overline{RPS.YP}} = 0.0000001505\ YP1 + 0.0000001423\ YP2 + 0.000575.$
                (17.771)   (26.052)   (24.696)

   $c\bar{R}^2 = 0.997,\ c\ SEE = \$8.10\text{m},\ c\ D = 2.12.$

10. $NFS = -0.4628\ SM + 0.5389\ SM_{-1} + 0.3540\ IMN + 0.0105\ IMN_{-1}$
          (4.962)   (5.000)   (2.147)   (0.167)

    $$- 0.1240\ BNF_{-1} + 0.4652\ NFS_{-1} + 87.4306.$$
        (2.964)   (3.223)   (1.433)

    $\bar{R}^2 = 0.805,\ SEE = \$26.78\text{m},\ D = 1.99.$

11. $M = 0.1039\ GNP - 91.2031\ \overline{RGS} + 0.2958\ (\overline{PLEX} + PLEN) + 0.975\ M_{-1}$
       (15.305)   (5.187)   (2.930)

    $$+ 313.8806.$$
       (4.469)

    $c\bar{R}^2 = 0.999,\ c\ SEE = \$46.32\text{m},\ c\ D = 1.72.$

12. $SEP = 0.1035\ \overline{ITR}\ (C - \overline{CR}) + 40.6097.$
         (77.630)   (11.714)

    $\bar{R}^2 = 0.992,\ SEE = \$6.07\text{m},\ D = 1.98.$

13. $TAR = 0.00006802\ IMN^2 + 29.8772 + 0.375\ \hat{u}_{-1}.$
         (30.540)   (20.128)

    $\bar{R}^2 = 0.985,\ SEE = \$2.12\text{m},\ D = 2.00.$

14. $ITSL = -37.1066 + 0.04823\ HGNE + 0.158\ \hat{u}_{-1}\ .$
        (9.543)   (53.562)

    $\bar{R}^2 = 0.989,\ SEE = \$5.80\text{m},\ D = 1.97.$

15. $\ln GPFC^* = -1.6479 + 0.003920\ \overline{TIME} + 3.0290\ \ln NNF/NNF_{-1}$
          (1.019)   (2.234)   (7.386)

          $+ 1.1540\ \ln NNF_{-1} + 0.596\ \hat{u}_{-1}.$
          (5.154)

$\overline{R}^2 = 0.998, SEE = 0.0076, D = 1.96.$

$\overline{TIME} = 100$ in 1958.3, 101 in 1958.4, 102 in 1959.1, etc.

16. $VAC = 0.2063\ (NNF - NNF_{-1}) + 0.7975\ VAC_{-1} + 2.292 + 0.432\ \hat{u}_{-1}.$
          (6.783)   (16.184)   (1.229)

$\overline{R}^2 = 0.964, SEE = 2.06('000), D = 1.80.$

17. $U = \dfrac{1444.37}{VAC} + 0.2445\ U_{-1} + 9.113 + 0.768\ \hat{u}_{-1}.$
          (12.034)   (3.794)   (2.479)

$\overline{R}^2 = 0.988, SEE = 2.68('000), D = 2.36.$

18. $\dfrac{W - W_{-4}}{W_{-4}} = W_1(L)\ \overline{BD} + W_2(L)\ \overline{MTDC} + 0.008050\ \dfrac{VAC}{U}$
                                                        (1.225)

          $+ 0.0790\ \left(4\dfrac{PC_{-1} - PC_{-2}}{PC_{-2}}\right) + 0.003035 + 0.647\ \hat{u}_{-1}.$
          (1.552)   (0.596)

$\overline{R}^2 = 0.903, SEE = 0.0064, D = 2.09.$

$W_1(L)$ Sum = 0.008751; Ave. = 0.333	$W_2(L)$ Sum = 0.007440; Ave. = 0.631
W_0 0.005833 (10.095)	W_0 0.004074 (5.709)
W_1 0.002917 (10.095)	W_1 0.002232 (5.908)
	W_2 0.000939 (2.094)
	W_3 0.000195 (0.530)

19. $\dfrac{WH - WH_{-4}}{WH_{-4}} = W(L)\ \dfrac{W - W_{-4}}{WH_{-4}} + 0.01622\ \dfrac{VAC}{U}$
                                                          (3.627)

          $+ 0.007854\left(4\dfrac{VAC/U - (VAC/U)_{-1}}{(VAC/U)_{-1}}\right) + 0.1574\left(4\dfrac{PC_{-1} - PC_{-2}}{PC_{-2}}\right)$
          (4.898)   (1.943)

          $+ 0.005388.$
          (1.839)

$\overline{R}^2 = 0.895, SEE = 0.0072, D = 1.78.$

$W(L)$ Sum = 0.9753; Ave. = 0.513

W_0 0.5775 (6.010)
W_1 0.2951 (6.702)
W_2 0.1026 (1.656)

20. $PHG = W_1(L)ULCN + W_2(L)(0.0708\overline{ITI}) + 0.009029\ \dfrac{VAC}{U} - 0.09189$
                                                      (1.147)   (1.175)

          $+ 0.785\ \hat{u}_{-1}.$

$\overline{R}^2 = 0.995, SEE = 0.004, D = 2.10.$

$W_1(L)$ Sum = 1.7559; Ave. = 2.700

W_0 0.3043 (2.384) W_4 0.2258 (4.911)
W_1 0.2985 (4.614) W_5 0.1831 (3.348)
W_2 0.2835 (16.139) W_6 0.1313 (2.625)
W_3 0.2592 (10.555) W_7 0.0702 (2.210)

$W_2(L)$ Sum = 0.3859; Ave. = 2.219

W_0 0.0917 (0.183) W_4 0.0408 (0.148)
W_1 0.0780 (0.245) W_5 0.0296 (0.108)
W_2 0.0650 (0.272) W_6 0.0191 (0.083)
W_3 0.0526 (0.211) W_7 0.0092 (0.066)

21. $$PC = W_1(L)ULCN + W_2(L)(0.1122\,\overline{ITI}) - \underset{(0.006)}{0.000038}\,\frac{VAC}{U} + 0.1364 + \underset{(1.748)}{0.920}\,\hat{u}_{-1}.$$

   $\bar{R}^2 = 0.994$, $SEE = 0.003$, $D = 1.81$.

$W_1(L)$ Sum = 1.3467; Ave. = 2.493.

W_0 0.2705 (2.726) W_4 0.1599 (4.260)
W_1 0.2475 (4.906) W_5 0.1245 (2.837)
W_2 0.2214 (13.961) W_6 0.0861 (2.161)
W_3 0.1922 (8.813) W_7 0.0446 (1.767)

$W_2(L)$ Sum = 0.3948

W_0 0.7955 (2.346) W_4 −0.2089 (1.267)
W_1 0.2969 (1.527) W_5 −0.1749 (1.452)
W_2 −0.0113 (0.063) W_6 −0.1032 (1.562)
W_3 −0.1671 (0.903) W_7 −0.0322 (1.663)

Notes:

(i) The figures in brackets under coefficients are t statistics.

(ii) $\bar{R}^2$ is the coefficient of determination (squared multiple correlation) adjusted for degrees of freedom. $c\bar{R}^2$ denotes the "comparable" $\bar{R}^2$ indicating goodness of fit in terms of original units.

(iii) SEE is the standard error of estimate. $c\,SEE$ is the standard error in original units.

(iv) D is the Durbin-Watson d-statistic. $c\,D$ is the d-statistic for original units.

Identities

1. $C \equiv CMV + COD + CND + \overline{CR}.$
2. $IM \equiv IMN + \overline{IMC} + \overline{IMG} + \overline{IMP}.$
3. $GPNF \equiv C + ID + NFS + IOB + IOPE + \bar{E} - IM.$
4. $GNP \equiv GPNF + \overline{GPF}.$
5. $WSNF \equiv 13\,WH\dfrac{NNF + \overline{NDEF}}{1000}.$
6. $Y \equiv YP + \overline{CB} - TPL - \overline{ODT}.$
7. $YP \equiv YPNW + WSNF.$
8. $SM \equiv C + ID + IOB + IOPE + \bar{E} - IM.$
9. $ITAX \equiv SEP + TAR + \overline{ITOC} + ITSL - \overline{SUBS}.$
10. $GPFC \equiv GPNF - ITAX.$
11. $ULCN \equiv 0.9875\,\dfrac{13WH.NNFN}{GPFC^*},$

   where $\ln NNFN = \dfrac{1}{1.0520}(\ln GPFC^* - 6.3540 - 0.0047\,\overline{TIME}).$

   The factor 0.9875 equates the mean value of $ULCN$ with that of ULC, unit labour costs.

   ULC, unit labour costs.

   $TIME$ = 100 in 1958.3, 101 in 1958.4, etc.

   $GPFC^*$ (real $GPFC$) is obtained endogenously from PHG through an identity involving exogenous price deflators for IM, $\overline{EXPO}$, $\overline{FS}$ and $\overline{GPF}$ and corresponding expenditure flows.

12. $KIDD \equiv 0.995\,KIDD_{-1} + ID$ ($KIDD = \$8400m.$ in June 1958).
13. $KMVD \equiv 0.98\,KMVD_{-1} + CMV$ ($KMVD = \$900m.$ in June 1958).
14. $KODD \equiv 0.97\,KODD_{-1} + COD$ ($KODD = \$2700m.$ in June 1958).
15. $KIOB \equiv 0.99\,KIOB_{-1} + IOB$ ($KIOB = \$4387m.$ in June 1958).
16. $KIOP \equiv 0.967\,KIOP_{-1} + \overline{IOPE}$ ($KIOP = \$5041m.$ in June 1958).
17. $BNF \equiv BNF_{-1} + NFS + \overline{NSVA}$ ($BNF = \$3207m.$ in June 1958).
18. $GNE \equiv C + ID + NFS + IOB + IOPE + \overline{E} - \overline{EXPO} + \overline{GPF}.$
19. $GNEA \equiv GNE - \overline{ADGE} - ID - IOB - NFS - \overline{FS}.$
20. $PBAL \equiv (HGNE - C)/(HGNE/PHG - C/PC).$
21. $PLEN \equiv \overline{PCUR}*.PBAL - \overline{IMG} + \overline{CB} - TPL - ITAX.$

Definition of variables

All variables expressed as money values are defined in $ million at current prices; other units are as specified. Seasonally adjusted quarterly data have been used throughout except for award wages, W, and major decision magnitudes, BD and $MTDC$. Variables in real terms are denoted by an asterisk (*).

$\overline{ADGE}$	Public authority capital expenditure on building and construction plus government imports of goods and services (payments basis) plus imports of civil aircraft; $(\overline{PCAB}*.PBAL + \overline{IMG} + \overline{ICA})$ in simulation
$\overline{BD}$	National Wage Case decision magnitude (percent)
BNF	Book value of non-farm stocks
$\overline{CB}$	Cash benefits to persons; $(\overline{CB}*.PC)$ in simulation
C	Personal consumption expenditure − total
CMV	− motor vehicles
COD	− other durables
$\overline{CR}$	− rent
CND	− other non-durables
$\overline{CPIR}$	Consumer price index − rent component
$\overline{DIS}$	Statistical discrepancy
$\overline{DSSK}$	Dock strike dummy variable; U.K. dock strike: -26 in December quarter 1967, $+26$ in January quarter 1968; U.S. dock strike: -31 in March quarter 1969, $+9$ in June quarter 1969, $+22$ in September quarter 1969; zero elsewhere
$\overline{E}$	Non-farm exogenous demand; $((\overline{FE}* + \overline{PCAP}* + \overline{PCUR}*)PBAL + \overline{EXPO} + \overline{FS} + \overline{DIS} - \overline{GPF})$ in simulation
$\overline{EXPO}$	Exports of goods and services
$\overline{FE}$	Financial enterprises net current expenditure
$\overline{FS}$	Increase in value of farm stocks (excluding stock valuation adjustment)
$\overline{GPF}$	Farm gross product at factor cost
$GPFC$	Non-farm gross product at factor cost
$GPNF$	Non-farm gross product (including net indirect taxes)
GNP	Gross national product (excluding stock valuation adjustment)
GNE	Gross national expenditure
$GNEA$	Adjusted gross national expenditure $(GNE - \overline{ADGE})$
$HGNE$	Home produced GNE $(GNE - \overline{FS} - \overline{DIS} - IM)$

ID	Gross private fixed capital expenditure – dwellings
IOB	– other new building and construction
IOPE	– all other (plant and equipment)
IM	Imports of goods and services – total
$\overline{IMC}$	Imports of civil aircraft
$\overline{IMG}$	Government imports (payments basis)
IMN	Imports of goods and services – endogenous
$\overline{IMP}$	Imports of petroleum
ITAX	Indirect taxes less subsidies (net indirect taxes)
$\overline{ITOC}$	Indirect taxes, other Commonwealth
$\overline{ITI}$	Index of statutory rate of sales, excise and payroll taxes and customs duties on excisable products
$\overline{ITR}$	Index of statutory rate of sales, excise and payroll taxes
ITSL	Indirect taxes, State and Local
KIDD	Stock of dwellings
KIOB	Stock of other new building and construction investment
KIOP	Stock of plant and equipment investment
KMVD	Stock of motor vehicles
KODD	Stock of other durables
M	Volume of money (deposits plus notes and coin in the hands of the public) at end of quarter (average of Wednesdays in last month)
$\overline{MTDC}$	Metal Trades decision magnitude (percent)
$\overline{NDEF}$	Defence personnel ('000)
NFS	Increase in value of non-farm stocks (excluding stock valuation adjustment)
NNF	Wage and salary earners in non-farm employment (excluding defence) ('000)
$\overline{NSVA}$	Non-farm stock valuation adjustment
$\overline{ODT}$	Other direct taxes
PBAL	Implicit deflator for non-consumption home-produced *GNE*
$\overline{PCAP}$	Gross fixed capital expenditure by public authorities and enterprises
$\overline{PCAB}$	*PCAP* on building and construction
$\overline{PCUR}$	Net current expenditure by public authorities (payments basis)
PHG	Implicit price deflator for home-produced *GNE*
PC	Implicit deflator for personal consumption expenditure
PLEN	Quasi-budget deficit
$\overline{PLEX}$	Change in primary liquidity of private sector, excluding quasi-budget deficit, i.e. Balance of payments position of private sector (gold and foreign exchange – Commonwealth overseas transactions) – Budget domestic surplus (exogenous components) + Wheat Board credits + Rural credits advances + Reserve Bank miscellaneous + (adjustment).
	Or: Increase in *LGS* assets and *SRD*'s of banks and public (All assets except Commonwealth securities measured as average of Wednesdays in last month of quarter; securities are on last day basis) – *PLEN*
$\overline{RGS}$	Theoretical yield on 2 year rebateable bonds (percent)
$\overline{RMFD}$	Maximum rate of interest on fixed deposits (percent)
$\overline{RPS}$	100 plus percentage levy on personal income tax
SEP	Sales, excise and payroll tax collections
SM	Domestic non-farm sales
$\overline{STMV}$	Rate of sales tax on motor vehicles (proportion)

$\overline{STOD}$	Rate of sales tax on other durables (proportion)
$\overline{SUBS}$	Subsidies payable
TAR	Indirect taxes, customs duties
TPL	Tax payable on non-farm personal income
U	Persons registered for employment with the CES ('000)
$ULCN$	Normal unit labour costs (proportion)
VAC	Vacancies registered with the CES ('000)
$VWFB$	Vacancies less 1% of NNF (where positive) ('000)
W	Award wages ($ per week)
WH	Average weekly earnings of non-farm wage and salary earners ($)
$WSNF$	Non-farm wages, salaries and supplements
Y	Non-farm personal disposable income (including estate and gift duties)
YP	Non-farm personal income (excluding cash benefits)
$YP1$	YP from September quarter 1958 to September quarter 1966, zero elsewhere
$YP2$	YP from December quarter 1966 onwards, zero elsewhere
YPP	Previous peak level of Y over last 8 quarters
$YPNW$	Non-farm personal income less $WSNF$

References

[1] S. Almon, "The distributed lag between capital appropriations and expenditures", *Econometrica* 33, No.1 (January 1965).

[2] O. Eckstein and G. Fromm, "The price equation", *American Economic Review* 58, No.5 (December 1968).

[3] V.W. FitzGerald, "Dynamic properties of a non-linear econometric model", in: this volume, p. 169.

[4] G. Fromm and P. Taubman, *Policy simulations with an econometric model* (Washington, Brookings Institution, 1968).

[5] R.J. Gordon, "The Brookings model in action: a review article", *Journal of Political Economy* 78, No.3 (May 1970).

[6] G.R. Green with M. Liebenberg and A. Hirsch, "Short, and long-term simulations with the O.B.E. econometric model". Paper presented to the Conference on Econometric Models of Cyclical Behaviour, Cambridge, Mass. Mimeo., 1969.

[7] K. Hancock, "Earnings drift in Australia", *Journal of Industrial Relations* 8, No.2 (July 1966). Reprinted in: *Australian Labour Economics, Readings,* edited by J.E. Isaac and G.W. Ford (Melbourne, Sun Books, 1967), pp. 222–254.

[8] J.F. Helliwell, H.T. Shapiro, G.R. Sparks, J.A. Stewart, F.W. Gorbett and J.R. Stephenson, *The structure of RDX2,* Bank of Canada Staff Research Studies, No. 7 (Ottawa, Bank of Canada, 1971).

[9] C.I. Higgins, "Award wages and earnings – interim report". One of a series of discussion papers on the development of a quarterly econometric model, Canberra, Commonwealth Treasury. Mimeo., 1971.

[10] C.I. Higgins. "A wage-price sector for a quarterly Australian model". Original version of paper presented to the Australasian Conference of Econometricians, Monash University, Mimeo., 1971.

[11] J.P. Nieuwenhuysen and N.R. Norman, "Wages policy in Australia: issues and tests", *British Journal of Industrial Relations* 9, No.3 (November 1971).

[12] J.D. Pitchford, "An analysis of price movements in Australia 1947–68", *Australian Economic Papers* 7, No.11 (December 1968).

[13] E.A. Russell, "Wages policy in Australia", *Australian Economic Papers* 4, Nos.1 and 2 (June–December 1965). Reprinted in: Isaac and Ford (eds.) *op. cit.*, pp.174–203.

[14] K.E. Schott and K.M. Sweeny, "Price equations for Australia", *Research Discussion Paper No.8.* Sydney, Reserve Bank of Australia. Mimeo., 1970.

SIMULATION EXPERIMENTS WITH A QUARTERLY MACROECONOMETRIC MODEL OF THE U.S. ECONOMY *

Arnold ZELLNER
University of Chicago

and

Stephen C. PECK
University of California, Berkeley

1. Introduction

The "Econometric Model-Building Industry" has produced a number of econometric models purporting (a) to represent the operation of national economies, (b) to help with the problem of forecasting, and (c) to assist in appraisal of proposed alternative economic policies. Unfortunately, few of these models have been subjected to strenuous testing. In fact many models have been presented to the economics profession and to others with relatively little known about their economic and statistical properties. In view of this unfortunate circumstance, it is not surprising that many have been somewhat bearish in their attitudes toward large-scale econometric models.[1]

Let us review some of the criteria that have been employed in an effort to check out the properties and performance of econo-

* Research financed in part by the Social Science Research Council, the Federal Reserve Bank of Chicago, and the H.G.B. Alexander Endowment Fund. This paper was written while the first author was Visiting Ford Research Professor in the Department of Economics, University of California, Berkeley. The second author's affiliation at that time was with the University of Chicago.

[1] See e.g., Gordon [3], Griliches [4], and Meiselman [6].

metric models. First, most are in agreement that econometric models should reflect sound and tested economic principles. While it is true that many models do reflect some economic principles, it is often the case that model-builders do not provide a clear enough exposition of the theoretical principles and the support for them so as to convince users of their merits. In addition, it must be noted that there are serious deficiencies in theory concerning economic dynamics, expectations, the role of money, speculative behavior, etc. Thus it seems fair to conclude that econometric model-building is not simply the application of tested and secure economic principles in the analysis of the behavior of national economies. Rather econometric model-building activities represent in part additional exploration and testing of a conjunction of economic hypotheses relating to the behavior of consumers, investors, government officials and markets.

Second, the statistical procedures employed to check out the properties and performance of models usually leave much to be desired for a variety of reasons. It is the case that models containing literally hundreds of parameters or more are implemented with relatively small samples of aggregated data. Since large sample procedures are used for estimation and testing, it is practically impossible at present to appraise small sample properties of statistical procedures that have been applied. Further complications arise from the fact that the same body of data is used for screening alternative versions of equations as well as for estimation of "final" versions. This "pre-testing" at present results in final estimates with unknown properties. The same can be said of estimates which reflect an informal use of a priori information. Add to these complications the fact that not much is known about the appropriate quantities to compute in comparing alternative versions of an equation and the fact that tests of one equation's formulation are not independent of those for other equations and the conclusion which emerges is that not much is known about the statistical properties of the "final" estimates of any macroeconometric model.

Third, the forecasting abilities of some econometric models

have been studied.[2] While this is indeed important, it must be realized that often econometric models are checked out in this dimension under the assumption that exogenous variables' values in the forecast periods are known without error. Also the number of forecasts that have been compared with actual outcomes has been small in many cases. Thus, it is the case that few, if any, econometric models have been subjected to thorough tests of forecasting ability.

Last, simulation techniques can be employed to study the properties of econometric models. While this approach is quite straightforward for linear models, its application to nonlinear models requires special solution algorithms which have only recently been programmed for use and which still have relatively unexplored convergence properties. In the past, many models presented to the profession have dynamic properties which were and still are unknown. Aside from possible computational problems, the fact that a model's dynamic properties are unknown means that it is nothing more than a black box that probably should be marked "unsafe for use".

The above points are indeed depressing. Ideally, we would like to have a set of formal, well-tested techniques for model building and model evaluation. Since such formal techniques are currently not available, the best we can do at present, it seems, is to use an *informal*, judgmental approach which some have described as an iterative research strategy.[3] Such a strategy involves use of economic theory and whatever other information is available to formulate an initial model. The initial model should be subjected to statistical testing, mathematical analysis, strenuous simulation analysis and forecasting tests. Given the results of such analyses, unsatisfactory parts of the model can often be pin-pointed and reformulated. Then again statistical, mathematical and simulation analyses, along with additional forecasting tests, can be performed in an effort to attain an improved version of the model. In these

---

[2] See e.g., Zarnowitz [7].

[3] A fuller description of such a model-building strategy is presented in Hamilton et al. [5].

analyses, it is desirable to employ as much new data and information as possible. Again reformulation may be necessary followed by additional analyses. While this iterative approach seems to be an obvious one, it appears that few model-building efforts to date have incorporated it.

In the present paper, we report results of two sets of simulation experiments with a version of the Federal Reserve-MIT-Penn Quarterly Econometric Model of the U.S. Economy.[4] This model features the final demand and financial sectors of the U.S. economy and incorporates several important policy control variables. Our simulation experiments can be viewed as a contribution to the on-going work to enhance understanding of and to effect improvements in the model. In the first set of experiments, we subject the model to symmetric increases and decreases in an important monetary and then a fiscal policy control variable. Our objectives are to determine the extent to which induced changes in the model's endogenous variables are symmetric and/or linear. Symmetry is of interest for its own sake while a finding of linearity or near linearity may be useful in efforts to simplify the model's structure. Also, since the effects of both relatively small and large changes are reported, we gain information on both the local and global properties of the model. We believe that it is very important to understand local and global properties of a model before it is used for serious policy analysis.

In the second set of experiments, we set up conditions such as to make the model produce a major depression. Again our objective is to provide a check on the global properties of the model and to discover possible weaknesses in its formulation. In particular, we shall be concerned about whether the movements of the model's important variables during the course of the depression are reasonable.

Before turning to the results of our simulation experiments, we provide a brief overview of the version of the Federal Reserve-MIT-Penn model that we employed.

---

[4] Some earlier experiments are reported in Ando and Modigliani [1], and in de Leeuw and Gramlich [2].

2. Brief overview of the model[5]

The variant of the Federal Reserve-MIT-Penn model used in our experiments, denoted Version 4.1 and dated April 15, 1969, incorporates 171 equations that are classified by type and by sector in table 1. From the information in table 1, we see that a large num-

Table 1
Classification of equations of version 4.1 by sector and type

Sector	Number of equations	Behav-ioral	Tech-nical	Empir-ical	Defini-tional
I. Final demand	44	17	5	2	20
II. Income distribution	26	2	1	2	21
III. Tax and transfer	21	0	11	1	9
IV. Labor market	13	2	0	1	10
V. Prices	32	2	0	8	22
VI. Financial	35	19	0	2	14
Totals	171	42	17	16	96

ber of equations, 96 out of a total of 171, fall in the definitional category which includes accounting identities, mathematical transformations of variables, and equations defining variables. With respect to the 16 empirical relations, 8 appear in the price sector incorporating the assumption that price indexes for components of GNP are proportional to the implicit deflator for GNP. Of the 17 technical relations, 11 are institutional relations in the Tax and Transfer Sector, while 6 are depreciation and capital consumption equations. The remaining 42 equations are behavioral equations most of which are in the Final Demand and Financial Sectors.

The Final Demand Sector's 17 behavioral equations relate to the following categories: consumption (2); investment in plant and equipment (7); housing (3); state and local government (3); inventory investment (1); and imports (1). Consumption and consumer

---

[5] A listing of the model's equations appears in a document titled *Version 4.1,* dated 4/15/69, accompanied by a document titled *Alphabetical Listing of Variables.* The summary presented in this section is a condensation of Zellner [8].

durable goods expenditures (ex housing) are treated separately as are also producers' expenditures on plant and on equipment.

The 19 behavioral equations in the financial sector include separate demand equations for currency, demand deposits, and free reserves. In addition, there are relations that generate a treasury bill rate, a corporate bond rate, life insurance reserves, a municipal bond rate, a mortgage rate, and a dividend-stock price ratio. These and other equations attempt to portray certain aspects of the operation of commercial loan markets, commercial banks, saving and loan associations, and mutual savings banks. It is probably the case that this is the most detailed financial sector of any macro-econometric model currently in operation.

Three important policy control variables in the model are unborrowed reserves plus currency in the hands of the public (M), the federal personal income tax rate (T), and federal government expenditures (G). These are the policy control variables that play a key role in our simulation experiments described below.

3. Linearity and symmetry experiments

The objective of this set of experiments is to determine the extent to which the model's responses are linear and/or symmetric. With respect to linearity of responses, if responses are found to be approximately linear over a relevant region of the variable space, then it may be useful to consider working with a linearized version of the model that would represent a significant simplification of the model. On the other hand, if important, reasonable, non-linear responses are encountered, then, of course, linearization of the model may involve intolerable errors. With respect to symmetry of responses, it is of interest from an economic point of view to discover asymmetric responses of the model. For example, does a two percentage point increase in the federal personal income tax rate produce the same absolute change in the unemployment rate as does a two percentage point decrease? Are there downward rigidities present in the model which make for asymmetric responses? Or are there floors and/or ceilings which produce asymmetries? These are interesting questions that we think should be considered in relation to any econometric model. Our experiments throw some light on these issues in connection with the FB-MIT-Penn econometric model.

Our experimental conditions are as follows. The model, with parameters estimated with quarterly data, was run out for the period 1964I–1966II, 10 quarters, using historically observed values for initial conditions and exogenous variables. The model's outputs for this run, called the *base run*, are compared with outputs of other runs in which certain of the exogenous policy variables are changed from their actually observed values. In our experiments we introduced the following changes in exogenous policy control variables: unborrowed reserves plus currency in the hands of the public, M, was changed by ± 1, ± 3, and ± 5 billions of dollars and the federal personal income tax rate, T, was changed by ± 2 and ± 5 percentage points. In the case of each change in M and T, the 1964I value and subsequent historically observed values were changed by the indicated amounts. For example, with respect to a 2 percentage point increase in the federal personal income tax rate, the historically observed rates for every quarter in the period 1964I–1966II were increased by 2 percentage points and fed into the model, along with other historically given inputs, to yield the model's outputs. To give the reader an indication of the relative sizes of the above changes, we note that unborrowed reserves plus currency varied from about 53 billion in 1964I to about 60 billion in 1966II while the federal personal income tax rate's value is given in our data as 20.59% in 1964I and 19.53% in 1966II.

In figure 1, the base run input for M and base run output for selected major variables are plotted. Also shown in figure 1 are plots of deviations from the base run for experiments in which M was increased by 1 billion dollars and in which M was decreased by 1 billion dollars. A deviation from the base run for a variable y in quarter t is defined by

$$\delta y_{t,\Delta} = y_{t,\Delta} - y_{t,b} \tag{6.1}$$

where $y_{t,b}$ = value of y in the tth quarter for the base run, and

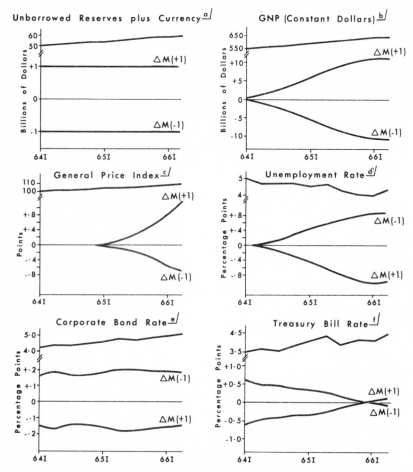

Fig.1. Base run and deviations from base run outputs for selected variables for the period
1964I–1966II for money changes of plus and minus one billion dollars. At the top of
each panel is plotted the behavior of the variables during the base run and in the bottom
of each panel the deviations from the base run. – Footnotes are presented in the
Appendix at the end of the paper.

$y_{t,\Delta}$ = value of y in the tth quarter for a simulation experiment in
which a policy control variable was changed by Δ units.

Below we shall use the deviations defined in (6.1) to construct
descriptive measures of symmetry and linearity. In figure 2, we
present base run input for T, the federal personal income tax rate,

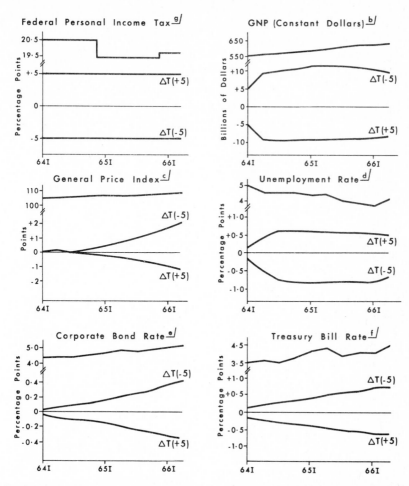

Fig.2. Base run and deviations from base run outputs for selected variables for the period 1964I–1966II for tax rate changes of plus and minus 5 percentage points. – Footnotes are presented in the Appendix at the end of the paper.

base run output for the same variables as in figure 1, and deviations from the base run associated with experiments in which T was changed by plus and minus 5 percentage points. The information in figures 1 and 2 provides the reader with a visual display of the paths of the output variables given the historically observed input variables, the base run, and for selected changes in the variables M and T.

A visual inspection of figure 1 indicates a remarkable degree of symmetry in the model's output responses to symmetric one billion dollar changes in M. For example, the upward and downward deviations of GNP in constant dollars from the base run are almost identical in magnitude. The variable displaying the greatest asymmetry is the general price level variable (implicit deflator for GNP). In 1966II, this variable's value is about 1.2 percentage points above the base run value given $\Delta M = +1$, while its value in 1966II is -0.61 percentage points below the base run value given $\Delta M = -1$. Thus the model appears to incorporate assumptions producing greater upward than downward price flexibility. This property of the model apparently reflects the non-linear asymmetric dependence of the employee compensation variable on the unemployment rate. Since the general price level is related to the employee compensation variable in a "mark-up" equation, the effects of the aforementioned asymmetric nonlinearity are reflected in the behavior of the general price level.

In figure 2, the model's responses to very large changes in the federal personal income tax rate, namely $\Delta T = \pm 5$ percentage points, are displayed. For these very large changes, the model's outputs display more asymmetry than was the case in figure 1. The results indicate that a tax cut of 5 percentage points, $\Delta T = -5$, produces larger deviations from the base run than does a tax increase of the same magnitude for all variables included in figure 2. However, the amount of asymmetry is not large in many cases, a surprising result in view of the large size of the tax rate changes, $\Delta T = \pm 5$. Again the variable displaying a good deal of asymmetry is the general price level. For $\Delta T = -5$, its deviation from the base run in 1966II is about 1.9 percentage points, while for $\Delta T = 5$, it is about -1.0 percentage points.

To characterize the degree of symmetry of the model's responses to symmetric changes in input variables, such as M and T, we first define a deviation from symmetry in output of a variable, say y, as

$$\gamma_t = \delta y_{t,\Delta} + \delta y_{t,-\Delta} \qquad (6.2)$$

where $\delta y_{t,\Delta}$ and $\delta y_{t,-\Delta}$ are deviations from the base run defined in (6.1). The mean absolute deviation from symmetry is then simply given as the arithmetic average of the $|\gamma_t|$'s, $t = 1, 2, ..., 10$, that is,

$$\bar{\gamma} = \sum_{t=1}^{10} |\gamma_t/10| . \tag{6.3}$$

To provide a relative measure of symmetry, we introduce the following absolute deviation from the base run

$$\phi_t = [\,|\delta y_{t,\Delta}| + |\delta y_{t,-\Delta}|\,]/2 . \tag{6.4}$$

Then the mean absolute distance from the base run, called *DIST*, is given by

$$DIST = \sum_{t=1}^{10} \phi_t/10 . \tag{6.5}$$

Finally, our relative measure of symmetry, called *SYM*, is

$$SYM = \bar{\gamma}/DIST . \tag{6.6}$$

Note that

$$SYM = \sum_{t=1}^{10} |\gamma_t| / \sum_{t=1}^{10} \phi_t = \sum_{t=1}^{10} |\gamma_t/\phi_t|\phi_t / \sum_{t=1}^{10} \phi_t ,$$

a weighted average of the ratios $|\gamma_t/\phi_t|$ with the ϕ_t's serving as weights. A value of *SYM* close to zero denotes symmetry in the response of an output variable while a large value indicates a lack of symmetry.

In table 2, we present calculated values of *SYM* and *DIST* for changes in T of $\pm\,2$ and $\pm\,5$ percentage points and for changes in M of $\pm\,1$ billion dollars. The results associated with $\Delta T = \pm 2$ indicate a remarkable degree of symmetry for all variables except the implicit price deflator for GNP. For example, *SYM* = 0.075 for price

Table 2
Calculated values of symmetry and distance measures for selected endogenous variables [a]

Changes in T and M	Measure [b]	Endogenous variables [c]					
		Price-deflated GNP	Current GNP	Implicit deflator for GNP	AAA corp. bond rate	Treas. bill rate	Unemployment rate
$\Delta T = \pm 2$	SYM	0.075	0.110	0.241	0.066	0.072	0.098
	DIST	4.113	5.537	0.194	0.069	0.181	0.264
$\Delta T = \pm 5$	SYM	0.188	0.281	0.604	0.156	0.185	0.247
	DIST	10.206	13.983	0.522	0.175	0.456	0.664
$\Delta M = \pm 1$	SYM	0.061	0.128	0.492	0.078	0.120	0.137
	DIST	7.022	8.812	0.219	0.169	0.320	0.460

[a] See text for explanation of conditions employed in simulation experiments.
[b] *SYM* and *DIST* are explained in the text.
[c] The symbols employed in the model for the variables shown below are: XOBE, XOBE$, PXB, RCB, RTB and ULU, respectively. The Office of Business Economics definition of GNP is the one employed. The treasury bill rate is the rate on 90 day bills while the unemployment rate is the percentage of the civilian labor force unemployed.

deflated GNP indicating that the mean deviation from symmetry, $\bar{\gamma}$, is 7.5% of *DIST* which for this variable is about 4.1 billion dollars. For the implicit price deflator for GNP, $SYM = 0.241$ indicating that the mean deviation from symmetry, $\bar{\gamma}$, is 24.1% of *DIST* which for this variable is 0.194 index points. For the larger changes, $\Delta T = \pm 5$, we note a general increase in the values computed for *SYM* with again that for the GNP price deflator being the largest. Its value is also largest in the experiments for which $\Delta M = \pm 1$. The conclusion that emerges from the plots in figures 1 and 2 and the measures in table 2 is that for changes $\Delta T = \pm 2$ and $\Delta M = \pm 1$, the model's outputs for the variables studied are quite symmetric with the exception of those for the implicit price deflator for GNP. For the large changes, $\Delta T = \pm 5$, the degree of asymmetry is large for the implicit price deflator for GNP and increased somewhat for the other variables considered.

With respect to symmetry of outputs and in other respects, it is important to report the results of experiments in which the following changes in M were tried: $\Delta M = \pm 3$ and $\Delta M = \pm 5$ billions of dollars. For experiments with $\Delta M = 3$ and $\Delta M = 5$, both fairly substantial quarterly changes, the model failed to converge to a solution. While we can speculate about the reasons for this failure to converge, at present this is still an open problem.[6] Thus these experiments revealed an extremely important asymmetry in the model's performance, one that deserves further attention in our opinion.

We next take up the problem of appraising the extent to which the responses of the model to changes in T and in M are linear. To illustrate our approach to this problem, consider the responses of a variable, say y, to changes in M, namely, $\Delta M = 1$ and $\Delta M = 3$ billion dollars. We computed the deviations from the base run, defined in (6.1), that is $\delta y_{t,1}$ and $\delta y_{t,3}$. Then

$$\eta_t = \delta y_{t,3} - 3\delta y_{t,1} \qquad (6.7)$$

was computed for each of the 10 quarters of our output, $t = 1, 2,$ ..., 10. The η_t's are measures of departures from linearity. To obtain a relative measure of linearity, we compared $\bar{\eta} = \Sigma_{t=1}^{10} |\eta_t|/10$ with the following distance measure:

$$DIST = \sum_{t=1}^{10} \frac{1}{2}[|\delta y_{t,3}| + 3|\delta y_{t,1}|]/10 . \qquad (6.8)$$

Thus, our relative measure of linearity (or nonlinearity) is:

$$LIN = \bar{\eta}/DIST \qquad (6.9)$$

with $DIST$ defined in (6.8). Note that if responses are perfectly linear, $LIN = 0$. Calculated values of LIN and $DIST$ for selected

---

[6] From intensive study of the simulation program's output, we tentatively concluded that an interest rate was forced to be negative on these runs and that the program refused to compute the logarithm of a negative number.

Table 3
Calculated values of linearity and distance measures for selected endogenous variables [a]

Changes in T and M	Meas- ure [b]	Endogenous variables [c]					
		Price- deflated GNP	Current GNP	Implicit deflator for GNP	AAA corp. bond rate	Treas. bill rate	Unem- ployment rate
$\Delta T = -5, -2$	LIN	0.046	0.088	0.223	0.049	0.062	0.074
	DIST	10.917	15.274	0.610	0.184	0.483	0.720
$\Delta T = 5, 2$	LIN	0.068	0.085	0.157	0.041	0.052	0.077
	DIST	9.572	12.531	0.396	0.164	0.425	0.606
$\Delta M = -5, -1$	LIN	0.131	0.180	0.606	0.108	0.163	0.180
	DIST	31.947	37.849	0.636	0.929	1.740	1.967
$\Delta M = -5, -3$	LIN	0.068	0.086	0.277	0.048	0.073	0.085
	DIST	30.910	36.001	0.516	0.956	1.789	1.870
$\Delta M = -3, -1$	LIN	0.065	0.096	0.345	0.058	0.090	0.097
	DIST	19.778	23.619	0.424	0.543	1.004	1.227

[a] See text for explanation of conditions employed in simulation experiments.
[b] LIN and DIST are explained in the text.

changes in T and M and for selected output variables are shown in table 3.

With respect to the changes in T shown in table 3, we see that the responses of the general price level (implicit deflator for GNP) depart most from linearity as measured by LIN. For other variables, the values of LIN are rather small, ranging from about 0.04 to 0.09. As regards the changes in M, again the general price level's responses are found to be quite nonlinear with values of LIN equal to 0.606 for $\Delta M = -5, -1$, 0.277 for $\Delta M = -5, -3$, and 0.345 for $\Delta M = -3, -1$. For $\Delta M = -5, -3$ and $\Delta M = -3, -1$, values of LIN for other variables are quite small indicating that the model's responses for these variables are approximately linear. Thus we may conclude that for changes of 3 points or less in T and downward changes of about 2 or 3 billion in M, the variables that we studied responded almost linearly with the exception of the general price level variable.

4. Major depression experiments

As in the experiments reported in section 3, the model was run out beginning in 1964I. The input variable M, unborrowed reserves plus currency in the hands of the public, a major policy control variable, was fed into the model in such a way as to create a major depression. The assumed path for M is shown in figure 3. M remains fairly constant for 6 quarters and then is moved downward by 5% per quarter for 5 quarters. For the remaining 10 quarters, M was kept constant in value. In our first experiment, other exogenous variables were given their historically observed values for the period 1964I–1969I.

The behavior of M, described in the preceding paragraph, did indeed produce a major depression. As can be seen from the plots in figure 3, price-deflated GNP falls considerably. The unemployment rate jumps from about 5% to about 12%. In broad outline, these variables' behavior seems reasonable given the strong downward movement in M. However, the behavior of other variables – see figure 3 – seems unusual in the following respects:

(1) The implicit deflator for GNP barely turns down, and at no time is the level of the deflator lower than its level in 1964I, even though the model has produced a 12% unemployment rate, and a substantial decline in real GNP.

(2) The AAA corporate bond rate and the treasury bill rate both move up to extremely high levels, to about 15% in each case. In addition we note that the differential between these two rates changes drastically during the course of the major depression.

(3) The federal government deficit moves up to astronomical levels, about 50 billion dollars; also the net deficit of the state and local governments increases to about 11 billion dollars.

To investigate the possibility that the huge deficits that appeared in our first experiment might have been responsible for the strange behavior of interest rates and the price level, we reduced federal government expenditures and increased grants in aid to state and local governments. Two experiments were performed along these lines; in one the previously described downturn in the money series was combined with a large fiscal downturn (DLF in

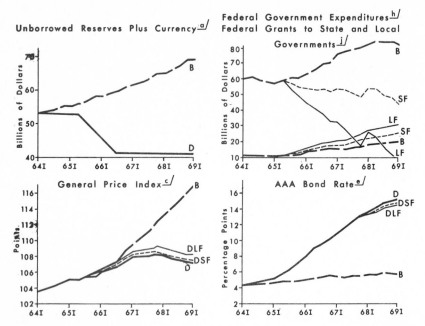

Fig.3. Base and depression runs' outputs for selected variables for the period 1964I–1969I. The first two panels indicate the behavior of the policy variables in the experiments. Each curve is referenced by a letter. B refers to the behavior of the money and fiscal variables during the base run. D refers to the behavior of the money series during the depression run. SF and LF refer to the behavior of the fiscal variables in the runs to reduce the budget deficits. SF stands for a small fiscal downturn and LF for a large fiscal downturn. In the remaining seven panels are plotted the endogenous variables in which we are particularly interested. If a series is referenced by a B, it is the behavior of the variable during the base run. If a series is referenced by a D, it is the behavior of the variable during the depression run when the money variable is constrained to follow the path indicated by D in the first panel. If a series is referenced by a DSF it is the behavior of the variable when the money variable follows the path indicated by D in the first panel, and the fiscal variables follow the path indicated by SF in the second panel; hence DSF refers to the behavior of endogenous variables in the "depression and small fiscal downturn run". DLF is to be interpreted similarly. – Footnotes are presented in the Appendix at the end of the paper.

figure 3), and in the other with a smaller fiscal downturn (DSF in figure 3). The paths of the fiscal variables are shown in the second panel of figure 3; the paths of the other variables are shown in the other panels of figure 3. Even though federal government expenditures were reduced enormously in these two experiments, we note

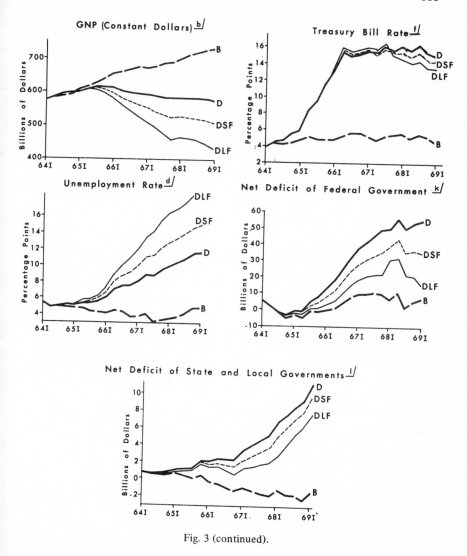

Fig. 3 (continued).

that the behavior of interest rates is still very similar to that encountered in the first depression experiment. Also the path of the price level is not changed very much relative to the depression run, and the change that does occur runs contrary to our intuition; GNP in constant dollars falls more than in the depression run, and

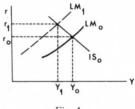

Fig. 4

yet the price level does not fall as much. Last we note that even with a large reduction in government spending, the deficits are still rather large. It may be that the tax revenue functions of the model are producing too large a decline in tax revenues given the large fall in output and income.

We do not claim to have full explanations of the anomalies reported above. However, the heuristic "IS-LM curve analysis" illustrated in figure 4 may be relevant. Given the initial schedules, LM_0 and IS_0, equilibrium income and the interest rate are Y_0 and r_0, respectively. With our drastic decline in M, the LM curve shifts upward to the left to LM_1 producing a high interest rate r_1 and a substantially lower level of income Y_1 *under the assumption that the IS curve does not shift.* Possibly, the IS curve associated with the model shifts downward to the left but not enough to offset the upward shift in the LM curve with the result that the interest rate rises while income falls. Such an effect may be due to the fact that changes in anticipations of consumers and investors are not adequately incorporated in the model's consumption and investment equations. If such factors are important, and many believe that they are, and had been incorporated in the consumption and investment equations, it may be that the IS curve would show a greater downward shift to the left producing a lower rather than a higher interest rate and an even lower level of income. Further work with the model is needed to check out the reasonableness of the above tentative explanation for some of the anomalies encountered in our major depression experiments with the model.

5. Summary and conclusions

In this paper we have presented the view that understanding the local and global properties of econometric models is extremely important. Further, we have provided some measures of symmetry and linearity that may be useful in characterizing properties of models' responses. In addition, we have stressed the importance of exercising a model strenuously in simulation experiments in order to discover possible model defects. To illustrate application of these methods and principles, we reported results of experiments with the Federal Reserve-MIT-Penn quarterly econometric model of the U.S. economy. For the conditions we employed and for the output variables considered, we found that the model's local responses were quite symmetric and fairly linear with the exception of the responses of the general price level. From our major depression experiments, that bear on certain global properties of the model, we found that the model can indeed yield a major depression. However, the depression behavior of the price level and interest rates yielded by the model appears to us to be rather strange. We suggest that this problem be studied further and that more attention be given to incorporating changes in expectations in the equations of the model. Finally, we hope that our results will be of use to those who are continuing work to improve the Federal Reserve-MIT-Penn quarterly model of the U.S. economy.

Appendix

There follows a list of the full title of the variables graphed together with the variable name by which they are identified in the model.

[a] Unborrowed reserves at member banks plus currency outside of banks (ZMS).
[b] GNP (O.B.E. definition) (XOBE).
[c] Price deflator for non-farm business product (PXB or PNF).
[d] Unemployment rate (ULU).
[e] Corporate bond rate (RCB).
[f] Treasury bill rate (RTB).
[g] Effective rate of Federal personal income tax (UTPF).
[h] Federal government expenditures on goods and services (EGF).

^{j} Federal grants-in-aid to state and local governments (GFS).
^{k} Net deficit of Federal government (GDSF).
^{l} Net deficit of state and local governments (GDSS).

References

[1] A. Ando and F. Modigliani, "Econometric analysis of stabilization policies", *American Economic Review* 59 No.2 (Papers and Proceedings issue, May 1969) 296–314.

[2] F. de Leeuw and E.M. Gramlich, "The channels of monetary policy", *Federal Reserve Bulletin* (June 1969).

[3] R.J. Gordon, "Short and long term simulations with the Brookings model: a comment", in: *Econometric models and business cycles,* edited by B. Hickman (New York, National Bureau of Economic Research, 1971).

[4] Z. Griliches, "The Brookings model volume: a review article", *Review of Economics and Statistics* 1 (May 1968) 215–234.

[5] H.R. Hamilton, S.E. Goldstone, J.W. Milliman, A.L. Pugh, E.R. Roberts and A. Zellner, *Systems simulation for regional analysis: an application to river basin planning* (Cambridge, Mass., MIT Press, 1969).

[6] D. Meiselman, "Comment on 'Econometric analysis of stabilization policies' by Albert Ando and Franco Modigliani", *American Economic Review* 59, No.2 (Papers and Proceedings issue, May 1969) 318–321.

[7] V. Zarnowitz, "Econometric model simulations and the cyclical characteristics of the U.S. economy", Paper prepared for presentation to the Second World Congress of the Econometric Society, Cambridge, England, September 1970.

[8] A. Zellner, "General description of the Federal Reserve-MIT-Penn quarterly econometric model of the U.S. economy" (Version 4.1–4/15/69), M.S., University of Chicago, September 1969.

DYNAMIC PROPERTIES OF A NON-LINEAR ECONOMETRIC MODEL *

V.W. FITZGERALD

Bureau of Census and Statistics, Canberra

1. Introduction

This paper reports a study undertaken to establish dynamic properties of a non-linear econometric model. The model studied is a version of the quarterly National Income Forecasting (NIF) model, which is being constructed at the Commonwealth Treasury and the Bureau of Census and Statistics. This version is the same as that set out in an appendix to the paper by Dr. C.I. Higgins in this volume [14], except that it does not include the newly developed price-wage-employment sector which is the subject of that paper; the differences are specified in section 4 below. The NIF model is not yet fully developed in some sectors which might be expected to contribute significantly to the model's dynamic behaviour; thus, this is a preliminary study.

There are many ways in which the dynamic properties of a model may be summarized and the choice here was motivated by considerations of utility in the context in which the NIF model is

* The author wishes to thank Professor R.D. Terrell for helpful advice and comments in the early stages of this work. Thanks are due also to A. Johnson, R. Svanberg and M. Joyce for assistance with programming and in the preparation of the experiments, and to the IBM Systems Development Institute, Canberra, for the provision of excellent computing facilities. – This study is part of the joint model-building project of the Commonwealth Treasury and the Bureau of Census and Statistics; C.I. Higgins and V.W. FitzGerald are the respective principal investigators. However, statements made in the paper are the responsibility of the author and do not necessarily reflect the views of the employing organisations.

being used and developed. Since a very early stage in its development, versions have been assembled for regular use in short-term
forecasting and policy analysis within an existing institutional
framework, described briefly in [13]. The results of the present
study were in part intended to be directly usable in this work; thus
the summary measures chosen include confidence envelopes which
may be placed around forecasts made with the model and estimates of the model's dynamic responses to incremental changes in
exogenous variables, particularly policy instruments. While these
short-term time-domain characteristics are relevant to the immediate uses of the model, other measures may be more revealing
when attention is focussed on the model's behaviour over longer
periods. For example, it may be of interest to establish whether
the structure of the model implies that its endogenous variables
will display cyclical fluctuations of the sort found in historical
data; or, there may be interest in the implied leads or lags between
pairs of variables. The answers provided to such questions will be
of particular interest when the model is a growing one, as this
implies a continual process of making choices between alternate
specifications for areas of the model's structure.

Investigation of the short-term time-domain characteristics of
dynamic econometric models is not a new area of study; a great
deal of basic work on impact and dynamic multipliers, simulation
of policy packages and so on has been done.[1] Recent studies have
paid increasing attention to *stochastic* simulation experiments, in
which random error terms with appropriate sampling properties
are generated. By replicating the experiments, the investigator may
compute estimates of the low-order moments of the joint probability distribution of the values of each of the endogenous variables in each of a number of forecast periods, conditional on given
initial conditions, given model parameters and assumed projections
of exogenous variables; hence confidence ranges for forecasts may
be constructed.[2] For linear models, such information may instead
be computed from known analytical results regarding conditional

[1] See for instance Goldberger [5] and Adelman and Adelman [1].
[2] See for instance Nagar [21].

forecasts and their probability distributions; see for instance Goldberger [5] and Goldberger et al. [6]. However, with a non-linear model these results can be applied only to a linear approximation, which might not be readily obtainable. Since most modern econometric models are non-linear, simulation methods retain a place in the evaluation of short-term time-domain characteristics of large models.

In recent years, the attention of investigators has also been focussed on the longer-term cyclical behaviour implicit in econometric models. As in other disciplines concerned with stochastic and dynamic systems, it was realized that time-domain analysis of these questions presented intractable problems but that they were eminently amenable to analysis in the frequency domain, that is by means of spectrum and cross-spectrum analysis. For a linear system, analytical expressions for frequency response characteristics are available[3], although the use of these expressions for a large model may involve a heavy computing burden in inverting large complex-valued matrices at each frequency. The application of these analytical results to a non-linear system again entails the derivation of a linear approximation tailored to the particular system at hand, which may be difficult to obtain. Moreover, a linear approximation may imply patterns of dynamic behaviour which seriously distort those implicit in the original non-linear model. These considerations, together with questions of computing convenience, may make it preferable to use simulation experiments[4] to determine the frequency response patterns of a model.

The results obtained in the present study are derived from simulation experiments of two kinds: deterministic and stochastic, both of which involve holding some of the inputs to the model fixed while others are subjected to shocks. In the case of deterministic simulation, the shocks are usually simple impulse functions employed to trace out in the time-domain the dynamic responses to individual inputs. A stochastic simulation experiment on the other hand involves generating for each time period a vector of

[3] See for instance Howrey [15, 16, 18].
[4] For such a study, see Green et al. [8].

random shocks with sampling properties the same as those of the residuals encountered during consistent estimation of the model. Stochastic simulation experiments are *replicated*, although fixed sets of parameters, initial conditions and exogenous variables are maintained throughout each set of replications. These features enable the outcomes of the experiments to be processed to yield estimates of the confidence ranges applicable to forecasts made with the model. The model's frequency response patterns could be estimated from the outcomes of carefully designed simulation experiments of either kind; see for instance [20]. However, in this study it has been convenient to employ the replicated *stochastic* simulations in making spectrum and cross-spectrum estimates, after discarding some of the observations following the take-off point.

A further feature is added to the study by the use of a facility to switch the status of many of the variables from endogenous to exogenous, enabling experiments to be conducted which attempt to locate which parts of the model's structure give rise to aspects of its dynamic behaviour.

The following section of this paper deals briefly with linear models and serves to establish the terminology and notation which will be employed in succeeding sections dealing with non-linear systems.

2. Linear models

An econometric model such as the NIF model may be viewed as a system of non-linear stochastic difference equations with two classes of forcing function inputs – the exogenous variables and the error terms (random shocks). A sample time-path for an endogenous variable in such a system may then be regarded as combining three response components: a transient arising from initial conditions, a response to the exogenous variables and a response to the random shocks. This decomposition is an obvious one and corresponds to that encountered in solving *linear* inhomogeneous difference or differential equations. Since an investigation such as this entails isolating these component responses for analysis, it will be useful to proceed by first examining linear systems from this viewpoint.

It should be re-emphasized that throughout the study the estimated model parameters (including variances and covariances of the error terms) will be regarded as *fixed*.[5] The analysis procedures employed are not alternatives to the usual post-regression tests of significance for validating the estimation process[6]; rather, they provide means of measuring the inherent dynamic properties of a specified model with known parameters. This does not preclude using the procedures to conduct sensitivity analyses to reveal the effects of changing the given parameter values or to make comparisons between alternative specifications for areas of a model.

A sufficiently general model to consider is the following one, which incorporates a moving-average disturbance process[7]:

$$A_0 y_t + A_1 y_{t-1} + ... + A_p y_{t-p} = B_0 x_t + B_1 x_{t-1} + ... + B_q x_{t-q}$$

$$+ C_0 e_t + C_1 e_{t-1} + ... + C_r e_{t-r}, \quad (7.1)$$

where y_t is a $g \times 1$ vector of observations at time t on the endogenous variables, x_t is a $k \times 1$ vector of observations at time t on the exogenous variables, assumed *known* and non-stochastic, and e_t is a $g \times 1$ vector of temporally uncorrelated ("white noise") gaussian disturbances with contemporaneous covariance matrix Σ. The A_j, $j = 0, 1, ..., p$, the B_j, $j = 0, 1, ..., q$, and the C_j, $j = 0, 1, ...,$

---

[5] Since econometric models are usually specified and estimated as fixed-parameter models, it would be illogical to conduct stochastic simulation trials in which new sets of parameters are drawn *each period* from a suitable random population (as has sometimes been suggested). However, for some purposes it would "make sense" to draw a new set *each replication*. This approach has not been explored in this study.

[6] This point is discussed by Howrey and Kelejian [19].

[7] If an individual equation of the system were specified with an autoregressive residual u_t, say with $d(L)u_t = e_t$ (e_t serially uncorrelated), then multiplying both sides of the equation by the autoregressive operator $d(L)$ reduces it to a form compatible with (7.1). This simple procedure could also be applied if the residual u_t had the "mixed" specification $d(L)u_t = c(L)e_t$. If one (or more) of the equations in the model is an identity, it may be treated by making the corresponding row and column in Σ zero and by setting appropriate coefficients in $C(L)$ to zero. See Howrey [15], Appendix.

r, are (sparse) matrices of known coefficients with dimensions $g \times g$, $g \times k$ and $g \times g$ respectively. For normalization reasons C_0 is the unit matrix and A_0 will have ones on the diagonal. Using the lag operator L, defined by $L\,z_t \equiv z_{t-1}$ for any time-series z_t, (7.1) may be written more compactly as

$$A(L)y_t = B(L)x_t + C(L)e_t ,\qquad\qquad (7.2)$$

where, for instance,

$$A(L) = A_0 + A_1 L + ... + A_p L^p .\qquad\qquad (7.3)$$

$A(L)$ is a $g \times g$ matrix operator or "filter" whose elements are scalar polynomials in L; for example, the (i, j) element of $A(L)$ is

$$a_{ij}(L) = a_{ij0} + a_{ij1}L + ... + a_{ijp}L^p ,\qquad\qquad (7.4)$$

where a_{ijk} is the (i, j) element of A_k.

Now, regarding (7.2) as a system of stochastic difference equations with constant coefficients, it may be seen that a particular solution may be written down "at sight":

$$y_t^P = A^{-1}(L)B(L)x_t + A^{-1}(L)C(L)e_t \qquad\qquad (7.5)$$

$$= \quad y_t^X \quad + \quad y_t^E ,\qquad\qquad (7.6)$$

which consists of two parts, a particular solution corresponding to the exogenous variables, or "the response to the exogenous variables", and a particular solution corresponding to the disturbances, or "the stochastic response". The complete solution of (7.2) also contains a "transient" or complementary function, obtained by solving the homogenous equation

$$A(L)y_t = 0 .\qquad\qquad (7.7)$$

This transient is of the form $E\,V^t$, where V is an $m \times 1$ vector of roots, assumed distinct, of the auxiliary polynomial equation

$$v^m |A(1/v)| = 0 , \tag{7.8}$$

in which $|A(L)|$ represents the determinant polynomial, assumed to be of degree m, of the operator $A(L)$.[8]. The notation V^t signifies the vector each of whose elements is formed by raising the corresponding element of V to the power t. E is a $g \times m$ matrix of constants[9] which may be computed from the initial conditions, taken to be a set of p observations on the vector y_t made before the start time ($t = 1$) and assumed fixed. The complete solution is then

$$y_t = E V^t + A^{-1}(L)B(L)x_t + A^{-1}(L)C(L)e_t . \tag{7.9}$$

It is also assumed that all the roots of (7.8) are less than unity in modulus, so that the system is *stable* and the transient approaches zero or "dies out" as t increases, regardless of initial conditions. When sufficient time periods have elapsed for the transient to have died out, solutions recorded from that point onwards are called "steady-state" solutions and consist of the two particular solutions only. The period which ends at that point may be termed the "transient period" or "forecast period".

If a simulation program is available for solving the model (7.1) in successive periods it is a simple matter to isolate the component responses. For instance, the transient may be isolated by merely setting the values of x_t and e_t to zero in all time periods.[10] The transient and the response to the exogenous variables *together* form the "deterministic solution", obtained by setting to zero all e_t values. It will be seen that the deterministic solution is the *mean* (expected value) *time-path* of y_t, given the values of the exogenous variables in all periods, since the expected value of the stochastic response is zero for all t, even though this response may possess a rich autocorrelation pattern.

---

[8] m will be less than or equal to pg.

[9] If the assumption of distinct roots were relaxed, a column in E corresponding to a repeated root would have elements which are low-order polynomials in t.

[10] If the *level* is not important, the x_t may be held at some constant value (other than zero) in all periods.

Deterministic simulation may also be used to calculate *impact and dynamic multipliers,* i.e. the sequence of changes to the deterministic solution (mean time-path) for y_t which are induced by applying a "one-shot" or "impulse" change of one unit in a particular period, to the given series for a particular exogenous variable in x_t. It will be seen that this amounts to a calculation of the coefficients of each polynomial element of the corresponding column of the rational matrix operator $(A^{-1}(L)B(L))$. The sequence of coefficients of successive powers of L in any of these polynomial elements converges to zero at a rate similar to that displayed by the transient, since the model is stable. With a linear model, the use of this impulse-function "test signal" for tracing out filter coefficients may be performed in two ways. One way would be to set to zero the initial conditions, all of the e_t, and all of the elements of x_t except the particular one being tested; then this individual exogenous variable would be set to unity at $t = 1$ (say) and to zero elsewhere. The other way would be to do the calculation in two steps; first a deterministic simulation would be run using any given sequences for x_t, yielding a "control" solution; secondly, another deterministic simulation would be run with all inputs the same except for a unit change at $t = 1$ in a particular exogenous variable, yielding a "disturbed" solution. Subtraction of the control solution from the disturbed yields the required filter coefficients. Use of the impulse-function test signal on individual elements of e_t in one of these ways would yield the coefficients of the rational matrix filter $(A^{-1}(L)C(L)) = D(L)$.

Since the exogenous variables are assumed known and nonstochastic, it will be seen that the mean time-paths of the endogenous variables are then determined, and the only part of the complete solution (7.9) not pre-determined is the stochastic response, which will be re-named u_t:

$$u_t = A^{-1}(L)C(L)e_t \qquad\qquad (7.10)$$

$$= D(L)e_t . \qquad\qquad (7.11)$$

It is because the stochastic response may possess a very complicated autocorrelation pattern that time-domain analysis of its properties is usually restricted to the calculation of confidence intervals for short-term forecasts. These may be calculated from the outcomes of replicated stochastic simulations, or, if the coefficients of the polynomial elements of $D(L)$ have been calculated for the first few powers of L as indicated above, then the following method may be used.

Let $D(L)$ be expanded as

$$D(L) = D_0 + D_1 L + D_2 L^2 + \dots ,\qquad (7.12)$$

so that

$$u_t = D_0 e_t + D_1 e_{t-1} + \dots .\qquad (7.13)$$

Because the initial conditions on y_t are assumed fixed, those on e_t in (7.10), itself a set of difference equations, must be taken as fixed also. Thus without loss of generality we may take the values of e_t for t less than 1 (the start time) as zero. Thus the covariance matrix of u_t with u_{t+j} is given by

$$E(u_t\, u'_{t+j}) = E(D_0\, e_t\, e'_t\, D'_j) + E(D_1\, e_{t-1}\, e'_{t-1}\, D'_{j+1}) + \dots \qquad (7.14)$$

$$= D_0\, V_t\, D'_j + D_1\, V_{t-1}\, D'_{j+1} + \dots ,\qquad (7.15)$$

where

$$\begin{aligned} V_t &= \Sigma \quad \text{if } t \geqslant 1 ; \\ &= 0 \quad \text{if } t < 1 ; \end{aligned}\qquad (7.16)$$

and where $j = 0, 1, 2, \dots$.

The sequence of contemporaneous covariance matrices of u_t ($j = 0$; $t = 1, 2, \dots$) will converge in a stable model for sufficiently large t to a limiting matrix, the steady-state contemporaneous covariance matrix of the u_t process. Of course the lag covariance matrices ($j \neq 0$) will have steady-state limits also, and as j increases these steady-state lag covariance matrices will converge to the null matrix. In the present study, the expressions (7.15) have not been used so far; instead replicated stochastic simulations have been used to calculate contemporaneous variances of elements of u_t in forecast periods.

If the longer-term cyclical characteristics of the model are of interest, any analysis in the time-domain becomes intractable[11] and it becomes necessary to conduct the analysis in terms of the spectrum of the stochastic process (7.13). Since the D_j in the moving average representation (7.13) of u_t converge to the null matrix for large j, then in the steady-state u_t is a strictly stationary multi-channel stochastic process. The transfer function of the filter $D(L)$ is obtained formally by evaluating $D(L)$, considered as a polynomial in L with matrix coefficients, on the unit circle at $L = e^{-i\lambda}$. Then the $g \times g$ spectral matrix of the u_t process at frequency λ is given by[12]

$$F_{uu}(\lambda) = D(e^{-i\lambda}) \, F_{ee}(\lambda) \, D^*(e^{-i\lambda}) , \qquad (7.17)$$

where $D^*(e^{-i\lambda})$ is the conjugate transpose of $D(e^{-i\lambda})$ and $F_{ee}(\lambda)$ is the spectral matrix of the e_t process. Thus

$$F_{uu}(\lambda) = D(e^{-i\lambda}) \frac{\Sigma}{2\pi} D^*(e^{-i\lambda}) , \qquad (7.18)$$

for frequencies between $-\pi$ and π.[13]

If desired the spectral matrix may be expressed in terms of the original operators $A(L)$ and $C(L)$, where $D(L) = A^{-1}(L) \, C(L)$, but the use of the resulting expressions (the usual ones given in the literature) would entail inverting a large complex-valued matrix at each frequency. It seems preferable to use the deterministic simulation procedures suggested above to compute the coefficients of polynomial elements of $D(L)$, until they become negligibly

---

[11] This matter has been treated extensively elsewhere. See, for instance, Hannan [9].

[12] See, for instance, Fishman [4], chapter 2.

[13] Frequencies are measured in radians per time unit, where the time-unit is the interval between consecutive (equi-spaced) observations.

small, and then to employ (7.18).[14] Alternatively, one may *estimate* F_{uu} (λ) directly from steady-state stochastic simulations, a course which has been taken to date in this investigation, for reasons of computing convenience.

The diagonal elements of the spectral matrix are the auto-spectra of the stochastic responses of each of the individual endogenous variables. The auto-spectrum (or simply the spectrum) is the allocation over frequencies of the variance (or power) of the particular stochastic response. If the spectrum shows a concentration of variance about a particular frequency, for instance, this implies that the model's steady-state time paths for that particular endogenous variable will exhibit more-or-less regular fluctuations about the mean time path with the corresponding period and with an amplitude given from the spectrum. Hence alternate specifications or sets of parameters can be compared on the basis of, say, spectral power at business-cycle frequencies, and so on (see, for instance, [22]). Howrey [17] uses this approach to test the hypothesis that the U.S. economy has been more stable after World War II than before, by fitting a simple multiplier-accelerator model to both periods. Other measures, including leads and lags between pairs of variables, can also be obtained from the spectral matrix[15], but will not be discussed here.

3. Procedures for non-linear models

The preceding section discussed analytical results and simulation procedures which could be applied to measure dynamic properties of a *linear* model. For a *non-linear* model, there are no comparable analytical results which may be applied generally, and some of the numerical simulation procedures are not appropriate. For a particular non-linear model, it may be possible to derive analytical

[14] Evaluation of $D(L)$ at $L = e^{-i\lambda}$ implies taking the discrete Fourier transform of the sequence of coefficients of each polynomial element; this can be done very quickly using the Fast Fourier Transform — see [2, 3]. If preferred, only a subset of the rows of $D(L)$ need be used, so that some rows and columns of $F_{uu}(\lambda)$ are not calculated.

[15] Details may be found in standard texts on spectral analysis, e.g. Hannan [10].

results or a close linear approximation from a knowledge of the model's structure. Clearly, the first of these courses can not be considered a routine approach. The second course may be practical in some cases, and could be considered; however, particular types of non-linearities will defy attempts at linearization, and also there is no guarantee that patterns of dynamic behaviour displayed by an explicit linear approximation to a non-linear model will not be serious distortions of those implicit in the original model; little is known concerning the errors involved in replacing areas of the structure of large non-linear systems by linear approximations designed section by section. For these reasons, the view is taken here that the procedures chosen should *not* require the derivation of an *explicit* linear approximation to the model at hand. It must also be considered whether an (implicit) linear approximation *exists* for a particular non-linear system, and if so, under what conditions. First, however, it will be useful to examine what *is* known regarding non-linear models in original form.

The subject of dynamic properties of non-linear models is discussed by Howrey and Kelejian [19] and it will be sufficient to recall some of their results. The model considered by these authors has sufficient generality for their (mostly negative) conclusions to apply to most modern macro-models. The model is

$$y_t = A \, F(y_t, y_{t-1}, x_t) + B \, G(y_{t-1}, x_t) + Cx_t + e_t \, , \qquad (7.19)$$

in which y_t and e_t are $g \times 1$ vectors and x_t is $k \times 1$, and each has the same meaning as in the previous section. Only a single lag on y_t appears, the moving average operator on e_t has been omitted and the vector of known exogenous variables x_t appears unlagged only. A, B and C are matrices of known coefficients and $F(.)$ and $G(.)$ are vectors each of whose elements is a given function of the variables in parentheses. Many models (including the NIF model) contain equations whose *left-hand-side* dependent variables are known functions of the same type as $F(.)$ above; however, such a model is readily made compatible with (7.19) by suitable re-definition of variables and inclusion of identities.

The *reduced form* of the model (7.19) may be expressed as

$$y_t = J(y_{t-1}, x_t) + u_t, \tag{7.20}$$

where u_t is a vector of reduced form disturbances, whose expectation, conditioned upon the values of y_{t-1} and x_t, is zero, and $J(.)$ is the vector whose elements are the *conditional expectations of elements of* y_t, given y_{t-1} and x_t. $J(.)$ is given by

$$J(y_{t-1}, x_t) = A\, S(y_{t-1}, x_t) + B\, G(y_{t-1}, x_t) + Cx_t, \tag{7.21}$$

where the elements of $S(.)$ are the conditional expectations, given y_{t-1} and x_t, of corresponding elements of $F(.)$. The functions which make up $S(.)$ may involve the (known) contemporaneous variances and covariances of e_t (assumed gaussian); also, depending on the particular types of non-linear functions in $F(.)$, their conditional expectations may assume different functional forms. Thus the reduced form (7.20) can *not* in general be derived by solving the model equations (7.19) to obtain an expression for each of the current endogenous variables in terms of predetermined variables and structural disturbances only. To put it another way, the reduced form is *not* in general a solution of the system. Further, if the e_t in the structural form (7.19) are set at zero and the system is solved by *deterministic* simulation, the solutions obtained are *not* the mean time-paths given by successive application of (7.21), but may be expected to *diverge* systematically from those mean time-paths. However, replicated *stochastic* simulation experiments in which the structural form (7.19), including generated random error terms, is solved period by period, will yield unbiased estimates of (7.21) by averaging across replications. It is thus possible to measure in each period the biases separating the mean time-paths from the deterministic time-paths. Note, however, that even with linear models, the estimated mean time-paths from stochastic simulation may be unbiased predictors of the *expected* time-path of y_t, but *not* of the *actual values*; the relationship between actual y_t and the estimated mean time-paths is an errors-in-variables model — see [19].

Consider now the reduced form disturbances u_t. It will be clear from the preceding discussion that the elements of u_t are not linear combinations of the elements of e_t, are not obtainable by solving the structural form, but are *non-linear* functions of the structural disturbances. However, since non-linear functions of uncorrelated variables are in general correlated, then the u_t will in general be autocorrelated. Furthermore, the u_t may be heteroskedastic with respect to the pre-determined variables, even though the structural disturbances are assumed homoskedastic, and the u_t will not in general be gaussian. Thus, if the stochastic response of the model is defined (as before) as the deviation of a particular trial from the mean time-path, then this response will not in general be second-order stationary, even when the model is stable (i.e. its mean time-paths converge to constant levels when the exogenous variables are held constant).

It should not be concluded from this discussion that no analysis is possible for a non-linear model. Experience suggests that many models are only mildly non-linear within fairly wide ranges of economic conditions. It will be suggested below that this is true of the NIF model. In a particular case, however, it will be necessary to conduct a number of tests to establish whether a linear approximation exists, and if so, within what range of conditions; it will also be necessary to design simulation experiments carefully so as to achieve outcomes falling within that range of conditions. Unfortunately, no battery of tests exists which would establish objectively or conclusively whether or not a particular model may be regarded as approximately linear. This is so because approximate linearity can only be tested empirically in terms of a *number* of properties of the model's responses; thus subjective weights must be assigned to a number of (possibly conflicting) pieces of evidence in making an assessment. For instance, one might consider evaluating responses to increments in each exogenous variable at a number of points in the space of the exogenous variables. In practice, only a few points in that space can be considered, at which dynamic responses to impulse shocks (possibly at different levels and/or of opposite signs) are measured up to a selected time-horizon.[16] The preferred result is of course that dynamic responses

---

[16] Strictly speaking, these dynamic responses should be calculated as shifts in the

per unit shock be insensitive to all of these changes and to changes in the initial values of the endogenous variables.

As well as examining variations in responses to shocks in exogenous variables, one could examine in a similar manner the behaviour of the *stochastic* response over a suitable grid; this amounts to checking whether reduced form disturbances appear to be homoskedastic with respect to exogenous variables and initial conditions. Further tests may be employed to check other aspects of the stochastic response which depend on near-linearity of the model; for instance, second-order stationarity of the steady-state responses may be checked by (say) dividing the steady-state recording period in two and applying an F-test to estimated variances from the two half-periods. Finally, if the structural disturbances in a near-linear model are gaussian, then so also should be the stochastic response[17]; if it is not, then the behaviour of higher-order moments may be of some importance. However, this possibility is not explored here.

4. The experiments

This section discusses the methods used in the experiments and the results obtained to date. The model version used[18] represents

estimated mean time paths from *stochastic* simulation experiments. However, this is clearly impracticable, so that *deterministic* simulation would be used in the expectation that the *differences* between the biases in "control" and "disturbed" solutions, would be negligible.

[17] See Fishman [4] for suggestions on testing this.

[18] The model version investigated is the same as that set out in detail in an appendix to the paper in this volume by Dr. C.I. Higgins [14], *except* that the newly developed price-wage-employment sector discussed in that paper is excluded. This means that behavioural eqs. 15–21, and identities 5, 7, 11, 20 and 21 are omitted, and behavioural eq. 8 is replaced by:

8. Non-farm personal income (excluding cash benefits)

$$\frac{YP}{GPFC} = \underset{(12.726)}{0.8924} \left(\frac{YP}{GPFC}\right)_{-1} + \underset{(1.520)}{0.0876}$$

$$c\bar{R}^2 = 0.999$$
$$cSEE = \$25.3\text{m}$$
$$cD = 2.03$$

the NIF model as it was being used in forecasting and other work in June 1971, although a number of the equations, such as those for private business investment were typically modified in operation to allow for short-term factors not accounted for adequately in the model's structure.

The basic tool used in the experiments is a simulation program into which the fourteen behavioural equations[19] and sixteen identities are coded, and which solves the model iteratively[20] each period. The program incorporates a facility to hold the values of the exogenous variables constant throughout all periods, so that the exogenous response may be suppressed if desired. The program also incorporates an option to perform the calculation of dynamic multipliers by the two-step method mentioned in section 2. A control run is executed using given values for the input variables (errors and exogenous) in all periods; then a number of disturbed runs are executed in each of which a selected input variable is subjected to an impulse change in a selected period; finally, the control time-paths for the endogenous variables are subtracted from the disturbed paths to yield the required responses. Since the model is approximately linear only in a first-order Taylor sense in some bounded region surrounding the sample-period time paths for all variables, such responses *cannot* be calculated in one step in which the initial conditions and the inputs (except the one being tested) are all set to zero.

In deterministic simulation experiments, the program sets the error terms to zero in all periods, thus suppressing the stochastic response. In stochastic simulation experiments, the program generates a vector of inter-correlated random normal numbers for the error terms in each period. This is done by first generating a vector of random numbers uniformly distributed over the interval (0,1); then using an approximation to the inverse of the normal distribution function[21] this vector is transformed into a vector of uncor-

---

[19] Including error terms.

[20] Using the Gauss-Seidel method described in [23].

[21] This approximation is given by Hastings [11]. The approximation operates in the interval (½, 1−r), where r is a very small number, so that (0,1) is mapped onto that interval and a random sign is attached.

related random normal numbers with zero means and standard deviations unity. Finally, this vector is pre-multiplied by the (lower-triangular) Cholesky transform[22] of the estimated covariance matrix of the sample-period residuals to yield a vector of error terms with the required sampling properties. The option is also incorporated in the simulation program to use antithetic variables. If this option is used in stochastic simulation experiments, it results in the execution of the selected number of replications with one stream of random normal numbers, followed by the execution of the same number of replications with a new stream of random numbers which are the negatives of those in the first stream.

Tests for stationarity in mean were conducted by taking sets of initial conditions from the sample-period data and conducting deterministic simulation experiments in which the exogenous variables are held constant over a long simulation period (400 quarters). These tests showed that the system has some real and complex roots which are very close to unity in absolute value. In particular, the inclusion of the equations for private non-dwelling or "business" investment (*IOB* and *IOPE*, eqs. 5 and 6) gives rise to oscillations which die out extremely slowly, if at all, and which are still quite marked in the transients after 300 quarters[23], even though the transients appear to have reached equilibrium *levels* before that. Adverse results obtained to date with the model incorporating endogenous relationships for business investment have been interpreted as casting doubt on the simple accelerator mechanism specified at present for these equations, and investigations are proceeding aimed at finding alternate specifications for the factor demand area, including business investment. If the equations for business investment are "switched out", i.e. these expenditures are made exogenous, then the major sources of oscillatory

---

[22] The Cholesky or "square root" transformation of the sample-period covariance matrix is computed outside the simulation program using the algorithm given by Healy [12].

[23] One result of this has been that attempts to estimate spectra for the model with business investment endogenous have been unsuccessful, in that such estimated spectra have been "swamped" by a massive "spike" at a frequency near 4.0 years per cycle.

behaviour become the inventory equation (*NFS*, eq. 10) and the equation for dwelling investment (*ID*, eq. 4), but the oscillations are much more heavily damped and effectively disappear within about 40 quarters. In this reduced model the transients converge to equilibrium levels (within a tolerance which is small compared to standard errors) after about 80–100 quarters, and movements become imperceptible after about 150 quarters. For these reasons, *the numerical results reported below are for the reduced model with business investment exogenous, except for the short-term policy multipliers* given in table 1 and figures 4 and 5. In the steady-state stochastic simulation experiments, the length of the transient period was then deemed to be 150 quarters and that of the steady-state period 250 quarters (from $t = 151$ to $t = 400$). Examples of transients are presented in figure 1.

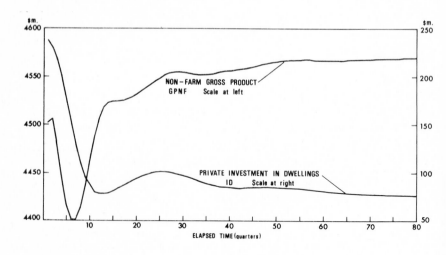

Fig.1. Examples of transient responses.

Tests of near-linearity have so far consisted mainly of measuring the dynamic responses over three years to impulse shocks of different sizes and of different signs applied to each of a set of policy

Table 1
Effects on non-farm gross product GPNF of impulse changes in public authority net current expenditure PCUR ($ millions)

Quarter	Changes in 1964I			Quarter	Changes in 1968I		
	−$15m	−$75m	+$75m		−$15m	−$75m	+$75m
1964I	−9.19	−46.08	45.89	1968I	−9.11	−45.60	45.49
II	−8.10	−40.66	40.27	II	−7.90	−39.63	39.39
III	−6.16	−30.97	30.50	III	−5.89	−29.65	29.36
IV	−5.12	−25.81	25.24	IV	−4.81	−24.26	23.95
1965I	−4.53	−22.84	22.25	1969I	−4.19	−21.17	20.83
II	−4.10	−20.70	20.09	II	−3.74	−18.93	18.56
III	−3.65	−18.47	17.84	III	−3.28	−16.65	16.28
IV	−3.08	−15.65	15.00	IV	−2.73	−13.88	13.49
1966I	−2.35	−11.97	11.63	1970I	−2.03	−10.40	10.02
II	−1.44	− 7.39	7.32	II	−1.19	− 6.20	5.82
III	−0.36	− 1.99	2.13	III	−0.23	− 1.37	1.01
IV	0.84	4.01	−3.68	IV	0.81	3.84	−4.18
1967I	2.09	10.30	−9.78	1971I	1.87	9.19	−9.50

instruments[24] at different places in the sample period. The results of these tests can only be suggestive, but are so far the main grounds on which the assumption has been made that the present version of the NIF model is approximately linear in a first-order Taylor sense. The results have been interpreted as showing that the time-forms of the dynamic responses and their magnitudes per unit shock are "reasonably" insensitive to the size and direction of the applied shock and to the choice of period in which it is imposed. Some results from these tests are given in table 1.

The stochastic simulation experiments conducted have two objectives — computation of short-term time-domain characteristics (apart from policy multipliers), and calculation of estimates of selected spectral statistics to provide a characterization of the model's stochastic responses. For the first objective, a three-year time horizon was selected and the initial conditions and forecast

---

[24] Including the level of public current spending (*PCUR*), the rate of levy on personal income tax (*RPS*), a sales tax change (affecting *STMV* and *ITR*) and an interest rate change (affecting *RMFD* and *RGS*). The maximum sizes of the applied shocks would represent quite dramatic changes in the respective policy instruments.

Table 2

Statistics for short-term forecasts from 1967IV for personal consumption expenditure on durables CD (80 stochastic replications with antithetic errors) ($ millions)

Quarter	Deter-ministic solution	Mean solution	Upper limit	Lower limit	Range	Var-iance	Standard deviation
1967IV	469.0	469.2	490.0	448.0	42.0	116.7	10.8
1968I	470.0	470.0	509.0	431.0	78.0	170.1	13.0
II	475.0	475.3	512.0	438.0	74.0	169.7	13.0
III	473.0	473.0	512.0	434.0	78.0	182.7	13.5
IV	484.0	483.5	515.0	452.0	63.0	215.4	14.7
1969I	500.0	499.8	531.0	468.0	63.0	196.7	14.0
II	511.0	510.9	546.0	476.0	70.0	222.0	14.9
III	522.0	522.0	569.0	474.0	95.0	336.0	18.3
IV	529.0	529.4	600.0	459.0	141.0	423.5	20.6
1970I	522.0	522.2	581.0	464.0	117.0	481.2	21.9
II	525.0	525.1	576.0	474.0	102.0	507.3	22.5
III	527.0	526.7	577.0	476.0	101.0	423.3	20.6
IV	543.0	543.4	599.0	488.0	111.0	311.7	17.7

values for the exogenous variables were taken from within the sample period. For each period chosen, a large number of stochastic replications[25] were executed and the results processed to yield estimates of the mean, range and standard deviation in each forecast quarter for each endogenous variable; in addition, each mean time-path is compared with a forecast obtained by deterministic simulation. Some of these results are shown in figure 2 and table 2.

For the second objective, initial conditions were again taken from the sample period, but the option mentioned above to hold the exogenous variables constant was employed. Steady-state stochastic responses were recorded after discarding 150 transient-period observations. In the experiments conducted to date, 250 steady-state observations have been found adequate to achieve good resolution of the spectral estimates; ten to twenty replications were employed in each experiment and the spectral estimation procedures used are based on those suggested by Tukey et al.

[25] 80 have been used in experiments reported here.

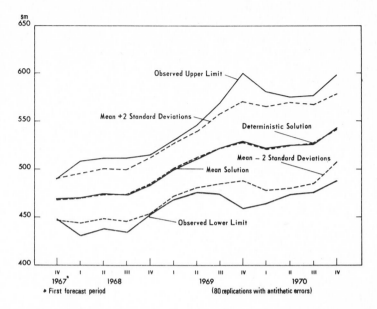

Fig.2. Confidence ranges for short-term forecasts of personal consumption expenditure on durables *CD*.

in [2] and [24]. For a particular replication, each series is pre-processed by the removal of a least-squares linear time trend, then a "taper" is applied at each end of the series, with weights rising smoothly from zero to one along a cosine curve at the left-hand end of the series, and falling to zero along the mirror-image curve at the right-hand end of the series. The fraction of the length of the series which is tapered determines the shape of the spectral window of the estimated spectra; a taper extending over one-tenth of the length at each end has been chosen here. After tapering, each series is augmented with zeros to bring its length to the nearest power of two (in this case, 256); then the series are taken in pairs and their discrete Fourier transforms obtained by the Cooley-Tukey algorithm [3], yielding complex amplitudes at the periodogram frequencies (128 in this case). To obtain the power spectra, the moduli of these complex amplitudes are averaged in groups of (say) 4; in the present case this gives 32 frequency bands, the first band above the zero frequency being centred at

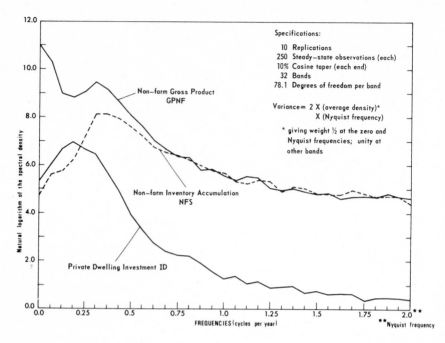

Fig.3. Examples of logarithms of power spectra of stochastic responses.

16 years per cycle. A selection of the power spectra obtained are shown in figure 3.

The results in figure 3 reveal some striking features. The stochastic response of Non-Farm Inventory Accumulation *NFS* shows a very pronounced peak in its spectrum in the neighbourhood of 2.7–3.2 years per cycle. This inventory cycle appears also in the spectrum of Non-Farm Gross Product *GPNF* which otherwise follows Granger's [7] "typical shape" for the spectrum of an aggregate economic variable. It should be noted that the *observed historical* behaviour of the endogenous variables may have been dominated by the forced response to exogenous variables, and that the contribution of the model's stochastic response to the observed sample-period variation in the endogenous variables cannot be uniquely determined. Thus one would not necessarily expect the spectra of the model's stochastic responses to have the shapes typically found in the spectra of the corresponding historical series.

The historical spectrum of Private Dwelling Investment *ID*, for instance, would in all probability be much closer to Granger's "typical shape" than to the shape found for the spectrum of the stochastic response of this variable, which shows a pronounced peak at 5.3 years per cycle, a peak which is not apparent in the stochastic response of Non-Farm Gross Product. Apart from these few features of interest, the spectral results to hand so far do not suggest a model which is rich in dynamic structure. However, as sectors at present being developed are incorporated into the model the picture will undoubtedly change.

One encouraging feature of the results is that the differences between forecasts made using deterministic simulation and average time-paths obtained from stochastic simulation appear to be negligible in the results obtained so far. A typical example of this may be seen in figure 2, which compared these forecasts for the series *CD*, Personal Consumption Expenditure on durables. Such results suggest that one is justified in using the computationally cheaper deterministic simulation procedures for the production of short-

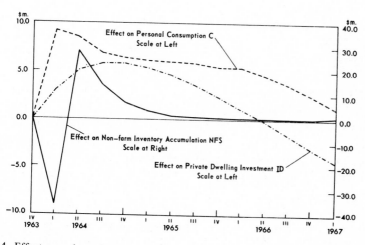

Fig. 4. Effects on three variables of a one-shot increase of $75m in public current expenditure *PCUR* in 1964I.

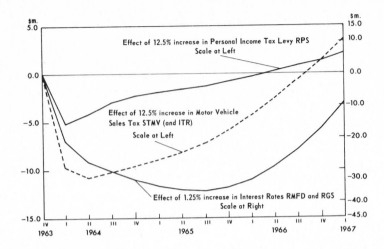

Fig.5. Effects on non-farm gross product of one-shot increases in various policy instruments in 1964I.

term forecasts and policy package simulations. Examples of policy simulations are given in figures 4 and 5 (as well as in table 1).

Interesting comparisons may be drawn between the speeds of response of Non-Farm Gross Product to changes in the four policies considered; it would also be interesting to compute the changes required to produce the same effect on Non-Farm Gross Product within (say) the first year – however, there is not space here to discuss these matters.

References

[1] I. Adelman and F.L. Adelman, "The dynamic properties of the Klein-Goldberger model", *Econometrica* 27 (1959) 596–625.

[2] C. Bingham, M.D. Godfrey and J.W. Tukey, "Modern techniques of power spectrum estimation", *IEEE Transactions on Audio and Electroacoustics* **AU-15** (1967) 56–66.

[3] J.W. Cooley and J.W. Tukey, "An algorithm for the machine calculation of complex Fourier series", *Mathematics of Computation* **19** (1965) 297–301.

[4] G.S. Fishman, *Spectral methods in econometrics* (Santa Monica, Calif., Rand Corporation, 1969).

[5] A.S. Goldberger, *Impact multipliers and dynamic properties of the Klein-Goldberger model* (Amsterdam, North-Holland Publishing Company, 1959).

[6] A.S. Goldberger, A.L. Nagar and H.S. Odeh, "The covariance matrices of reduced-form coefficients and of forecasts for a structural econometric model", *Econometrica* **29** (1961) 556–573.

[7] C.W.J. Granger, "The typical spectral shape of an economic variable", *Econometrica* **34** (1966) 150–161.

[8] G.R. Green with M. Liebenberg and A.A. Hirsch, "Short- and long-term simulations with the OBE econometric model". Paper prepared for the Conference on Econometric Models of Cyclical Behaviour, Cambridge, Mass., November 1969.

[9] E.J. Hannan, *Time series analysis* (London, Methuen, 1960).

[10] E.J. Hannan, *Multiple time series* (New York, John Wiley and Sons Inc., 1970).

[11] C. Hastings Jr., *Approximations for digital computers* (Princeton, University Press, 1955).

[12] M.J. Healy, "Multiple regression with a singular matrix", *Applied Statistics* **17** (1968) 10–17, and Algorithm AS6, 195–196.

[13] C.I. Higgins, "A model for national income forecasting". Paper presented to the Canberra Branch of the Economic Society of Australia and New Zealand, November 1970.

[14] C.I. Higgins, "A wage-price sector for a quarterly Australian model", in: this volume, p. 115.

[15] E.P. Howrey, "Dynamic properties of stochastic linear econometric models". Research Memo. No.87, Econometric Research Program, Princeton University (1967).

[16] E.P. Howrey, "Dynamic properties of a condensed version of the Wharton model". Paper prepared for the Conference on Econometric Models of Cyclical Behaviour, Cambridge, Mass., November 1969.

[17] E.P. Howrey, "Structural change and post-war economic stability: an econometric test", *Review of Economics and Statistics* **52** (1970) 18–25.

[18] E.P. Howrey, "Stochastic properties of the Klein-Goldberger model", *Econometrica* **39** (1971) 73–87.

[19] E.P. Howrey and H.H. Kelejian, "Dynamic econometric models: simulation versus analytic solutions". Paper presented at the Symposium on the Design of Computer Simulation Experiments, Duke University, Durham, N.C., October 1968.

[20] E.P. Howrey and L.R. Klein, "Dynamic properties of nonlinear econometric models". Paper presented at the Second World Congress of the Econometric Society, Cambridge, England, September 1970.

[21] A.L. Nagar, "Stochastic simulations of the Brookings econometric model", in: *The Brookings model – some further results,* edited by J.S. Duesenberry et al. (Amsterdam, North-Holland Publishing Company, 1969).

[22] T.H. Naylor, K. Wertz and T.H. Wonnacott, "Spectral analysis of data generated by simulation experiments with econometric models", *Econometrica* **37** (1969) 333–352.

[23] M.R. Norman, "Solving a non-linear econometric model". Paper presented to a meeting of the American Economic Association, Washington, December 1967.

[24] J.W. Tukey, "An introduction to the calculations of numerical spectrum analysis", in: *Advanced seminar on spectral analysis of time series,* edited by B. Harris (New York, John Wiley and Sons Inc., 1967), pp.25–46.

STOCHASTIC SIMULATION OF MACROECONOMETRIC MODELS: METHODOLOGY AND INTERPRETATION *

Eric R. SOWEY

University of New South Wales

PART 1. STOCHASTIC SIMULATION: A DISCUSSION ON METHODOLOGY

1. Validation by simulation

Macroeconometric model building involves several distinct steps. These are, in sequence: specification, identification, estimation, validation and finally application in some inferential fashion, usually *ex ante* forecasting or the comparative analysis of alternative policy proposals. It is with the fourth of these stages that we are presently concerned.

Validation of a model is here regarded as distinct from verification of the model. Indeed, verification – establishing whether the model is 'true' – is essentially a fruitless objective, since, after all, no conclusive evidence can ever be adduced about the precise way in which complex economic forces interact.

By validation, on the other hand, is understood simply determining whether the model fulfils well the demands made of it. It is not a question whether the model embodies strictly causal me-

* My warm thanks go to Dr. W.E. Norton and Mr. J. Henderson of the Reserve Bank of Australia for their generous assistance in providing me with the data and specification for the model examined in part 2 of this paper and for many helpful discussions. I am indebted also to Professors N.C. Kakwani, L.R. Klein and J.W. Nevile for their comments on a draft of this paper. – None of these people is responsible for any errors there may be here. Neither is our IBM 360/50 computer. Though it didn't always do what I wanted it to do, it always did exactly what I told it to.

chanisms, but rather whether the estimated model, with all its inherent imperfections, does an adequate job of prediction, both within and beyond the estimation period. To a degree, validation of the model within the estimation period is carried out at the estimation stage. Tests of significance on estimated coefficients, R^2 and the Durbin-Watson statistic, all provide information on the 'explanatory power' of the individual structural equations. But, especially in the case of a nonlinear model, it is not until all the separate members of the model are integrated and the entire model is solved that its quality over the estimation period is apparent. Holt ([24], p. 639) observes:

> 'The use of the same set of data (as were the basis for estimation) to test the model would appear somewhat questionable. However, ... it is quite possible for the individual equations ... to fit reasonably well, but when all the equations are solved jointly, errors may accumulate and a bad fit may be obtained.'

In a good forecasting model, of course, we expect that the solution path for the various endogenous variables will approximate quite closely their actual path, at least over the estimation period and a few subsequent periods. While it is always possible to compare actual and model solution values over the estimation period, this can be done beyond the estimation period only if the test is carried out after the *ex ante* forecast period has become the actual past. There remains, however, a difference between this approach and that used when the model is used to forecast the actual future. In the former case forecasts are made and evaluated conditional on the *true* values of exogenous variables, while in the latter, forecasts are conditional on *projected* values for those variables.

A model validated, however comprehensively, from historical data can never ensure the sustained quality of forecasts into the future. Primarily this is because of errors, just mentioned, in projecting the exogenous variables and the possibility of massive structural change occurring, but also on account of a variety of other errors, whose source will be described briefly in the second part of this paper. It follows that *ex ante* forecasting with a macroeconometric model must be looked on as very much a short-run affair.

It is clear, then, that the process of validation must be regarded as, at best, a close approximation to the unattainable ideal of verification. Nonetheless, it is reasonable to believe that a model which has shown itself to be valid in the historical context and, hence, has presumably captured the leading attributes of the economy's underlying structure, will yield more reliable forecasts in the short term than a model that has not been so validated.

Now, for a static (lagless) model that is entirely linear in the variables, it is almost trivially simple to derive the reduced form and hence obtain the period-by-period solution by substituting successive sets of values for the exogenous variables. Deriving the solution path for endogenous variables is only slightly more difficult in the case of a dynamic (lagged) model, linear in the variables. In this case, the dynamic structure of the model will be represented in a series of (probably non-homogeneous) difference equations, which can be solved explicitly by standard analytical methods (see Goldberg [18]). Depending on the relative sizes of the coefficients in the difference equations, the time path of solutions for the endogenous variables will exhibit smooth growth or decline, or some oscillatory pattern.

The distinctive feature of the analytical procedure used for the above two classes of models is that a perfectly general solution is obtained. That is, it is possible to determine directly the model solution values for a particular period, given only the values of exogenous variables demanded by the specification, and without reference to solution values in any prior period.

Most realistic macroeconometric models are nonlinear to some extent and hence do not fit into the categories just described. For a dynamic model composed of simultaneous nonlinear difference equations, an analytical solution for all the endogenous variables will ordinarily be unobtainable and resort must be had to some numerical solution technique. Such a technique does not yield a general form of solution: instead, the solution values for each period must be 'cranked out' successively (preferably with computer assistance). Evidently it also is not possible to deduce *a priori* the dynamic characteristics of the model. The model's dynamic structure can be inferred only from examination of the time-pattern of solutions, computed period by period.

The synthetic representation of reality by sequential solution of a mathematical model, conditional on estimates of the model's parameters and on actual or supposed values of the exogenous variables, is commonly termed simulation. It will be understood, then, that simulation is particularly relevant for the validation and analysis of dynamic nonlinear econometric models. This is not to say that simulation techniques cannot be applied to fully linear models: simply that

'once the classical regression tests concerning the parameters and the residuals of (such) an econometric model have been carried out, the results of further tests of the model via comparisons of linear functions of the historical and simulated values of the endogenous variables over the period of estimation contain no additional information about the validity of the model' (Howrey and Kelejian [26], p.303).

2. Simulation categories

Simulation, applied in the evaluation of macroeconometric models, has a number of assignable attributes which govern the interpretation to be given to the results derived. These attributes are drawn from three independent dichotomous categories:

(a) one-step or dynamic simulation;
(b) deterministic or stochastic simulation;
(c) control or experimental simulation.

The choice made in each of these categories has implications that deserve further discussion.

2.1. One-step vs. dynamic simulation

In one-step simulation, the model is solved, each period, using actual values for the lagged endogenous variables, whereas in dynamic simulation, previous solution values are used for the lagged endogenous variables. Thus, dynamic simulation displays the model's inherent dynamic characteristics, whilst in one-step simulation, the model is continually constrained to follow closely the actual path of the endogenous variables.

Which mode of simulation is preferable? This question is, of course, relevant only to a prediction period in the actual past (which may possibly include an interval of historical future, as reckoned from the last estimation period). The answer depends on the purpose of the investigation. If the objective is validation, then dynamic simulation offers a more exacting test of the model's stability, and hence its capacity to follow the sequence of recorded events. Since, moreover, the dynamic solution path usually tends to diverge progressively from the true path, owing to cumulation of discrepancies, it is possible from graphical examination of the two time paths for each endogenous variable to draw conclusions about the quality of different parts of the model's specification. Thereby, selective alterations can be made to the model in an attempt to improve its *ex post* predictive capacity. However, once the model is judged satisfactory in its tracking of past period values and a single period forecast into the actual future is sought, greater accuracy will be obtained by one-step simulation.

2.2. Deterministic vs. stochastic simulation

Whether simulation is to be stochastic or deterministic is another matter for consideration. Indeed, this question is of considerable significance in the methodology of simulation and, after brief discussion here, will be taken up again in section 3, below.

The standard scheme for specifying behavioural equations in econometrics assigns a random disturbance (additively or multiplicatively) to the combination of explanatory variables. The inclusion of this stochastic component can be justified in a variety of ways (Johnston [29], p.10): it is this component that necessitates the application of statistical methods in econometric analysis. The presence of stochastic elements in each behavioural equation of the model specification raises the question whether their effect should not also be embodied when simulating. In other words, should not simulation be stochastic? The alternative would be that each disturbance be assigned its certainty equivalence expectation, namely zero, in which case simulation would be deterministic.

Stochastic simulation requires that a random shock, drawn from a prespecified multivariate distribution, be applied to each behavioural equation when the model is solved. The joint distribution from which these stochastic elements are drawn should, naturally, reflect the true model structure as fully as possible. Accordingly, in addition to mirroring the population variances of each equation's disturbance, the joint distribution should also preserve the inter-equation covariance pattern of the disturbances and even their within-equation serial correlation structure.[1]

Techniques for setting up a matrix of disturbances with the required properties have been devised by Nagar [36] and Mc-Carthy [33]. Both methods are based on transformation of the computed residuals from the estimated model. McCarthy's method is the more elegant and is also computationally simpler. For these reasons, it was chosen for the stochastic simulations described in part 2 of this paper.

Certainly there is no assurance that the shocks assigned in one stochastic simulation run with a model will coincide in magnitude and sign with the true disturbances. So that, given the results of a single deterministic and a single stochastic run, there is no basis for presuming that the latter will better describe reality than the former. The key characteristic of stochastic simulation, however, is that replicated simulations produce a distribution of outcomes for each period. Such a distribution provides valuable information for

---

[1] The remarks made earlier, concerning the use of analytical solution procedures for a linear model, related to the model's deterministic solution. If a stochastic solution is desired, the same analytical methods are still valid, but they will then be applied to a structure which includes a matrix of synthetically generated stochastic elements with the properties just noted.

statistical analysis — the nature of which will be examined presently.

2.3. Control vs. experimental simulation

Finally, in our account of categories of simulation, we deal with
control and experimental simulations. A control simulation is one
performed with all variable values as actually measured and all
regression coefficients as actually estimated. The results of this
mode of simulation form the basis of comparison for any further
simulation experiments, in which certain coefficients and/or certain variable values may deliberately be modified. Such further
simulations are termed experimental simulations and are of two
kinds, which we may call "perturbed model" and "policy" simulations.

The estimated equation coefficients in an econometric model
are, of course, random variables and it is open to enquiry what
effect small changes (say, within one standard error) in these coefficients may have on the model solution values. Similar reasoning applies to projected values of the exogenous variables, to
which small perturbations may be applied and the consequent
effects on *ex ante* model solutions examined. The point of such
perturbed model simulations is to discover whether the econometric model being analysed has any marked tendencies to insta-
bility and to what degree it is sensitive to moderate displacements
in its estimated parameters and exogenous inputs. Extreme sensitivity, if not directly attributable to the true state of the world,
bodes ill for the continuing successful use of the model for short
term forecasting.

When changes are made to specific policy instruments among
the exogenous variables, simulation enables the effect of the
implied economic policies to be explored, compared and contrast-
ed. Such policy simulations are of interest when performed *ex
post,* for the information they provide on various tax and expenditure multipliers and on 'what might have been done', but their
real worth rests on the insights they can give about the course of
events in the future. It is certainly less costly to evaluate and rank

policy alternatives, even imperfectly, with a carefully validated, up-to-date and reasonably disaggregated model than to embark directly on a course of policy action whose eventual quantitative effects on target variables can only be hazarded.

The number and variety of different possible perturbed model and policy simulations that might be carried out with any particular model is, quite clearly, almost limitless. In the case of policy simulation, for instance, the instrument variables might be modified singly, in pairs, in threes etc. Also, one may wish to try out several different levels of every policy variable and to examine the effects of impulse (or short-term) changes and of sustained changes in these variables.

A systematic procedure for the performance and analysis of such compound simulation experiments is provided by the statistical principles of experimental design. Discussion of these principles is, however, beyond the scope of the present paper: skeleton surveys with useful bibliographies are to be found in papers by Hunter and Naylor [27] and Naylor et al. [38].

3. The significance of stochastic simulation

We examine now the merits of stochastic simulation and the grounds on which it may be preferred to deterministic simulation.

What is probably the earliest example of stochastic simulation in a macroeconometric context, viz. the study of cyclical behaviour by Fisher [10], shows the possibility of generating cycles in income by subjecting the two behavioural equations of a simple three-equation macroeconometric model to exogenous random shocks. Without the shocks, the model's response over time was found to be continuously damped. Fisher's results are theoretical evidence in support of the conception that business cycles are predominantly induced by random disturbances in the economy – a credible notion first propounded by Frisch [13] on the basis of the remarkable work of Slutsky [46], and vigorously endorsed by Haavelmo [20] among others. More recently, Adelman and Adelman ([2], pp. 619–20), examining the Klein-Goldberger model, concluded:

'... the behaviour of the model is remarkably stable, as evidenced by the fact that the solution resumes its unperturbed equilibrium growth trend even after a strong exogenous disturbance.

On the other hand, when random shocks of a realistic order of magnitude are superimposed upon the original form of the Klein-Goldberger equations, the cyclical fluctuations which result are remarkably similar to those described by the NBER as characterizing the United States economy.'

And Evans et al. [9], investigating the Wharton model, found similarly that 'the cyclical behaviour of most variables in the system became more measurable in the stochastic than in the nonstochastic simulations'.

These studies (though the last ranges considerably more widely) all deal with the application of a *single* stochastic simulation in verifying the Slutsky effect in macroeconometric systems. This, indeed, has been historically the prime motive for stochastic simulation. But stochastic simulation has more to recommend it.

As was earlier pointed out, simulation emerges as the principal tool for assessing the performance of nonlinear econometric models. A specific attribute of stochastic simulation, not shared by deterministic simulation, is the possibility of *replicating* the simulation experiment over the same time path, incorporating a different set of generated random shocks each time. The resulting set of replicated simulations provides a cross-section distribution of simulated values for each time period. Valuable information may be derived from these distributional data and, by the application of a variety of inferential techniques, many pertinent conclusions may be drawn. The single sequence generated by deterministic simulation, on the other hand, precludes such analyses.

Techniques specifically appropriate to the analysis of replicated stochastic simulations include: establishment of tolerance intervals for validation and prediction, and performance of significance tests and multiple rankings for policy comparisons. These are considered in the next section.

At the simplest level, the series of values obtained by averaging stochastic simulations over replications in each period (the 'mean stochastic simulation') may be regarded as a measure alternative to the deterministic simulation for validating a model and for *ex ante* forecasting.

It is apparent that, in a dynamic *ex post* simulation with a lagged model, the mean stochastic simulation will not commonly coincide with the actual endogenous variable values when several replications are performed. But neither, in all likelihood, will a deterministic simulation. Unfortunately, there are no general practical criteria to determine which of the two simulation paths will approach more closely the actual values in any particular period. It would seem reasonable, therefore, to examine the historical fit of both the deterministic and the mean stochastic simulation results and decide pragmatically which alternative to adopt when *ex ante* forecasts are sought.

And yet, from a theoretical viewpoint, the matter is more subtle than this. In a most perceptive paper [26], Howrey and Kelejian have demonstrated under very general conditions that deterministic simulation of a nonlinear model yields results that are (even asymptotically) biased from values that would in theory be obtained from the reduced form. There is, however, no such asymptotic bias for the expectation of replicated stochastic simulations. These results, whilst not conclusive for the practical finite sample case, at least 'suggest that the properties of dynamic nonlinear models should not be studied in terms of nonstochastic simulation procedures' ([26], p.309).

Stochastic simulation, then, has the following four significant attributes:

(1) A single stochastic simulation can be used to assess a model's dynamic response over future periods, when it is the 'profile' of the time path that is of interest, rather than the exact time path values.

And for a replicated stochastic simulation:

(2) The mean over replications is a practical alternative to deterministic simulation and may frequently accord better with actually observed values.

(3) There is scope for using a variety of inferential techniques that exploit the richer information content of two-dimensional data.

(4) A desirable asymptotic property obtains in relation to the theoretical reduced form of the true model specification.

4. Evaluating simulations

In empirical work, the actual generation of simulated model results is no more than a preliminary. These results will reveal little of significance unless analysed further. Some form of graphical representation of the actual and simulated time-series is usually considered indispensable.

Rather surprisingly, very many reports of computer simulation experiments go little beyond a discussion of the points of interest revealed by visual inspection of these graphs. Much more detailed information is derivable by computing a variety of summary measures, some of which can be tested for significance using established statistical techniques. The techniques that are appropriate differ according as the objective of the simulation is the validation of the model (by comparing the *ex post* forecast series with the actual values of selected endogenous variables), or the evaluation of alternative policy proposals in the *ex ante* domain.

4.1. Historical validation

First, for the task of historical validation, we discuss
    (a) analytical measures without statistical significance points;
    (b) analytical measures whose significance can be tested.

(a) *Non-testable measures*:
(1) Given series which are sufficiently long to display a number of clearly defined cyclical movements, it is possible to compare their period and timing with standard 'reference cycles', where these have been established. Though an object of research in the U.S.A. since the early 1940's, specification of reference cycles has

been undertaken only quite recently in Australia. Of particular interest here is the paper by Bush and Cohen [6]. The goodness of fit of a particular series to the relevant reference series may be expressed by means of an index of conformity, defined and applied in Adelman and Adelman ([2], p.618). The approach is also well illustrated in the study by Moore et al. [35]. Reference cycle comparisons have not been attempted in part 2 of this paper owing to the comparative shortness of the simulation period examined there.

(2) To measure the degree of absolute correspondence of simulated and actual series, one may use the well-known root mean square error.

$$\text{R.M.S.E.} = \left[\frac{1}{T} \sum_{t=1}^{T} (P_t - A_t)^2 \right]^{\frac{1}{2}}, \qquad t = 1, 2, ..., T \ ;$$

where P_t = predicted (deterministic or mean stochastic) value in period t, and A_t = actual value in period t.

This is rather a crude measure. For one thing, it does not discriminate between 'overpredictions' and 'underpredictions' of the same magnitude and, furthermore, it is quite uninformative on the degree of correspondence of turning points between actual and simulated series. In part 2 the R.M.S.E. measure has been employed in dimensionless terms (to facilitate comparisons between different variables) in the form:

$$\left[\sum (P_t - A_t)^2 / \sum A_t^2 \right]^{1/2} .$$

(3) Another goodness-of-fit criterion, which implicitly measures the accuracy of turning point predictions, has been given by Theil ([47], pp.28, 40–43, 59). This is the so-called inequality statistic. There is, in fact, a whole family of inequality statistics. Each one compares the model's accuracy in predicting changes with the accuracy that would be attained using some particular 'naive' (mechanistic) forecasting rule.

Two such inequality statistics are

$$T_1 = \frac{\sum(p_t - a_t)^2}{\sum a_t^2} \qquad \begin{array}{l} T_1 = 0 \text{ if } p_t = a_t \text{ (for all } t); \\ \quad 1 \text{ if } p_t = 0 \text{ (for all } t); \end{array} \qquad (8.1)$$

$$T_2 = \frac{\sum(p_t - a_t)^2}{\sum(a_t - a_{t-1})^2} \qquad \begin{array}{l} T_2 = 0 \text{ if } p_t = a_t \quad \text{(for all } t); \\ \quad 1 \text{ if } p_t = a_{t-1} \text{ (for all } t); \end{array} \qquad (8.2)$$

where p_t = predicted % change between periods t and $t-1$; and a_t = actual % change between periods t and $t-1$ (percentage rather than simple changes being used to facilitate comparisons between different variables).

Each of these statistics has the value zero when changes are predicted perfectly in both magnitude and direction. T_1 and T_2 have the value unity when, respectively, the naive 'no change' model and the naive 'same change' model is valid. Values greater than 1 indicate that the model's predictions of change are poorer even than those given by the corresponding mechanistic formula. It is clearly desirable to have values of T_1 and T_2 as close to zero as possible. Theil ([47], pp. 40–43) has, on quite restrictive assumptions of normality and independence, derived the large sample variance of T_1. This result cannot be applied with any confidence for significance testing in small sample cases.

(4) In place of the two naive models that underlie the inequality statistics mentioned, one may substitute more complex variants with greater predictive power. Comparison with such variants would constitute a more stringent test of the model. Theil ([47], p.59) proposes, as an alternative mechanistic criterion for comparison, the sum of squared deviations from the *average* realization over a number of past periods.

Mincer and Zarnowitz ([34], pp. 32–38) and Zarnowitz ([49], ch.6) suggest yet another criterion: the sum of squared prediction errors from an autoregressive structure with a specified number of lags. The particular length of lag might be chosen so that the prediction error is minimised. Though these writers are concerned with evaluating so-called 'business forecasts', their idea is no less applicable to the evaluation of forecasts from econometric model simulations.

All the measures[2] just quoted involve accumulating forecast errors by squaring them. It is also possible to accumulate the errors in modulus form, as Moore et al. do in [35]. It should be noted that this latter method, perhaps inappropriately, attaches equal weight to both large and small forecast errors.

(b) *Statistically testable measures*:

(1) The relation between actual and predicted levels of a variable may be written

$$A_t = P_t + u_t , \tag{8.3}$$

where the random variable u_t is the forecast error. If the population average value of u_t is zero, the prediction procedure is termed 'unbiased'.

Now, in a simple linear regression of A_t on P_t,

$$A_t = \alpha + \beta P_t + v_t , \tag{8.4}$$

the least squares estimator of β is

$$b = \frac{\sum (P_t - \bar{P})(A_t - \bar{A})}{\sum (P_t - \bar{P})^2} ,$$

where the barred symbols represent sample means. Substituting from (8.3),

$$b = \frac{\sum (P_t - \bar{P})(P_t + u_t - \bar{P} - \bar{u})}{\sum (P_t - \bar{P})^2} = 1 + \frac{\sum (u_t - \bar{u})(P_t - \bar{P})}{\sum (P_t - \bar{P})^2} .$$

---

[2] In exploratory evaluation of an econometric model's characteristics through simulation, attributes other than goodness of fit to historical data may be of interest. For example, measures of linearity and symmetry of response in experimental simulation are proposed by Zellner [50] in the present volume.

Hence, only when u_t and P_t are uncorrelated (i.e., when forecast errors are not systematically related to the magnitudes predicted) do we have

$$\beta \, (= \text{plim } b) = 1 \, .$$

If this is the case, the prediction procedure is termed 'efficient'. It follows that if the prediction procedure is both unbiased and efficient

$$\alpha = 0 \, ,$$

where $\alpha = \text{plim } a = \bar{E}(A_t) - \beta.\bar{E}(P_t)$ and $\bar{E}$ indicates asymptotic expectation.

To examine the attributes of predictions from model simulation, we may regress actual on predicted values and then (on the reasonable supposition that u_t, v_t are normal and on the less tenable assumption that variable values do not have severe serial correlation) make:

(i) an F-test on the joint null hypothesis $\{\alpha = 0, \beta = 1\}$. Acceptance of this hypothesis implies that predictions are both unbiased and efficient. Rejection of the hypothesis indicates separate tests:

(ii) a t-test of the hypothesis $E(A_t) = E(P_t)$, for unbiasedness.

(iii) a t-test of the hypothesis $\beta = 1$, for efficiency.

The choice of the regression of A_t on P_t, rather than conversely, is prompted by the desire to be able to apply an optimal linear correction to predictions, should the above tests all prove significant. The matter is discussed in Theil ([47], pp. 34–36). These significance tests may be applied in parallel fashion to an estimated regression of relative change in A_t on relative change in P_t.

(2) All the foregoing measures, whether testable or not, are equally applicable to a deterministic or a mean stochastic simulation sequence. There is, however, a further evaluative measure which, by its very nature, refers specifically to the data generated by a replicated stochastic simulation. This is the nonparametric tolerance interval. An $\alpha\%$ tolerance interval with coverage P and upper and lower limits L_1 and L_2, based on a sample of size n, is an

interval such that the probability is $\alpha\%$ that in repeated sampling at least a proportion P of the population from which the sample was drawn will lie between L_1 and L_2. This concept was introduced by Wilks [48], who showed, moreover, that the tolerance interval may be defined independently of the form of the population distribution. As a particular case, the limits L_1 and L_2 can be taken at the endpoints of the sample range. Then it can be shown that α, P and n are related by the result:

$$\frac{\alpha}{100} = 1 - nP^{n-1} + (n-1)P^n .$$

Thus, for each time period, the maximum and minimum of a set of replicated stochastic simulations define a tolerance interval whose coverage, P, can be determined for fixed n (number of replications) and specified α. The need to solve a nonlinear equation for P can be averted by using a nomograph linking α, n, P such as is given in Gumbel ([19], p.105). For example, for $n = 20$ and $\alpha = 98\%$ the value of P is found to be 0.927. One can be 98% confident that, on average, the limits of the replication range contain 92.7% of the population density. Conversely, one may determine the number of replications required for a tolerance interval having prespecified α and P. Thus, the number of replications performed in a stochastic simulation experiment, commonly decided on purely *ad hoc* grounds, is here shown to be rationally determinable.

Evidently, for appropriately chosen α, n, P, the maximum and minimum of the stochastic simulation runs represent informative boundaries in comparison with which the model's fit to historical data can be evaluated. Should the actual values, period by period, not lie within the interval defined by the maximum and minimum of the replicated simulations, then the model may be regarded as being significantly in error. The caveat must be expressed that the tolerance interval for each time period must be considered in isolation. Because of correlation between successive time-series values, comparisons between periods are likely to be invalid.

Indeed, the problem of serial correlation over time bedevils most attempts to construct testable measures of the goodness of fit and predictive accuracy of simulations. For this reason, Gadd and Wold's [17] Janus quotient, for example, is of limited usefulness. Not only are the usual parametric tests invalid *across time periods,* so also are nonparametric tests which, but for serial correlation, would be quite appropriate. The paired sign test and the Wilcoxon paired two-sample test are cases in point (see Bradley [5], p. 171).

An analytically significant feature of replicated stochastic simulation is that the several simulation runs can be generated independently. Hence, reliance can be placed in the results of tests performed *across replications.* Such tests are especially valuable for comparing the consequences of alternative policies in *ex ante* simulations.

4.2. Comparing alternative policies

When endogenous variable values are forecast several periods into the future under different policy assumptions but towards some common goal, it is usually not very enlightening to compare the forecast time paths period by period. Of greater significance are comparisons of some summary measure of each simulation's characteristics, e.g., the mean or variance over time or, perhaps, the mean square deviation from some subjectively-rated optimal time-path approach to the target. Then each policy simulation is replicated n times, random shocks being generated independently between replications. The summary measure is computed for each replication and a sample of n independent values from the population distribution of that measure results. Suppose k alternative policies are conceived of; then the problem is to select appropriate statistical procedures for making comparisons among the k samples of size n.

For testing the homogeneity of means the usual one-way analysis of variance model is appropriate. If variances are to be tested for equality across the k samples, Bartlett's test (see Anderson and Bancroft [3]) may be used. More elaborate techniques, however, are available. The joint testing of all pairs of differences of means is a problem in multiple comparisons. And the ordering, according to the summary measure specified, of the policies that will on balance of probability perform best, second best, etc. in actuality, is a problem in multiple ranking. This is a statistical problem, since it is not certain that a ranking by sample magnitudes necessarily corresponds with the conceptual ranking of the underlying populations.

It must be noted that these parametric procedures are all quite strongly dependent on an assumption of normality of population distributions that cannot always be supported. It may, however, be possible to apply transformations that endow the test statistics with a closer approximation to normality. Alternatively, the use of distribution-free tests (e.g. the Kolmogorov-Smirnov test for comparing means) may be contemplated, though their scope is rather more limited.

Procedures for comparing alternative policies on the basis of replicated stochastic simulation will not be pursued further here. Reference is made to the papers by Naylor, Wertz and Wonnacott [39] and Kleijnen and Naylor [30] in which the techniques mentioned above, especially multiple comparison and multiple ranking, are surveyed in greater detail.

4.3. Spectral analysis

Spectral methods are a powerful means for deducing the dynamic properties of a linear econometric system from information contained in the matrix of computed residuals after estimation. Nonlinear models are amenable to these techniques, provided that they are first linearized approximately. The paper by Howrey [25] shows well how effective use may be made of a spectral analytic approach, in lieu of stochastic simulation of the model. However, spectral analysis is concerned primarily with determining the nature of the model's general dynamic properties, rather than with the specific time-path values its component endogenous variables may trace out.

For analysis of nonlinear models which are not readily linearized, spectral methods complement rather than contend with stochastic simulation. In particular, for evaluating alternative policies, comparisons over policies of the spectra of de-trended target variables are likely to be informative. Such comparisons will be more precise if confidence intervals for the true spectra are constructed around estimated spectra. The relevant techniques are discussed in most expositions of time series analysis: in the context of simulation, reference to articles by Naylor et al. [40] and Fishman and Kiviat [11] is specifically appropriate. An application of such methods is to be found in this volume FitzGerald [12]).

It is well to sound a caution on the use of spectral analysis in the evaluation of simulations. The requirements of stationarity are fairly exacting and not easily satisfied in work with empirical data. Heuristic 'treatment' of the data may be necessary to render them suitable for spectral analysis. Moreover, most of the statistical tests of significance that can be made are only approximate and their validity for small samples is not clearly established.

5. Experiences with stochastic simulation in macroeconometrics

The application of simulation techniques to the analysis of macroeconometric models is by no means well established. In particular, the exploration of model properties and policy implications through stochastic simulation seems, at least until a year or so ago, to have been almost totally neglected. Apart from the previously cited business cycle study by Adelman and Adelman [2] and its sequel [1] relating to longer cycles, the investigation by Duesenberry et al. [7] appears to have been the only publication prior to 1969 involving stochastic simulation in a macroeconometric context. All these writers employ stochastic simulation solely to examine their models' propensity to generate cyclical responses.

In 1969, Nagar's stochastic simulation [36] of the Brookings Model was published, and a conference was sponsored by the N.B.E.R. [41] in the course of which numerous stochastic simulations of the larger U.S. macroeconometric models were reported [9, 15, 35]. These simulation experiments are much more ambitious than those previously referred to. The N.B.E.R. Conference papers illustrate the utility of both deterministic and stochastic simulation and underline the practical significance of the latter, especially in longer term simulations.

Nonetheless, little use has yet been made of the statistical information embodied in replicated simulation data. Statistical testing of inferences from simulation is uncommon even in the most recent studies cited. And the *ex ante* evaluation of alternative policies on the basis of formal significance tests, as suggested in the previous section of this paper, still awaits application. Such techniques for evaluation are a valuable adjunct to the elegant but statistically inconclusive procedures advocated by Fromm and Taubman ([16], ch.5). And they are germane also to the more flexible approach to policy evaluation of Helliwell et al. ([21], p. 396) who recognise that

'... the one-by-one examination of policies forces us to ignore what is perhaps the most important aspect of the problem, namely, the choice of a mix of policies most appropriate in the light of several conflicting policy goals. In these circumstances the most powerful and fast-acting policies may not be at all appropriate; for what is needed is a range of policies with differential effects on the various target variables.'

6. Summary

The presence of stochastic disturbances in the specification of behavioural equations suggests that their influence be reproduced synthetically when simulating. This was the initial proposition in support of stochastic simulation of nonlinear models. Essentially, this proposition implies that, in the absence of randomly assigned shocks, simulation solutions will in some way be biased. Indeed, it is not a valid counter-argument that the representation of individual disturbances may be neglected because their average effect on solutions is zero. For, as Klein and Goldberger ([31], p. 75) observe, 'although disturbances are individually zero, on the average, their covariation need not be zero on the average. In a linear structural model, the error term of the (reduced form) equation is a linear function of error terms in the original structural equations, but in a nonlinear system this is not true. The (reduced form) equations will depend upon nonlinear functions of the separate disturbances and, in general, the estimated covariances of these disturbances will have to be taken into account.'

This thesis is proved by Howrey and Kelejian, in the course of their analytical study [26] referred to earlier. For the same reason, the possibility that disturbances may be serially correlated should also not be overlooked.

In addition to this asymptotic argument for stochastic simulation, there are a number of more practical justifications. Apart from measures based on replicated simulation data, there are virtually no measures of the goodness of fit or predictive accuracy of a nonlinear econometric model that are amenable to reliable tests of significance. The value of being able to assess statistically inferences drawn from simulation results must be rated highly. In fact, as examination of recent macroeconometric simulation studies has revealed, little use has as yet been made of the fruitful analyses that stochastic simulation data make possible. This may be largely because stochastic simulation is rather more laborious than deterministic simulation, and also more expensive in terms of computation costs. If, however, the potential of stochastic simulation is properly exploited for fuller information and the accurate interpretation of experimental conclusions, then its utilisation is amply vindicated.

PART 2. STOCHASTIC SIMULATION OF THE RESERVE BANK MODEL: RBA1

7. Introductory

Macroeconometric model building is still in its infancy in Australia, but is progressing vigorously. The first model of the Australian economy was presented by Nevile [42] (with 11 equations in annual terms) only a decade ago. Since then no fewer than five other models of the economy have appeared, that could be described as medium-sized (say, 15 equations or more). These are the work of Kmenta [32], Ironmonger and Kumar [28], Nevile [43], Higgins and FitzGerald [22] and Norton [44]. They each have between 18 and 21 equations except the last which has over 50. The last two of these models are cast in quarterly terms, the remainder in annual terms. For short-term forecasting and policy analysis quarterly models are, by virtue of their temporal disaggregation, intrinsically better suited than annual models. And, indeed, the two quarterly models cited were designed for just such purposes.

Some results of stochastic simulation of a version of Norton's model are reported below. This model, designated RBA 1, is a product of on-going research at the Reserve Bank of Australia. The model was first defined in January 1971; since then it has gone through considerable development. Hereafter, discussion of RBA 1 is to be understood as referring to the version of May 1971[3].

RBA 1 is a quarterly nonlinear model with 55 simultaneous equations, of which 24 are behavioural equations. There are 50 fully exogenous variables. Considerable use is made of distributed lag specifications and of multiplicative seasonal effects. The data used for estimation are seasonally unadjusted and expenditure variables are expressed in real terms at constant 1966–67 prices. A few variables appear in current price terms also. All indices in the model are relative to a base of 1.000 for 1966–67. Ordinary least squares were used for estimating the model, generally over the period 1959(1) to 1969(4). In seven cases, data limitations necessitated a shorter estimation period, but it was never shorter than 1963(2)–1969(4).

8. Simulation procedure

The model RBA1 has been simulated stochastically over the esti-

---

[3] A revised version of RBA 1 appears in chapter 3 of this volume.

mation period 1963(2)–1969(4) and for a further four quarters, using true values of the exogenous variables. The objectives of these simulations are:

(a) to assess the model's goodness-of-fit to past data (including four periods of the historical future) and hence to point up parts of the model where respecification may be desirable.

(b) to examine the model's differential behaviour under dynamic and one-step simulations.

(c) to compare the mean stochastic simulation path for selected endogenous variables with the deterministic simulation path, in order to discover whether either is systematically superior for point prediction.

Stochastic simulation has, as was explained in part 1, special value for the statistical comparison of alternative economic policies. No comparative analysis of stochastic policy simulations with RBA1 has been undertaken, however, since the model's specification has not yet reached a settled state. In these circumstances, the high cost in terms of computer and human time render such analysis unjustifiable.

The model was solved for values of the endogenous variables each period by means of the iterative algorithm known as the Gauss-Seidel method. This algorithm, originally devised for solving a set of simultaneous linear equations, is readily adaptable to the nonlinear case, as Fromm and Klein [14] describe. The Gauss-Seidel method has the drawback that convergence of the solution values in successive iterations is not assured. Unfortunately the formal conditions for convergence are of little more than theoretical value. However, in the computations actually performed, correspondence to five significant figures between successive iteration solutions was always attained within 22 iterations.

The effect of random shocks was simulated by means of pseudorandom numbers. These numbers were obtained by generating a set of independent standard normal variates using the method of Box and Muller [4], and then transforming these variates by the method of McCarthy [33] into normal variates having the same asymptotic variance-covariance structure as the true model disturbances.

Each stochastic simulation experiment was replicated 20 times. As explained in section 4.1 above, the maximum and minimum of these replicated values define, for each time period, a 98% tolerance interval with coverage 92.7%. These values were judged to specify a suitable tolerance region, consonant with reasonable computational cost, for validating the model's goodness-of-fit to actual data. It should be borne in mind that, with the tolerance coefficient fixed at 98%, coverage could be increased to 96.3%, for example, but only at the cost of doubling the number of replications. As the 100% coverage asymptote is approached, the relationship between increase in coverage and increase in number of replications required becomes more and more disproportionate.

Computer execution time on the IBM 360/50 for 20 replications, each one of which consisted in solving the model's 55 equations iteratively over 31 quarters, averaged 20 minutes. Input and output setup times for the computations occupied a little over two minutes. Thus each replication took just under a minute to perform.

9. Simulation results for validating RBA1

From the results of dynamic stochastic simulation of RBA1 over the period 1963(2)–1970(4) various summary measures were computed for evaluating the model's goodness of fit to historical data. These measures are presented in tables 2 and 3 for 20 selected endogenous variables, details of which are set out in table 1.

A comparison of the test statistics in columns 4–6 of tables 2 and 3 suggests that, by and large, the model more efficiently predicts percentage changes in endogenous variables than the actual levels of those variables. An interesting exception to this appears to be the set of implicit price deflators, most of which are more efficiently predicted as levels than as changes.

The changes in question are principally seasonal movements. Over the simulation period (1963–70), no marked peaks or troughs occurred in the level of general economic activity in Australia and it remains to be seen whether the foregoing conclu-

Table 1
20 endogenous variables from RBA1

Variable	Symbol	Units	Estimation R^2	Estimation SEE
Gross national product, current prices	$GNP	$mill.	–	–
Gross national product	GNP	$mill.	–	–
Consumption of non-durables	CND	$mill.	0.997	22.50
Consumption of motor vehicles	CMV	$mill.	0.963	11.40
Construction investment	IC	$mill.	0.910	12.33
Dwellings investment	ID	$mill.	0.985	6.85
Inventory investment	IH	$mill.	0.721	47.26
Imports	IMA	$mill.	0.983	22.60
Implicit GNP deflator	PGNP	1966-7 = 1.00	–	–
Implicit deflator for dwellings	PD	1966-7 = 1.00	0.998	0.32
Implicit non-durables deflator	PND	1966-7 = 1.00	0.997	0.37
Implicit deflator for "other durables" (apart from motor vehicles)	POD	1966-7 = 1.00	0.888	0.49
Average weekly earnings	WE	1966-7 = 1.00	0.996	0.97
Civilian employment	EMP	'00, 000	0.999	11.74
Civilian unemployment	U	'00, 000	–	–
Personal disposable income	YPD	$mill.	–	–
Gross operating surplus of companies	GOSC	$mill.	–	–
Private sector's demand for advances	ADVO	$mill.	0.914	28.33
Private sector's demand for currency	CURR	$mill.	0.995	8.22
Money stock	M	$mill.	–	–

Notes:
1) Apart from $GNP, all expenditure variables are in constant 1966–67 prices.
2) A dash in the R^2 and standard error of estimate (SEE) columns indicates that the corresponding variable is determined by an identity.

sion would be sustained in relation to longer run cyclical movements.

Unbiasedness of the prediction procedure is upheld in virtually every case, in view of the insignificance of the statistic t_B.

The actual and simulation paths for each variable, when graphed, reveal very few cases where the actual path lies consistently within the tolerance region delimited by the maximum and minimum stochastic simulation paths. Two cases are illustrated in figures 1 and 2. For *CURR* the actual path lies within and very close to the tolerance region, but this is not so in the case of *CMV*.

Table 2
Analysis of stochastic simulation for levels

Sym-bol	Regression of actual on predicted value		Test statistics (B = bias, E = efficiency)			Dimen-sionless RMSE	Maximum coeff. of var. (%)
	Intercept	Slope	Joint F	t_B	t_E		
(1)	(2)	(3)	(4)	(5)	(6)	(7)	(8)
$GNP	111.41	0.98	2.94	1.51	1.85	0.015	0.28
GNP	164.07	0.97	1.25	0.87	1.32	0.019	0.41
CND	338.04	0.88	9.13*	1.63	3.80*	0.023	0.47
CMV	86.70	0.55	17.64*	0.72	5.85*	0.113	3.01
IC	3.04	0.98	0.14	0.41	0.33	0.065	0.53
ID	15.22	0.95	1.61	1.05	1.44	0.037	1.75
IH	3.73	0.90	0.53	0.43	0.94	0.435	note (4)
IMA	162.15	0.80	6.08*	0.79	3.36*	0.072	1.19
PGNP	0.04	0.96	0.83	0.47	1.20	0.015	0.23
PD	0.06	0.94	1.78	0.70	1.74	0.015	0.36
PND	0.00	1.00	0.05	0.31	0.03	0.012	0.23
POD	−0.70	1.69	48.93*	1.47	9.45*	0.009	0.15
WE	−0.03	1.03	2.25	0.27	2.10*	0.013	0.19
EMP	1.97	0.95	4.90*	1.17	2.85*	0.010	0.17
U	0.51	0.17	>99.99*	1.24	17.68*	0.681	note (4)
YPD	61.75	0.98	2.90	1.71	1.64	0.013	0.21
GOSC	32.27	0.96	1.89	1.08	1.60	0.039	1.09
ADVO	102.53	0.96	2.49	1.46	1.65	0.030	0.55
CURR	24.45	0.98	0.89	0.86	1.02	0.020	0.85
M	107.72	1.00	7.56*	3.95*	0.07	0.032	0.86

Notes:
1) Entries in cols. 2−7 are based on the mean stochastic simulation results.

2) The F-test has (2,29) degrees of freedom; t_B has 30 degrees of freedom; t_E has 29 degrees of freedom. The one-tail 5% significance point for F = 3.33. The two-tail 5% significance point for t_B = 2.04 and for t_E = 2.05. Asterisks mark values significant at the 5% level.

3) Entries in col. 7 are obtained by the formula: root(mean square error/mean square actual value).

4) Each entry in col. 8 is the maximum over 31 quarters of the coefficient of variation calculated for each quarter across 20 replications. For variables IH and U the maximum is not given, since it is very much distorted in each case by an exceptionally small mean value. The median coefficient of variation for these variables is 6.26% and 7.78% respectively.

Table 3
Analysis of stochastic simulation for % changes

Symbol	Regression of actual on predicted % change		Test statistics (B = bias, E = efficiency)			Inequality statistics	
	Intercept	Slope	Joint F	t_B	t_E	T_1	T_2
(1)	(2)	(3)	(4)	(5)	(6)	(7)	(8)
$GNP	0.03	1.02	0.57	0.45	0.97	0.110	0.068
GNP	0.14	1.01	0.17	0.51	0.29	0.167	0.103
CND	−0.15	1.03	0.51	0.57	0.83	0.162	0.090
CMV	1.49	0.55	2.98	0.73	2.31*	0.951	0.600
IC	0.55	1.06	0.24	0.45	0.53	0.485	0.270
ID	0.53	0.86	0.35	0.41	0.72	0.683	0.571
IH	824.74	0.17	1.52	0.69	1.59	1.025	0.721
IMA	0.17	0.78	1.71	0.49	1.78	0.635	0.414
PGNP	0.59	0.34	21.65*	0.26	6.57*	0.995	0.896
PD	0.58	0.25	21.99*	0.70	6.54*	0.753	0.930
PND	0.69	0.26	14.73*	0.31	5.41*	0.521	1.091
POD	−0.01	1.90	2.19	0.78	1.93	0.820	0.710
WE	0.06	1.03	0.27	0.44	0.59	0.235	0.136
EMP	0.19	0.80	1.80	0.29	1.87	0.325	0.406
U	8.29	0.08	>99.99*	0.80	32.33*	5.461	3.305
YPD	0.01	1.02	1.04	0.41	1.38	0.090	0.054
GOSC	0.73	0.89	1.28	0.30	1.57	0.401	0.211
ADVO	−0.05	0.94	0.64	0.75	0.85	0.340	0.268
CURR	0.07	1.02	0.22	0.52	0.41	0.239	0.177
M	0.38	0.91	1.58	0.91	1.52	0.305	0.247

Notes:

1) Values in this table are derived from computations on relative first differences of variables, of the form $100(p_t-p_{t-1})/|p_{t-1}|$. The modulus in the denominator is necessary to preserve correct signs in all cases for the direction of change. Simulation results are represented by the mean stochastic simulation.

2) The F-test has (2,28) degrees of freedom; t_B has 29 degrees of freedom; t_E has 28 degrees of freedom. The one-tail 5% significance point for F = 3.34. The two-tail 5% significance point for t_B = 2.05 and for t_E = 2.05. Asterisks mark values significant at the 5% level.

3) T_1 (col.7) is the inequality statistic for the "no change" alternative prediction rule; T_2 (col.8) for the "same change" alternative prediction rule.

On the other hand, the simulated paths show very good correspondence in phase with the ups and downs of the actual seasonal movements. These observations corroborate the earlier conclusion that the model is more reliable for predicting changes than levels.

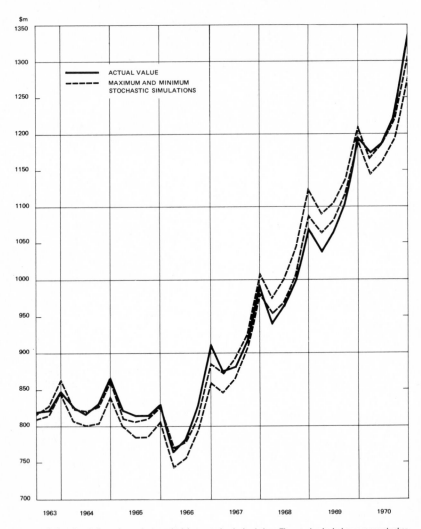

Broken lines indicate the maximum and minimum stochastic simulations. The actual series is shown as an unbroken line. The deterministic simulation and the mean stochastic simulation are virtually coincident and their difference would be beyond resolution in this chart. For clarity, neither series has been plotted — both would be located approximately midway on the vertical scale between the plotted maximum and minimum stochastic simulations.

Fig. 1. Actual and simulated time paths of private sector's demand for currency (*CURR*) — (dynamic simulation).

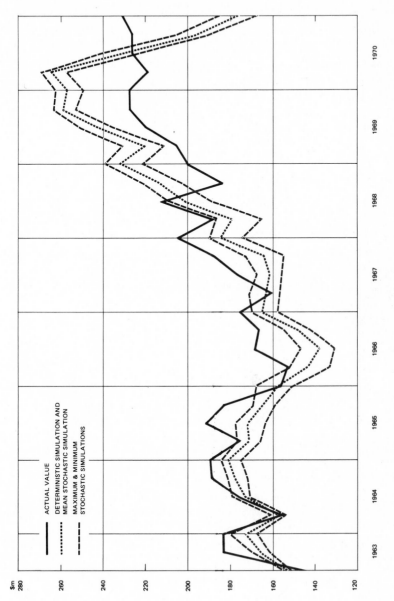

Fig. 2. Actual and simulated time paths of consumption of motor vehicles (*CMV*) – (dynamic simulation).

For almost all the variables under examination, the two Theil inequality statistics have values less than 1.0. In particular, the inequality statistics are very low for the aggregates $GNP and GNP, giving formal confirmation that the purpose of national income forecasting in Australia is far better served by a structural econometric model than by a simple mechanistic prediction rule.

The test statistics, root mean square errors and inequality statistics, when compared across variables, highlight imperfect model specifications: IH, CMV and U, in particular, draw one's attention. Inventory investment (IH) is a highly volatile quantity, whose rapid fluctuations are difficult to explain really well in a regression structure. The possibility of substantial errors of measurement in the series for inventories exacerbates the prediction problem.

The abrupt downturn in 1970 in the simulated series for consumption of motor vehicles (CMV, fig. 2) is probably due to inaccuracies in recent values of some exogenous variables. Yet, even with this qualification, it appears that the CMV equation needs to be modified to account better for the irregularity of the amplitude of seasonal swings.

Unemployment (U) presents a special problem. For some periods in 1969–70, the simulated series takes on impermissible negative values. Since U is determined by an identity relating the total labour force (exogenous) and the employed labour force (EMP), the problem becomes that of respecifying the employment equation. The required adjustment is rather a delicate one, since it is a local rather than a general tendency to overprediction that must be corrected. It is instructive to note that EMP itself has relatively unremarkable summary measures and that the value of R^2 for its estimation in single equation form is very high!

Percentage prediction errors for a number of variables are shown in table 4. The predictions are for the year 1970, which is in the model's historical future. The absence of cumulating overprediction in the dynamic simulation values suggests that RBA1 is quite a stable model in the short run. Moreover, the prediction errors are generally not large, indicating that the model is reasonably effective for short-term forecasting. Table 5 provides illustrative numerical data relating to $GNP for general comparison of

Table 4
Prediction errors (%) for dynamic and one-step simulation
(+ overprediction; − underprediction)

		1970(1)	1970(2)	1970(3)	1970(4)
$GNP	Dynamic	+3.0	+3.2	+1.7	−0.2
	One-step	+2.8	+3.1	+1.1	−0.6
IMA	Dynamic	+9.1	+5.4	+12.0	+7.6
	One-step	−0.9	−6.3	+0.5	−3.7
PGNP	Dynamic	−1.8	+1.8	+4.4	+1.7
	One-step	−1.4	+1.4	+3.3	−0.5
EMP	Dynamic	+2.1	+1.7	+1.7	+0.8
	One-step	+0.7	−0.01	+0.4	−0.3
YPD	Dynamic	+3.6	+2.5	+1.6	+0.05
	One-step	+2.8	+1.4	+0.7	−0.7
M	Dynamic	−2.1	−3.2	−5.0	−6.2
	One-step	−2.8	−1.3	−1.2	−1.2

deterministic and stochastic simulation results. For most of the simulations performed with RBA1, deterministic and mean stochastic simulation results were as closely in agreement as in table 5.

10. Sources of numerical inaccuracy

Successful quantitative analysis with a macroeconometric model requires recognition of possible origins of inaccuracy in final results. Errors of measurement, redefinitions of economic aggregates and periodic revisions to official statistics have, as Holden [23] demonstrates, considerable effect on forecasting accuracy. To these sources of error must be added the incommensurable consequences of model misspecification and coefficient bias in estimation with small samples. All these influences affect the quality of the model, independently of inaccuracies that may be introduced during simulation.

When simulating by computer, rounding errors in numerical cal-

E.R. Sowey

Table 5
Dynamic control simulation of RBA1, 1963(2)–1970(4). Analysis of simulations for variable $GNP

Year + qrtr	Actual value	Determin. simulation	Stochastic simulation				Actual % change	Determin. % change	Stoch. % change
			Mean stoch. simulation	Maximum value	Minimum value	Standard deviation			
1963(2)	3869.00	3937.94	3938.24	3941.95	3935.34	2.04	0.00	0.00	0.00
1963(3)	4335.00	4317.15	4318.87	4328.77	4308.87	5.66	12.04	9.63	9.66
1963(4)	5011.00	5040.47	5044.03	5062.86	5021.34	10.85	15.59	16.75	16.79
1964(1)	4279.00	4288.30	4290.73	4303.95	4273.01	7.96	-14.61	-14.92	-14.93
1964(2)	4339.00	4364.88	4370.06	4388.61	4344.82	10.86	1.40	1.79	1.85
1964(3)	4754.00	4798.54	4800.47	4816.58	4778.69	9.31	9.56	9.94	9.85
1964(4)	5466.00	5519.10	5518.29	5536.27	5496.59	10.04	14.98	15.02	14.95
1965(1)	4790.00	4902.82	4901.90	4919.85	4884.94	9.09	-12.27	-11.17	-11.17
1965(2)	4776.00	4845.96	4843.55	4865.28	4820.01	10.23	-0.29	-1.16	-1.19
1965(3)	5086.00	5170.14	5165.48	5182.99	5150.36	9.99	6.49	6.69	6.65
1965(4)	5680.00	5686.72	5682.50	5718.48	5656.06	13.65	11.68	9.99	10.01
1966(1)	4911.00	4873.87	4871.19	4905.33	4854.91	12.54	-13.54	-14.29	-14.28
1966(2)	4971.00	4933.21	4929.05	4966.43	4907.70	14.04	1.22	1.22	1.19
1966(3)	5385.00	5268.44	5267.49	5302.78	5242.13	14.63	8.33	6.80	6.87
1966(4)	6215.00	6125.60	6126.01	6160.27	6106.07	13.70	15.41	16.27	16.30
1967(1)	5578.00	5589.08	5588.29	5616.64	5573.33	13.40	-10.25	-8.76	-8.78
1967(2)	5492.00	5455.73	5454.90	5486.95	5433.73	14.38	-1.54	-2.39	-2.39
1967(3)	5803.00	5703.55	5702.74	5726.96	5671.60	15.42	5.66	4.54	4.54
1967(4)	6672.00	6556.51	6559.20	6584.47	6534.55	13.30	14.98	14.95	15.02
1968(1)	5727.00	5637.26	5642.46	5675.04	5618.50	13.98	-14.16	-14.02	-13.98
1968(2)	5974.00	5899.38	5904.58	5931.54	5880.15	14.38	4.31	4.65	4.65
1968(3)	6409.00	6458.03	6459.98	6488.50	6432.70	16.99	7.28	9.47	9.41
1968(4)	7568.00	7535.75	7538.21	7565.90	7495.29	16.79	18.08	16.69	16.69
1969(1)	6524.00	6585.06	6586.29	6620.18	6546.27	17.25	-13.79	-12.62	-12.63
1969(2)	6680.00	6709.97	6711.36	6746.13	6670.03	18.13	2.39	1.90	1.90
1969(3)	7201.00	7354.70	7355.27	7382.76	7330.44	13.30	7.80	9.61	9.59
1969(4)	8111.00	8225.24	8225.84	8257.58	8204.18	15.43	12.64	11.84	11.84
1970(1)	7221.00	7442.38	7439.64	7469.62	7423.02	12.59	-10.97	-9.52	-9.56
1970(2)	7505.00	7746.54	7745.22	7778.11	7723.62	14.18	3.93	4.09	4.11
1970(3)	7913.00	8049.53	8046.86	8074.42	8017.45	13.50	5.44	3.91	3.89
1970(4)	8728.00	8713.53	8709.03	8740.49	8681.35	14.20	10.30	8.25	8.23

culation are of principal concern (Ramsey [45]). This points to the need for evaluating carefully the arithmetic precision of the computer being used and suggests the use of extended precision whenever the option is available. The matter is particularly important in the case of dynamic simulation, where inaccuracies in the solutions for one period are propagated through all subsequent period solutions.

Extrapolation of exogenous variables when the model is used for forecasting gives rise to yet further inaccuracies. The construction of 'closed' models, in which the only predetermined variables are lagged endogenous, would eliminate the difficulty, but is probably impracticable in most cases. In a model such as RBA1, with 50 exogenous variables, the risk of sizable prediction errors stemming from inaccurate extrapolations becomes quite substantial.

Though the sources of error just briefly surveyed cannot usually be eliminated, their influence on the accuracy of simulation results may often be diminished by careful attention to detail.

11. Conclusion

In discussing stochastic simulation in principle and in practice we have been concerned with demonstrating the attributes of this technique and the sorts of conclusions that one may draw by its use in connection with macroeconometric models. We make no claim for its absolute primacy in every respect. Indeed, consideration of cost must figure very strongly in deciding whether to undertake replicated stochastic simulation for evaluating nonlinear econometric models. The alternative, deterministic simulation, is clearly much cheaper in terms of computer time. When deterministic and mean stochastic simulation results are in close correspondence (as was the case in validation of RBA1), a researcher may be quite willing to forgo some additional information by relying on deterministic simulation.

But the weighing of information against cost may not always dictate economy. Then, the use of stochastic simulation can yield results which are not only more detailed but are also fully assessable in terms of statistical reliability.

References

[1] I. Adelman, 'Long cycles – a simulation experiment', in: *Symposium on simulation models,* edited by A.C. Hoggatt and F.E. Balderston (South-Western, 1963), pp. 152–181.

[2] I. Adelman, and F.L. Adelman, 'The dynamic properties of the Klein-Goldberger model', *Econometrica* 27 (1959) 596–625.

[3] R.L. Anderson, and T.A. Bancroft, *Statistical theory in research* (New York, McGraw-Hill, 1952).

[4] G.E.P. Box and M. Muller, 'A note on the generation of random normal deviates', *Annals of Mathematical Statistics* 29 (1958) 610.

[5] J.V. Bradley, *Distribution-free statistical tests* (Englewood Cliffs, Prentice Hall, 1968).

[6] M.G. Bush and A.M. Cohen, *The indicator approach to the identification of business cycles.* Reserve Bank of Australia, Occasional Paper No. 2, 1968.

[7] J.S. Duesenberry, O. Eckstein and G. Fromm, 'A simulation of the U.S. economy in recession', *Econometrica* 28 (1960) 749–809.

[8] J.S. Duesenberry, et al. (eds.), *The Brookings model: some further results* (Amsterdam, North-Holland, 1969).

[9] M.K. Evans, L.R. Klein and M. Saito, 'Short run prediction and long run simulation of the Wharton model', in N.B.E.R. [41].

[10] G.H. Fisher, 'Some comments on stochastic macroeconomic models', *American Economic Review* 42 (1952) 528–539.

[11] G.S. Fishman and P.J. Kiviat, 'The analysis of simulation generated time series', *Management Science* 13 (1967) 525–557.

[12] V.W. FitzGerald, 'Dynamic properties of a non-linear econometric model', in: this volume, p. 169.

[13] R. Frisch, 'Propagation problems and impulse problems in dynamic economics', in: *Economic essays in honour of Gustav Cassel* (London, Allen & Unwin, 1933).

[14] G. Fromm and L.R. Klein, 'Solutions to the complete system', in: J.S. Duesenberry et al. (eds.) [8], chapter 11.

[15] G. Fromm, L.R. Klein and G.R. Schink, 'Short and long term simulations with the Brookings model', in N.B.E.R. [41].

[16] G. Fromm and P. Taubman, *Policy simulations with an econometric model* (Amsterdam, North-Holland, 1968).

[17] A. Gadd and H.O. Wold, 'The Janus Quotient: A Measure for the Accuracy of Prediction', in: H.O. Wold (ed.), *Econometric Model Building* (Amsterdam, North-Holland, 1964).

[18] S. Goldberg, *Introduction to difference equations* (New York, Wiley, 1961).

[19] E.J. Gumbel, *Statistics of extremes* (Oxford, University Press, 1958).

[20] T. Haavelmo, 'The inadequacy of testing dynamic theory by comparing theoretical solutions and observed cycles', *Econometrica* 8 (1940) 312–321.

[21] J.F. Helliwell, L.H. Officer, H.T. Shapiro and I.A. Stewart, 'Econometric analysis of policy choices for an open economy', *Review of Economics and Statistics* 51 (1969) 383–398.

[22] C.I. Higgins and V.W. FitzGerald, 'A model for national income forecasting', roneoed, Canberra, 1970. (A revised version of this model appears in: this volume, p.115.)

[23] K. Holden, 'Effect of revisions to data on two econometric studies', *The Manchester School* 37 (1969) 23–37.

[24] C.C. Holt, 'Validation and application of macroeconomic models using computer simulation', in: *The Brookings quarterly model of the U.S. economy*, edited by J.S. Duesenberry et al. (Amsterdam, North-Holland, 1965).

[25] E.P. Howrey, 'Stochastic properties of the Klein-Goldberger model', *Econometrica* 39 (1971) 73–88.

[26] E.P. Howrey and H.H. Kelejian, 'Simulation versus analytical solution: the case of econometric models', in: Naylor [37], chapter 12.

[27] J.S. Hunter and T.H. Naylor, 'Experimental designs for computer simulation experiments', *Management Science* 16 (1970) 422–434. (Reprinted with modifications in Naylor [37], ch. 6.)

[28] D. Ironmonger and S. Kumar, 'Econometric models of the Australian economy'. Presented at the First Australian Conference of Economists, roneoed, Melbourne, 1970.

[29] J. Johnston, *Econometric methods* (New York, McGraw-Hill, 2nd ed., 1972).

[30] J.P. Kleijnen and T.H. Naylor, 'The use of multiple ranking procedures to analyze simulations of business and economic systems', in: *Proceedings of the American Statistical Association* (Business and Economic Statistics Section), 1969, pp. 605–615.

[31] L.R. Klein and A.S. Goldberger, *An econometric model of the United States, 1929–1952* (Amsterdam, North-Holland, 1955).

[32] J. Kmenta, 'An econometric model of Australia', *Australian Economic Papers* 5 (1966) 131–164.

[33] M.D. McCarthy, 'Some notes on the generation of pseudo structural errors for use in stochastic simulation studies', Appendix to M.K. Evans et al. [9] in N.B.E.R. [41].

[34] J. Mincer and V. Zarnowitz, 'The evaluation of economic forecasts', in: *Economic forecasts and expectations*, edited by J. Mincer. Studies in Business Cycles no. 19 (National Bureau of Economic Research, 1969), chapter 1.

[35] G.H. Moore, C. Boschan and V. Zarnowitz, 'Business cycle analysis of econometric model simulations', in N.B.E.R. [41].

[36] A.L. Nagar, 'Stochastic simulation of the Brookings model', in: J.S. Duesenberry et al. (eds.) [8], chapter 12.

[37] T.H. Naylor, *Computer simulation experiments with models of economic systems* (New York, Wiley, 1971).

[38] T.H. Naylor, D.S. Burdick and W.E. Sasser, 'Computer simulation experiments with economic systems: the problem of experimental design', *Journal of the American Statistical Association* 62 (1967) 1315–1337.

[39] T.H. Naylor, K. Wertz and T.H. Wonnacott, 'Some methods for evaluating the effects of economic policies using simulation experiments', *Review of the International Statistical Institute* 36 (1968) 184–200.

[40] T.H. Naylor, K. Wertz and T.H. Wonnacott, 'Spectral analysis of data generated by simulation experiments with econometric models', *Econometrica* 37 (1969) 333–352.

[41] National Bureau of Economic Research (N.B.E.R.), *Econometric models of cyclical behaviour,* edited by B. Hickman. Conference on Income and Wealth Series no.36, 2 volumes, 1972.

[42] J.W. Nevile, 'An econometric model of the Australian economy', *Australian Economic Papers* 1 (1962) 79–94.

[43] J.W. Nevile, 'An Australian econometric model', in: *Fiscal policy in Australia—theory and practice* (Cheshire, 1970), chapter 5.

[44] W.E. Norton and J.F. Henderson, 'The structure of a model of the Australian economy', in: this volume, p. 49.

[45] J.B. Bamsey, 'Errors in digital computers: their effect on the results of econometric analysis', *Econometrics Workshop Paper 6715,* Michigan State University, June 1968.

[46] E. Slutsky, 'The summation of random causes as the source of cyclic processes', *Econometrica* 5 (1937) 105–146 (Originally published in Russian in 1927).

[47] H. Theil, *Applied economic forecasting* (Amsterdam, North-Holland, 1966).

[48] S.S. Wilks, 'Determination of sample sizes for setting tolerance limits', *Annals of Mathematical Statistics* 12 (1941) 91–96.

[49] V. Zarnowitz, *An appraisal of short-term economic forecasts,* Occasional Paper no. 104 (N.B.E.R., 1967).

[50] A. Zellner and S.C. Peck, 'Simulation experiments with a quarterly macroeconometric model of the U.S. economy', in: this volume, p. 149.

PART 2

MONETARY SECTOR MODELS

REAL BALANCES AND OUTPUT: A PRODUCTIVITY MODEL OF A MONETARY ECONOMY *

L. McGREGOR

Monash University

and

A.A. WALTERS

London School of Economics and Political Science

1. Introduction

The formulation of a satisfactory theory of a monetary economy presupposes the identification of an appropriate role for money itself, and of the motivations that govern the behaviour of its holders. A community that organises its affairs along monetised lines in preference to barter must perceive some advantages in the arrangement; and in general terms it is not difficult to recognise at least the more obvious of these. But the successful accommodation of the implications of monetisation within a formal theoretical framework is a different matter. Too often the attempt yields results that are intuitively unsatisfying, or even apparently inconsistent with the existence of money. For example in James Tobin's innovatory attempt [17] to introduce monetary considerations into a neoclassical growth model, the outcome is a *reduction* in per capita output and consumption, as compared with the barter situation.[1] Clearly this result fails to capture the essential econo-

---

* We have benefited from very useful discussions with our colleagues at Monash University and the London School of Economics. We are particularly grateful to Milton Friedman who pointed out some errors in an earlier draft of this paper. The usual absolutions are however due.

[1] See Tobin [17] and [18].

mic forces underlying the use of money.[2]

The most familiar procedure for analysing the behaviour of a monetary economy is to regard money balances as an argument of the utility function of the consumer. This approach is exemplified by modern attempts, most notably that of Patinkin [13], to integrate monetary and value theory upon Walrasian general equilibrium foundations. The difficulty in this procedure is to preserve the characteristic 'moneyness' of money from an operational point of view. As Clower [3] has argued, technically money enters Patinkin's formal system in essentially the same way as other goods, and hence is analytically indistinguishable from those other goods as a source of effective demand. Accordingly, he insists, 'what presently passes for a theory of a money economy is in truth descriptive of a barter economy'.[3]

An alternative approach, which we adopt in the present paper, is to acknowledge directly the social productivity of money by treating it explicitly as a factor of production, with a role analogous to that of labour or of physical capital. Though this conception of the role of money is evidently congenial in principle to many economists[4], its implications have not so far been seriously explored.[5] Here we attempt an initial step in this direction, within the framework of a comparatively elementary macrostatic equilibrium model.

2. The productivity of money

The basis of a productivity approach to monetary analysis is the notion that money is desired and held, not for its own sake but as an

---

[2] See also Robert Crouch's comments in his contribution to this volume [5].

[3] Clower [3], p. 3.

[4] See, in particular, Bailey [1], pp. 59ff.; Patinkin [13], chapter VII; Levhari and Patinkin [12], pp. 737ff.; Johnson [10], pp.40ff.

[5] Martin Bailey acknowledges that 'there is no question that [cash balances] are a factor of production', and that to treat them as such in an analytical system would affect the properties of that system. But he dismisses the issue as empirically unimportant (Bailey [1], pp. 59–61). It is not made clear upon what evidence this judgment is based. We return to this question below.

intermediate good, for the services it can provide. It is held, that is, for its capacity to generate real income. At the most general level, this notion can be justified along revealed preference lines. The fact that money balances are actually held at a positive (opportunity) cost may be taken to imply that they provide some return, or real income, sufficient to compensate for that cost.

Such an interpretation seems to have its most natural application in the case of business enterprises. It is evident that in so far as they facilitate increased specialization and efficiency of resource allocation, the money balances of firms contribute to the production and distribution of commodities in the same way as the physical factors labour and capital; and that therefore those balances should enter with the other factors into the firms' production function.[6] From this point of view, the demand for money balances, like the demand for other factors of production, derives purely from profit maximising considerations in the business enterprise sector.

There is a corresponding argument for treating the household sector symmetrically. Here cash balances provide yields reflected in increased leisure, improved timing of consumption patterns, greater sense of security, and the like. The psychic income of households is determined by the time-stream of goods and services achievable with given levels of real money balances. *Ceteris paribus* an increase of real money balances, brought about for example by a fall in the price level with the same stock of nominal money, will enable households to achieve a higher level of satisfaction than before. This clearly means that individual psychic incomes have increased and so aggregate real income is greater. We cannot escape the conclusion that real aggregate income is a function of the stock of real money balances. Accordingly, such balances held by households can be interpreted conveniently as an input into the household production function — an input that is necessary in order to produce the observed stream of consumption. The utility of the household is achieved from the

---

[6] Levhari and Patinkin [12] introduce real balances into an aggregate production function in the context of an equilibrium growth model, confining the argument solely to balances held by the business sector.

stream of goods and services consumed; money balances serve merely as the intermediator in exchange.

For these reasons we treat all cash balances, whether held by households or by firms, as a factor of production entering an aggregate production function

$$\frac{Y}{P} = \phi \left(N, K, \frac{M}{P} \right) ,$$

where Y/P is real output, and N, K and M/P are inputs of labour, real capital and real money balances respectively. Each individual economic entity, whether firm or household, will adjust its real cash balances so that their marginal productivity is equal to the marginal opportunity cost of such balances. Ignoring the intractable problems of aggregation, and assuming that each entity faces a constant opportunity cost, in equilibrium the marginal product of aggregate real cash balances $\partial\phi/\partial(M/P)$ will be equal to common opportunity cost.[7]

One form of such a production function is illustrated in figure 1. We assume that the quantities of labour and capital employed are fixed at $N = N_0$ and $K = K_0$ and then plot real output Y/P as it varies with real balances M/P. The level of output rises as real balances rise. The curve starts not at the origin but at some intercept representing the output level of the economy under barter conditions $(Y/P)_{min}$. Total real output reaches a maximum, $(Y/P)^*$, at $(M/P)^*$, where the marginal productivity of real balances becomes zero. As an equilibrium state, this would correspond to a zero marginal private opportunity cost of real cash balances. If it be assumed — and this is the standard supposition — that the marginal social cost of cash balances is zero, then $(M/P)^*$ is the optimum (real) money supply.

Provided that real balances can be left idle, and on the assumption that storage costs are negligible, it seems sensible to regard the function as a constant at $(Y/P)^*$ beyond $(M/P)^*$. Thus it may be supposed that if the cost of holding real balances is zero, an increase in the real money supply will result in the accumulation of higher

---

[7] Provided, as we assume formally below, that the second derivative is non-positive.

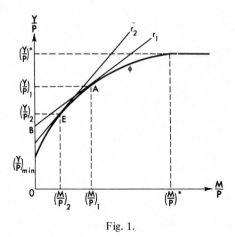

Fig. 1.

money stocks with no effect at all on output. Money balances are a free good or factor with zero shadow price.

Alternatively it might be argued that the accumulation of additional money balances will require a diversion of factors to guard and administer them, so that the production function turns down beyond $(M/P)^*$. [8] We do not adopt this assumption in the present model, though the consequences of doing so can be readily examined if one wishes to pursue the point.[9]

In equilibrium, the first differential of the function illustrated in figure 1 is equal to the opportunity cost of money — i.e., the real rate of interest (r). If, for example, the interest rate is 20% per annum, then the equilibrium production-money relationship can be formed by the line of a slope 1 : 5 such as BA, which is just tangential to the function at A. In this case a real income of $(Y/P)_1$ and a real money stock of $(M/P)_1$ are consistent with an interest rate r_1 of 20% per annum.[10] At the higher interest rate r_2, the tangency at E represents

[8] Friedman [6], pp. 17–18. For a detailed consideration of this 'Region III' of output functions, see Tangri [16].

[9] Various alternative forms of this production function could be hypothesised. While we consider the relationship discussed in this section to be plausible on *a priori* grounds, ultimately, of course, the issue is an empirical one.

[10] The special case of constant marginal productivity of money over a wide range of output, say from $(Y/P)_{min}$ to $(Y/P)^*$, would yield indeterminacy, with corner solutions at $(Y/P)_{min}$ and $(Y/P)^*$.

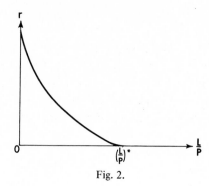

Fig. 2.

the corresponding equilibrium situation.

Assuming a continuously decreasing marginal productivity, the demand for money may be shown directly as in figure 2. With employment and the capital stock given, and with output variable, it shows the quantity of real balances demanded (L/P) for any given level of the real interest rate.[11]

Alternatively, it may be used to show the real rate of interest consistent with a given level of real balances, in the light of the prevailing productivity of money. As the interest rate approaches very high levels, the demand for real balances approaches zero, and the economy moves towards a state of barter. At a zero rate of interest money becomes a free good, so that when the demand curve meets the axis at $(L/P)^*$ any additional real balances are simply absorbed and left idle with a shadow price of zero.

---

[11] Although we assume price flexibility, in order to sustain as nearly as possible the parallel with more conventional macroeconomic models in the income-expenditure tradition we do not in this paper distinguish the (*ex ante*) real from the nominal interest rate. This is tantamount to assuming a unitary aggregate elasticity of expectations with respect to observed price change. By contrast, see Friedman [8], who adresses the problem in an explicitly dynamic framework. We do not pretend that this is a very satisfactory way of dealing with the relation between real and nominal interest rates. At a practical level, an obvious difficulty arises in that while it is not hard to conceive of the real interest rate falling to zero, the notion of the nominal rate doing so, with the implication of infinite bond prices, is simply not acceptable. This asymmetry might be rationalised in a variety of ways. It might be argued that at low levels of the real interest rate there is.a necessary divergence between it and the nominal rate, such that the unitary elasticity of expectations assumption cannot be retained. In this case we may suppose that a positive floor to the money interest rate is set by a 'liquidity trap' type of phenomenon, or by the rate of return on real capital. We hope to develop this issue in another paper.

3. The model

There are various lines along which the implications of the foregoing argument might fruitfully be explored. In this paper we restrict ourselves to introducing the productivity of money into the framework of an aggregative static equilibrium model. We neglect the overseas sector, and the budgetary activities of government.

3.1. Elements of the model

Consider an economy comprising households and business enterprises. Its aggregate real income or output is defined to include suitably deflated measures of the actual observed value of all market transactions in final goods and services, plus the imputed value of the non-marketed final services yielded by real assets and money balances. Output possibilities are determined by the general production function

$$\frac{Y}{P} = \phi \left(K, N, \frac{M}{P} \right) ,$$

where Y is output at current prices, K is the real capital stock, N is labour input, M is the nominal money stock, and P is an index of the average price level. We have emphasised the variety of possible forms of this production function. However, in order to add concreteness to the present analysis we here impose upon it a number of restrictions which seem to be neither implausible nor unduly stringent. Specifically, we assume the function to be continuous and twice differentiable, with the following properties:

$$\frac{Y}{P} > 0 \quad \text{for} \quad \left(\frac{M}{P} \right) = 0 ; \tag{9.1}$$

$$\partial \left(\frac{Y}{P} \right) / \partial \left(\frac{M}{P} \right) > 0 \quad \text{for} \left(\frac{M}{P} \right) < \left(\frac{M}{P} \right)^{*} ; \tag{9.2}$$

$$\partial^2 \left(\frac{Y}{P}\right) \Big/ \partial \left(\frac{M}{P}\right)^2 \leqslant 0 \qquad (9.3)$$

such that

$$\partial \left(\frac{Y}{P}\right) \Big/ \partial \left(\frac{M}{P}\right) = 0 \qquad \text{for } \left(\frac{M}{P}\right) \geqslant \left(\frac{M}{P}\right)^* . \qquad (9.4)$$

We have suggested earlier that if storage costs of money are ignored, there seems to be no practical reason to suppose that the marginal productivity of money should ever become negative, since excess balances could be simply left idle without interfering with the efficiency of the productive process. We also assume

$$\partial \left(\frac{Y}{P}\right) \Big/ \partial N > 0 ; \qquad (9.5)$$

$$\partial^2 \left(\frac{Y}{P}\right) \Big/ \partial N^2 \leqslant 0 ; \qquad (9.6)$$

$$\frac{\partial^2 (Y/P)}{\partial K \, \partial (M/P)} > 0 ; \qquad (9.7)$$

$$\frac{\partial^2 (Y/P)}{\partial N \, \partial (M/P)} > 0 . \qquad (9.8)$$

Throughout the following we ignore the fact that current investment adds to the capital stock, and treat the latter as fixed. Furthermore, in order to focus more directly on the role of money in our system, we also assume a given level of employment. (The model can be readily adapted to accommodate variable labour inputs.) Thus we have $K = K_0$ and $N = N_0$, so that

$$\frac{Y}{P} = \phi \left(K_0, N_0, \frac{M}{P}\right) . \qquad (9.9)$$

Households sell their factor services to business firms in return for money income, which may be allocated to the purchase from firms of commodities and bonds, and to the accumulation of cash balances. The commodities purchased by households in any period fall into two classes: durables and non-durables. Durable goods are assets acquired for the flow of services that they yield over time; in many respects, therefore, they, and the expenditure decisions involving them, are more nearly comparable to investment than to other consumption purchases. We accordingly classify them, together with the capital accumulation of firms, as part of the community's aggregate investment.

Consumption is correspondingly defined as the sum of the physical non-durable goods and services absorbed by households, and the (imputed) flow of final services provided by the real and monetary assets held by them. Saving, as usual, is that part of the income stream not diverted to consumption. *Ex post,* it is matched by the accumulation of inventories, plant and equipment, and consumer durables. Since saving (S/P) is undertaken partly to finance expenditure on household durables, we allow that it may be potentially sensitive to the rate of interest r, as well as to income, and adopt the savings function

$$\frac{S}{P} = S\left(\frac{Y}{P}, r\right),$$ (9.10)

where $[\partial(S/P) / \partial(Y/P)] > 0$, and $\partial(S/P) / \partial r \geqslant 0$.

As already observed, investment comprises the capital formation of firms and the purchase of consumer durables. We take the demand for the former to be influenced by familiar marginal efficiency of capital considerations, and the latter by the opportunity cost of holding wealth in this form. Accordingly, aggregate investment demand is assumed to be inversely related to the interest rate. For full consistency, however, our approach to the treament of money implies that the investment function be extended to incorporate a direct 'real balance' effect upon the demand for capital goods.

Given that real money balances contribute positively to total productive capacity, it follows that changes in the quantity of those balances give rise to variations in the average, and, by virtue of the cross-elasticity assumptions (9.7) and (9.8), the marginal productivities of the other factors. Specifically, an increase in real balances has the effect of shifting the capital-output relationship so that any given capital stock yields a higher level of output and marginal product than before. The likely effect of such a shift is to raise the expected incremental rate of return attributable to any level of capital input. This in turn raises both the optimum capital stock, and the optimum rate of change of the existing capital stock, at the prevailing rate of interest. In terms of formal investment theory, the increased physical productivity of capital due to the additional real balances shifts both the marginal efficiency of capital and the marginal efficiency of investment functions, thereby raising the equilibrium rate of investment at every interest rate.

There is thus established a link, quite separate from that operating through the interest rate itself, connecting the level of investment demand to the real money supply.[12] We accordingly formulate the

[12] The foregoing argument applies to the business component of investment. A similar result could be developed for the household component, along lines recently discussed by Patinkin [14]. As already indicated, throughout this model we suppose that durable consumer goods are also treated as capital accumulation and depreciated in the usual way. An increase in the supply of real balances will therefore induce consumers to extend their purchases of consumer durables to maintain a balanced asset portfolio. But here we prefer to keep to the production function interpretation of events. An alternative way of developing the point is by writing

$$K^d = \psi\left(r, \frac{Y}{P}\right),$$

where the desired capital stock is a function of the price of capital r and the expected level of real output. The change in the desired stock in this model in response to arbitrary changes in the interest rate and real balances is found (ignoring costs of adjustment) as

$$dK^d = \frac{\partial \psi}{\partial r}\, dr + \frac{\partial \psi}{\partial (Y/P)}\, d\left(\frac{Y}{P}\right).$$

But

$$d\left(\frac{Y}{P}\right) = \left[\partial\left(\frac{Y}{P}\right) \middle/ \partial\left(\frac{M}{P}\right)\right] \cdot d\left(\frac{M}{P}\right).$$

This shows that the change in desired capital stock depends on the change of the rate of interest and the change of money balances. The adjustment of the actual stock of capital in response to changes in the desired stock can be specified as one of the general class of fractional adjustment processes which depend on the cost of speeding up or slowing down the rate of investment.

investment function in real terms as

$$\frac{I}{P} = I\left(r, \frac{M}{P}\right),$$ (9.11)

where $\quad\dfrac{\partial(I/P)}{\partial r} < 0$,

and $\quad\dfrac{\partial(I/P)}{\partial(M/P)} > 0$.

We derive the demand for money as outlined in the previous section. The marginal real return attributable to a given stock of real money balances is reflected in the first derivative $\partial(Y/P)/\partial(M/P)$ of the production function; while the prevailing interest rate reflects the opportunity cost of holding those balances. Given the assumption that $\partial(Y/P)/\partial(M/P)$ is a declining function of M/P, monetary equilibrium is achieved when

$$\frac{\partial(Y/P)}{\partial(M/P)} = r.$$

From this equilibrium condition is derived the demand function for real balances shown in figure 2:

$$\frac{L}{P} = L(r),$$ (9.12)

where $\quad\dfrac{\partial(L/P)}{\partial r} < 0$.

The nominal money supply is treated as a parameter of the system, determined by the monetary authority[13]; i.e., initially,

$$M = M_0.$$ (9.13)

---

[13] While it would be possible to include the interest rate as a variable influencing the nominal supply of money, there seems to be no strong empirical reason for doing so.

As a first approximation it is convenient to think of this money supply as a pure 'outside' fiat currency.

The essential relationships of the model may now be assembled as follows:

$$\frac{Y}{P} = \phi \left(K_0, N_0, \frac{M}{P} \right) ; \tag{9.9}$$

$$\frac{S}{P} = S \left(\frac{Y}{P}, r \right) ; \tag{9.10}$$

$$\frac{I}{P} = I \left(r, \frac{M}{P} \right) ; \tag{9.11}$$

$$\frac{L}{P} = L(r) ; \tag{9.12}$$

$$M = M_0 . \tag{9.13}$$

3.2. Equilibrium characteristics

Equilibrium from the production side is given by (1). For equilibrium in the commodities market it is required that

$$S \left(\frac{Y}{P}, r \right) = I \left(r, \frac{M}{P} \right) ; \tag{9.14}$$

and in the money market that

$$\frac{M_0}{P} = L(r) . \tag{9.15}$$

Eq. (9.14) represents a family of the familiar Hicksian *IS* functions. For any given M/P, it indicates the various combinations of interest rate and real income level consistent with the clearing of the commodities market. The larger M/P, the 'higher' is the *IS* curve in the conventional configuration, indicating the increased output that is necessary, at any given interest rate, to satisfy the additional investment demand induced by those balances. The slope of each *IS* curve is determined by the marginal propensity to save $\partial(S/P)/\partial(Y/P)$ and by the responsiveness of investment and saving to the interest rate as reflected in $\partial(I/P)/\partial r$ and $\partial(S/P)/\partial r$ respectively. The shift of the curve for a given change in real balances is determined by the value of $\partial(I/P)/\partial(M/P)$.

There is no conventional *LM* function associated with the single, productivity-oriented demand for money in this model. With fixed employment, and a continuously declining marginal productivity of real balances, there is only one output associated with a given rate of interest. In place of the *LM* function of the standard model, we combine eqs. (9.9) and (9.10) to yield the rather different, composite equilibrium relationship

$$\frac{Y}{P} = g(r) \,, \tag{9.16}$$

signifying optimality with respect both to the holding of real balances and to their utilisation in production. We designate this production-optimum-money relationship the *POM* function.

The *POM* function can be expected to have a generally negative slope, reflecting the fact that as the interest rate falls the community will be induced to hold greater real balances, thus imposing the need for higher rates of ouput to justify the productive application of those holdings. In the limit, where $r = 0$ and $M/P = (M/P)^*$, output is at its maximum $(Y/P)^*$. As the interest rate increases to very high levels, the demand for money as a factor of production is driven towards zero, and the economy approaches the low level of production $(Y/P)_{min}$ typically associated with a barter form of organization.

The equilibrium characteristics of the system as a whole are determined by the interaction of the *POM* and *IS* curves, and hence depend upon the precise shapes of these curves. In an unrestricted world, there can be no guarantee of a unique solution. In principle it is conceivable, for example, that a case may arise like that illustrated

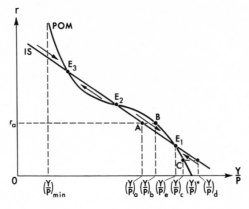

Fig. 3.

in figure 3. Assume for this purpose that the real balance effect upon investment is negligible [$\partial(I/P)/\partial(M/P) = 0$], so that the IS curve is uniquely identified for all M/P. Each of the intersections E_1, E_2, or E_3 implies that the demand for real money balances is satisfied by the available supply; that those money balances are fully employed; and that the output thus produced is absorbed by aggregate demand. Accordingly, all three represent viable equilibrium states of the system.

It must be noted, however, that in the normal case where [$\partial(I/P)/\partial(M/P)$] > 0, these three equilibria cannot exist simultaneously; for they are all associated with different quantities of real balances, which involve different IS curves. Even allowing for this it is still possible that the system may be simultaneously consistent with a low-, an intermediate-, and a high-output equilibrium. But for a given shape of the IS curve, the probability of this occurring decreases the less pronounced are the inflexions in the POM function, and the greater is the elasticity of the investment function with respect to real balances (which tends to shift the IS curve out of the multiple-intersection range as real balances change). On the other hand, an appropriate nonlinearity of the IS curve could also give rise to multiple solutions.

3.3. Stability of the system

In order to establish stability properties we next examine the question of disequilibrium behaviour.[14] Disequilibrium may involve violation of any of the relations (9.9), (9.14) and (9.15), or any combination of them. Let us take each case in turn, considered independently.

Output cannot exceed the constraint imposed by the production function (9.9). On the other hand, it may fall short of the level appropriate to the current stock of real balances. This implies an inefficient organisation of production.[15] Competitive pressures will tend to induce an expansion of output, thus restoring equilibrium directly, while any attempt to convert the currently unused cash balances into bonds will tend to reduce the interest rate.

Monetary disequilibrium involves positive or negative excess demand for real balances at the ruling interest rate. The former case implies that the interest rate is below its equilibrium value. As holders attempt to adjust their asset position by converting bonds to cash the interest rate rises, reducing the excess demand for money and bringing the market toward equilibrium. The adjustment is symmetrical in the contrary case of an initial negative excess demand.

In the commodities market, disequilibrium involves inequality between production and aggregate demand. In the typical Keynesian analysis, this is resolved in one of two ways, depending upon the existence of excess capacity. At less than full employment (the fixprice model), disequilibrium is eliminated simply by an appropriate adjustment of output. Under full employment conditions the burden of adjustment falls wholly on the price level.[16] Here

[14] The question of stability cannot strictly be resolved without reference to some explicit, fully specified dynamic adjustment mechanism prescribing the disequilibrium behaviour of the model. However, here we follow the less rigorous procedure of conventional static equilibrium theory, and attempt to infer stability properties on the basis simply of plausible, *ad hoc* assumptions concerning directions of change of the relevant variables.

[15] At the current level of output the marginal productivity of real balances exceeds their marginal cost.

[16] Friedman has recently offered an extended discussion of this issue ([7], pp. 207–12).

we regard both possibilities as part of the general adjustment mechanism. A positive excess demand for commodities, $[I(r, M/P) - S(Y/P, r)] > 0$, may be an incentive to increase production; but it is also an incentive to increase prices, which has the desired effect of reducing aggregate demand. In the contrary case the opposite pressure will be exerted on these variables.

In the light of these considerations let us now examine the stability of the system about E_1 (figure 3). Consider a point A where output, at $(Y/P)_a$, is below its equilibrium value $(Y/P)_e$. For ease of exposition, assume for the moment that $[\partial(I/P)/\partial(M/P)] = 0$, so that the IS function shown in figure 3 is defined for all price levels. At A, although output is correctly adjusted to aggregate demand (since the point is on the IS curve), it does not represent an efficient utilization of the existing money supply, which is capable of sustaining the higher level of output indicated by the POM curve at r_a. Accordingly, an attempt will be made to dispose of the excess money balances; or to raise production, say towards $(Y/P)_b$, in order to absorb available capacity; or both.

Suppose the initial reaction is confined to the adjustment of output. This carries the system to B, where monetary and production equilibrium prevails, but where aggregate demand, equivalent only to $(Y/P)_a$ at the current interest rate, is insufficient, by the amount $[(Y/P)_b - (Y/P)_a]$, to clear the commodities market. If this excess supply is now met simply by a decrease of prices (again to choose but one of the available possibilities), then the real money supply M_o/P increases, causing an increase in productive capacity due to the productivity of money, and a downward interest rate adjustment in the money market. Both of these effects are revealed in the movement from B towards E_1 along the POM curve. At the same time, the declining interest rate induces additional demand, until eventually the entire system comes to equilibrium at E_1.

There are obvious variants of this analysis. It might be argued that demand considerations dominate those of productive capacity so that instead of raising output from $(Y/P)_a$ to $(Y/P)_b$ in order to activate idle cash balances, the more plausible behaviour would be to keep output adjusted to demand, while attempting to release excess money balances. The effect of this response would be to drive down the interest rate, increasing aggregate demand and carrying the economy down along its *IS* curve from *A* towards E_1. Meanwhile the falling interest rate enables additional cash balances to be used efficiently, thus increasing productive capacity as shown by the *POM* curve. Eventually capacity and demand will correspond at E_1.

More generally, the adjustment process might be expected to move on more than one front, with any combination of the price level, the interest rate and the level of output operating simultaneously as equilibrating variables. All such cases, however, may be analysed along the lines of the preceding paragraphs, and can be shown to give the same result: E_1 is stable with respect to local downward displacements of income.

Now consider *C* as a typical displacement in the other direction [points to the right of the *POM* curve are excluded by eq. (9.9)]. Since output is constrained, the excess demand for commodities $[(Y/P)_d - (Y/P)_c]$ generates rising prices. The associated reduction in the real money supply forces a reduction in output and drives the economy back along the *POM* curve towards E_1. Simultaneously, the rising interest rate causes aggregate demand to decline at a faster rate than output (given the relative slopes of the curves) until the two come to equality at $(Y/P)_e$.

The equilibrium at E_1 is thus stable (in the restricted sense specified earlier) with respect to all local disturbances. Parallel reasoning establishes that E_3 is also fully stable, while E_2 is unstable for all disturbances. These properties are indicated by the directional arrows in figure 3.

It should be emphasised again that there is no reason to suppose that the multiple equilibrium case is in any sense "normal". Further, as we have argued earlier, for a given production function the likelihood of this case arising diminishes the more sensitive is the *IS* curve to variations in real balances. Accordingly, in extending the foregoing analysis now to accommodate the influence of real balances upon investment, we concentrate on single-solution configurations of the model. Consider the case illustrated in figure 4, with the *IS* curve at $IS(M_0/P_1)$ and the economy operating at

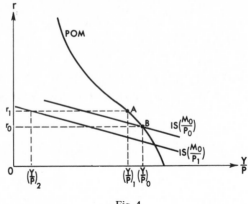

Fig. 4.

A.[17] This would mean production in excess of demand to the extent of $[(Y/P)_1 - (Y/P)_2]$. Suppose that this excess production is met by a reduction of prices. With the nominal money supply fixed, this price adjustment implies an increase in real balances, which has in turn two consequences. First, total productive capacity will rise, enabling the economy to move out along its *POM* curve. Second, the *IS* curve will move to the right as aggregate demand increases, due to the real balance term in the investment function. The effect of these forces is to produce a convergence to an equilibrium state; for the one tends to increase the actual level of output, and the other to decrease the level required for equilibrium, so that the two adjustments will ultimately bring the economy to rest at some point like *B*. A similar convergence can be shown to operate in the reverse direction, where the economy produces initially above the equilibrium output $(Y/P)_0$.

[17] We assume throughout that the *IS* curve does not cut the *POM* curve from above, thereby giving rise to a single unstable equilibrium.

4. Behaviour of the model

4.1. The neutrality of money

Central to the model outlined in section 3 is the notion that money plays a positive role in determining the overall productive performance of the economic system. A state of barter reflects a less efficient organization of the community's physical resources than that which is possible under monetary arrangements; and, up to a point, the higher the degree of monetisation (defined, for example, in terms of the ratios $(M/P)/K_0$ and $(M/P)/N_0$), the greater is the productive potential of those other resources. [18] In this fundamental sense, the characteristic feature of the model is the non-neutrality of money.

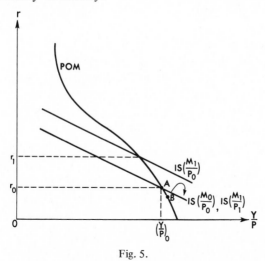

Fig. 5.

Such propositions relate, however, to money defined in real terms. It does not follow that output can be simply regulated through variations in the nominal money supply. Consider the situation illustrated in figure 5, with the economy initially in equi-

[18] Crouch's model [5] in which money is seen as a labour-augmenting technological innovation, appears to comprehend only the special case of an optimal degree of monetisation.

librium at a point like A. We have already shown such an equilibrium to be stable with respect to local displacements in either direction. It can now be seen to be similarly stable with respect to an exogenous monetary disturbance.

Assuming, as usual, that price adjustments are not instantaneous, then an increase in the nominal money stock means, in the first instance, a corresponding increase in the real value of that variable. The productivity effect of this increment to the real money supply enables a movement out along the *POM* function, raising the productive potential of the system, say to B. At the same time, aggregate demand is stimulated by any fall in the interest rate and by an upward shift of the *IS* function. The relative magnitudes of these responses are such as to create excess demand at all interest rates lower than r_1, so that prices begin to rise. This reduction in real balances will continue, shifting the *IS* function to the left, on the one hand, and reducing productive capacity on the other, until the economy returns to its original equilibrium state at $(Y/P)_0$ and r_0. The net effect of increasing the nominal money supply is simply to raise the price level equiproportionately, while leaving the equilibrium values of the real variables unchanged. In this sense, money is neutral. This conclusion is of course equivalent both to the pure classical result, and to the Keynesian result for an increase in the money supply in a full employment situation. [19]

The implication in our model is that where an equilibrium exists at a positive interest rate, any attempt to stimulate economic activity by means of an increase in productive real balances is bound to be defeated by the accompanying demand reaction. Without imposing some artificial constraint upon aggregate demand, the optimum (real) quantity of money cannot be achieved.

The neutrality of money, in this comparative-statics sense, does not mean, however, that monetary changes cannot produce significant effects upon the behaviour of the system. We have shown

[19] However, unlike the Keynesian model (at least in the general case outside the liquidity trap), output here is invariant also with respect to a (nominal) monetary contraction.

that the new equilibrium, achieved after the system has fully accommodated itself to a change in the nominal money stock, is identical with the old in terms of real output. But there is no reason to suppose that this accommodation will necessarily take place quickly or smoothly; and good reason to suppose that it will be accompanied by transitory output variations. Indeed, from a practical, real-world point of view, the most interesting repercussions of monetary disturbances are likely to be those associated with just such transitory adjustment paths.

We cannot here undertake a detailed analysis of the disequilibrium dynamics that underly this extremely important aspect of the behaviour of the model. But we can derive some general insight into the sort of repercussions that might be expected. A monetary expansion, reflected initially in both the nominal and the real value of the money supply, throws the system immediately into a state of disequilibrium characterised by both excess demand for commodities, and excess productive capacity. Both supply and demand considerations call for a higher rate of production. A natural response, then, would be an increase in output towards *B* (figure 5). The short-term effect of the increased money stock is to stimulate the economy. However, as figure 5 shows, given the elasticities of the functions no feasible increase in output can alone eliminate excess demand in the commodities market. Sooner or later, therefore, price adjustments must take place. As prices rise, the real money balances decline, output is constrained, by the productivity effect of that money stock, to fall back towards its original level; and is encouraged to do so by the concomitant reduction of demand.

The pattern emerging from this brief qualitative sketch of the adjustment process is consistent with reported empirical findings. [20] It makes an interesting comparison also with David Hume's classic description of the response to a monetary stimulus. In the short run, Hume points out,

we find, that, in every Kingdom, into which money begins to

[20] See, for example, Friedman [7], pp. 216–17. See also Friedman [6], chapter 12.

flow in greater abundance than formerly, everything takes a new face: labour and industry gain life; the merchant becomes more enterprising, the manufacturer more diligent and skilful, and even the farmer follows his plough with greater alacrity and attention. [21]

But, in my opinion, it is only in this interval or intermediate situation, between the acquisition of money and rise of prices, that the increasing quantity of gold and silver is favourable to industry. [22]

4.2. Changes in aggregate demand

Autonomous changes in aggregate demand cause corresponding shifts in the *IS* curve. Consider an outward shift, say from IS_0 to IS_1 in figure 6. The immediate effect is to create excess demand

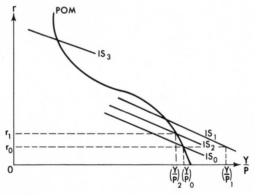

Fig. 6.

amounting to $[(Y/P)_1 - (Y/P)_0]$ at the current interest rate. As we have shown previously for such a disequilibrium, price, output and demand adjustments will be such as to bring about a new equilibrium at $(Y/P)_2$ on IS_2. This is an apparently perverse result: in the face of an increase in demand, output falls. The explanation lies in the fact that the rising prices brought about by excess

[21] Hume [9], p. 37.
[22] Hume [9], p. 38.

demand in the commodities market reduces the real money supply and thus, since money is a factor of production, reduces real output. [23]

It is interesting to note that a sufficiently large increase in demand (shown by IS_3) can so far outstrip the ability to produce that any attempt to increase the real money stock is effectively destroyed by price inflation, so that the economy is forced towards a virtual barter equilibrium. Under such circumstances, however, one would expect that since real balances are so valuable, the long term effect would be to produce substitutes for money; we touch upon this below, in section 4.3. A substantial contraction of demand, on the other hand, could produce the optimum result discussed earlier.

4.3. Changes in technology

Any change in technology will affect productive capacity. Specifically, a change in the technology of the monetary system, leading to either more or less intensive use of real balances per unit of output, will mean a shift of the production function (1). This is likely to cause a concomitant shift in the demand-for-money function, and will certainly cause a shift in the *POM* function. Increased monetary efficiency will lift the *POM* curve, tending to raise output and to reduce the equilibrium interest rate. The introduction of less efficient monetary arrangements will have the opposite effects.

5. Quantitative considerations

The practical, as distinct from the theoretical interest of the foregoing analysis turns primarily upon the precise econometric characteristics of the production function (1). We have noticed earlier (footnote 5, above) that Bailey [1], for example, recognises the appropriateness of including real money balances in the produc-

[23] It will be recalled that we are at present assuming fixed employment of labour as well as of capital.

tion function; but after suggesting the possibility, he goes on to ignore the effects since "for the most part the change in real income will be too small a magnitude to be taken seriously". [24] If that were indeed the case then there would be little point in pursuing the analysis further. [25] It is therefore worth doing a rough check to try to deduce what the effects are likely to be.

The issue depends critically on the elasticity of substitution between real balances and other factors of production in the aggregate production function. Three cases can be usefully distinguished.

As a first possibility we may take the Leontief-Marx case of a proportional production function with zero elasticity of substitution. Then if real balances are the scarce factor a given percentage decline in the real money supply must give rise to the same percentage decline in real output. [26] Clearly if we assumed this sort of production function it could only be correct for a limited range of output. In particular such a model cannot comprehend the concept of a positive and finite rate of output under pure barter conditions. Nevertheless it is useful as an archetype at the aggregative level. [27]

The second archetype is the extreme assumption of perfect factor substitution. Any increase in real money balances may simply substitute for labour and capital. Again such conditions could not conceivably hold over any substantial range of output — indeed they carry the nonsensical implication that the optimum

[24] Bailey [1], p. 61.

[25] It is interesting to observe that in the revised edition of his book, Bailey expresses no such reservations about the empirical significance of the point; [2], pp. 54–56.

[26] If we assumed, on the other hand, that the economy comprised industries each with a zero elasticity of substitution but with different cash requirements per unit of output, a change in the quantity of real money balances would in general result in a change in the output mix. We do not intend to examine this aspect of the problem in this paper.

[27] It might be held to result in conditions approximating to those of the Cobb-Douglas in the long run; see below. It may appear that one rather surprising supporter of the view that there is zero elasticity of substitution between money balances and other factors of production is Keynes himself. In the *General Theory* he says: "The second *differentia* of money is that it has an elasticity of substitution equal, or nearly equal, to zero; which means that as the exchange value of money rises there is no tendency to

quantity of real balances is infinite. Income could always be increased effortlessly by substituting money, which (as an approximation) costs nothing to produce, for labour and capital.

The third case is a Cobb-Douglas type of production function where the elasticity of substitution between real money balances and other factors of production is unity. Some idea of the reaction of the economy to an increase in real balances in such a case, where capital and labour are fixed, can be obtained as follows. Let velocity, Y/M, be 2 and the rate of interest 0.10. Then the share of "return" attributable to money balances in total output is α (the coefficient of real balances), where, from the Cobb-Douglas relation,

$$\alpha = r\frac{M}{Y} = \frac{0.1}{2} = 0.05 \ .$$

(Note that if we write velocity as equal to unity during slump conditions and we reduce the interest rate during the slump to 0.05 we get the same result.) Under such conditions, with perfect competition and constant returns, we would therefore expect that a 10% reduction in real balances would be reflected in a 0.5% reduction in output.

Choosing between the no-substitution, perfect substitution and Cobb-Douglas variants is a matter that should properly wait upon analysis of the data. However, perhaps we can venture some suggestions towards a preliminary selection at this stage. In the first place, we are concerned primarily with the *short*-run effects of a fall or rise in real balances. The substitution possibilities in the short run are likely to be very small indeed. One might therefore

substitute some other factor for it..." ([11], p. 231). But Keynes is not talking about the cost of real money balances in the sense of an increase in the interest rate (which is what we mean by the cost of money). He is talking about the *"exchange value"* of *nominal* money. The marginal utility of nominal money rises and falls *pari-passu* with the price level and so there is no tendency to substitution. Keynes' proposition is therefore no more and no less than a statement of the absence of a money illusion. In spite of the reference to "factor" substitution he did not imply that money and other factors had a zero elasticity of substitution in the *production* function. Indeed the concept of a money-in-the-production-function approach seems quite outside the framework of Keynes' analysis.

expect a Leontief-Marx assumption to be a fair approximation to the reactions of the economy within one or perhaps even two years. Secondly one would expect an increasing degree of substitution to be possible as time goes on, but it is unlikely to be as large as the Cobb-Douglas elasticity. Evidence from aggregate and industry production functions generally suggests values of the elasticity considerably less than unity. [28] In fact one would expect that under the impetus of reduced balances there would be incentives to produce innovations that economise on money stocks — to make money go further. Consequently, the production function would be induced to shift over time.

These arguments then lead us to conclude that in the *short* run the reaction of real output to a change in real balances will not be "too small a magnitude to be taken seriously". [29] It will be noted that analytically it is the *short* run reaction that is important. [30] In the longer run, in the absence of other changes, we would expect a movement in prices that would restore real balances to their former level.

Some idea of the order of magnitude of the short-run reaction of the economy of the United Kingdom to a change in real balances may be inferred from Sheppard's results [15]. In the postwar years a 10% increase in real balances has been associated with a 5—9% rise in the level of real income. [31] These are the results from annual data of a regression which is contemporaneous and includes the rate of interest; thus they are not ideal for our purposes. Quarterly data however, for the period 1956—67, which include the change in the interest rate, give similar results. [32]

[28] Walters [19].

[29] Bailey [1], p. 61.

[30] We have noted incidentally the distributional effects of a change in the money stock if industries differ in the extent to which they employ real balances in production. Thus in a period of contraction, firms that relied heavily on money balances would find themselves squeezed more than others. The money-hungry firms would try to attract money balances away from others in order to maintain production and profits. This distributional effect of a monetary squeeze, and in particular the differential effects on large and small firms, has been much discussed in recent years.

[31] Sheppard [15], pp. 84—85.

[32] This result was contributed by Dr. Charles Goodhart of the Bank of England. See Sheppard [15], p. 85, note to table 5.5.

We would not regard these data as powerful evidence in favour of our hypothesis. But again, there is perhaps enough to suggest that the *POM* effect should not be lightly dismissed.

References

[1] Martin J. Bailey, *National income and the price level: a study in macrotheory* (New York, McGraw-Hill, 1962).

[2] Martin J. Bailey, *National income and the price level: a study in macroeconomic theory*, 2nd ed. (New York, McGraw-Hill, 1971).

[3] Robert Clower, 'A reconsideration of the microfoundations of monetary theory', *Western Economic Journal* 6,1 (December 1967) 1–8. Reprinted in Clower, [4], pp. 202–11.

[4] R.W. Clower (ed.), *Monetary theory: selected readings* (Harmondsworth, Middlesex, Penguin, 1959).

[5] Robert Crouch, 'A new approach to the monetisation of neoclassical growth models', in this volume, p. 285.

[6] Milton Friedman, *The optimum quantity of money and other essays* (Chicago, Aldine, 1969).

[7] Milton Friedman, 'A theoretical framework for monetary analysis', *Journal of Political Economy* **78**, 2 (March/April 1970) 193–238.

[8] Milton Friedman, 'A monetary theory of nominal income', *Journal of Political Economy* **79**, 2 (March/April 1971) 323–37.

[9] David Hume, 'Of money', in: *David Hume: writings on economics*, edited by Eugene Rothwein (London, Nelson, 1955), pp. 33–46.

[10] Harry G. Johnson, 'Inside money, outside money, income, wealth and welfare in monetary theory', *Journal of Money, Credit and Banking* **1**, 1 (February 1969) 30–45.

[11] J.M. Keynes, *The general theory of employment, interest and money* (London, Macmillan, 1936).

[12] David Levhari and Don Patinkin, 'The role of money in a simple growth model', *American Economic Review* **58** (September 1968) 713–53.

[13] Don Patinkin, *Money interest and prices*, 2nd ed. (New York, Harper and Row, 1965).

[14] Don Patinkin, *On the nature of the monetary mechanism* (Wicksell Lectures, Stockholm, Almquist and Wicksell, 1967).

[15] D.K. Sheppard, *The growth and role of U.K. financial institutions, 1880–1962* (London, Methuen, 1971).

16] O.P. Tangri, 'Omissions in the treatment of the law of variable proportions', *American Economic Review* **56**, 3 (June 1966) 484–93.

[17] James Tobin, 'Money and economic growth', *Econometrica* **33**, 4 (October 1965) 671–84.

[18] James Tobin, 'The neutrality of money in growth models: a comment', *Economica* (N.S.) **34**, 133 (February 1967) 69–72.

[19] A.A. Walters, 'Production and cost functions: an econometric survey', *Econometrica* **31**, 1–2 (January-April 1963) 1–66.

THE SUPPLY PRICE OF CAPITAL IN MACROECONOMIC MODELS *

John HELLIWELL
University of British Columbia

Gordon SPARKS
Queen's University

and

Jack FRISCH
Princeton University

1. Introduction

Although the supply price of capital plays a key role in theoretical models of the link between financial markets and output and the price level, quantitative models have generally utilized crude approximations to this variable based on nominal interest rates and stock market dividend/price ratios. In this paper, we report on our efforts to measure the supply price of capital more precisely, in both nominal and real terms, and to make use of it within aggregate econometric models of the Canadian and Australian economies. The Canadian results are used within the quarterly model RDX2 described elsewhere in this volume [5].

* The Canadian work was carried out while Helliwell and Sparks were part-time consultants to the Research Department of the Bank of Canada. The Australian work was done while Frisch was an officer and Helliwell a visiting economist in the Reserve Bank of Australia. We are grateful to Jim Dingle of the Bank of Canada for help with the Canadian data and experiments, and to Peter Boxall of the Reserve Bank for revising the Australian data and re-estimating the Australian equations. Responsibility for the contents of the paper rests solely with the authors.

In section 2, the theoretical basis of the concept is discussed and an equation is derived relating the market value of the stock of real capital to the interest rate, current earnings and the expected rate of increase in the price level. This relationship is used in section 3 to obtain empirical estimates of the supply price of capital in Canada and, as a by-product, the expected rate of inflation. The Australian empirical work is described in section 4. In section 5 we describe some of the more important actual and potential uses for the measures of the supply price of capital and the expected rate of inflation within macroeconomic models. The concluding section suggests further developments, and contains a chart of estimated supply prices of capital, in real and nominal terms, for Australia and Canada.

2. The concept of the supply price of capital

2.1. Definition and relationship to investment

In a number of recent writings (see for example [10], [11]), James Tobin has led the way in formulating a theory of the link between financial markets and real investment that breaks away from the implicit Keynesian assumption that bonds and real capital are perfect substitutes in the portfolios of investors. He advocates a general approach to monetary analysis which allows for a spectrum of assets, ranging from money to real capital, whose rates of return are determined by the interaction of demand and supply. In this framework, Tobin argues that:

> "The strategic variable − the ultimate gauge of expansion or deflation, of monetary tightness or ease − is the rate of return that the community of wealth-owners requires in order to absorb the existing capital stock (valued at current prices), no more, no less, into their portfolios and balance sheets. This rate may be termed the supply price of capital" ([10], p. 35).

A fundamental distinction is made between the supply price of capital (ρ), which is the rate of return on the stock of capital in existence at a particular point in time, and the conventional notion of the marginal efficiency of capital (mec), which represents the rate of return on newly produced capital goods. The former is determined by the asset preferences of investors and the relative supplies of competing assets, while the latter is determined by the stock of physical capital already in existence in conjunction with technology, prices of other factors and the price of output. Investment in newly produced capital goods is seen to depend on the relationship between these two rates of return. If ρ is lower than the mec, there will be an incentive to add to the existing stock by undertaking new investment expenditure, in excess of that required to offset depreciation, until equilibrium is restored through a fall in the mec. Looking at this process from an alternative point of view, there is an incentive for new investment when the market value per unit of the existing stock of capital exceeds its reproduction cost. Such a disequilibrium can, of course, persist for an extended period of time because of the lag involved in putting new plant and equipment in place. In the converse situation, in which ρ is above the mec, gross investment will fall to zero and remain there until depreciation reduces the capital stock to the point where equality between ρ and the mec is restored.

2.2. Relationship to the share market

Since the stock market represents the primary institutional vehicle for trading equities in the existing stock of real capital, the supply price of capital held by corporations can be viewed as the rate of return on unlevered shares. From the point of view of corporate investment decisions it is equivalent to the cost of capital as defined by Modigliani and Miller [8] in the context of their well-known theorem which states that the market value of a firm is independent of the proportions of debt and equity in its capital structure. The Modigliani-Miller analysis provides an alternative but equivalent view of the key role of the supply price of capital in investment decisions. They argue that a firm will maximize the market value of its shares by undertaking those projects which yield a return greater than or equal to the capitalization rate applied by investors to the future earnings stream of the firm. Their capital structure proposition provides an important supplement to Tobin's analysis since it implies that the supply price of capital remains the fundamental variable even when debt issue is used to finance investment. The interest rate on bonds is irrelevant except in so far as it influences the supply price of capital via some degree of substitutability between bonds and equities in financial portfolios. This conclusion is of course strictly valid only in the Modigliani-Miller world which abstracts from corporation taxes and market imperfection.

Modigliani and Miller also emphasize the role of uncertainty with respect to the future earnings stream from real capital as the basic source of the imperfect substitutability between it and other assets. Differences in capitalisation rates among firms are attributable to differences in risk, and firms with the same capitalisation rate are said to be in the same "risk class" ([8], pp. 265–67). Since our empirical estimates are based on an aggregate over all firms, we implicitly assume that proportions of the total market value of real capital accounted for by firms in different risk classes remain constant over time.

2.3. A simple model

Given the expected future earnings stream, x_t, and the supply price of capital, ρ, the market value of the stock of real capital, v, is simply the present discounted value given by

$$v = \int_0^\infty e^{-\rho t} x_t \, dt .$$

(10.1)

If the earnings stream is assumed to grow at a constant rate, g, beginning at an initial level x, this integral reduces to:

$$v = \frac{x}{\rho - g} ;$$

(10.2)

or

$$\rho = \frac{x}{v} + g.$$ (10.3)

Since g and ρ are not directly observable, we eliminate ρ from (10.3) by introducing a reduced-form equation derived from the supply and demand for real capital. The demand is assumed to depend on ρ and the long-term bond rate, r. The relative supply is represented by the ratio of the earnings from real capital to interest paid on government debt, h; that is, $\rho v/h$, or equivalently,

$$\frac{x + gv}{h}.$$ (10.4)

Thus our reduced-form equation is of the form

$$\rho = f(r, \frac{x + gv}{h}, e),$$ (10.5)

where e is an error term representing omitted variables.

Combining (10.3) and (10.5) we obtain the following relationship:

$$\frac{x}{v} + g = f(r, \frac{x + gv}{h}, e).$$ (10.6)

The remaining nonobservable variable, g, is assumed to be related to the expected rate of increase of the price level as represented by a distributed lag function of past rates of change; that is

$$g = \sum_{i=0}^{n} w_i \dot{p}_{-i} + u,$$ (10.7)

where $\dot{p}_{-i}$ is the rate of change of the price level lagged i periods and u is an error term. This assumption is discussed below.

2.4. *The market value of real capital and the expected rate of inflation*

The expected rate of inflation is taken to be the principal determinant of the expected rate of growth of earnings for the following reasons. First, it should be noted that the relevant stream of earnings is that which is expected to accrue to holders of the existing stock and excludes earnings generated by future additions to the capital stock financed by new saving. Thus, future growth in output will not affect g unless there is a concomitant change in the capital share. If productivity gains are accompanied by proportional increases in the real wage rate, inflation-induced capital gains will be the only source of earnings growth.

Under the above hypothesis concerning the determination of g, our model as expressed in (10.6) becomes a relationship determining the share market earnings/price ratio in terms of the interest rate, the expected rate of inflation, and the relative supply variable. It is interesting to compare this with an alternative approach, used in a number of recent studies, which derives a measure of the expected rate of inflation by relating the nominal interest rate to past rates of change of the price level.[1] Since this approach purports to be a theory of interest rate determination, it introduces the difficult theoretical problem of specifying the determinants of the real rate of interest. (For attempts to do this, see [2], [7] and [9]). Furthermore, this approach is not in the spirit of Tobin's framework since it implicitly assumes that in equilibrium the bond rate and the rate of return on real capital are equal (or differ by a constant risk premium) and are independent of relative supplies. Our approach attempts to get at the expected rate of inflation via the relationship between bond and stock yields adjusted for the effect of changes in relative supplies.

---

[1] See Yohe and Karnosky [12] for an example of this approach and a review of earlier studies.

3. Estimation of the supply price of capital using Canadian data

3.1. Estimation of a time series for the market value of real capital

A time series for the market value of domestic business fixed capital assets and inventories was obtained by applying to the aggregate book value of these assets a valuation ratio obtained from balance sheet and stock market data for the seventy-six largest nonfinancial corporations whose shares have been traded on Canadian stock exchanges continuously since 1955. An estimate of aggregate book value was obtained by accumulating business investment expenditure at historic cost and deducting depreciation at the declining balance rates specified for tax purposes (5% per annum for structures and 20% per annum for machinery and equipment).

The market value of the capital assets of the firms in our sample was estimated by assuming that the market values of financial assets and liabilities are equal to book values. Thus, given the market value of the firms' equity, the market value of capital assets can be calculated as follows:

Market value of capital assets = Market value of equity − Net financial assets at book value.

An aggregate valuation ratio was then obtained by dividing total market value of capital assets of firms in the sample by total book value. The market value of the capital stock for all firms (VKB) was estimated by applying this ratio to aggregate book value.

3.2. Empirical results

For purposes of empirical estimation, eq. (10.6) was written in the form

$$r - \frac{x}{v} = \alpha + \beta \frac{x + gv}{h} + g + e . \tag{10.8}$$

Substituting from (10.7) and rearranging terms, we obtain

$$r - \frac{x}{v} = \alpha + \beta \frac{x}{h} + (1 + \beta \frac{v}{h}) \sum_{i=0}^{n} w_i \dot{p}_{-i} + e + \beta \frac{v}{h} u \ . \tag{10.9}$$

Since this relationship is nonlinear in the parameters, the least squares estimates were obtained by an iterative procedure. Almon polynomial constraints were employed to estimate the weights in the distributed lag. The variables used were as follows:

r: long-term Government of Canada bond rate.

x: four-quarter moving sum of corporate profits after taxes, corporate interest paid, net income of nonfarm unincorporated business less imputed labour income, and income of government business enterprises.

v: average of the beginning and end of quarter market value of the business capital stock.

h: four-quarter moving sum of interest paid on government debt.

$\dot{p}$: four-quarter percentage rate of change of the Consumer Price Index.

Using quarterly data for the period 1956–68, the following equation was obtained, and is presented in the format of eq. (10.8):

$$r - \frac{x}{v} = \underset{(3.35)}{2.028} - \underset{(-7.98)}{0.9122} \frac{x + gv}{h} + \sum_{i=0}^{11} w_i \dot{p}_{-i} \ .$$

w_i: *Lag distribution on* $\dot{p}$

(third degree polynomial, constrained to pass through zero at $t-12$)

Lag	Weight	t-ratio
D	0.1577	(0.93)
1	0.0633	(0.92)
2	0.0113	(0.25)
3	−0.0068	(−0.09)
4	0.0010	(0.01)

Lag	Weight	t-ratio
5	0.0262	(0.37)
6	0.0607	(1.10)
7	0.0963	(2.26)
8	0.1245	(2.75)
9	0.1373	(2.47)
10	0.1263	(2.18)
11	0.0833	(1.99)
Sum	0.8811	(4.54)

$SEE = 0.511, \bar{R}^2 = 0.786, D/W = 0.60.$

R^2 for $v = 0.93, D/W = 0.60.$

The numbers in brackets are t-values of estimated coefficients, or of sums of estimated coefficients. Below the standard error of estimate (SEE), $\bar{R}^2$, and Durbin/Watson statistic (D/W) for the estimated equation, we report a pseudo R^2 and a Durbin/Watson statistic calculated from the estimated and actual values of v, the share market value of business fixed assets and inventories. The R^2 for v was calculated as one minus the ratio of the sum of squared errors to the sum of squared deviations from the mean for the actual values. This formula is strictly speaking inappropriate when the series do not represent actual and predicted values from a regression with a constant term. However it gives an indication of the explanatory power of the equation in terms of the market value of the business capital stock.

3.3. Real and nominal measures of the supply price of capital

The distributed lag weights obtained were used to construct a series for the expected rate of change of consumer prices ($PCPICE$).

A time series to represent ρ can be derived in two different ways. From the definition eq. (10.3), ρ can be estimated as the sum of x/v and $PCPICE$. From eq. (10.8), on the other hand, we can derive ρ as $[r - \alpha - \beta (x + gv)/h]$. If there were no error terms in eqs. (10.7) and (10.8), these two definitions would be equivalent. In the absence of any specific information concerning the relative size of the errors, we take a simple average of the alternative expressions to derive a time series we call *RHO*. The corresponding measure of the supply price of capital in real terms, *RHOR*, is obtained by subtracting *PCPICE* from *RHO*.

4. Estimation of the supply price of capital using Australian data

4.1. Obtaining a time series for the market value of real capital

The basic method used is the same as that for the corresponding Canadian series for *VKB*. The sample of firms used is slightly smaller, but the basic criteria used for inclusion are similar—continuous trading on Australian stock exchanges since 1956, and total assets of each firm greater than $25 million at the end of the sample period. The exact procedures used are described in section 6 of [4].

4.2. Types of equation estimated

The experiments with Australian data involved several generalisations of the basic model used with the Canadian data.

In addition to using a four-quarter moving sum of actual profits to define the normalised profits stream (x), we have also tried explicit stationary expectations processes involving extrapolative and regressive elements. Both the extrapolative and regressive elements are assumed to have exponentially declining weights and are applied to data for the current and preceding eleven quarters. This leaves three parameters to be estimated: the rates of decline of the extrapolative and regressive elements and a parameter determining the relative importance of the extrapolative and regressive components.

We also assessed an alternative specification of the function linking the relative supply variable to the rates of return on government bonds and business assets. The linear version used in the

Canadian case takes the form:

$$r - \rho = \alpha + \beta \left(\frac{x + gv}{h}\right) + e .$$
(10.10)

The Australian experiments have also employed a constant elasticity approximation in which the ratio of the rates of return depends linearly on the ratio of the relative supplies:

$$\frac{\rho}{r} = \alpha + \beta \left(\frac{x + gv}{h}\right) + e .$$
(10.11)

This equation is transformed before estimation by multiplying through by r, and decomposing ρ according to $\rho = x/v + g$, so that:

$$\frac{x}{v} = -g + \alpha r + \beta r \left(\frac{x + gv}{h}\right) + er .$$
(10.12)

Two further developments involved making the price expectations weights depend on current values of factors influencing future prices, and allowing for portfolio substitution between Australian and foreign equities. Both of these supplementary features substantially improved the fit of the model, and will therefore be explained in more detail in the next section describing the estimated equations.

4.3. Empirical results

In this section we first describe briefly the empirical counterparts to the variables in the theoretical model, and then present the estimated equations.

v: Market value of business fixed assets and inventories. The Australian equations use VKB, the end-of-quarter market value of business fixed assets and inventories, to represent v. The Canadian equations use the average of the beginning and end of quarter values for VKB. (The chief reason for this difference is that the

Canadian interest rate is the average over the quarter, while the Australian interest rate is the average for the last week of the quarter. Thus both models employ definitions for v that provide corresponding valuation dates for bonds and shares.)

x: Four-quarter moving sum of company net operating surplus, after company tax, plus a synthetic series for the net operating surplus of unincorporated business. (See [1] for details, as well as for some results using an alternative definition of x.)

r: Interest rate on long-term government bonds. 10-year theoretical yield on Commonwealth securities.

h: Four-quarter moving sum of total interest payments on the government debt, excluding payments on foreign-currency debt (which is assumed to be entirely foreign-held).

p: Four-quarter percentage rate of change of the Consumer Price Index.

$RYPUS$: Earnings yield on U.S. shares (dividend/price ratio from *MPS* model, multiplied by ratio of aggregate profits to dividends).

$RYPUK$: Earnings yield on U.K. shares (from U.K. *Financial Times*).

$RYPUKUS$: Average of U.K. and U.S. earnings yields ($RYPUKUS$ = 0.5 $RYPUK$ + 0.5 $RYPUS$).

The first results to report are negative. None of the synthetic series for expected profits provide equations whose fit and structure are as good as those from models using a four-quarter moving sum of profits to represent x. Furthermore, in neither of the two functional forms fitted did the relative supply variable perform very satisfactorily. Its coefficient was generally insignificant, and sometimes of perverse sign. The strongest role for the relative supply variable is obtained from eq. (10.9) with the following results (sample period 3Q58–4Q69):

$$r - \frac{x}{v} = \underset{(-6.98)}{3.35} - \underset{(-1.88)}{0.0116} \frac{x + gv}{h} + \sum_{i=0}^{11} w_i \dot{p}_{-i} \, .$$

w_i: lag distribution on $\dot{p}$

(third degree polynomial constrained to pass through zero at $t-12$)

Lag	Weight	t-ratio
0	0.0475	(0.52)
1	0.0646	(1.63)
2	0.0722	(3.09)
3	0.0721	(2.24)
4	0.0659	(1.82)
5	0.0553	(1.71)
6	0.0420	(1.73)
7	0.0276	(1.51)
8	0.0140	(0.66)
9	0.0027	(0.10)
10	−0.0045	(−0.15)
11	−0.0060	(−0.28)
Sum	0.4534	(2.36)

$SEE = 0.970, \bar{R}^2 = 0.320, D/W = 0.26.$

R^2 for $v = 0.773, D/W = 0.27.$

Below the statistics for the estimated equation we report the R^2 and Durbin/Watson statistic calculated from the estimated and actual values of *VKB*, the share market value of business fixed assets and inventories. There is marked serial correlation of the residuals in the estimated equation and in the calculated series for the share market value of business fixed assets and inventories (v or *VKB*). The sum of the distributed lag weights on past price changes is about half as great as in the Canadian model.

Estimation of the function in the form suggested by eq. (10.12) produced a worse explanation for *VKB*. Much better results, however, are obtained when allowance is made for substitution between Australian, U.K. and U.S. equities in foreign portfolios, and for price expectations to be influenced by current values of variables likely to affect future prices. The former influence is captured by a weighted average of U.K. (*RYPUK*) and U.S. (*RYPUS*) earnings yields on equities. Several pairs of weights were assessed, but the best result, in terms of the R^2 between VKB and v, is obtained with weights of 0.5 attached to each yield. Adding the foreign rates of return markedly improves the residual properties of the equation without apparently disturbing the estimates of domestic price expectations. The results including the relative supply variable, with an insignificant positive coefficient, are reported in [1]. Without the supply variable, the estimated equation using data for the period 3Q58–4Q69 is:

$$r - \frac{x}{v} = \underset{(-15.8)}{-3.394} + \sum_{i=0}^{11} w_i \dot{p}_{-i} - \underset{(-13.3)}{0.7908} RYPUKUS$$

w_i: lag distribution on $\dot{p}$

Lag	Weight	t-ratio
0	−0.0523	(−1.52)
1	0.0342	(2.05)
2	0.0873	(9.01)
3	0.1127	(10.26)
4	0.1158	(9.60)
5	0.1021	(9.22)
6	0.0772	(8.52)
7	0.0465	(5.78)
8	0.0156	(1.69)
9	−0.0100	(−0.92)
10	−0.0248	(−2.26)
11	−0.0233	(−3.00)
Sum	0.4810	(5.62)

$SEE = 0.437, \bar{R}^2 = 0.862, D/W = 1.23.$

R^2 for $v = 0.966, D/W = 1.55.$

The coefficient on the weighted average of foreign yields indicates that the Australian supply price of capital would rise by about 0.4% in response to a 1% rise in either of the foreign equity yields.

Several determinants of prices were tested as determinants of the weights in the expectations process. The only definite improvement came from the ratio of the number of registered vacancies to the number of unemployed. These results are reported in [1]. Doubts about the validity of the implied price expectations weights in this equation lead us to prefer the simpler equation reported above.

The estimates of *RHO* and *RHOR* for Australia, as shown in figure 1 of section 6, are derived, using the procedure outlined in section 3.3, from the equation that excludes the relative supply variable and includes *RYPUKUS*.

5. Some roles for the supply price of capital

The primary concern of this section is with uses for the series for *RHO* and *RHOR*, the nominal and real measures of the supply price of capital. The derived series for *PCPICE*, the expected rate of change of consumer prices, has fairly obvious roles to play in wage determination equations. The advantage of *PCPICE* over measures defined within other equations is that the financial markets providing the raw material have fewer bars to rapid price adjustment than almost any others in a macro-model. Thus the observed prices for bonds and shares provide up-to-date information about the expectations in the minds of asset holders. If a sensible series for expected price changes can be wrested from these data, it may be suitable for use elsewhere in the model, even if the decision-making group is not the same in the other equations.

We proceed now to consider how *RHO* and *RHOR* might be employed in the various sectors of a macroeconomic model.

5.1. Investment

In section 2 we described how differences between *RHO* and the mec provide a measure of the incentive to add to the stock of real capital.

In the recent or forthcoming versions of Canadian and Australian models, this mechanism is specified in more detail. In RDX2, the level of investment is determined by a distributed lag on the product of a desired capital/output ratio and the gap between expected output and the currently preferred level of output taking into account the capital/output ratio embodied in each surviving vintage of the capital stock. In the Australian context, a non-vintage version of the model appears to be preferable. In both models, *RHO* appears as one component of the expected cost of capital services used in the choice of cost-minimising capital/output ratios. Because the expectations processes used to define expected wage costs are supposed to take adequate account of future growth of wage rates, the price of capital services includes *RHO* rather than *RHOR*. (For details see chapter 3 of [6] for Canada, and [3] for Australia.)

In these schemes, the mec is represented by expected output, the expected price of capital goods, depreciation rates, expected wage rates, and tax factors. At present, the two models do not make explicit use of *VKB/KB$*, the ratio of the market value to the reproduction cost of the stock of business capital. Some experiments have been done, in the Australian context, in which this ratio influences the speed with which an indicated capital shortage is made up. To date this type of variable-weight lag distribution has been empirically weaker than fixed-weight lag distributions and other forms of variable-weight distributions.

5.2. Consumption

Viewed from one side, *RHOR* is the supply price of capital, measured in real terms, while from the other side it is the real rate of return on savings invested in equities. Thus *RHOR* can be used to define the rate of intertemporal transformation open to savers, measured after company tax but before personal tax. As such, it can enter the variables defining the prices of capital services entering the equations for consumer expenditure on dwellings, motor vehicles, and other durables. It can enter directly, as an opportunity cost, in the equations explaining consumption of non-durables and of services from durable goods.

The equations presented in sections 3 and 4 are used within their respective macro-models to solve for *VKB*, the market value of business assets. The time series for *VKB* is part of the aggregate market value of wealth, and thus may help to define a series for expected nonwage income (aggregate wealth times *RHOR* provides one such measure). Changes in the market value of wealth, less the current flow of new savings, may be used to define a time series for revaluation gains and losses for inclusion in consumption equations.

The exact ways in which *RHOR* and the market value of wealth ought to influence the aggregate split between consumption and savings have not been fully explored. The new-found possibility of distinguishing changes in the discount rate from changes in expected earnings exposes richer alternatives to the usual tests of "life-cycle" and "permanent income" models constructed on the assumption of an unchanged discount rate.

Conceptually, the life cycle model depends upon current and expected wage income, and differences between the actual and desired levels of assets. The stock of assets is important as a source of nonwage income, and as a pool of consumption power to be spent over the life cycle. The usual tests of the hypothesis include wage income and the value of assets, taking no account of possible changes in the discount rate. There are three main causes of changes in the market value of assets: a change in the expected stream of returns from the stock (which can be interpreted as a change in the "real" stock of assets), a change in the discount rate, and a change induced by a change in the desired stock of assets and brought about through savings or dissavings. According to the basic hypothesis, each of these changes influences consumption differently. Thus a full test of the hypothesis requires more than just wage income and the value of assets as independent variables.

The most straightforward way of using the data for *RHOR* and the market value of wealth to disentangle these influences might be to specify *RHOR* times wealth as the expected stream of returns from the stock and the cumulant of changes in the market value of wealth, net of asset changes arising from new savings, as the measure of discrepancy between the actual and desired stock of assets. To make this latter definition more precise, it would be desirable to split actual savings into intended and unintended components to allow a buffer stock role for assets in the life cycle hypothesis. "Unintended" savings out of wage income could be defined as the difference between actual and expected (or "permanent") wage income, less any current consumption expenditure out of that difference. The influence of changes in the discount rate on the rate of saving would be modelled either by explicit representation of the desired stock of assets (in turn dependent on the discount rate) or simple inclusion of *RHOR* in the consumption equation. For strict application of the framework, consumption expenditure must be defined to include nondurables and services only, including imputed services from consumer durables used by the owner.

The "permanent income" hypothesis can also be generalised to take account of the separate measures of the discount rate and the market value of wealth. Permanent and transitory wage income would have their usual definitions. Permanent property income would be *RHOR* times the market value of wealth. One measure of transitory property income would be the difference between current property income (as recorded in the national accounts) and permanent property income. But this ignores revaluation gains and losses, and relies on a mixture of cash income and roughly imputed items. It would probably be better to use current revaluation gains and losses, as defined in the previous paragraph, or some short distributed lag of them, as the sole measure of transitory property income. *RHOR* would play a direct role in representing the possibilities for intertemporal substitution in consumption.

The specifications suggested above are not the only ways of fitting *RHOR* and the market value of wealth into a consumption sector, but they do suggest some possible starting points. To use *RHOR* to represent the discount rate applicable to estimates of expected income from all private sector assets may be risky, because *RHOR* may be too much influenced by current interest rates and company profits. If so, then the derived measure for expected nonwage income may be unduly influenced by current changes in interest rates. This risk is least for those parts of wealth, such as government bonds, whose market values can be made to depend in the appropriate way upon current interest rates. If all bonds were consols, for example, the market value would decrease proportionately as much as the interest rate decreased, and the relevant measure of expected property income would be unchanged. But for the bulk of assets, whose values are measured at replacement cost, any increase in *RHOR* implies an increase in expected non-wage income. With respect to adjustments in the stocks of such assets, it should no doubt be true that the flow of services from the marginal unit should be forthcoming at the rate *RHOR*. But there is nothing to force the average expected flow of services from, say, the replacement value of the existing stock of dwellings to move proportionately with *RHOR*. Thus, it might be appropriate to use a long moving average of *RHOR*, or perhaps some weighted average of *RHOR* and other assumed rates of return, when approximating the expected income from aggregate private sector wealth.

5.3. International capital flows

Direct investment flows from one country to another ought to depend upon the marginal efficiency of capital and the supply price of capital in both countries (as well as in other countries, for that matter). Within the Canadian and Australian models, the levels of investment expenditure are used directly in the direct investment equations, thus obviating the need for independent measures of the mec. The supply prices of capital in the two countries are then used to determine what fraction of a country's capital investment will be financed by direct investment from the second country.

International portfolio investment in equities does not depend on the mec, but rather on supply prices of capital (the rates of return on equity investment) in the two countries, possibly with separate consideration given to recent capital gains experience in the two countries.

When international capital flows are being determined, should the supply price of capital be measured in real or nominal terms?

An international *RHO* differential is distinguishable from a *RHOR* differential only to the extent that *PCPICE* differs in the two countries. In the long run, if exchange rates are expected to move so as to offset any international differences in inflation rates, the *RHOR* differential is the correct one to employ. If exchange rates are pegged, or if there are other factors restricting movements towards purchasing power parity, then the *RHO* differential may be relevant for all investment decisions over a horizon shorter than the expected lifetime of the current exchange rate.

5.4. Price formation

Some price equations for RDX2 have employed a normal unit capital costs variable, equal to marginal capital costs per unit of normal output (*UGPPS*). The marginal cost of capital is the imputed cost of capital services (measured as a proportion) times the replacement value of the capital stock. The cost of capital services is separate for each type of capital, and is equal to the sum of *RHO* and the depreciation rate, with adjustments made for the effects of corporation taxes. The conceptual difference between this normal unit capital costs variable and the normal unit labour costs variable is that the latter uses wages actually paid while the former approximates a marginal cost. To the extent that prices are determined by average rather than marginal outlays, unit labour costs may act more quickly, and with a larger total effect, than unit capital costs. This is what happens in an equation for the price of construction materials. In an early equation for the main consumer price, normal unit labour and capital costs were entered jointly as a unit factor cost variable. Simulation experiments showed higher interest rates to have a net inflationary effect, probably because the cost effect of higher interest rates was over-estimated by our treatment of average unit labour costs and marginal unit capital costs on equal terms.

6. Further developments

The equations developed for the Canadian and Australian models provide satisfactory predictions of the market value of equities, and empirically useful measures of the supply price of capital and

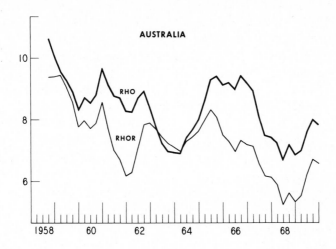

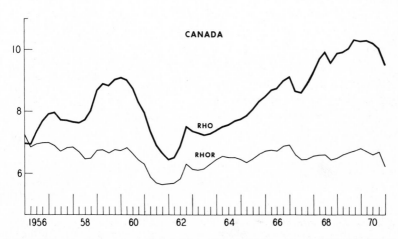

Fig.1. Estimated supply prices of capital in nominal (*RHO*) and real (*RHOR*) terms for Australia and Canada. *RHO* – *RHOR* = *PCPICE*, the expected annual percentage rate of change in the Consumer Price Index.

the expected rate of increase in consumer prices. However, we suspect that it may be possible to find expectations processes for profits and for prices that would allow us to be more confident that we are dividing changes in the market value of equities correctly between changes in the discount rate (ρ), changes in the 'normal' current level of profits (x), and changes in the expected rate of growth of profits (g).

We have performed a number of experiments in which g is determined not only by expected price changes but also by expected changes in the distribution of business earnings between labour and capital. So far, these experiments have suggested that changes in income shares have not influenced g, but better measurement of the relevant shares may alter this result.

The major problems with our present Australian equation results lie in the small sum of weights defining expected price changes (*PCPICE*) and the poor performance of the relative supply variable. The chief worry about the Canadian equation is caused by its highly autocorrelated errors. Despite these difficulties, the derived measures of the real and nominal supply prices of capital, and the series for the share market value of business assets, have proved useful elsewhere in both macro-models.

To conclude on a quantitative note, we have prepared figure 1 showing the values of *RHO* and *RHOR* derived from the currently preferred equations for both countries. The Canadian estimates for *RHO* and RHOR are smoother than the Australian numbers because the Canadian series are based on averages of beginning and end-of-quarter values for v, while the Australian series use only the end-of-quarter values.

References

[1] Peter Boxall and John Helliwell, *The share market value of business assets, price expectations, and the supply price of capital.* Reserve Bank of Australia, Research Discussion Paper No. 23, December 1971.
[2] M.S. Feldstein and O. Eckstein, 'The fundamental determinants of the interest rate', *Review of Economics and Statistics* **52** (November 1970) 363–375.

[3] R.G. Hawkins, *Interrelated factor demands: a preliminary study.* Reserve Bank of Australia, Research Discussion Paper No. 22, October 1971.

[4] John Helliwell and others, *Quarterly estimates of private sector wealth.* Reserve Bank of Australia, Research Discussion Paper No. 18, August 1971.

[5] John Helliwell, Fred Gorbet, Ian Stewart and Don Stephenson, 'Some features and uses of the Canadian quarterly model RDX2', in: this volume, p. 27.

[6] J.F. Helliwell, H.T. Shapiro, G.R. Sparks, I.A. Stewart, F.G. Gorbet and D.R. Stephenson, *The structure of RDX2.* Bank of Canada Staff Research Studies, No. 7 (Ottawa, Bank of Canada, 1971).

[7] M.W. Keran, 'Expectations, money and the stock market', *Federal Reserve Bank of St. Louis Review* **53** (January 1971) 16–31.

[8] F. Modigliani and M.H. Miller, 'The cost of capital, corporation finance and the theory of investment', *American Economic Review* **48** (June 1958) 261–97.

[9] T.J. Sargent, 'Commodity price expectations and the interest rate', *Quarterly Journal of Economics 83* (February 1969) 127–40.

[10] J. Tobin, 'Money, capital and other stores of value', *American Economic Review* **51** (May 1961) 26–37.

[11] J. Tobin, 'A general equilibrium approach to monetary theory', *Journal of Money, Credit and Banking* **1** (February 1969) 15–29.

[12] W.P. Yohe and D.S. Karnosky, 'Interest rates and price level changes, 1952–69', *Federal Reserve Bank of St. Louis Review* **51** (December 1969) 18–38.

A NEW APPROACH TO THE MONETISATION OF NEOCLASSICAL GROWTH MODELS *

Robert CROUCH
University of California, Santa Barbara

Existing models of money and growth have intuitively implausible implications. According to Tobin [11], who must be credited with the first attempt to monetise a neoclassical barter growth model, monetisation *reduces* steady state growth income per capita y, the wage rate w, and the capital-labor ratio k, while it *increases* the real rate of interest r.[1] As Levhari and Patinkin [6] have pointed out, this contradicts the classically vaunted advantages said to be associated with the introduction of money into a barter economy. Monetisation is *not* supposed to make us worse off. Why, after all, if it does make us worse off, as Tobin's hypothesis implies, introduce money in the first place? In response to this dilemma, Levhari and Patinkin have shown, using an amendment to Tobin's hypothesis first suggested by Johnson [4], that it is *possible* (they claim no more) that the monetisation of a neoclassical barter model *may* increase y, w, and k. However, in the context of the Johnson-Levhari-Patinkin (hereinafter, JLP) model, and for plausible values of its parameters, it can be shown that such increases in y, w, and k are contingent upon a rate of inflation in excess of ten percent per annum compound. For lower rates of inflation, Tobin's conclusions prevail. Thus, according to the JLP model, we must be prepared to accept a high rate of inflation before the

* I would like to thank Robert Clower, Harry Johnson, P.D. Jonson, Alvin Marty, Frank Milne, and the participants in the second Australasian Conference of Econometricians, Melbourne, 1971, for their helpful comments and suggestions on an earlier version of this article whilst absolving them all of any residual error.

[1] See Tobin [11] and [12].

introduction of money redounds to our benefit. This would have surely raised the eyebrows of classical economists.

Both these models are beset by other difficulties. Tobin's model is crucially dependent on monetisation being by way of the introduction of *outside* fiat money. The model predicts *nothing* when monetisation is by an inside bank money. The JLP model also predicts *nothing* when socially *optimal* inside bank money arrangements are adopted. For this model to have substantive implications when inside bank money is introduced, the monetary arrangements have to be socially sub-optimal.

I find the implications of both the Tobin and the JLP models intuitively implausible. This paper takes a radically new approach to the monetisation of neoclassical growth models. It treats monetisation as a *technological innovation*. As a consequence, monetisation is shown to imply an *unambiguous increase* in y, w, and k. Monetisation leaves us indubitably better off. Moreover, money is shown to be neutral given the assumed monetary institutions. This, of course, is a very neoclassical conclusion.

1. The neoclassical barter model bench-mark

The impact of monetisation on the steady state growth equilibrium values of the variables of a neoclassical model is conveniently measured against the steady-state growth equilibrium values of the variables in a neoclassical barter model. Assuming a well-behaved constant returns to scale production function (excluding technological progress), a labor force growing at a constant proportional natural rate n, a proportional saving function, and that all saving is invested, such a model is represented by eqs. (11.1) – (11.4) in table 1, where Y = income, K = the capital stock, L = the supply of labor, S = saving, s = the propensity to save, and I = investment. From these equations it is easy to show that steady-state growth occurs when $sf(k) = nk$ (where $y = f(k)$ is the intensive form of the production function). The steady-state growth equilibrium values of the variables are conveniently illustrated by figure 1. For the neoclassical barter model in steady state growth, income per capita

Table 1
Comparison of four growth models

	Barter model		Tobin's model		JLP's model		The proposed model	
Equations	$Y = F(K, L)$	(11.1)	$Y = F(K, L)$	(11.5)	$Y = F(K, L)$	(11.5)	$Y = F(K, \gamma L)$	(11.1')
	$L = L_0 e^{nt}$	(11.2)	$L = L_0 e^{nt}$	(11.6)	$L = L_0 e^{nt}$	(11.6)	$L = L_0 e^{nt}$	(11.2)
	$S = sY$	(11.3)	$Y_d = Y + \dfrac{d(M/P)}{dt}$	(11.7)	$Y_d = Y + \dfrac{d(M/P)}{dt} + \dfrac{M}{P}(r+\pi)$	(11.7')	$S = sY$	(11.3)
	$I = \dfrac{dK}{dt} = S$	(11.4)	$\dfrac{M}{P} = \lambda Y$	(11.8)	$\dfrac{M}{P} = \lambda Y$	(11.8)	$I = \dfrac{dK}{dt} = S$	(11.4)
			$S = sY_d$		$S = sY_d$	(11.9)	$\dfrac{M}{P} = \lambda Y$	(11.8)
			$S = \dfrac{dK}{dt} + \dfrac{d(M/P)}{dt}$		$S = \dfrac{dK}{dt} + \dfrac{d(M/P)}{dt}$	(11.10)		
Steady-state growth equilibrium condition	$sf(k) = nk$		$[s - (1-s)\lambda n]f(k) = nk$ $\sigma_1 f(k) = nk$		$\{s[1 + \lambda(\pi + n + r)] - \lambda n\}f(k) = nk$ $\sigma_2 f(k) = nk$		$s\gamma f(k\gamma^{-1}) = nk$	

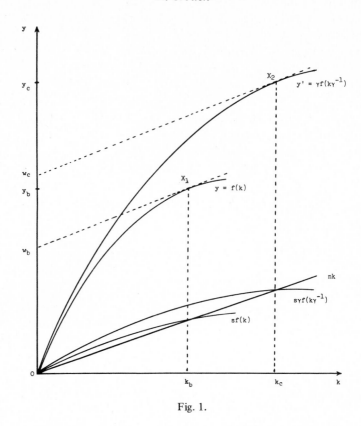

Fig. 1.

is y_b (b for barter), the wage rate is w_b, and the capital-labor ratio is k_b.

2. The monetary arrangements

Assume that monetisation occurs by way of the introduction of an *inside* bank money. In particular, assume the creation of just one monopoly bank which is the creature of the government. When the government wishes to increase the money supply, it makes a head subsidy (or transfer payment) to everybody with one hand by crediting their bank accounts but, at the same time, with the other hand, so to speak, informs them that they are in debt to the monopoly bank by an equal amount. Conversely, when the government wishes to decrease the supply of money, it levies a head tax on everybody and takes payment by debiting their bank accounts and, at the same time, informs them that their indebtedness to the monopoly bank has been decreased by an equal amount. This caricature of a banking system is intended to broadly represent a normal commercial banking system in which when the money supply is increased private indebtedness to the banks also increases, and when the money supply is decreased private indebtedness to the banks also decreases.[2] We assume that the administration of this monetary mechanism is a costless operation, i.e. the social cost of supplying money is zero.

The rate of return to holding real money balances M/P of this inside bank variety is zero. This is easy to see. Assume a given inside bank money stock. Now when the price level decreases, for example, the value of real money balances increases but so does the real value of indebtedness *pari passu*. Thus, the change in wealth is zero. It follows that the change in wealth per unit of time (which is, by definition, the change in income from this source) is also zero. As a result, the change in income per unit of real balances (which is, by definition, the rate of return on real balances) is also zero. Thus, with inside bank money, disposable income is not affected when real money balances change whether such a change is brought about by a change in M or in P. Consequently, eq. (11.7) of Tobin's model (which *is* the appropriate specification of disposable income Y_d in an outside money model) is an *in*appropriate specification of disposable income when money is of the inside variety.[3]

Furthermore, with inside money it is not possible to save by accumulating real money balances since, if real money balances change (due to a change in M or P), there is an inevitable change in real indebtedness to the bank *pari passu* in the same direction. In

---

[2] Caricature though it may be, it is no more 'unrealistic' than the monetary arrangements underlying Tobin's *outside* fiat money model.

[3] Levhari and Patinkin [6] also discuss a model in which money is treated as a *producer's* good. That model is not discussed here. Attention is focussed here only on the model in which they treat money as a *consumer's* good.

effect, there is an equal amount of *dis*saving collectively. Thus, eq. (11.10) of Tobin's model (which is a correct specification of the saving relationship in an outside money model) is an *in*appropriate specification of the saving relationship when the model is predicated on inside money.

Eqs. (11.7) and (11.10) are the *unique* features of Tobin's model (compared with the barter model). But these *both* depend on his outside money assumption. Thus, Tobin's model explains *nothing* when monetisation is by way of an inside money.

The JLP model differs from Tobin's model only in eq. (11.7′), which includes the term $(M/P)(r+\pi)$. According to their hypothesis, real money balances generate a 'utility yield' (or 'amenity yield' or 'convenience service') which is a component of disposable income. This imputed income from money is equal to the quantity of real money balances held multiplied by the opportunity cost of holding money at the margin.[4] This opportunity cost depends on the monetary specifications of the model. The opportunity cost of holding money is the difference between the rate of return on alternative assets (real capital) r and the rate of return on money. With non-interest bearing outside money, the rate of return on real balances is equal to the negative of the rate of change of the price level, i.e. $-\pi$, where $\pi = (1/P)(dP/dt)$. Thus, the opportunity cost of holding money is $r-(-\pi)=r+\pi$, the money rate of interest. With non-interest bearing inside money, the rate of return on real balances equals zero (as argued above) so the opportunity cost of holding them is simply r. As written, then, (11.7′) assumes a non-interest bearing outside money. For a non-interest bearing inside money model it would read $Y_d = Y + (M/P)r$.

It has been assumed that inside money is costless to produce. For a social optimum, therefore, it should also be costless to hold. This can be arranged simply by having money balances (and the offsetting indebtedness) bear interest at the rate r. This makes the opportunity cost of holding money zero. Consequently, society

---

[4] Johnson [4] originally suggested that this imputed income from money should be measured by the integral under the demand curve subtended by the quantity of real balances held. However, the text follows Levhari's and Patinkin's [6] approach to the specification of this yield.

would demand to hold the satiety quantity of real balances where their marginal utility has fallen to zero (which is achieved by appropriate adjustment of the price level). With the marginal utility value imputed to money driven to zero, (11.7′) degenerates to $Y_d = Y$. Thus, the JLP model collapses into the barter model when monetisation is by way of the introduction of socially optimal inside money arrangements. Presumably, therefore, it can predict nothing about the impact of monetisation in such circumstances.

3. Monetisation as a technological innovation

Are we to conclude, therefore, that monetisation by way of socially optimal inside bank money arrangements is without any effect? The answer is 'no' if monetisation is regarded as a technological innovation.[5] Is there any justification for such an approach? I believe there is. Even in a one commodity barter model, several types of exchanges must still occur. First, labor must barter its services with firms in exchange for commodity earnings. Second, labor, which *owns* the capital stock even though it is *held* by firms, takes its commodity earnings and, since it is a net saver in the aggregate, negotiates commodity loans with firms. This inevitably involves another set of barter transactions between households and firms since any particular firm may have borrowed capital from workers not in its employ. Third, since inventory holding is not explicitly included in the barter model, if labor receives its commodity earnings only at discrete intervals while it consumes

---

[5] It transpires that the hypothesis that monetisation is equivalent to a technological innovation has been independently advanced by two other economists. When I arrived at the Melbourne Conference, Mr. P.D. Jonson, University of Melbourne, handed me an unpublished note in which he argues that 'the invention of ... money should be regarded as a once for all technical change' [5], and I recently came across a note by Douglas Purvis, Queen's University, which suggests that the introduction of money 'would bring about a once-for-all shift in the production function...' [8, p. 380, fn. 20]. I find it encouraging that others have independently arrived at the same conclusion as I did. It seems that the theory of economic growth is particularly prone to simultaneous, independent, discoveries. Harrod and Domar, Solow and Swan, and the mass discovery of the Golden Rule spring to mind as cases in point.

continuously (i.e., there is lack of synchronization), firms and labor must be engaging in commodity exchanges in the payments interval. Fourth, although labor is a net saver, individuals may have different time preferences. This implies another batch of commodity exchanges as labor re-shuffles its consumption stream. (Since the wage rate and the interest rate are constant in steady-state growth, there is no opportunity for income straightening, given perfect foresight.) All in all, then, even a one commodity barter model does involve a lot of bartering with all the search costs that that implies. Some fraction of the effort of the labor force employed by firms is, therefore, devoted to this activity. The main advantage classically vaunted in favor of monetising a barter economy is that the labor effort devoted to bartering is thereby eliminated. On monetisation there is, effectively, an augmentation of the labor force from a *production* point of view. Labor can be switched from un(physically) productive bartering to physical production. In the words of Stein ([10], p. 90), "if there were no medium of exchange, then the inefficiencies of a barter economy would result. Labor and capital would have to be diverted from the production of goods to their 'distribution' in order to achieve the 'double coincidence of wants' ".[6]

This notion can be formally introduced into the neoclassical barter model by writing the production function (11.1'), where $\gamma = 1$ from $t = 0$ to $t = \theta$ (the period of barter) and $\gamma > 1$ from $t = \theta$ to $t = \infty$ (the monetary period). In the production function, then, monetisation is equivalent to a *one-shot* labor augmenting technological innovation. When money is introduced the benefits are reaped all at once and, from that moment on, the productive labor force is increased by the factor γ. Clearly, the larger the benefits to be reaped on monetisation, the larger is γ.

The model under construction is completed by eqs. (11.2) – (11.4) and (11.8). The first three of these equations are the familiar equations of the barter model. As explained in the previous section, no special re-definitions of disposable income and saving are required when monetisation is by inside bank money. Eq.

---

[6] See, also, Stein [10, p. 87, fn. 7].

(11.8) is the demand for money function. In the proposed model with socially optimal inside money arrangements, the liquidity preference parameter γ is independent of interest rates. The satiety quantity of real balances would always be held.[7] In the other two models, assuming non-interest bearing outside money, γ is inversely related to the money rate of interest $r + \pi$.

The constant returns to scale production function (11.1′) can be converted into its intensive form by dividing through by γL to obtain:

$$y = \gamma f(k\gamma^{-1}) \quad \text{and} \quad Y = \gamma L f(k\gamma^{-1}).$$ (11.11)

To find the steady-state growth equilibrium condition, the easiest way to proceed is to find the condition under which the capital-labor ratio is constant, i.e., $dk/dt = 0$. Proceed as follows:

$$\frac{1}{k} \cdot \frac{dk}{dt} = \frac{1}{K} \cdot \frac{dK}{dt} - \frac{1}{L} \cdot \frac{dL}{dt} = \frac{1}{K} \cdot \frac{dK}{dt} - n \,,$$

since the growth rate of the labor supply is given as n. But $dK/dt = S = sY = s\gamma L f(k\gamma^{-1})$, using (11.3), (11.4), and (11.11). Thus,

$$\frac{1}{k} \cdot \frac{dk}{dt} = \frac{s\gamma L f(k\gamma^{-1})}{K} - n \,.$$

On multiplying through by $k = K/L$ and setting $dk/dt = 0$, one obtains

$$s\gamma f(k\gamma^{-1}) = nk$$ (11.12)

as the steady-state growth equilibrium conditions.

The post-monetisation situation relative to the barter situation is illustrated graphically in figure 1. Since monetisation is being interpreted as a one-shot labor augmenting technological innova-

---

[7] When interest is not paid on inside money, λ in the proposed model would be inversely related to r.

tion, the intensive production function $y' = \gamma f(k\gamma^{-1})$ applicable after monetisation is a radial projection of the intensive production function $y = f(k)$ applicable during the barter era. (That labor augmenting technological progress makes successive intensive production functions radial projections of the previous intensive production function is well known.) Both the output-capital ratio and the profit rate are, consequently, the same at X_1 and X_2. This is required, of course, by the definition of labor augmenting technological progress. Since $y' = \gamma f(k\gamma^{-1})$ is everywhere above $y = f(k)$ it follows immediately that $s\gamma f(k\gamma^{-1})$ must be everywhere above $sf(k)$. Consequently, it is inevitable that $s\gamma f(k\gamma^{-1})$ intersects nk to the right of where $sf(k)$ intersects nk. Thus, it is immediately apparent that monetisation, when viewed as a technological innovation, must lead unambiguously to higher steady-state growth values of income per capita y_c, the wage rate w_c, and the capital-labor ratio k_c. (The interest rate is unchanged.) These conclusions appear to be much more consistent with the classical arguments vaunted in favor of monetising a barter economy.

Since $0 < s < 1$ and both λ and n are positive by assumption, σ_1 in Tobin's model is unambiguously less than s. Consequently, when graphed, $\sigma_1 f(k)$ will always lie below $sf(k)$ and, therefore, intersect nk to the left of where $sf(k)$ intersects nk. This is why Tobin's model implies y, w, and k unambiguously *decrease* after monetisation. In the JLP model (assuming non-interest bearing outside money), σ_2 is *not* necessarily less than s. Thus, $\sigma_2 f(k)$ *may* intersect nk to the *right* of k_b, which would imply that y, w, and k *rise* after monetisation. However, consider σ_2 in the form $[s+s\lambda(\pi+n+r) - \lambda n]$. This is greater than s if $s\lambda(\pi+n+r) > \lambda n$, that is, if $s(\mu+r) > n$, where μ is the proportional rate of change in the supply of money $(1/M)(dM/dt)$ (since, in steady-state growth, $\mu = \pi + n$). The value of μ necessary to maintain this inequality can be worked out for any given set of plausible values of s, r, and n. With s, r, and n equal to 0.1, 0.5, and 0.02, respectively, for example, the value of μ necessary to maintain the inequality is 0.15. Thus, for σ_2 to exceed s and monetisation to raise y, w, and k, the rate of growth of the supply of money must approximate 15% (and inflation proceed at about 13% or, say, 10% in a model including technological progress).

4. The neutrality of money

In the context of growth models, money is neutral *in a comparative static sense* if the real variables are independent of one-shot injections of money (before and after which injection the rate of growth in the supply of money μ is unchanged). Money is neutral in this sense in Tobin's model, the JLP model, and the proposed model since the steady-state growth equilibrium conditions for all three are in no way affected by the *level* of the money supply from which the constant rate of growth in the money supply proceeds. It is interesting to note that the proposed model is also independent of changes in liquidity preference λ. The other two monetised models are not, however, since inspection of *their* steady-state growth equilibrium conditions reveals that they are clearly dependent on λ. In the proposed model, if λ increased, say, *ceteris paribus*, indicating increased liquidity preference, the only repercussion would be a fall in the price level P until the new desired level of real money balances, for the given level of income, was established.

Money is neutral *in a growth sense* if the real variables are independent of changes in the rate of growth of the money supply μ. Money is not neutral in this sense in either Tobin's or the JLP model. The reason is simple. In steady state-growth $\mu - n = \pi$. Thus, when μ is increased, for example, so is π. This raises the money rate of interest $r + \pi$ and this increase in the money rate of interest decreases λ. And this change in λ clearly affects the steady-state growth equilibrium condition. The foregoing piece of analysis is applicable to Tobin's model only. In the JLP model, $(\partial\sigma_2/\partial\mu) = (\partial\sigma_2/\partial\lambda)(\partial\lambda/\partial\pi)(\partial\pi/\partial\mu)$, which has an ambiguous sign since, although $\partial\pi/\partial\mu = 1$ and $\partial\lambda/\partial\pi < 0$, $\partial\sigma_2/\partial\lambda = s(\mu+r) - n$, which is of unknown sign and might be zero. However, in general it is not zero and, therefore, $\partial\sigma_2/\partial\mu \neq 0$. Thus, money will not be neutral in a growth sense in their model.

Money *is* completely neutral in a growth sense in the proposed model. This is obvious by inspection of (11.12). Nothing in that equation is in any way dependent on the rate of growth of the supply of money μ. *After* it is introduced, money is a complete

veil; changes in its rate of growth have no real repercussions what-
soever. Especially noteworthy is the fact that the rate of interest is
independent of μ (which it is *not* in either Tobin's or the JLP
model). The real (or natural) rate of interest is completely independent of purely monetary phenomena. This is a very neoclassical conclusion. In this model, the famous neoclassical propositions
about neutrality of money (see Patinkin [9] *passim*) carry over
into a growth context. In the last analysis, the underlying reason
why money is neutral in the model being proposed is that the
model *dichotomizes*. That is to say, it is separable into a real
sector, eqs. $(11.1')$ – (11.4), and a monetary sector, eq. (11.8). It
is well-known from Patinkin [9] that dichotomy implies neutrality (although the reverse is not true). As will have been apparent
from the technique by which the model was solved in the previous
section, the real sector equations (only) generate all the steady-
state growth values of the real variables. Then, with Y and λ given,
M sets P via (11.8). Looking at it another way, the real sector
equations generate the steady-state growth values of the real variables; then, since $\mu - n = \pi$ must also hold in this model in steady-
state growth, setting μ sets π and, most important, changes in π
have no feedback effects into the real sector (which they *do* in
Tobin's and the JLP model).[8]

---

[8] The neutrality of money is preserved in the proposed model when interest is *not*
paid on money as long as the imputed liquidity yield from money is not included in
disposable income. Arguments in favor of such an exclusion have been advanced. Consider Bailey ([1], p. 875), '... the imputable income due to cash balances will appear in
some other measurable form. Either the holder's leisure will increase, or the same total
non-cash resource employment will produce more. If so, the services of cash balances
should be imputed as the resource input, but not as an output, for to do so would be
double counting.' And also Marty ([7], p. 258), '... people desire money to spend rather
than to hold and ... no utility should be imputed to real balances (cash is then treated solely
as an argument in the production function).' A third argument might run along the
following lines. In steady-state growth equilibrium, all markets clear. Therefore, assuming,
as we are, zero transactions costs in all markets, all goods are equally (perfectly) liquid in
the sense that they can be traded without loss. Why, then, attach a special 'liquidity yield'
to the money good? Money is demanded, to use, simply because it is the medium of
exchange. On this last argument for the exclusion of the liquidity yield of money from
disposable income see Friedman ([3], p. 26, fn. 19). – For a critical treatment of the idea
that real balances have a utility yield see Stein ([10], pp. 94–96).

The optimal rate of growth of money implied by the proposed model is clear. Since money is neutral and incapable of influencing real variables, the rule should be to set μ equal to the natural rate of growth. This sets $\pi = 0$ and price stability is preserved. This rule corresponds to 'Friedman's vintage (5%) rule' of [2] as opposed to 'Friedman's new (2%) rule' of [3].

In conclusion of this section, three things are worth drawing attention to. First, for those wedded to the neoclassical economic paradigm, it is comforting to have a theory of money and growth in which, when socially optimal inside money institutions are established, (a) monetisation is unambiguously advantageous[9] and (b) money is, thereafter, neutral. Through pains-taking scholarship, Patinkin [9] has demonstrated the conditions required for money to be neutral in a *comparative static* model. One thing emerges quite clearly from his discussion; namely, money will only appear neutral in such models after a good deal of time has elapsed. But the long-run is the domain of growth. It would be tragic indeed if, having proved these neoclassical neutrality propositions for comparative static models, they could not be carried over into a growth model which is more appropriate to their long-run habitat. Second, it is standard practice when discussing technological innovation in growth models to assume such innovations are exogenous and use no real resources. With its infinitesimal production costs, *inside* bank money fulfills this criterion perhaps better than any other type of technological innovation imaginable. Third, the one-shot labor augmenting technological innovation represented by monetisation does not affect the steady-state growth rate. It merely affects the levels of the relevant variables from which such growth proceeds. In this regard, it obviously bears some analogy to the impact of a change in the propensity to save in neoclassical growth models.

[9] Recall that, with such socially optimal inside money arrangements, both Tobin's model and the JLP model predict that monetisation has no effect.

5. Monetisation as a technological innovation continued

Monetisation might, alternatively, be regarded as a one-shot capital-augmenting technological innovation or a one-shot capital- *and* labor-augmenting technological innovation. The appropriate production functions then become (11.1″) or (11.1‴), respectively:

$$Y = F(\beta K, L) \quad \text{or} \quad y = f(\beta k) \qquad (11.1'')$$

with $\beta = 1$ from $t = 0$ to $t = \theta$ and $\beta > 1$ from $t = \theta$ to $t = \infty$;

$$Y = F(\beta K, \gamma L) \quad \text{or} \quad y = \gamma f(\beta k \gamma^{-1}) \qquad (11.1''')$$

with $\beta = \gamma = 1$ from $t = 0$ to $t = \theta$ and $\beta, \gamma > 1$ from $t = \theta$ to $t = \infty$. (To impose Hicks-neutrality at monetisation simply set $\beta = \gamma > 1$ in the monetary period.) In each case the models are completed by eqs. (11.2) − (11.4) and (11.8). It is then easy to show, by setting $dk/dt = 0$, that the steady-state growth equilibrium condition in the first case is $sf(\beta k) = nk$ and, in the second case, $s\gamma f(\beta k \gamma^{-1}) = nk$. Moreover, it is also easy to show that, in both cases, monetisation will still lead to an *unambiguous increase* in y, w, and c. In addition, money will continue to be neutral in a comparative static and a growth sense in both alternative models since both models also dichotomise.

In summary, then, no matter whether monetisation is regarded as labor-augmenting, capital-augmenting, or both labor- and capital-augmenting, assuming socially optimal inside monetary institutions are established, monetisation is always unambiguously advantageous and, thereafter, money is neutral. This paper has assumed monetisation by way of an inside money in order to maintain a sharp confrontation with the Tobin and JLP models. However, there is no reason why monetisation by way of an outside fiat money should not also be regarded as a technological innovation. The way would then be open to synthesize the Tobin or JLP model with the proposed model. All that is required is the substitution of the production function (11.1′), or (11.1″) or (11.1‴), for (11.1) in their models. In such a synthesized model, money would not be neutral and monetisation would not leave us unambiguously better off. However, for reasonable values of the parameters in σ_1 (or σ_2) and plausible guesses at the sizes of γ (and/or β), the probability is high that we would be better off after monetisation.

References

[1] M.J. Bailey, 'Comment: optimum monetary growth', *Journal of Political Economy* (July – August 1968).

[2] M. Friedman, *A program for monetary stability* (Fordham University Press, 1959).

[3] M. Friedman, *The optimum quantity of money* (Aldine, 1969).

[4] H.G. Johnson, *Essays in monetary economics* (Cambridge, Mass., 1967), chapter IV.

[5] P.D. Jonson, 'Money and economic growth: the Tobin model extended'. Unpublished paper, University of Melbourne, April, 1971, p. 2.

[6] D. Levhari and D. Patinkin, 'The role of money in a simple growth model', *American Economic Review* (September 1968).

[7] A.L. Marty, 'Notes on money and economic growth', *Journal of Money, Credit, and Banking* (May 1969).

[8] D.D. Purvis, 'Introducing useful money into a growth model', *Canadian Journal of Economics* (August 1971).

[9] D. Patinkin, *Money, interest, and prices*, 2nd ed. (New York, Harper and Row, 1965).

[10] J.L. Stein, 'Monetary growth theory in perspective', *American Economic Review* (March 1970).

[11] J. Tobin, 'Money and economic growth', *Econometrica* (October 1965).

[12] J. Tobin, 'Comment', *Economica* (February 1967).

A CONTINUOUS DISEQUILIBRIUM MODEL OF UNITED KINGDOM FINANCIAL MARKETS *

C.R. WYMER

London School of Economics and Political Science

1. Introduction

Until recently the estimation of differential equation systems in econometrics has been neglected but a consideration of such estimators is interesting and, as this paper shows, probably worthwhile. The reason for formulating a system of differential equations rather than a discrete system is based on the proposition that at a highly disaggregated level the behaviour of the economy can be represented more accurately by a continuous model which is recursive. Such a system allows a more satisfactory treatment of the problem of the length of interval between observations and thus the distinction between lagged endogenous and dependent variables, the independence of the disturbances on the equations, and the distribution of time lags in the system. A recursive model can be given a causal interpretation and allows the structural and behavioural functions of the system to be identified.

The estimation of the continuous system has been considered elsewhere [1–3]. [1] This estimator, which approximates the differ-

* This paper is based on a Ph.D. Thesis in the University of London [3]. I am indebted to Professor J.D. Sargan for his help and encouragement during the preparation of the thesis, and I am grateful to Professors W.M. Gorman and A.R. Bergstrom for their comments on this paper. I should like to acknowledge both the financial support of a Commonwealth Scholarship during my study at the LSE, and the assistance of the Atlas Computer Laboratory, Chilton, which provided the computing facilities. In particular my thanks are due to Mr. M.E. Claringbold of the Laboratory for his help with the computation.

[1] A paper by the author entitled 'Econometric Estimation of Stochastic Differential Equation Systems' is to be published shortly in *Econometrica*.

ential equation system by a non-recursive discrete model with the
same structural form thus allowing *a priori* restrictions to be included without difficulty, is biased but the bias is known, in general, to be small [2]. Although the disturbances in the discrete
model are a moving average process of order one less than the
order of the differential system, they can be approximated by a
process which is independent of the coefficients of the model so
that the variables of the system may be transformed to eliminate
the moving average. Full information maximum likelihood estimates of the parameters of the approximate model are obtained as
well as estimates of the eigenvalues of the system.

In this paper a multi-sector dynamic model of financial markets
is specified which allows portfolio adjustment processes to determine holdings of securities (defined to include all financial assets
and liabilities) and market adjustment processes to determine
prices or rates of interest. The behaviour functions of these sectors
and the market adjustments within the model will usually assume
a recursive form. Such a model does not require the economy to
be in equilibrium at any point of time but instead assumes a
non-tâtonnement process where the adjustment function depends
on the excess supply or demand of securities of each sector. This
does not preclude the model from being in equilibrium which
would occur if the adjustment was very fast but estimates of a
model would show this only if the model is continuous.

2. Dynamic models of financial markets

It is assumed that for each economic unit behaviour functions can
be derived from the maximisation of some utility function subject
to a wealth constraint such that if supply and demand of all factors of production and all commodities are assumed to be realised,
and if the economic units can be aggregated into sectors, demand
(with supply considered as negative demand) or desired interest
rate functions for all financial assets can be specified for each
sector. These behaviour functions will include all variables relevant
to the sector's objective function and exogenous, or at least pre-

determined, to that sector. It is further assumed that stock and interest rate adjustment functions may be specified for each security and each sector, where for each sector the adjustment function for holdings of each security depends on the excess demands for all securities held by that sector or on the excess of desired over actual interest rates of those securities; and for each security the interest rate adjustment function depends on the excess demands for all securities by all sectors or on the excess of desired over actual interest rates of those securities.

It is considered that such an economic system may be specified as a continuous recursive model especially if the sectors in the system are sufficiently disaggregated. The model can then be given a causal interpretation and the structural functions of the system will be identified. In formulating the model, however, some constraints may have to be imposed on the form of the behavioural and expectations functions in the model.

A model such as this may not, however, be estimated by simultaneous methods without imposing non-linear across equation restrictions. It was necessary to simplify the model in order to identify and estimate the structural functions without the use of across equation restrictions.[2] In particular each adjustment function was specified to include only one excess demand or supply function or one excess interest rate function. If more than one excess demand function were allowed in each adjustment function, restrictions would need to be imposed across equations in estimation, and if the same variable occurred in each excess demand function restrictions may need to be imposed within the equation. These restrictions on the parameters would be non-linear in general. For a similar reason, no explicit expectations functions were intro-

---

[2] The exclusion of non-linear restrictions was made necessary by the computer program used to estimate the model. This program, code-named SIMUL, was developed by the author to find full information maximum likelihood estimates of a linear model, and in particular of the discrete approximation to the continuous system, subject to linear restrictions only on the coefficients. However, the author has since developed another program, RESIMUL, to find full information maximum likelihood estimates of a model where the coefficients in the system are any functions of the set of parameters of the model. This allows non-linear restrictions within and across equations. The results of this work will appear elsewhere.

duced and, in addition, restrictions on the behaviour functions due to the utility optimisation assumptions were neglected.

For each sector the demand function can be considered as being determined subject to a wealth constraint, and as holdings need not equal demand but are subject to the same constraint each sector must have at least one security which acts as a residual to satisfy this constraint. Almost by necessity this security or group of securities must be very liquid. If it is assumed that for the jth sector the holdings of the ith security $B_{ij}(t)$ are adjusted to the excess demand for that security then

$$DB_{ij}(t) = h_{ij}[\hat{B}_{ij}(t) - B_{ij}(t)] , \qquad i = 1, ..., m \text{ (say)}, \qquad (12.1)$$

where a circumflex denotes a desired value and D is the differential operator d/dt. If one of these securities (say) $B_{1j}(t)$ is the sector residual in the short run, the adjustment process (12.1) is true only for $i = 2, ..., m$, and changes in the residual are given by the wealth identity. If the sector is assumed to wish to keep its holdings of this residual security as near as possible to desired holdings then some other asset, say $B_{2j}(t)$, might be adjusted to absorb the excess demand for $B_{1j}(t)$ rather than being adjusted to its own excess demand. Thus the adjustment function for $B_{2j}(t)$ becomes

$$DB_{2j}(t) = h_{2j}[\hat{B}_{1j}(t) - B_{1j}(t)] , \qquad (12.2)$$

but $B_{1j}(t)$ is still given by the identity. It could be argued that the excess demand for $B_{1j}(t)$ should be included in the adjustment function of all other securities, but if this is the case then it is considered that in the adjustment function for securities which are not highly liquid, or not close substitutes for $B_{1j}(t)$, the effect of any excess demand for $B_{1j}(t)$ would be small and could be neglected. A similar argument can be made against including other excess demands in a particular adjustment function.

If a sector has a strong influence over the interest rate for a particular security $B_{2j}(t)$ either because it can fix the interest rate directly in some way or because it is a leading operator in the market for the security then holdings of that security may be considered as exogenous by that sector, and the interest rate adjustment function approximated by

$$Dr_2(t) = f_2[\hat{B}_{2j}(t) - B_{2j}(t)] \ . \tag{12.3}$$

If this security is a close substitute for the sector residual $B_{1j}(t)$ and if the sector does not have a significant influence over the interest rate $r_1(t)$, then holdings of $B_{2j}(t)$ may be a function of the excess demand for $B_{1j}(t)$ as in (12.2). In this way excess demands in one market can influence interest rates in some other market.

Another restriction on the adjustment function in the model is that for each security at all points of time total holdings are zero. For each security therefore it is assumed that there is at least one sector which absorbs the excess stock of the security in the market but in order to do this it is likely that this sector or group of sectors will need to exercise a strong influence on the yield of that security. Other sectors may also have some influence on this yield but this effect is likely to be small; their influence is assumed to act through the demand for other securities rather than directly on the interest rate of this particular security. If the market is non-competitive, however, some economic units may be able to fix interest rates, so that the adjustment of interest rates need not be governed by the excess demand for the security but by the behaviour of the price-leaders in the market. The interest rate adjustment functions can be interpreted therefore either as an approximation to a competitive market structure where one sector is dominant in a particular market, or as a non-competitive structure where one sector can control the interest rate directly.

In the models estimated below the behaviour functions are assumed to contain current variables only and not expectations. In this system the adjustment function takes the form

$$D^2 X_i(t) = \beta[\hat{X}_j(t) - X_j(t)] - \alpha D X_i(t) + u_i(t) \ , \tag{12.4}$$

where $X(t)$ refers to holdings of some security $B(t)$ or to some interest rate $r(t)$, $\hat{X}(t)$ is the desired value of $X(t)$ and i and j may be the same. $u_i(t)$ is a disturbance term specified as white noise. This function could be considered to be derived from

$$DX_i(t) = \int_0^\infty \alpha e^{-\alpha\theta} \gamma [\hat{X}_j(t-\theta) - X_j(t-\theta)] \, d\theta + \omega_i(t) , \qquad (12.5)$$

which gives

$$D^2 X_i(t) = \alpha\gamma [\hat{X}_j(t) - X_j(t)] - \alpha DX_i(t) + (D+\alpha)\omega_i(t) . \qquad (12.6)$$

Although formally (12.6) is similar to (12.4), it is evident that if (12.5) is the correct model and $\omega_i(t)$ is white noise, then (12.6) is not correct since the derivative of white noise does not exist. In order to escape this problem the adjustment function is specified as (12.4) with $u_i(t)$ being white noise elements. The behaviour function $\hat{X}(t)$ may contain an additive white noise disturbance without affecting the model. Such a system corresponds to the second order differential equation system

$$D^2 y(t) = A_1 Dy(t) + A_2 y(t) + Bz(t) + u(t) , \qquad (12.7)$$

where $y(t)$ is a vector of endogenous variables, $z(t)$ is a vector of exogenous variables and A_1, A_2 and B corresponding matrices of coefficients of the model. In the system estimated here A_1 is diagonal.

3. A model of the United Kingdom financial markets

This model of a part of the United Kingdom financial market consists of a system of adjustment functions for holdings of securities and for interest rates, with a demand or supply function or a desired interest rate function being specified for each security. As the behaviour functions are specified as linear, the partial derivatives with respect to any variable in the function is given by the coefficient of that variable, and the sign of this coefficient can usually be determined from economic theory. The expected signs are shown with the model. In order that the behavioural parameters in the model should be identifiable and able to be estimated with the appropriate restrictions, each behaviour function occurs only once in the model. In the model below the stochastic disturbance terms have been omitted for convenience.

Although on theoretical grounds behaviour functions should include all variables relevant to the sector's objective function and exogenous to that sector as noted above, the behaviour functions specified here have been restricted further to include only those variables which are expected to be most significant in each function. Although this is the model for which detailed estimates are given, the less restricted and theoretically more justifiable model was also estimated and is discussed at the end of the paper. It will be seen that the less restricted model does appear to be significantly better but to present the detailed estimates of that model would be lengthy, confusing and unnecessary at this stage. The emphasis throughout this paper is placed on the dynamic structure of the system rather than on the specification of particular demand and supply functions.

In this study the economy was divided into a public sector, including only the government and monetary authorities; a private sector consisting of a personal sector, a (non-financial intermediary) corporate sector, a (non-banking) financial intermediary sector, a banking sector, and the discount houses; and an external sector. Unfortunately, in the initial model lack of satisfactory data required that the first three subsectors of the private sector be aggregated, and initially most of the external sector was eliminated from the system. As noted above, this is a study of only the financial markets of the economy with real variables being considered exogenous.

The notation of the model is:

(i) The letter plus first subscript denotes the type of security or interest rate.

(ii) The second subscript denotes the sector holding or issuing the security: specifically, 1 denotes discount houses, 2 the (domestic) banking sector and 5 the private non-banking sector. (The absence of a second subscript denotes a total value.)

(iii) A circumflex over a variable denotes a desired value or corresponding behavioural function.

The variables in the system are:

B_3^* Total bills excluding official external holdings.

B_1^* Treasury bills excluding official external holdings.

B_2 Other bills.

B_{31} Bills held by discount houses.

B_{32} Bills held by banking sector.

B_{15} Bills held by private sector.

B_6^* Government securities excluding official external holdings.

B_{61} Government securities held by discount houses.

B_{62} Government securities held by banking sector.

B_{65} Government securities held by private sector.

D_{02} Deposits of banking sector.

A_{12} Advances of banking sector.

L_{02} Liquid assets held by banking sector.

M_{02} Cash and balances at Bank of England of banking sector.

M_{31} Money at call and deposits held by discount houses.

M_{32} Money at call of banking sector.

M_{12} Money at call of banking sector held by discount houses.

M_{35} Money at call of banking sector held by private sector.

M_{15} Money at call of private sector held by discount houses.

r_0 Bank Rate.

r_1 Treasury bill discount rate on allotment.

r_2 Treasury bill re-discount rate (market rate).

r_3 Call-money rate.

r_4 Gross redemption yield on short-term Government securities (0–4 years maturity).

r_5 Gross redemption yield on long-term Government securities (15–20 years maturity).

r_6 Gross flat yield on 3½% War Loan (undated stock).

r_9 New York Federal Reserve Bank Rate.

ER Gold and Convertible Currency Reserves.

EX Exports of goods and sevices.

EI Imports of goods and services.

Y_{pg} Gross domestic product of the private sector.
I_g Investment of the Government sector.
I_p Investment of the private sector.
C_g Government expenditure on goods and services.
T_y Direct and indirect taxation.
U Unemployment.
p Gross domestic product implicit price deflator.

The model, with a brief description of the structure of the system, is:

(i) *Authorities*
The adjustment functions for the total volume of Government securities and Treasury Bills (excluding official external holdings) are assumed to depend on the excess supply of those securities by the authorities.

$$D^2 B_6^*(t) = \beta_1 [\hat{B}_6^*(t) - B_6^*(t)] - \alpha_1 DB_6^*(t) \, ,$$

$$\hat{B}_6^*(t) = \delta_{11} r_6(t) + \delta_{12} ER(t) + \delta_{13} U(t) + \delta_{14} I_g(t) \, , \qquad (12.8)$$

where $\alpha_1, \beta_1 > 0$; $\delta_{11}, \delta_{12}, \delta_{13} < 0$; $\delta_{14} > 0$.

$$D^2 B_1^*(t) = \beta_2 [\hat{B}_1^*(t) - B_1^*(t)] - \alpha_2 DB_1^*(t) \, ,$$

$$\hat{B}_1^*(t) = \delta_{21} r_2(t) + \delta_{22} ER(t) + \delta_{23} U(t) + \delta_{24} B_{61}(t) \, , \qquad (12.9)$$

where $\alpha_2, \beta_2 > 0$; $\delta_{22}, \delta_{23} < 0$; $\delta_{21}, \delta_{24} > 0$.
The adjustment function for Bank Rate is assumed to depend on the excess of desired over actual Bank Rate

$$D^2 r_0(t) = \beta_3 [\hat{r}_0(t) - r_0(t)] - \alpha_3 Dr_0(t) \, ,$$

$$\hat{r}_0(t) = \delta_{31} ER(t) + \delta_{32} U(t) + \delta_{33} r_9(t) \, , \qquad (12.10)$$

where $\alpha_3, \beta_3 > 0$; $\delta_{31}, \delta_{32} < 0$; $\delta_{33} > 0$.

(ii) *Discount houses*

It is considered that the discount houses absorb the residual market Treasury Bills and take their money at call as given by the banking and private sectors; the residual asset of their portfolios will, therefore, be Government securities.

$$B_{61}(t) = M_{31}(t) - B_{31}(t) .\tag{12.11}$$

The Treasury Bill discount and rediscount rates are assumed to be functions of the excess demand by the discount houses for bills and money at call.

$$D^2 r_1(t) = \beta_4 [\hat{B}_{31}(t) - B_{31}(t)] - \alpha_4 Dr_1(t) ,\tag{12.12}$$

$$\hat{B}_{31}(t) = \delta_{41} r_0(t) + \delta_{42} r_1(t) + \delta_{43} r_2(t) + \delta_{44} r_3(t) + \delta_{45} B_{61}(t) ,$$

where $\alpha_4 > 0$; $\beta_4 < 0$; $\delta_{41}, \delta_{43}, \delta_{44} < 0$; $\delta_{42}, \delta_{45} > 0$.

$$D^2 r_2(t) = \beta_5 [\hat{M}_{31}(t) - M_{31}(t)] - \alpha_5 Dr_2(t) ,\tag{12.13}$$

$$\hat{M}_{31}(t) = \delta_{51} r_0(t) + \delta_{52} r_1(t) + \delta_{53} r_2(t) + \delta_{54} r_3(t) + \delta_{55} B_{61}(t) ,$$

where $\alpha_5, \beta_5 > 0$; $\delta_{51}, \delta_{52}, \delta_{55} > 0$; $\delta_{53}, \delta_{54} < 0$.

(iii) *Banking sector*

It is assumed that the banks have a short-term and a longer-term portfolio with the latter consisting of 'liquid assets', Government securities and advances, and the former holdings of cash and balances at the Bank of England, money at call, and Treasury and other bills. Cash is assumed to be the residual of the shorter term portfolio and 'liquid assets' the residual of the longer term portfolio, with deposits being exogenous to the banking sector.

$$M_{02}(t) = L_{02}(t) - M_{32}(t) - B_{32}(t) ,\tag{12.14}$$

$$L_{02}(t) = D_{02}(t) - B_{62}(t) - A_{12}(t) .\tag{12.15}$$

The adjustment function for money at call is specified as depending on the excess demand for cash and balances at the Bank of England, and the adjustment function for Treasury and other bills depends on the excess demand for those bills.

$$D^2 M_{32}(t) = \beta_6 [\hat{M}_{02}(t) - M_{02}(t)] - \alpha_6 DM_{32}(t) ,$$

$$\hat{M}_{02}(t) = \delta_{61} r_3(t) + \delta_{62} D_{02}(t) , \qquad (12.16)$$

where $\alpha_6 > 0; \beta_6 < 0; \delta_{61} < 0; \delta_{62} > 0$.

$$D^2 B_{32}(t) = \beta_7 [\hat{B}_{32}(t) - B_{32}(t)] - \alpha_7 DB_{32}(t) ,$$

$$\hat{B}_{32}(t) = \delta_{71} r_2(t) + \delta_{72} r_3(t) + \delta_{73} L_{02}(t) , \qquad (12.17)$$

where $\alpha_7, \beta_7 > 0; \delta_{71}, \delta_{73} > 0; \delta_{72} < 0$.

Holdings of Government securities are assumed to be a function of the excess demand for liquid assets, and advances may be specified as a function of the excess supply of advances by the banks.

$$D^2 B_{62}(t) = \beta_8 [\hat{L}_{02}(t) - L_{02}(t)] - \alpha_8 DB_{62}(t) ,$$

$$\hat{L}_{02}(t) = \delta_{81} r_2(t) + \delta_{82} r_4(t) + \delta_{83} D_{02}(t) , \qquad (12.18)$$

where $\alpha_8 > 0; \beta_8 < 0; \delta_{81}, \delta_{83} > 0; \delta_{82} < 0$.

$$D^2 A_{12}(t) = \beta_9 [\hat{A}_{12}(t) - A_{12}(t)] - \alpha_9 DA_{12}(t) ,$$

$$\hat{A}_{12}(t) = \delta_{91} r_0(t) + \delta_{92} r_4(t) + \delta_{93} D_{02}(t) , \qquad (12.18')$$

where $\alpha_9, \beta_9 > 0; \delta_{91}, \delta_{93} > 0; \delta_{92} < 0$.

The banks, as the major suppliers of money at call, are assumed to have a significant influence over the money at call rate which is assumed to adjust to the excess supply of money at call by the banks. Also, as the banks are leading operators in the short term Government securities market the short term rate on these secur-

ities is assumed to adjust to the excess demand of the banks for
Government securities.

$$D^2 r_3(t) = \beta_{10} [\hat{M}_{32}(t) - M_{32}(t)] - \alpha_{10} Dr_3(t) ,$$

$$\hat{M}_{32}(t) = \delta_{101} r_2(t) + \delta_{102} r_3(t) + \delta_{103} L_{02}(t) , \qquad (12.19)$$

where $\alpha_{10} > 0; \beta_{10} < 0; \delta_{101} < 0; \delta_{102}, \delta_{103} > 0$.

$$D^2 r_4(t) = \beta_{11} [\hat{B}_{62}(t) - B_{62}(t)] - \alpha_{11} Dr_4(t) ,$$

$$\hat{B}_{62}(t) = \delta_{111} r_0(t) + \delta_{112} r_4(t) + \delta_{113} D_{02}(t) , \qquad (12.20)$$

where $\alpha_{11} > 0; \beta_{11} < 0; \delta_{111} < 0; \delta_{112}, \delta_{113} > 0$.

(iv) *Private sector*

In the model below advances to the private sector are assumed
to adjust according to the excess demand for advances so that
(12.18′) does not hold.

$$D^2 A_{12}(t) = \beta_{12} [\hat{A}_{12}(t) - A_{12}(t)] - \alpha_{12} DA_{12}(t) ,$$

$$\hat{A}_{12}(t) = \delta_{121} r_0(t) + \delta_{122} EX(t) + \delta_{123} EI(t) + \delta_{124} I_p(t) , \quad (12.21)$$

where $\alpha_{12}, \beta_{12} > 0; \delta_{121} < 0; \delta_{122}, \delta_{123}, \delta_{124} > 0$.

The next equation is an approximation to the identity which
determines deposits of the banking sector. [3]

$$D[D_{02}(t)] = DA_{12}(t) + DER(t) - DB_{65}(t) + C_g(t) - T_y(t) + I_g(t) . \tag{12.22}$$

---

[3] This equation is only an approximation to the portfolio identity of the private
sector. In particular, receipts and payments rather than income and expenditure variables
should be included, and a number of very short term securities have been omitted. These
include money at call loaned by the private sector to the discount houses, holdings of
Treasury Bills by the private sector, holdings of commercial bills by the banks and
discount houses, and holdings of Tax Reserve certificates. Adequate data are not available for the earlier part of the sample period to enable the true identity to be used.

The private sector is assumed to have a significant influence over the long-term Government security rate which is specified as a function of the excess demand for these securities by the private sector.

$$D^2 r_6(t) = \beta_{13}[\hat{B}_{65}(t) - B_{65}(t)] - \alpha_{13} Dr_6(t) ,$$

$$\hat{B}_{65}(t) = \delta_{131} r_0(t) + \delta_{132} r_6(t) + \delta_{133} Y_{pg}(t) + \delta_{134} D_{02}(t)$$
$$+ \delta_{135} p(t) , \tag{12.23}$$

where $\alpha_{13} > 0; \beta_{13} < 0; \delta_{132}, \delta_{133}, \delta_{134} > 0; \delta_{131}, \delta_{135} < 0.$

(v) *Market clearing identities*

Money at call of the banks held by the private sector, and money at call of the private sector held by the discount houses is assumed to be exogenous.

$$M_{31}(t) = M_{12}(t) + M_{15}(t) , \tag{12.24}$$

$$M_{12}(t) = M_{32}(t) - M_{35}(t) . \tag{12.25}$$

The discount houses are assumed to absorb the residual of the Treasury and commercial bills market.

$$B_3^*(t) = B_1^*(t) + B_2(t) , \tag{12.26}$$

$$B_{31}(t) = B_3^*(t) - B_{32}(t) - B_{15}(t) . \tag{12.27}$$

The private sector is assumed to absorb the residual of the Government securities market.

$$B_{65}(t) = B_6^*(t) - B_{61}(t) - B_{62}(t) . \tag{12.28}$$

The first three adjustment functions are those which depend on the excess demand or supply of securities or the excess of desired over actual interest rates of the authorities. (12.8) specifies that

total Government securities, excluding official holdings by overseas authorities, adjust according to the excess supply of those
securities, but it may be noted that such an equation is statistically
equivalent to a system in which issues of Government securities
depend on the excess of desired over actual interest rates. It is
assumed, therefore, that the action of the authorities can be form-
alized by specifying a decision function which determines either
the desired supply of Government securities and Treasury Bills, or
the desired rate of interest.

As the authorities announce the volume of Treasury Bills for
tender some time before the discount houses and other intermediaries make their bid for the Bills, and since the discount
houses 'cover the tender' of the issue, the authorities are likely to
determine the supply of Bills rather than the interest rate, although the interest rate will be taken into account in this supply
function. The authorities can enter the market at any time, however, and buy 'tender' or sell 'tap' Bills, so they will exert a continuous influence on either the stock of Treasury Bills or their yield.

It is more likely, perhaps, that the authorities will have a desired
interest rate function, rather than a supply function for medium
and long-term Government securities, and so will buy and sell
securities to try to maintain this rate. When the authorities are
absorbing stock, however, a supply function may be more plausible. In either case, the authorities will determine the actual stock
in the market so that the adjustment functions can be specified as
in (12.8) and (12.9). The adjustment function (12.9) is continuous
since although the issue of new Bills to the market is largely dis-
continuous the function represents the continuous influence of
the Bank of England.

It is assumed that holdings of Treasury Bills by the private and
external sectors are determined by these sectors leaving the discount houses and banks to balance demand and supply in the
market while attempting to reach their desired position. The discount houses take up all surplus bills issued by the Treasury tender, but may rediscount with either the banks or the Bank of
England, or borrow from the Bank of England to help finance
their holdings. The banks do not tender for Treasury Bills on their

own account, but meet requirements only by rediscounting bills for the discount houses or the private sector, and always hold the Bills until maturity. But the banks can influence the supply of bills offered to them since they supply money at call and short notice to the discount houses to finance their holdings of bills and securities.

It could be assumed that the banks have demand functions for each of the assets which they hold but that the deposits of the banks are determined by the private sector. Thus the decision function of the banks would allow these desired holdings to be determined simultaneously as functions of the yields on all securities, the expected yields, the expected rate of capital gain and the level of deposits. It seems reasonable to consider cash as the 'residual' in the banks' portfolio but the banks will wish to keep this as close as possible to the desired level because, although a minimum quantity is necessary for transactions, its return is zero.

A perhaps more plausible description of the banking system can be found if the banks are assumed to make relatively infrequent (long-term) decisions on their holdings of total liquid assets, Government securities and advances, and to make more frequent (short-term) decisions regarding their holdings of individual liquid assets. The liquid assets of the banks are defined as cash and balances at the Bank of England, money at call and short notice, Treasury Bills and other bills. For simplicity, bills other than Treasury Bills will be neglected at this stage since they can be introduced later without affecting the basic model.

Within the 'longer-term' portfolio of the banks it is considered that the residual will be 'liquid assets' as in (12.15). Since 'liquid assets' usually have a lower return than other assets of the banks, and as the risk involved is often no greater than, for example, short term bonds, it seems likely that banks will wish to keep 'liquid assets' as near as possible to desired holdings. As short-term Government bonds are highly liquid but are not included in the conventional 'liquid assets' of the banks, the banks can change their holdings of 'liquid assets' by selling bonds to the discount houses who finance these additional holdings by borrowing money at call from the banks. The banks will have the same total liquid

assets defined to include short bonds, as before, but a higher proportion of these will be in the 'liquid assets' group. This is for-
malised in (12.18) such that the adjustment of Government securities held by the banks is a function of the excess demand for
liquid assets as suggested in (12.2). Cash and balances at the Bank
of England will be the residual liquid asset (12.14), and thus the
overall residual asset of the banks, but since money at call is
virtually as liquid as cash, and has a positive return, holdings of
money at call are specified as adjusting to the excess demand for
cash (12.16).

If it is assumed as in (12.16) that the banks determine the
supply of money at call, that the supply of money at call from the
private sector to the discount houses is determined by the private
sector, and that the discount houses absorb the residual Treasury
Bills in the market (12.27), then the residual of the discount
houses is likely to be advances and rediscounts by the Bank of
England. It was found, however, that the adjustment process here
was very rapid, and with the data used could not be determined
statistically, so that such advances were omitted from the model.
This leaves holdings of short term Government bonds as the residual of the discount houses as in (12.11).

There are several possible sets of equations which may represent
the link between the banking sector and the discount houses. In
this model it was assumed that holdings of Treasury Bills by the
banks is a function of their excess demand for Treasury Bills
(12.17), that the call money rate is a function of the excess supply
of money at call by the banks (12.19), and that the rediscount
rate is a function of the excess demand for call money by the
discount houses (12.13). This formulation is partially due to the
simplifying restrictions placed on the adjustment processes for
estimation purposes. It would be expected that the excess demand
or supply of each sector should enter into each interest rate adjustment function. Thus the market rate for Treasury Bills would be
determined not only by the excess demand of the discount houses,
but also by the excess demand of the banking and private sectors,
and so this rate would be a function of excess total demand. If it is
accepted that some sectors are likely to be more sensitive than

others to their excess demand, or have a greater influence on the market rate, then the rate of interest could still change if some sectors were out of equilibrium even though total excess demand was zero. In specifying the model it was assumed that the discount houses and the banks have a very strong influence on the discount and rediscount rates and the effect of disequilibrium in the holdings of Treasury Bills by other sectors is likely to be negligible in comparison with this.

Similarly the rate on call money should be a function of the excess supply of money at call by the banks and the excess demand for money at call by the discount houses. But the banks are likely to use money at call as their behavioural short term residual, as has been assumed, only if they have a strong influence over the call money rate. The interdependence of money at call and Treasury Bill rediscounts by the banks may, however, make the assumption that the call money rate is a function of the excess demand for money at call by the discount houses and the rediscount rate is a function of the excess supply of money at call by the banks equally plausible. The functions specified for rediscount and call money rates should be considered as approximations to general market adjustment functions and not as the adjustment functions of a particular sector; any choice between the approximations specified will be based on statistical grounds.

In the model above the discount rate on Treasury Bills is assumed to adjust according to a behaviour function of the discount houses and not to be a market adjustment function. This follows from the structure of the discount market in the United Kingdom. There is no theoretical reason, however, why the roles of the excess demand for Treasury Bills by the discount houses, and the excess demand for money at call by the discount houses, should not be reversed.

Finally, deposits of the private sector at the banks and advances by the banks to the private sector must be considered. The rate of interest charged on advances is in most cases Bank Rate plus 1% with a minimum of 5%. In the earlier part of the sample period the banks had 'surplus' liquid assets and thus it is likely that advances were demand determined, that is a function of the excess demand of the private sector rather than a function of the excess supply of the banks. In the latter part of the period, however, more and more stringent restrictions seem to have been imposed by the authorities, and under these conditions advances may be supply determined. This desired supply may not be the potential supply of the banks but rather the supply under the constraint of some 'request' from the authorities. Since the interest rate is tied to Bank Rate, under conditions of excess demand the banks will need to use some form of selective control which would be strengthened as actual lending increases to desired lending, but to the extent that banks wish to maintain goodwill advances will still be made.

Therefore, given that the banks desire a certain level of liquid assets the amount of securities held by the banks follows from the advances made. If advances increase, liquid assets will decrease and to some extent deposits will increase as in (12.22); this increase in deposits will partly offset the decrease in liquid assets but the proportion of liquid assets in the portfolio will have fallen. This will be counteracted by a shift from Government securities so the major restraint on any increase in advances is the holdings of short bonds by the banks. Thus the volume of advances may be determined according to some supply function such as (12.18'). Although it is suggested that over the period considered here advances were demand determined (12.21), despite the sometimes stringent requests of the authorities, supply functions have also been specified.

It is also assumed that the private sector has desired demand functions for the other securities which it holds but only deposits and holdings of Government securities and Treasury Bills are considered here. It is specified in (12.28) that the private sector absorbs the residual Government securities in the market, and although this may not be particularly realistic it is likely that some sector of the private sector, such as non-banking financial intermediaries, may in effect do so. As with Treasury Bills the rate of interest on these securities would depend on the individual excess demands for each sector holding Government securities but it will be assumed that the excess demand of the private sector has the greatest effect giving (12.23).

In most discussions on the volume of money in the economy it is presumed that the authorities have some control over the supply of money and by taking appropriate action can directly increase or decrease this volume by some significant amount; or it is assumed that the private sector has a demand function for money and that actual holdings are adjusted to this. In the model here it is assumed that these supply and demand functions do exist, but instead of assuming that the volume of money is adjusted to either this desired supply or desired demand it is specified as the residual financial asset of the private sector (12.22). Thus an increase in the volume of money will equal the sum of Government payments less Government receipts from the private sector, the increase in the volume of advances, the decrease in Government securities held by the private sector, and export receipts less import payments by the private sector. Transactions within the private sector do not affect the volume of money as a whole but would change the holdings of subsectors of this sector. The private sector may, however, take some action to change its money holdings, such as by changing holdings of advances or bonds; or subsectors of the private sector may increase their demand for commodities or investment goods.

4. Estimates of the model and its economic significance

Full information maximum likelihood estimates of three subsystems of the model above are presented below.[4] The first model is of the London Clearing Banks estimated using monthly data for the period 1952–66; another model includes the discount houses and the banking sector (consisting of the London Clearing Banks, the Scottish banks and the Northern Ireland banks) and is estimated using quarterly data for 1952–66; a third model introduces

---

[4] Standard errors are given in parentheses beneath the estimates of the coefficients.

Model 1: Structural estimates (data: monthly, 1952–66)
Banking sector

1. $D^2 M_{32}$ = $-8.048\, DM_{32}$ + $13.965\, M_{02}$ − $16.673\, D_{02}$ − $0.307\, r_3$
        (1.855)   (2.885)   (3.435)   (0.105)

2. $D^2 B_{32}$ = $-3.410\, DB_{32}$ − $0.904\, B_{32}$ + $0.138\, r_2$ − $0.173\, r_4$
        (0.496)   (0.176)   (0.075)   (0.089)

3. $D^2 B_{62}$ = $-3.152\, DB_{62}$ + $0.818\, L_{02}$ − $0.671\, D_{02}$ − $0.047\, r_2$
        (0.460)   (0.170)   (0.146)   (0.017)

4. $D^2 r_0$ = $-4.552\, Dr_0$ − $0.092\, ER$ − $0.086\, U$ − $0.605\, r_0$ + $0.136\, r_9$
        (0.526)   (0.055)   (0.039)   (0.113)   (0.049)

5. $D^2 r_3$ = $-4.343\, Dr_3$ + $0.165\, M_{32}$ + $1.085\, r_2$ − $1.581\, r_3$
        (0.495)   (0.066)   (0.247)   (0.292)

6. $D^2 r_4$ = $-6.164\, Dr_4$ − $0.387\, B_{62}$ + $0.665\, r_2$ − $1.270\, r_4$
        (1.018)   (0.151)   (0.207)   (0.331)

7. M_{02} = $4.014\, L_{02}$ − $0.978\, M_{32}$ − $2.005\, B_{32}$

8. L_{02} = $2.631\, D_{02}$ − $0.631\, B_{62}$ − $1.120\, A_{12}$

the private (non-banking) sector and the authorities into the second model but excludes the discount houses, and this was estimated using quarterly data for the period 1955–66.

In the model presented here the variables are those defined above[5], and the observations used are deviations about seasonal means of the logarithms of the original observations. Since the model is log-linear, and as a linear estimator is to be used, the identities were approximated by a Taylor series expansion at the mean. The estimates are those of the approximate discrete model [2, 3] so that if x_t refers to observations on a stock, interest rate or price variable at time t, the notation used is such that

$$D^2 x = (1-L)^2 x_t \ , \qquad Dx = \tfrac{1}{2}(1-L^2)x_t \ , \qquad x = \tfrac{1}{4}(1+L)^2 x_t \ ,$$

$$(12.29)$$

[5] A full definition of the economic series used is given in [3].

Model 2: Structural estimates (data: quarterly, 1952–66)
Banking and discount houses sectors

---

1. $\quad D^2 M_{32} = -7.406\, DM_{32} + 2.182\, M_{02} + 2.262\, L_{02} + 0.229\, r_3$
$\qquad\qquad\quad (1.884) \qquad\quad (0.479) \qquad\quad (0.757) \qquad (0.160)$

2. $\quad D^2 B_{32} = -2.399\, DB_{32} - 1.352\, B_{32} + 1.298\, r_2 - 1.204\, r_3$
$\qquad\qquad\quad (0.467) \qquad\quad (0.307) \qquad\quad (0.346) \qquad (0.337)$

3. $\quad D^2 B_{62} = -2.901\, DB_{62} + 1.650\, L_{02} - 1.174\, D_{02} - 0.176\, r_2$
$\qquad\qquad\quad (0.574) \qquad\quad (0.205) \qquad\quad (0.173) \qquad (0.055)$

4. $\quad D^2 r_0 \;\; = -3.328\, Dr_0 \; - 0.269\, ER - 0.099\, U - 0.775\, r_0 + 0.118\, r_9$
$\qquad\qquad\quad (0.431) \qquad\quad (0.084) \qquad (0.070) \qquad (0.199) \qquad (0.063)$

5. $\quad D^2 r_1 \;\; = -3.201\, Dr_1 \; + 0.725\, M_{31} - 0.495\, B_{31} - 0.861\, r_0 - 6.179\, r_1 + 6.054\, r_2$
$\qquad\qquad\quad (0.391) \qquad\quad (0.222) \qquad (0.169) \qquad (0.314) \qquad (1.293) \qquad (1.328)$

6. $\quad D^2 r_2 \;\; = -3.543\, Dr_2 \; + 0.047\, M_{31} + 1.428\, r_1 - 0.975\, r_2 - 1.126\, r_3$
$\qquad\qquad\quad (0.502) \qquad\quad (0.200) \qquad (1.316) \qquad (1.361) \qquad (0.565)$

7. $\quad D^2 r_3 \;\; = -4.341\, Dr_3 \; + 0.211\, M_{32} + 2.745\, r_2 - 3.379\, r_3$
$\qquad\qquad\quad (0.600) \qquad\quad (0.101) \qquad (0.517) \qquad (0.598)$

8. $\quad D^2 r_4 \;\; = -3.031\, Dr_4 \; - 0.393\, B_{62} + 1.165\, r_2 - 1.817\, r_4$
$\qquad\qquad\quad (0.571) \qquad\quad (0.133) \qquad (0.298) \qquad (0.389)$

9. $\quad B_{61} \;\; = \;\; 2.620\, M_{31} - 1.595\, B_{31}$

10. $\quad M_{31} \;\; = \;\; 0.605\, M_{12} + 0.385\, M_{15}$

11. $\quad B_{31} \;\; = \;\; 3.921\, B_3^* - 2.058\, B_{32} - 0.735\, B_{15}$

12. $\quad M_{02} \;\; = \;\; 3.574\, L_{02} - 0.904\, M_{32} - 1.641\, B_{32}$

13. $\quad M_{12} \;\; = \;\; 1.411\, M_{32} - 0.118\, M_{15}$

14. $\quad L_{02} \;\; = \;\; 2.658\, D_{02} - 0.683\, B_{62} - 1.125\, A_{12}$

---

where L is the lag operator; and if x_t is a flow variable, then the notation is

$$Dx = (1 - L)x_t, \qquad x = \tfrac{1}{2}(1 + L)x_t. \tag{12.30}$$

Thus, although D is not the differential operator but merely a symbol in the presentation of structural estimates for each model, it can be interpreted as the differential operator since the estimates are those of an approximation to the differential equation system.

Model 3: Structural estimates (data: quarterly, 1955–66)
Authorities, banking and private sectors

1. $D^2 B_6^* = -3.508\, DB_6^* - 2.559\, B_6^* + 0.082\, U + 0.052\, I_g - 0.077\, r_6$
   $\ (0.867)\ (0.641)\ (0.032)\ (0.027)\ (0.103)$

2. $D^2 B_{62} = -3.071\, DB_{62} - 1.572\, D_{02} + 2.052\, L_{02} + 0.038\, r_2 - 0.131\, r_4$
   $\phantom{2.\ D^2 B_{62} =}\ (0.789)\phantom{\,DB_{62}}\ (0.590)\phantom{\,D_{02}}\ (0.710)\phantom{\,L_{02}}\ (0.113)\ (0.222)$

3. $D^2 A_{12} = -1.981\, DA_{12} - 0.612\, A_{12} + 0.255\, I_p + 0.217\, EI - 0.295\, r_0$
   $\phantom{3.\ D^2 A_{12} =}\ (0.485)\phantom{\,DA_{12}}\ (0.146)\phantom{\,A_{12}}\ (0.113)\ (0.139)\ (0.090)$

4. $D^2 r_0 = -2.205\, Dr_0 - 0.576\, ER - 0.164\, U - 0.802\, r_0 + 0.404\, r_9$
   $\ (0.399)\ (0.248)\ (0.136)\ (0.263)\ (0.160)$

5. $D^2 r_4 = -2.718\, Dr_4 - 0.240\, B_{62} + 1.829\, D_{02} + 1.123\, r_0 - 2.402\, r_4$
   $\ (0.452)\ (0.143)\phantom{\,B_{62}}\ (0.443)\phantom{\,D_{02}}\ (0.296)\ (0.503)$

6. $D^2 r_6 = -4.422\, Dr_6 + 3.273\, B_{65} - 0.640\, D_{02} + 0.529\, p + 0.742\, r_0 - 2.932\, r_6$
   $\ (1.019)\ (1.426)\phantom{\,B_{65}}\ (0.307)\phantom{\,D_{02}}\ (0.318)\ (0.235)\ (0.717)$

7. $D^2 D_{02} = 0.123\, D^2 A_{12} - 0.367\, D^2 B_{65} - 0.011\, D^2 ER - 0.117\, DT_y + 0.110\, DC_g + 0.061\, D$
   $\phantom{7.\ D^2 D_{02} =}\ (0.072)\phantom{\,D^2A_{12}}\ (0.161)\phantom{\,D^2B_{65}}\ (0.014)\ (0.019)\ (0.063)\ (0.024)$

8. $L_{02} = 2.654\, D_{02} - 0.614\, B_{62} - 1.254\, A_{12}$

9. $B_{65} = 1.207\, B_6^* - 0.037\, B_{61} - 0.162\, B_{62}$

The continuous form of the adjustment functions may be written

$$D^2 X_1(t) = \alpha\beta[\hat{X}_2(t) - X_2(t)] - \alpha DX_1(t)\, , \qquad (12.31)$$

where α is the rate of adjustment and β is the adjustment coefficient on the excess demand (or supply) for $X_2(t)$ in the adjustment function for $X_1(t)$. Estimates of these parameters (see table 1) and of the parameters of the demand (or supply) function (see table 2) have been derived from the estimates above; as the model above is in logarithmic form the coefficients in the demand (or supply) function are elasticities.

These results may be considered firstly for the inference which may be drawn from the model regarding the structure of financial markets in the United Kingdom and secondly for the implications concerning the estimation of continuous systems. It is necessary,

Table 1
Estimates of parameters of adjustment functions

Adjustment function	Rate of adjustment			Adjustment coefficient		
	Model 1	Model 2	Model 3	Model 1	Model 2	Model 3
M_{32}	8.048 (1.855)	7.406 (1.884)		−1.735 (0.109)	−0.294 (0.033)	
B_{32}	3.410 (0.496)	2.399 (0.468)		0.265 (0.051)	0.563 (0.147)	
B_{62}	3.152 (0.460)	2.900 (0.574)	3.071 (0.789)	−0.259 (0.042)	−0.569 (0.048)	−0.668 (0.122)
A_{12}			1.981 (0.485)			0.309 (0.076)
B_6^*			3.508 (0.867)			0.730 (0.171)
r_0	4.552 (0.526)	3.328 (0.431)	2.205 (0.399)	0.133 (0.023)	0.233 (0.063)	0.364 (0.125)
r_1		3.202 (0.391)			0.155 (0.055)	
r_2		3.543 (0.502)			−0.013 (0.056)	
r_3	4.343 (0.495)	4.341 (0.600)		−0.038 (0.015)	−0.049 (0.024)	
r_4	6.164 (1.018)	3.032 (0.572)	2.718 (0.452)	0.063 (0.024)	0.130 (0.045)	0.088 (0.053)
r_6			4.422 (1.019)			−0.740 (0.323)

however, to consider this statistical inference in conjunction with the alternative hypotheses which were tested in order to find a model which is statistically significant and consistent with economic theory. The hypotheses tested here concerned the dynamic structure of the model, the form of the adjustment functions, and the specification of the demand functions.

Since the true lag structure of the adjustment function cannot

Table 2
Estimates of demand, supply and interest rate functions

(i) Authorities:

Variable	Model	Elasticity with respect to:				
		r_6	r_9	ER	U	I_9
$\hat{r}_0$	1		0.224 (0.075)	−0.152 (0.090)	−0.137 (0.060)	
	2		0.153 (0.089)	−0.347 (0.130)	−0.127 (0.087)	
	3		0.504 (0.219)	−0.718 (0.385)	−0.204 (0.155)	
$\hat{B}_6^*$	3	−0.030 (0.036)			0.032 (0.008)	0.019 (0.008)

(ii) Discount houses:

Variable	Model	Elasticity with respect to:				
		r_0	r_1	r_2	r_3	M_{31}
$\hat{B}_{31}$	2	−1.739 (0.916)	−12.478 (3.850)	12.225 (3.891)		1.464 (0.358)
$\hat{M}_{31}$	2 [a]		−30.565 (137.919)	20.889 (102.884)	24.109 (98.528)	

(iii) Banking sector:

Variable	Model	Elasticity with respect to:					
		r_0	r_2	r_3	r_4	L_{02}	D_{02}
$\hat{M}_{02}$	1			0.022 (0.006)			1.194 (0.021)
	2			−0.105 (0.065)		1.036 (0.200)	
$\hat{M}_{32}$	1		−6.586 (2.394)	9.573 (3.392)			
	2		−13.015 (5.780)	16.019 (7.164)			

Table 2 (continued)

Variable	Model	Elasticity with respect to:					
		r_0	r_2	r_3	r_4	L_{02}	D_{02}
$\hat{B}_{32}$	1		0.152 (0.077)		−0.191 (0.092)		
	2		0.960 (0.297)	−0.891 (0.287)			
$\hat{L}_{02}$	1		0.056 (0.019)				0.821 (0.064)
	2		0.107 (0.028)				0.712 (0.077)
	3		−0.019 (0.056)		0.064 (0.105)		0.766 (0.109)
$\hat{B}_{62}$	1 [b]		1.720 (0.587)		−3.286 (0.839)		
	2 [b]		2.961 (0.818)		−4.618 (1.050)		
	3 [b]	4.679 (2.482)			−10.013 (5.244)		5.539 (4.271)

(iv) Private sector:

Variable	Model	Elasticity with respect to:					
		r_0	r_6	D_{02}	I_p	EI	p
$\hat{A}_{12}$	3	−0.483 (0.128)			0.417 (0.179)	0.355 (0.196)	
$\hat{B}_{65}$	3	−0.227 (0.079)	0.896 (0.353)	0.196 (0.231)			−0.162 (0.135)

[a] In this model the adjustment coefficient of the excess demand function in the adjustment function for $r_1(t)$ is significant and positive and for $r_2(t)$ is insignificant and negative. This affects the estimates of the parameters of the demand function.

[b] In each model the adjustment coefficient of the excess demand function in the adjustment function for $r_4(t)$ is significant and positive. This affects the signs of the estimates of the parameters of the demand functions.

be settled theoretically, although it is possible to give reasons for using one form rather than another, two specifications of these functions were tested. In a preliminary study the economic structure of the model was taken as similar to that above but with the adjustment function specified as an unlagged adaptive function giving a first order differential equation system. A series of alternative demand functions were specified but these did not yield a set of satisfactory (in the sense of significant coefficients with the expected signs) maximum likelihood estimates. The simple adjustment process was rejected, therefore, and the lagged adjustment model used.

Another set of tests concerned the dynamic economic structure of the system such as the specification of which variables adjust to which excess demands. This was tested, however, only to a very limited extent so that, in general, the structure of the model relies almost entirely on economic theory and in particular monetary theory and a consideration of institutional behaviour. For some adjustment functions, however, it was difficult to distinguish *a priori* which excess demands or supply could be expected to be significant and so tests were made of some alternative hypotheses.

One set of tests of alternative hypotheses concerning the dynamic structure of the system was made in Model 2 in an attempt to determine the effect of the discount houses. It was assumed throughout that money at call and Treasury Bills held by the discount houses were both exogenous to the discount houses, and that Government securities held by the discount houses were the residual in their portfolio. In fact the residual in this portfolio is advances and discounts by the Bank of England but as it is Government securities which are close to maturity which are discounted and as the Bank acts as lender of last resort it is plausible to assume that holdings of Government securities are the residual. It was necessary to do so owing to the lack of satisfactory data.

The specification first tested and eventually accepted was that the adjustment function for the discount rate $r_1(t)$ depends on the excess demand for Treasury Bills held by the discount houses and that the rediscount rate $r_2(t)$ is a function of the excess demand for money at call held by the discount houses. One formulation which was rejected was that the discount rate was a function of the excess demand for money at call by the discount houses and the rediscount rate a function of the excess demand for Treasury Bills. Another specification made the discount rate $r_1(t)$ a function of the excess demand for Government securities since these are considered as the residual of the discount houses, and a further formulation reversed the roles of the supply and demand for money at call making the rediscount rate a function of the excess supply of call money by the banking sector and the call money rate a function of the excess demand for money at call by the discount houses. The latter two hypotheses were also rejected. It was found that the adjustment functions for the discount and rediscount rates were fairly unstable and the specification of these functions must still be considered as rather tentative.

Alternative structures of the system with respect to bank advances were also tested. An adjustment function depending on the excess supply of advances by the banking sector was tried in both Model 1 and Model 3 and rejected in both cases. The hypothesis that bank advances are demand determined could not be rejected, and later trials with an extended version of Model 3, which allowed discounts of accepting houses and advances of overseas banks as substitutes for commercial bank advances did not enable this conclusion to be changed. This latter formulation assumed total advances to be determined according to some adjustment function of excess demand by the private sector with advances of the commercial banks being supply determined and with overseas banks and accepting houses lending the residual, but the supply function specified for the commercial banks could not be accepted.

The other structural equation which was tested with respect to an alternative hypothesis was the adjustment function for the long-term interest rate $r_6(t)$ in Model 3. Initially separate functions for the medium term rate $r_5(t)$ and $r_6(t)$ were specified depending on either excess demand for Government securities by the private sector or excess demand for deposits by the private sector. This dynamic structure was rejected after a series of trials and in Model 3 only one function is specified.

Alternative demand and supply functions differing only in the interest rates and holdings of securities were also specified and estimated. Theory suggests a wide range of interest rates some of which will be insignificant in a given function and out of the set of rates which are likely to be significant a smaller set of rates which are actually statistically significant within the sample may be found given the overall structure of the model. For any given function no more than three interest rates were tried at any one time, and in most cases it soon became obvious which were the significant rates. In general these agreed with what might be expected given the institutional structure of the system. This testing of various specifications of demand functions did not preclude simultaneous testing of the dynamic structure of the system. It was found that if an adjustment function was relatively well determined such results would often hold over a wide range of alternative formulations of functions elsewhere in the system.

A model such as this has applications for theoretical study, for forecasting and for policy purposes. The structure of the financial sector of the economy can be studied as well as the effects of some changes in the structure. As the system is in equilibrium when all excess demands are zero an equilibrium point can be estimated for any set of values of exogenous variables by solving the set of equations

$$B_{ij}(t) = \hat{B}_{ij}(t) \qquad \text{and} \qquad r_i(t) = \hat{r}_{ij}(t)$$

for all endogenous holdings of securities and interest rates. Moreover, the model can give an indication of the path of each endogenous variable over time, given the exogenous variables, as well as the time required to move from one equilibrium point to another. This allows policy makers to predict the results of some policy or to compare alternative policies.

Some general observations on the model can be made but these hyptheses would require more thorough testing before they could be considered generally acceptable. These comments, of course, are made only in the context of the model and for the sample period. It will be shown below that the models are consistent or 'almost consistent' with the observed data but this does not preclude other systems also from being consistent.

This study rejects the hypothesis that a major determinant of total issues of Government securities by the authorities (including the Bank of England) is the interest rate on these securities; whenever this interest rate was included in the supply function for the securities its coefficient was not significantly different from zero.

The hypothesis that advances are determined by the banking sector is also rejected, as indicated above; and a variable indicating direct pressure on the banks by the authorities to reduce advances was not significant.[6] As this model does not disaggregate advances to the private sector the allocation of advances between subsectors of the private sector cannot be considered; directives of the authorities may affect this distribution. The directives, however, have no significant effect on either the total supply of or demand for advances.

The hypothesis that the demand for advances is a function of Bank Rate cannot be rejected, however, and an estimate of its elasticity is -0.5. This gives the authorities significant control over advances of the private sector, and suggests that if the rate on advances was set by the banks they would have a strong influence over demand. It is interesting that recently some banks have become more flexible in setting the rate on advances and it is suggested that this may be caused by these banks being unable to control advances despite the strong pressure put on them by the authorities. This study cannot reject the hypothesis that such a move would enable the banks to influence advances. The other major determinants of advances are private sector real investment and imports with elasticities of demand estimated as 0.4 and 0.35 respectively.

The authorities may wish to control the supply of money defined as cash and deposits; excluding the effect of Government receipts and payments which depend on real sector variables, and the external sector, the remaining factors causing changes in the volume of money are changes in private sector holdings of Government bonds and changes in advances. The authorities can influence

---

[6] This series was compiled by Mr. R.F.G. Alford of the London School of Economics.

advances by Bank Rate; it is much more difficult, however, for them to influence private sector holdings of Government securities. It is assumed here that the authorities can control, subject to a lagged function, the total holdings of Government securities but not their distribution. In the model, however, the point estimate of the interest elasticity for private sector holdings of securities is 0.9 and is significantly different from zero. As the private sector absorbs the residual securities in the market it appears that the authorities can, by increasing the supply of securities, encourage the private sector to increase its holdings but only at a higher rate of interest.

Although this study does not investigate the effect of financial behaviour on real variables it does have some implications for monetary policy. A prerequisite for effective monetary policy is that the authorities can exercise significant and predictable control over certain financial variables such as interest rates, the availability of credit and some forms of liquidity, in particular the volume of money. The estimates above suggest that the control of the authorities over advances and deposits is limited. The authorities do not appear to be able to control supply of advances by the banks as is often supposed, but they can influence demand through the use of Bank Rate to the extent that the rate charged on advances is linked to Bank Rate. Even if the authorities do have some control over advances, however, their control over deposits is more tenuous and depends very heavily upon the interest rate effect on holdings of Government securities. Moreover, advances are one form of credit available to the private sector over which the authorities are expected to have a high degree of control; the opportunity of the private sector to use other forms of credit would make monetary policy less effective.

If monetary policy is to be useful, however, not only must the authorities' control of certain financial variables be sufficiently predictable and rapid, but also changes in these variables must have the desired effect on the real variables at which the policy is directed. In order to investigate this a complete model of the economy would be required showing the way in which real variables are influenced by financial behaviour as well as the feed-back from the real sector to the financial variables.

Table 3
Eigenvalues of fitted models

Model 1 – Banking sector			Model 2 – Banks and discount houses				Model 3 – Authorities, banking and private sectors			
Eigen-values	Standard error	Damping period	Eigenvalues	Standard error	Damping period	Period of cycle	Eigenvalues	Standard error	Damping period	Period of cycle
−0.137	0.025	7.3	−0.146	0.110	6.9		−0.383	0.141	2.6	
−0.173	0.060	5.8	−0.252	0.075	4.0		−0.392	0.315	2.6	
−0.214	0.053	4.7	−0.274	0.445	3.6		−0.460	0.227	2.2	
−0.290	0.063	3.4	−0.822	0.296	1.2		−1.598	0.589	0.6	
−0.403	0.081	2.5	−2.209	0.789	0.6		−1.745	0.543	0.6	
−2.426	2.271	0.4	−2.441	0.776	0.4		−2.520	1.022	0.4	
−2.979	0.514	0.3	−3.076	0.464	0.3		−2.755	0.864	0.4	
−3.120	0.528	0.3	−7.129	2.016	0.1		−3.563	1.324	0.3	
−3.945	0.529	0.3	−0.449 ± 0.066i	0.266, 0.116	2.2	95.1	−0.883 ± 0.215i	0.263, 0.202	1.1	29.2
−4.415	0.533	0.2	−1.282 ± 0.422i	0.267, 0.672	0.8	14.9	−1.361 ± 0.752i	0.226, 0.339	0.7	8.4
−5.614	4.142	0.2	−3.550 ± 0.515i	0.542, 0.121	0.3	12.2				
−5.950	1.031	0.2	−1.621 ± 2.172i	0.196, 0.317	0.6	2.9				

A further difficulty in controlling the system is that although the lag in the effect of changes in the target or policy variables on the control variables may be short any action may produce cyclical fluctuations; in the models here these cycles are quite long but are heavily damped (see table 3)[7]. The real eigenvalues are also quite small so that their damping period is short. It is interesting that these models should produce such long cycles considering the nature of the system. Model 2, for example, is concerned solely with the banks and discount houses yet includes cyclical fluctuations of about nine months, three and four years and a much longer cycle, which is significant at the 5% level. Although this long cycle does not occur in Model 3 the sample period for this model was only 12 years, whereas for Model 2 it was 15 years. Model 3 does, however, have a significant six or seven year cycle as well as a two year one. All except the 20 year cycle are heavily damped.

The imposition of over-identifying restrictions on the model, if correct, increases the efficiency of the estimator, but if incorrect the estimates will be inconsistent. The likelihood ratio was used to provide a set of tests on the restrictions used in the model. The very restricted Model 1, or Model 1a, with 25 coefficients, was estimated as above. A less restricted system, Model 1b, with 40 coefficients, was then estimated by specifying each demand function in the adjustment functions of the banks to be a function of Bank Rate r_0, Treasury Bill market rate r_2, call money rate r_3, short-term Government security rate r_4, and deposits D_{02}. Thus the demand functions are approximately those required by economic theory with each function depending on variables exogenous to the particular sector. The Bank Rate adjustment functions of the authorities, the structure of the adjustment functions of the banks and the identities were unchanged. Finally the unrestricted reduced form (excluding the identities), with 126 coefficients, was used to provide a test of all the over-identifying restrictions.

---

[7] The eigenvalues and their asymptotic standard errors, and other properties of the eigensystem, were found by a program, code-named CONTINEST, developed by the author [3].

Table 4
Likelihood ratio χ^2 statistic of over-identifying restrictions

	Degrees of freedom	χ^2 statistic	$\chi^2_{0.01}$	$\chi^2_{0.05}$
Model 1:				
(a) Restricted demand	101	216	135	124
(b) Unrestricted demand	86	79	118	107
Model 2:				
(a) Restricted demand	220	595	271	255
(b) Unrestricted demand	194	589	242	227
Model 3:				
(a) Restricted demand	159	191	203	189
(b) Unrestricted demand	146	169	188	175

Similar tests were made of the over-identifying restrictions in Models 2 and 3. Models 2b and 3b were estimated with 'unrestricted' demand functions, depending on all interest rates and other variables exogenous to the particular sector, but with the same dynamic structure and adjustment functions as Models 2 and 3 respectively. The unrestricted reduced forms were also estimated to give the likelihood of the just-identified models. The χ^2 statistics required to test the over-identifying restrictions on each model calculated from the ratio of the likelihood of the restricted model to the likelihood of the just-identified model are given with the corresponding confidence limits at the 1% and 5% levels of significance for a one tailed test.

The estimates of Models 1a and 1b, 2a and 3a generally satisfy economic theory and the propositions made above concerning the dynamic structure of the system. Moreover, the likelihoods of Models 1b and 3a are not significantly different from those of the just-identified models so that the over-identifying restrictions on these models are consistent with the sample. Model 1a, and also Models 2a and 2b, satisfy economic theory but the over-identifying restrictions on these models are not consistent with the sample and although the estimates of the coefficients of Model 1a often have a smaller variance than those of Model 1b the differences are not necessarily significant. It is considered that the specification of the less restricted demand functions, depending on all interest rates and holdings of securities which are determined exogenously to the sector, is preferable to the use of a more restricted function.

The over-identifying restrictions in the models estimated in this study are due, however, not only to the form of the adjustment functions and the dynamic structure of the financial markets suggested above but also to the assumptions concerning the continuity of the system and the discrete approximation to the continuous model. It is considered, therefore, that these estimates support the assertion that financial markets in the United Kingdom can be represented by a non-tâtonnement model which is continuous and recursive and that this system can be approximated by the discrete model derived in [1−3] and used here.

References

[1] A.R. Bergstrom, 'Non-recursive models as discrete approximations to systems of stochastic differential equations', *Econometrica* (1966) pp. 173−182.
[2] J.D. Sargan, 'Some discrete approximations to continuous time stochastic models', forthcoming, *Journal of the Royal Statistical Society*.
[3] C.R. Wymer, 'Econometric estimation of stochastic differential equation systems with applications to adjustment models of financial markets'. Unpublished Ph.D. thesis, University of London, 1970.

Other references:

T.C. Koopmans, 'Models involving a continuous time variable', in: *Statistical inference in dynamic economic models,* edited by T.C. Koopmans, Cowles Commission for Research in Economics, Monograph 10 (New York, John Wiley and Sons, 1950), pp. 384−389.
T. Negishi, 'Market clearing processes in a monetary economy', in: *The theory of interest rates,* edited by F.H. Hahn and F.P.R. Brechling (London, Macmillan, 1965), pp. 159−161.

Report of the Committee on the Working of the Monetary System, Cmnd. 827 (London, HMSO, 1959).

SHORT-RUN MONETARY ADJUSTMENTS IN
THE AUSTRALIAN ECONOMY, 1952–70

Richard ZECHER*

University of Chicago

Existing studies of monetary behavior in Australia have adopted, more or less intact, the hypotheses that have proved fruitful in studying U.S. monetary behavior. Money demand relations have been estimated in single equation form (Dewald [3]) and as part of a larger scale model (Norton [11]), and 'St Louis' type estimates have been made of the effects of past monetary change on current income (Dewald and Kennedy [4]). The results of these tests, where they are directly comparable, on occasion differ quite radically from results of studies for the U.S. economy.

Theories of monetary adjustment in an open economy on fixed exchange rates dating from Hume's famous specie flow mechanism, with numerous refinements by Meade [8], Johnson [6], and Mundell [10], among others, suggest that the money adjustment process in a closed economy differs in several respects from the process in an open economy. Central to this difference is the role that reserve flows play in adjusting actual money stock to desired money stock. In Australia, and probably in most open economies with specialized central banks, this reserve flow cum money change mechanism is sometimes operative in the short-run and sometimes, due to central bank policies or other factors, inoperative.

In the present paper Australian monetary behavior is examined

* Much of the work on this paper was completed while the author was Special Visiting Lecturer at Monash University. The author wishes to thank Monash, and particularly Professor Don Cochrane, for providing a pleasant productive working environment, and J.S. Mallyon of the Reserve Bank of Australia for providing data and other assistance.

in two periods. One period is characterized by large, contemporaneous effects of reserve flows on changes in money. In this milieu, adjustment to equilibrium in the money market is expected to be rapid due to equilibrating changes in money supply.

The second period is characterized by zero correlation between contemporaneous reserve flows and changes in money. In this case the burden of adjustment in the money market falls, as in a closed economy, upon price, interest rate, wealth, and output changes. However, since prices and interest rates in an open economy on fixed exchange rates are closely linked to 'world' prices and interest rates, an open economy, particularly if it is a relatively small part of the world economy, may find that domestic prices and interest rates are little affected by domestic conditions. With most of the standard processes leading to monetary equilibrium either impaired or eliminated, monetary adjustment to equilibrium may be expected to proceed slowly in such an economy.

In section 1, a simple general equilibrium model is presented in order to clarify the assumptions of the study, and to show the adjustment processes that are assumed to be operating (a) when reserve flows affect money, and (b) when they do not. The bond and commodity market equations are not estimated in this paper, but I think it is nonetheless useful to write them out explicitly.

Section 2 reports the estimated relation between reserve flows and changes in money for two subperiods, 1952(I)– 1959(I) and 1959(II)– 1970(I). Data for these periods are then used to estimate the money demand equations reported in section 3. In summary, these results reveal reasonable income and interest rate elasticities and a rapid rate of adjustment for the period when reserve flows affect money, and the opposite results for the period when reserve flows do not affect money.

If the money market adjusts rapidly to full, long-run equilibrium by means of a change in the stock of money associated with reserve flows, all of the standard intermediate equilibria of a closed economy with changing interest rates, price of capital, output, etc., are avoided. Past changes in money in this case should have little relation to current changes in income. This is in fact the relationship found for the period when reserve flows affected

monetary changes. In the other period, when monetary adjustments were estimated to proceed very slowly, the relationship
between past changes in money and current changes in income is
similar to, but far from identical with, the 'St. Louis' type of
result for the U.S.A.

1. The model

The model describes an economy on fixed exchange rates with
three markets: commodities, bonds, and money. The purpose of
the model is to show the avenues of adjustment to equilibrium
open to an economy under some extreme assumptions about the
domestic price level and interest rate. These assumptions may be
concisely stated as

$$E(P_{Aus}, P_{World}) = 1.0 \quad \text{and} \quad E(i_{Aus}, i_{World}) = 1.0 , \quad (13.1)$$

that is, the elasticities of Australian prices and interest rates with
respect to an appropriate average of world prices and interest rates
are unity. In the long run, assumptions (13.1) are equivalent to the
familiar Purchasing Power Parity doctrine applied to a world of
fixed exchange rates. In the short-run these assumptions are not
easily defended, but they do capture an important, and I would
argue critical, difference between a country like Australia and a
'closed' economy like the U.S.A. Australia must take the world
price level as given and, since she cannot affect world prices, her
ability to change domestic prices is diminished or, under the extreme assumptions (13.1), nonexistent. The U.S.A., being much
larger relative to the world, can have appreciable influences on
world prices, and thus domestic U.S. prices should come closer to
performing the adjustment roles assigned to them in closed economies.

A milder short-run version of assumptions (13.1) is that the
smaller the country, the more important are the direct effects of
foreign prices and interest rates on domestic prices and interest
rates, and hence the less responsive will domestic prices and interest rates be to domestic conditions of disequilibria.

The commodity market is described by real private consumption demand c, real domestic autonomous expenditure including government and investment expenditures a, and real exports e. Consumption demand is given by

$$c = f(y, w) ; \tag{13.2}$$

where y = factor income; $w = \gamma_1 m + b + \gamma_2 k$; m = real money balances; γ_1 = fraction of real balances treated as wealth; b = real 'outside' bonds owned by Australians, where outside bonds include Australian government bonds and foreign bonds; k = real capital stock physically located in Australia; γ_2 = proportion of capital stock owned by Australians; and L = domestic labor supply.

The supply of domestically produced commodities is given by

$$y^s = g(k, L, P_{\text{Aus}}/P_{\text{World}}) , \tag{13.3}$$

with partial derivatives satisfying

$$g_k > 0 , \quad g_L > 0 , \quad g_{P_{\text{Aus}}/P_{\text{World}}} > 0 .$$

Under our assumptions, $P_{\text{Aus}}/P_{\text{World}}$ is fixed by instantaneous and complete adjustment of Australian prices to world prices.

The balance on trade account can be written as

$$e - im = y^s - c - a , \tag{13.4}$$

where im = real imports. Australians are assumed to be indifferent between domestic and foreign goods at the margin. Thus a one dollar increase in exports *ceteris paribus* is offset by a one dollar increase in imports, leaving the trade balance unaffected.

Real capital is assumed to be perfectly immobile, but income streams may be traded internationally in the form of bonds. Each bond is a promise to pay one dollar per year in perpetuity. It is convenient to write the bond market in terms of the net real demand for foreign bonds.

$$b^D = \frac{B^D}{P_{\text{Aus}}i} = j(y, w, i) - \frac{B^G}{P_{\text{Aus}}i} \qquad (j_y > 0, j_w > 0, j_i > 0) . \qquad (13.5)$$

$[P_{\text{Aus}}$ is used to calculate real bonds, although the appropriate P would be a weighted average of P_{Aus} and P_{World}.] The function j describes the stock demand for real, outside bonds; B^G is the policy determined number of one dollar income streams that are liabilities of the Australian government to the public, and $B^G/(P.i)$ is the real present value of these streams. All Australian govern-ment bonds are assumed to be domestically owned, thus b^D gives the stock demand for foreign bonds.

The demand for money is written as

$$\frac{M^D}{P_{\text{Aus}}} = l(y, w, i) \qquad (l_y > 0, l_w > 0, l_i > 0) . \qquad (13.6)$$

The supply of money is given two alternative and extremely sim-plified specifications in this paper.[1]

$$M^s = q(m, R, \bar{B}^G) , \qquad (13.7)$$

in which m is the 'money multiplier', and depends on the portfolio behavior of banks and the public, and on central bank policies governing interest rates and required reserves. R is reserves held by the central bank. $\bar{B}^G$ is the open market portfolio of the central bank which is equal to the amount of Australian government bonds owned by the bank. The signs postulated for partial deriva-tives are

$$q_m > 0 , \qquad q_R > 0 , \qquad q_{\bar{B}G} > 0 .$$

---

[1] Lachlan McGregor, Colin Burrows, and the present author are carrying out a de-tailed study of the Australian money supply process. An early result from that study allowed me to use a money stock definition in the present paper that conforms more closely to theory than does the published data. The major difference between the two series is that ours includes State government deposits at commercial and savings banks. These deposits constitute about 10% of the broadly defined money stock.

The two specifications of money supply are (a) that the total differential of q with respect to R is positive, and (b) that this differential is zero due to policy actions (or other changes) that perfectly offset the direct effects of reserve flows on changes in money stock.

Over the past twenty years Australia has typically had a positive trade balance in order to accumulate foreign income streams [(b) in terms of our model], and to a much smaller extent to enable reserves to accumulate. Short-run variations around the longer-run average position have been large, and it is these short-run variations that are the major concern of the present paper.

One type of shock to the model described in eqs. (13.1) – (13.7) results from an autonomous change in the world, and hence Australian, price level. Such a change upsets equilibrium in all three markets by decreasing the real value of bonds and money. In the commodity market, consumption demand falls leading to reduced imports and a more positive or less negative trade balance. In the bond market the real stock of outside bonds is reduced in proportion to the price change, and the demand for bonds is reduced by the total reduction in wealth multiplied by the wealth elasticity of demand for bonds. Under reasonable assumptions this will result in excess demand for bonds and lead to an increased rate of purchasing of foreign bonds.

Supply and demand both fall in the money market but, as in the bond market, supply is almost certain to fall more, leading to excess money demand. The immediate effect on the foreign accounts is to export more commodities and import more bonds and reserves. The inflow of bonds and reserves adds to the stock of bonds and, if reserve flows affect money supply, to the stock of money. The economy can reattain equilibrium without any domestically determined movement in either the price level or interest rate.

If reserve flows do not affect money stock, then equilibrium can only be reattained by a continuing inflow of bonds. If we maintain the assumption about fixed interest rates, this situation should also involve some change in the price of capital to bring about equilibrium in a total portfolio with relatively more bonds and less money.

The effects of exogenous changes in the interest rate, autonomous expenditures, and monetary policies may be derived from the model. In each such case, the adjustment to equilibrium is affected by the relation between reserve flows and changes in money stock. It is the major purpose of this paper to examine adjustments in the money market to shocks of any type, (a) under a regime where reserve flows have an immediate and substantial impact on money stock, and (b) where reserve flows have no immediate, and little intermediate effect on money stock.

If Australian prices and interest rates are not responsive to domestic conditions of disequilibrium, as we have assumed, and if reserve flows are not permitted to cause equilibrating movements in money stock [specification (b) of the supply of money], then the only means for eliminating monetary disequilibrium are bond imports or changes in the supply of commodities and income. Under such conditions we may expect adjustments of the money market toward equilibrium to be slow.

2. Two periods in recent Australian experience

The past two decades in Australia offer an amazing, and for our purposes very fortunate, contrast. In the first decade, 1951–60, contemporaneous reserve flows and changes in money stock are highly correlated and, in fact, reserve flows dominate all other factors in the quarter-to- quarter movements in money. During the second decade there is zero correlation between contemporaneous reserve flows and changes in money. The division between these two periods corresponds roughly with the establishment of the Australian Reserve Bank.

Simple regressions relating reserve flows and changes in money stock are reported below for the periods 1952(I) − 1959(I) and 1959(II) − 1970(I). These results show that net excess supplies in the commodity and bond markets, as reflected by reserve flows, had strong effects on money supply in the earlier period but no effect in the later period.[2]

[2] These results are not sensitive to the starting-point (1952(I)), the ending point (1970(I)) or to dividing points ranging several quarters around 1959(I).

Table 1
Changes in money and reserves [a]

Sample	Constant	Estimated coefficient	R^2	Durbin-Watson statistic	Standard error of estimate
1952(I) −1959(I)	73.0 (10.25)	0.52 (6.66)	0.59	1.58	41
1959(II)−1970(I)	198.0 (13.65)	0.132 (0.82)	0.016	0.78	95
1959(II)−1970(I)	101.0 (7.62)	0.19 (2.24)	0.17	1.01	87
1959(II)−1970(I)	100.0 (7.76)	0.18 (2.78)	0.16	1.05	85

[a] Left-hand variable is change in money; right-hand variable is reserve flow. t statistics are given in parentheses beneath the parameter estimates.

The last two rows in table 1 report the effects of two quarter and three quarter accumulations of reserves on the current change in money stock. That this effect remains small means that a state of net excess supply in the commodity and bond markets that persists for several quarters, and leads to a continuing accumulation of reserves, cannot be expected to lead to the expansion in money stock desired by the public.

3. The demand for money

One implication of our model is that the amount of time needed to reach equilibrium in the money market following a shock will be smaller when there are equilibrating movements in the money stock (changes in reserves and money are highly positively correlated), than when reserve flows have no effect on money stock. This implication is consistent with results obtained by fitting stock adjustment money demand equations of the following form:

$$\left[\frac{M}{P}\right]_t - \left[\frac{M}{P}\right]_{t-1} = b\left[l(y, i) - \left[\frac{M}{P}\right]_{t-1}\right]$$

$$= ba_0 + ba_1 y + ba_2 i - bM_{t-1} + e' , \qquad (13.8)$$

Table 2
Estimate of money demand functions, 1952(I)–1959(I) and 1959(II)–1970(I) [a]

Sample	Current income Y_t	Permanent income Y_t^P	12 year bond rate i_t	M_{t-1}	R^2	Durbin-Watson statistic	Standard error of estimate
1952(I)–1959(I)	0.738 (4.13)		−186 (−2.23)	−0.525 (−3.90)	0.39	0.48	93
1954(II)–1959(I) [b]		0.645 (3.33)	−285 (−2.78)	−0.390 (−2.57)	0.38	1.26	65
1959(II)–1970(I)	0.170 (1.48)		−188 (−5.91)	−0.055 (−0.952)	0.48	1.73	68
1959(II)–1970(I)		0.301 (2.02)	−228 (−5.56)	−0.112 (−1.58)	0.50	1.74	67

[a] t statistics are given in parentheses beneath the parameter-estimates.

[b] Due to extreme fluctuations in income during the Korean War, and to problems associated with the Australian devaluation just prior to the sample period, I have been reluctant to construct a permanent income series beginning closer to the period for which data are first available.

where current GNP and a measure of permanent income were tried as alternatives for y; i = 12 year government bond rate; and M = currency plus total deposits in commercial and savings banks, owned by the non-bank public and the State Governments.

In table 2 the estimated coefficients reported in the 'M_{t-1}' column support the prediction that monetary adjustment is rapid when money stock responds quickly to reserve flows, and adjustment is slow when reserve flows do not affect money stock. The estimated rate of adjustment for the more recent period, in fact, is not significantly different from zero at the 5% level.

The results for the earlier period in terms of income and interest rate elasticities are not greatly different from the estimates previously reported for the U.S.A. (Meltzer [9], Laidler [7]). Current income elasticity of money demand, calculated at the means of M/P and Y/P, is approximately + 2.34, and permanent income elasticity is + 2.87.[3] These elasticities are a bit higher than one

[3] In view of the very low value of the associated Durbin-Watson statistic, the former of these two estimates should be interpreted with due care.

would expect on the basis of findings in the U.S.A., and they reflect mainly the very rapid growth in interest bearing deposits in both commercial and savings banks. It is likely that these wealth elasticities are biased upwards by a misspecification that leaves out the effects of increasing rates of return on interest bearing deposits.

The interest rate elasticities of the first two equations are −0.25 and −0.53, both within the range of values estimated for the U.S. economy for long-term interest rates.

For the later period the implied wealth elasticities are about double those for the earlier period, and the interest rate elasticities are higher by a factor of about 10. These calculations are based on several coefficients that are not significantly different from zero.

If we believe the estimates for the period 1959–70, the money market is adjusting toward equilibrium at a very slow rate, if at all. However, the estimated equations for this period must, I believe, be discarded on the grounds that they are misspecified. Misspecification here arises from a violation of the elementary assumption in all demand studies that the market being studied is, in some sense, in equilibrium. Equilibrium, as in the present case, may involve an optimal rate of stock adjustment, but it is nonetheless a situation in which prices and/or quantities are changing in ways that will eliminate dissatisfaction. In the present case, little if anything is happening to eliminate monetary disequilibrium.

Our theoretical sensibilities may not be too badly offended to think of a money market constantly out of equilibrium, and more importantly one with no effective equilibrating movements in either prices or quantities, if the disequilibria tend to be small and if they tend to equal out over time in terms of excess demands and excess supplies. However, a large and persistent state of excess supply, for instance, will quickly exhaust international reserves, and must surely lead to monetary policy actions designed to reverse the reserve flow. Similarly, a large and persistent excess money demand will cause reserves to accumulate at an undesirable rate and lead to expansionary policies. 1970 was a period of extremely rapid reserve inflow (which we identify with an excess demand for money), causing the Australian stock of reserves to almost double! In such extreme cases the monetary authorities must either respond to the signals given by reserve flows by changing money supply, or else by changing the exchange rate.

4. *Effects of money on income*

The relationship between past and current changes in money and changes in current income is worth noting. When contemporaneous reserve flows and changes in money supply are highly positively related, we saw that the money market appears to approach equilibrium very rapidly. In this case changes in money in the past should have little relation to current changes in income. When excess demand or supply is quickly and *permanently* eliminated by equilibrating money stock changes, further adjustments over time are unnecessary.

From the results reported in table 3, there is no apparent relation between past changes in money and current changes in income for the period 1952(I) − 1959(I). For the more recent period, the effects of changes in money lagged one and two periods are positive and significantly different from zero.

The results for the later period suggest that disequilibrium in the monetary sector does have at least a lagged effect on prices, real output, or on both of these. This effect is smaller than similar estimates for the U.S.A., and it begins later (Andersen and Jordan [1]).

5. *Conclusions*

As we move from a closed economy or any economy on flexible exchange rates, to an open economy on fixed exchange rates, many aspects of the money adjustment process are altered. Price and interest rate movements, the two most important variables in monetary adjustments in a closed economy, become less responsive to domestic forces in an open economy. This tendency should increase the smaller the economy is relative to the world economy.

Table 3

Relation between current changes in income and current and past changes in money [a]

Sample	Constant	ΔM_t	ΔM_{t-1}	ΔM_{t-2}	ΔM_{t-3}	R^2	Durbin-Watson statistic	Standard error of estimate
1952(I)–1959(I)	+0.12 (1.95)	+1.40 (2.05)	−1.24 (−1.52)	+1.25 (1.52)	−0.50 (−0.70)	0.19	2.25	44
1959(II)–1970(I)	−2.20 (−0.21)	−1.12 (−0.11)	+1.60 (2.74)	+1.20 (2.06)	−0.43 (−0.78)	0.45	1.74	61

[a] t statistics are given in parentheses beneath the parameter estimates.

The decreased contributions of price and interest rate movements to the adjustment process in an open economy is offset by equilibrating reserve flows that operate directly to move money stock in the required direction. However, these reserve flows may be sterilized by the monetary authority. In this case a major source of equilibrating movements in money stock is eliminated.

The Australian experience offered a unique opportunity to test the effects on an open economy of eliminating the equilibrating effects of reserve flows. When reserve flows do not influence changes in money, the estimated speed of adjustment to equilibrium in the money market was very low. In fact, that estimate raised doubts about the assumption that the money market is in equilibrium *in any sense* in periods as short as one quarter.

When the reserve flow mechanism is operative, the estimated demand for money equation was similar to those reported for other countries. In addition, the estimated speed of adjustment was high and significantly different from zero.

The results reported in this paper suggest that techniques and hypotheses that have worked out well in closed economies cannot always be carried over, unaltered, to open economies. In the present case, the whole monetary adjustment process appears to depend on the presence or absence of an effective reserve flow cum money change mechanism of the type envisaged by Hume. The message implicit in this observation is that monetary studies in open economies should not be expected to duplicate results obtained in closed economies under all conditions, and certainly not in cases where the equilibrating effects of reserve flows are inoperable.

References

[1] Leonall C. Andersen and Jerry L. Jordan, 'Monetary and fiscal actions: a test of their relative importance in economic stabilization', *Review of the Federal Reserve Bank of St. Louis* (November 1968) 11–24.
[2] Gregory Chow, 'On the long-run and short-run demand for money', *Journal of Political Economy* 74 (April 1966) 111–131.
[3] William G. Dewald, 'The demand for money in Australia, 1952–1968'. Unpublished manuscript (1969).

[4] William G. Dewald and Robert V. Kennedy, 'Monetary and fiscal actions: some tests of their relative importance in Australia'. Paper read to the 41st Congress of the Australian and New Zealand Association for the Advancement of Science, Adelaide, August, 1969.

[5] Milton Friedman, 'The demand for money–some theoretical and empirical results', *Journal of Political Economy* **67** (June 1959) 327–351.

[6] Harry G. Johnson, *Money, trade, and economic growth: survey lectures in economic theory*, 2nd ed. (Cambridge, Mass., Harvard University Press, 1966).

[7] David E.W. Laidler, *The demand for money: theories and evidence* (Scranton, Pa., International Textbook Company, 1969).

[8] J.E. Meade, *The balance of payments* (London, Oxford University Press, 1951).

[9] Allan H. Meltzer, 'The demand for money: the evidence from the time series', *Journal of Political Economy* **71** (June 1963) 219–246.

[10] Robert A. Mundell, *International economics* (New York, The Macmillan Company, 1968).

[11] W.E. Norton, 'A model of the Australian economy: a progress report'. Occasional Paper No. 3A, Sydney, Reserve Bank of Australia, January 1970.

LIST OF PAPERS PRESENTED AT THE SECOND
AUSTRALASIAN CONFERENCE OF ECONOMETRICIANS,
MONASH UNIVERSITY, AUGUST 9–13, 1971

H.T. Burley (La Trobe University): "Production functions for Australian manufacturing industry".

Robert Crouch (University of California, Santa Barbara): "A new approach to the monetisation of neoclassical growth models".

R.S. Deane (Reserve Bank of New Zealand): "Macroeconometric relationships within New Zealand: a preliminary examination".

G.M. Feiger (Monash University): "Estimating capital and labour coefficients for 160 Australian manufacturing industries: model and preliminary remarks".

V.W. FitzGerald (Commonwealth Bureau of Census and Statistics, Canberra): "Dynamic properties of a non-linear econometric model".

S. Ganjarerndee (University of Sydney): "Effect of temporal aggregation on a model of the Australian monetary sector".

C. Gillion (New Zealand Institute of Economic Research): "The structural development of the New Zealand economy: an input-output model with prices".

R.G. Gregory (Australian National University): "Supply constraints and U.S. export of non-agricultural goods".

Tim Hazledine and Alan Woodfield (University of Otago): "Adjustment dynamics and short-run employment behaviour in New Zealand manufacturing".

John Helliwell (University of British Columbia), Gordon Sparks (Queen's University), and Jack Frisch (Princeton University): "The supply price of capital in macroeconomic models".

John Helliwell (University of British Columbia), Ian Stewart (Bank of Canada), Fred Gorbet (Bank of Canada), and Don Stephenson (Bank of Canada): "Some features and uses of the Canadian quarterly model RDX2".

C.I. Higgins (Commonwealth Treasury, Canberra): "A wage-price sector for a quarterly Australian model".

N.C. Kakwani (University of New South Wales): "On the bias in estimates of import demand parameters".

Derek Kent-Smith (Monash University): "A spectral regression analysis of the British Phillips curve".

L.R. Klein (University of Pennsylvania): "The treatment of undersized samples in econometrics".

S. Kim (University of Sydney): "An econometric model of Korea – application to estimating foreign resource requirements".

L. McGregor (Monash University) and A.A. Walters (London School of Economics): "Real balances and output: a productivity model of a monetary economy".

W.E. Norton and J.F. Henderson (Reserve Bank of Australia): "The structure of a model of the Australian economy".

Gary P. Sampson (Monash University): "Classifying productivity movements".

Lindsay Sheperd (Commonwealth Bureau of Roads, Melbourne): "An econometric analysis of car ownership and public transport use in Australian state capital cities".

Eric R. Sowey (University of New South Wales): "Stochastic simulation of macroeconometric models: methodology and interpretation".

Peter L. Swan (Monash University): "A model of demand and forecasts of annual sales of automobiles in Australia, 1949–80".

Ross. A. Williams (Monash University): "The impact of the cost of funds on housing completions: a variable weight distributed lag analysis".

C.R. Wymer (London School of Economics): "A continuous disequilibrium model of United Kingdom financial markets".

Richard Zecher (University of Chicago): "Short-run monetary adjustments in the Australian economy, 1952–70".

Arnold Zeller (University of Chicago) and Stephen C. Peck (University of California, Berkeley): "Simulation experiments with a quarterly macroeconometric model of the U.S. economy".

AUTHOR INDEX

SUBJECT INDEX